Civic Discourse and Digital Age Communications in the Middle East

edited by
Leo A. Gher
Southern Illinois University

and

Hussein Y. Amin
American University in Cairo

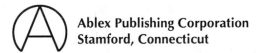
Ablex Publishing Corporation
Stamford, Connecticut

Copyright © 2000 by Ablex Publishing Corporation

Printed in the United States of America

Library of Congress Cataloguing-in-Publication Data

Civic discourse and digital age communications in the Middle East / edited by
Leo A. Gher and Hussein Y. Amin.
      p. cm.— (Civic discourse for the third millennium)
      Includes bibliographical references and index.
      ISBN 1-56750-472-8 (cloth) — ISBN 1-56750-473-6 (pbk.)
      1. Intercultural communication—Arab countries. 2. Civil society—
Arab countries. 3. Information superhighway—Arab countries. I. Gher, Leo A.
II. Amin, Hussein Y. III. Series.
HM1211.C58   2000
303.48'33'09174927—dc21   99–35518
                                              CIP

Ablex Publishing Corporation
100 Prospect Street
P.O. Box 811
Stamford, Connecticut 06904-0811

Nan, Julianna, Krista, Laurene and Mary Moynihan—my ever-constant sustainers

—L.A.G.

Ann, my wife; Adam, my son; Nouran, my daughter; and my parents—with love and respect.

—H.Y.A.

CONTENTS

Discourse III.   Cyberspace Digital Technologies: An Overview

Discourse IV.   Privatization of Media in the Middle East

Discourse V.   New Journalism: The Online Environment and Law

Global Forum: Dialogues for the Next Millennium

ACKNOWLEDGMENTS

Without invaluable assistance from many people this book would not have been finished in the 20th century. The authors wish to acknowledge especially the services of our graduate students at American University in Cairo and Southern Illinois University—particularly Byong Shin, Sirinthorn Kantakhom, Nan Luan, and Tara Kachgal. The coordinator of translations from Arabic to American English was Mohammed el-Nawawy, without whose facilitation the book would not have been possible. Moreover, we need to recognize and thank Nan Gher, who spent many hours as our syntax/semantics editor.

The authors also wish to express a heartfelt gratitude to the Arab–U.S. Association for Communication Educators (AUSACE), which graciously allowed us access to each of its conferences to promote this book and collect research materials. Furthermore, we want to thank Michael Prosser, Ablex's Civic Discourse for the Third Millennium series editor, for his considerable patience and guidance in the publication of this book. And lastly, with great respect, we acknowledge our friend and colleague, Dr. K. S. Sitaram, without whose patient mentoring this project would never have gotten the boost it needed in the beginning.

INTRODUCTION: FROM THE HEARTLAND OF AMERICA

Leo Avery Gher
Southern Illinois University

In classical Arabic I am called *agnabi*, which means foreigner. In colloquial Arabic the term is *khawaga*, which means foreigner as well, but may also be translated as "the one who does not know the culture" or, in some cases, may be interpreted more darkly as "the infidel." Obviously, the translation depends on the dialect or the regional origin of the speaker. The word *khawaga* is predominantly employed by the peoples of the Levant (eastern Mediterranean), while different words and phrases are spoken in the Maghreb region (northwest Africa), and still others are used in the Gulf territories. Regional dialects are nothing new, of course, but *khawagas* often view the Arabic language as being homogeneous. Of course, it is not. In a similar way, the Middle East is often portrayed as an autonomous land of Bedouin peoples, and this, too, is a notable misconception. To many Westerners, the concept of Pan Arabism (the Arabic version of the United States) is seen and understood to be the dream of all Arabs, which is another misunderstanding about the region. Arab states, as they now exist, are the contrivance of two European bureaucrats in the early part of the 20th century when Britain and France imposed imperial rule on the land. There are many misconceptions about the Middle East, but one sure thing is worth treasuring. It is a region of immeasurable diversity in politics, linguistics, government, economics, customs, and, most importantly, yet always just below the surface of everyday life, tribal culture. Arabic society is built upon patrimonial empowerment. The Middle East is also the nexus of three continents, and the sanctum of hundreds of religious sects, not just the three main, monotheistic faiths. Many arguments have been made that this is probably the most complex, variegated and mystifying realm on the planet.

For the most part, the Arab world is synonymous with the Middle East. It occupies a large geographical area, estimated at 13,738,000 square kilometers, which is equivalent to 10.8 percent of the earth's surface. The Arab world stretches from the shores of the Atlantic Ocean to the Persian Gulf (Labib, Quandiil, & Baker, 1983). The 1995 World Bank estimate projects that the population of the Middle East will reach 500 million in the first decade of the new millennium and will exceed 1 billion by 2100. Today, more than half of the region's population is under the age of 18, which means that the Arab world, plus Iran, will have to create close to 50 million new jobs in the coming years just to provide enough work for those who will enter the labor force. One World Bank economist, John Page, argues that the global economy is developing so rapidly that nations or regions that fail to make the required structural adjustments to compete for market share and capital investment are now liable to remain irrevocably poor (Miller, 1996).

There is considerable evidence of weak economics and slow development in the region. For example, in 1960 the average per capita income of the seven most prosperous Arabic states was slightly larger than that of the seven Asian Tigers (South Korea, Taiwan, the Philippines, Indonesia, Malaysia, Thailand, and Vietnam). By the early part of the current decade, however, per capita income of that same Arabic group was a mere U.S.$3,342, while that of the Asian Tigers exceeded U.S.$8,000. To further compound the economic problems, the Middle East attracts only 3 percent of today's worldwide foreign investment, whereas Asia garners 58 percent (Miller, 1996).

During the 20th century, the Middle East has witnessed fundamental changes on many levels. With the advent of World War I, several European governments entered the region, and imposed imperialism, nationalism, and Western values on Middle Eastern peoples. With each passing decade, the *khawaga* enforced alien ideas and bizarre transformations on Middle Eastern societies that had not previously been explored by Arabs. In the 1910s and 1920s, artificial lines were drawn on maps (the Sykes-Picot Agreement between Britain and France to settle colonial, governing disputes), and nations such as Syria, Lebanon, Iraq, Trans-Jordan, and Saudi Arabia were created where none existed before. By mid-century, European refugees had come to the region in droves to carve out the nation of Israel, and four tragic wars ensued. A decade later, global industrial powers discovered a sea of oil beneath the surface of the sands, and a dichotomy of superrich and ultrapoor Arabs evolved. In the 1960s, 1970s, and 1980s, Russia and the United States played out a chess game of superpower social science and protectorate politics. And in the final decade before the new millennium, American and European communication and entertainment conglomerates have invaded Middle Eastern homes and businesses with 24-hour-a-day Western television programs. Throughout this century global economics, Western cultural values, and the communications revolution have had profound effects on the social fabric of Arabic life.

Concerns expressed by Arabs about these changes are genuine. As seen through their eyes, the consistent flow of Western popular culture is a threat to their civilization. The sudden and addictive impact of occidental products such as video games, music CDs, computer software, films, and television programs has intensified their defensiveness. Islamic societies in general and Middle Eastern culture in particular are highly protective of ancient traditions, religious proprieties, and conservative values. Arabic and Islamic dominions are inseparable on these points, and are justifiably proud of the great cultural legacy preserved through the use of the Arabic language, Middle Eastern customs, and their media. Many Arab countries have responded to this infiltration through severe rules of censorship. The Freedom Forum has stated that censorship is rigorously applied in most countries of the Arab world (USIS, 1994). In the West, freedom of expression is a basic individual right that is protected by preeminent authority, but within many Arab societies, this form of censorship is easily tolerated and even expected as a form of civic responsibility.

Arabs have other concerns as well. Some countries are fearful of the danger of political and religious repercussions to this influx of alien values. An anti-West, Islamic fundamentalist reaction to the suddenly easy availability of pop culture products has been taking place for some time, and the predominant fear of certain governments within the region is the destabilization of other states. Islamic groups such as the Muslim Brotherhood disapprove of their members using the media, specifically television, which is felt to have a corrupting, immoral influence on Muslims. Public fear of these negative influences is well documented throughout the Middle East.

Another political concern has to do with some Arab governments' sensitivity to perceived unfavorable news reporting by international radio and television networks. The lack of skill within certain Arab administrations to cope with what is defined as negative reporting has caused jingoistic responses, such as the banning of satellite dishes in Saudi Arabia, or the refusal to develop the telecommunication infrastructures necessary to link Middle Eastern countries with the global information community. It is always important to remember that since broadcasting and media services in the Arab world are state-run activities, the misuse of these technologies during times of conflict may result in a type of communication warfare. But many technologies have already affected Arabic peoples in compelling ways. Modern international telecommunication services now assist in the free flow of information, and neither inter-Arab conflicts nor differences among groups will affect the direct exchange of services provided by global cyberspace networks. However, public dialogue has played almost no role in the process of developing a national communication system. It has been a one-way flow of information or aspiration, either from the West or from within the power structure of Arab states. All that is about to change.

A global community is emerging slowly, but surely, and the functional and structural components of all human societies are merging into a one-world economy, security system, communication infrastructure, and transnational assembly. Examples of this globalization process are evident everywhere. The Chrysler Corporation and Mercedes-Benz have partnered to exploit worldwide auto marketplaces; Arab Media Corporation has joined forces with the Kirch Television Group of Germany, Waleed Bin Talal, owner of EuroDisney, Silvio Berlusconi, the Italian film and television mogul, and the Richardson Broadcasting Consortium of South Africa to provide satellite television programming (*Multichoice*), which is now available on five continents; NATO military and UN forces have come together with a global vision to enforce security between warring states, or even among ethnic groups within states; the telecommunication systems of most sovereign states have come together to form a planetary information superhighway, as evidenced by the Internet and the World Wide Web; and international courts of law are being empowered by treaties that affect sovereign legislatures on every continent. The only societal component of importance that remains undiminished is the cultural component. But with considerable gusto, cultural factors such as tradition, custom, values, religion, and ethnic identity are being reexamined by peoples throughout the world. As we enter the new millennium, it would seem that human societies throughout the world are experiencing tectonic forces of opposite dimensions—those driving humanity together, and those pushing peoples apart. This is the state of affairs as we enter the 21st century. It is self-evident that we cannot go back to the past, nor can we change the tectonic forces that are moving us forward. We can, however, adapt.

One way to adjust to such change is to employ a special form of communications, which Dr. Amin and I call transnational civic discourse. Transnational civic discourse may be defined as a cross-border, citizen-to-citizen dialogue, on a nongovernmental level, conducted for the express purpose of seeking peace, understanding, security, and development for the mutual benefit of all. Civic discourse has been a part of our human community for a very long time, but it has always been constrained by national borders, language barriers, ethnic strife, and lack of mobility. With the advent of digital age communications, however, those hurdles are coming down. Cyberspace technologies allow for a world in which cross-border exchange and citizen-to-citizen dialogue are not merely possible, but are unavoidable. *Civic Discourse and Digital Age Communications in the Middle East* is one form of transnational civic dialogue that brings scholars, students, and citizens together in a multicultural setting to exchange ideas and discover possibilities.

With this in mind, whatever is defined as the Arab world is now challenged by a new world order. Digital communications, known collectively as the information superhighway, have come to the region with remarkable speed, and serious questions remain about the capabilities of Middle Eastern nations to take advantage of this cyberspace media. According to the March 5, 1999, NUA Internet Survey, 163 million people are online worldwide. The United States and Canada account for almost 100 million users alone, while the United Kingdom, Japan, and Germany make up the other members of the top five wired nations. The entire Arab world has an estimated online population of 780,000. In other words, about 30 percent of the North American population is online, while less than 3 percent of the entire Arab world is online, and future trends for online growth mirror the current data. On a planetary scale, online users will double to 320 million by the end of the year 2000, and will continue to explode to 720 million by 2005. Current estimates for Middle East connectivity remain stagnant in the near term, and, moreover, it must be acknowledged that most of the region is not hardwired for digital age services, unlike North America and Europe where telephone penetration exceeds 95 percent.

The issue of American-English literacy, the preeminent language of the information superhighway, is also a significant problem impeding mass penetration of Internet services. Throughout the Arab world, cumulative literacy is estimated at 60 percent, maximum, whereas the ability to read and write in American English is less than 6 percent (World Bank, 1998). Obviously, this means that even if the technical connectivity problem were solved, more than 90 percent of the population of the Middle East would not be able to convey their sentiments online because of the language barrier. Another limiting factor is the powerful cultural heritage of the "oral tradition," the preferred mode of communication among Arabic peoples. Western civilization has been molded by a written culture for about as long as the oral tradition in the Arab world, but too often Western eyes are oblivious to such facts, which will have a powerful effect on the development of Internet services. On the other hand, without any kind of control, censorship, or government approval, many people living in the Middle East do have access to international television networks and digital age communications such as the World Wide Web. Ordinarily, the construction of books such as this one are limited by time, geography, and professional association, but this is no longer the case in the digital age. Although this book represents an older, traditional form of communication, the entire compilation of the work was done via cyberspace linkages, allowing for academic research, essays in search of cross-border discussion, and personal observations to be submitted from four continents and 16 countries. There is now a great opportunity for political, economic, social, and cultural expansion within the Arab world. The potential for improvement is truly great. Imagine, for a moment, peace in the region—with 50 million skilled workers, a literate population, and a modern communication infrastructure in place. A golden age of development for the Middle East is possible with time and commitment from all.

HOW TO USE THIS BOOK

Civic Discourse and Digital Age Communication in the Middle East is divided into six sections that include a wide variety of critical exchanges on meaningful topics. Parts I through V present reseach projects that have been selected as the best reports of three international conferences of the Arab-U.S. Association for Communication Educators (AUSACE). The final section, "Global Forum: Dialogues for the Next Millennium," brings together a series of personal commentaries on the international state of affairs within a multicultural setting. These essays are not traditional academic reseach per se, but are based on personal experiences and shrewd observations over many years in the Middle East. Each brings a wealth of knowledge and understanding to the process of transnational civic discourse.

Civic Discourse and Digital Age Communication in the Middle East is primarily targeted to the university setting. Academic researchers, communication scholars, and graduate students will benefit from this cross-cultural approach to civic discourse. As a textbook, this book is best suited for courses in communication effects, sociology, cross-cultural studies, political science, management, law and regulation, international telecommunication studies, diplomacy, and government. Professional communicators will also find this book useful in dealing with different cultures and foreign affairs.

At the end of each chapter, the reader will find a set of five discussion questions about the research presentation at hand. These broad-based questions may be used to stimulate further discussion about important issues and future implications. Professors may also utilize the set of questions as test items, although answers are not provided.

Discourse I offers three fascinating reports concerning diplomacy, transnational communications, and mediated discourse. Marwan Kraidy, assistant professor at the University of North Dakota and former Lebanese journalist and writer, leads off this section with an on-ground investigation into the state of affairs of radio and television broadcasting in Lebanon after the war. Rasha Abdulla, lecturer at the American University in Cairo, next introduces the reader to one of the hot topics of the region with a critical examination of cross-cultural perspectives. Ms. Abdulla presents an absorbing thesis about the attitudes of Arab youth and MTV. And in the final report of this section, Mohammed el-Nawawy, assistant professor at the University of West Florida and former Middle East newspaper reporter, investigates one of the most important subjects in the world of telecommunication today: Internet pornography, morality, and constitutional law.

Discourse II presents three engaging compositions about Western cultural invasion, centering on the issue of whether it is myth or reality. Yahya Kamalipour, the director of Graduate Studies in communications at Purdue University, introduces us to his significant research on media images and stereotyping. Dr. Kamalipour analyzes American film portrayals of Arabs and Muslims globally, and Middle Eastern peoples in particular. Serious questions about ethics and civic responsibility are raised. Hana Noor al-Deen, professor of communication studies at the University of North Carolina-Wilmington, takes us to Algeria where she has completed a fascinating research project on Rai music and Algerian youth. A comparative reading with Rasha Abdulla's work on Arab youth and MTV is in order. Issam Mousa, professor at Yarmouk University in Jordan and the president of AUSACE, presents a fascinating report about how electronic media is produced in the West and the effects of these programs on universal attitudes across cultures.

Discourse III is an exhibition of five valuable research reports centering on cyberspace technologies and who wins and who loses in the global battle for audiences, customers, and capital resources. Ali Attiga, secretary general of the Arab Thought Forum, begins this section with a very important discussion about information technology, democracy, and development in the Middle East. James Danowski, associate professor at the University of Illinois-Chicago, presents an extensive report on worldwide telephone traffic in the Arab world. Researchers and coeditors Amin and Gher expose the reader to their far-ranging reseach on electronic media connectivity in Middle Eastern countries. This investigation is a continuing project, which shows the growth and development of digital communications over the past 4 years and projects future trends. Roger Gafke and Ronald Naeger, of the University of Missouri, demonstrate special teaching techniques that use the World Wide Web to edit journalism stories long distance. Shems Friedlander, the director of the Apple Center for Graphics Communications in Cairo, reports on the uses of digital technology in the construction of Arab newspapers.

Discourse IV furnishes the reader with three critical discussions pertaining to the privatization of media in the Middle East. Jihad Fakhreddine, media manager of the Pan Arab Research Center (PARC) in Dubai, outlines several critical issues dealing with economics in the Middle East and marketing communications. Much of his thesis comes from research on the electronic media conducted by PARC throughout the region. Walid Hashem, the managing director of Arab Media Corporation, with executive facilitation from Professor Gher, describes the managerial structure of Arab Radio and Television (ART). ART is an Arabic, seven-channel satellite television service that is distributed on five continents throughout the world. Chairman Safran al-Makaty of the Communication Department at Um al-Quara University in Mecca, and Drs. Boyd and van Tubergen of the University of Kentucky, detail a Q-study of attitudes and behaviors of Saudi viewers to D-B-S television programming in the Kingdom of Saudi Arabia.

Discourse V is a submission of four captivating investigations affecting new online journalism and legal ramifications from an international perspective. Carolyn Crimmins, associate professor in Communications at Georgia State University, investigates the problems associated with Palestinian press laws of 1995. Dr. Crimmins focuses on the relationship between Chairman Arafat and press freedom in the newly created territories in Israel. Yorck von Korff, a doctoral student from the University of Heidelberg, examines journalists' standards and personal ethics in the Middle East. The subject of a "living wage" for reporters in the region is the subject of comparison with Western principles. James Napoli, associate professor at the American University in Cairo, Carolyn Crimmins, and Leonard Teel, director of the Center for International Media Education at Georgia State University, compare and contrast recent Egyptian and Palestinian press laws, and describe how each affects professional journalism in the Arab world. And in the final research paper of the book, Mohammed el-Nawawy reveals the results of a comparative content analysis between American network news and the main newscasts of the Egyptian government. The subject of the study centers on the treatment of international news events in both countries. Biases are found in both nations, but the results contradict widely held opinions about the subject.

REFERENCES

Labib, S., Quandiil, H., & Baker, Y. A. (1983). *Development of communication in the Arab states: Needs and priorities*. Paris: UNESCO.

Miller, J. (1996). *God has ninety-nine names*. New York: Simon & Schuster.

NUA Internet survey [Online]. (1999, March 5). Available: http://www.nua.ie/surveys/

USIS Arabic Bulletin. (1994, May 4). Washington, DC: United States Information Agency.

World Bank Group [Online]. (1998, September). Available: http://www.worldbank.org/

INTRODUCTION: FROM THE BANKS OF THE NILE

Hussein Y. Amin
American University in Cairo

Historically, Middle Eastern governments have set the media agenda and have viewed radio and television as the most effective means of promoting their political, religious, cultural, and economic agendas. Since the introduction of electronic media in the Middle East, many governments have exercised severe rules of censorship, with only a few exceptions such as Morocco and Lebanon. Most Middle Eastern regimes give considerable credit to both radio and television, and promote the expansion of government-owned media empires that can be used as a tool to formulate public opinion, mobilize the public, and deliver the official line. At the beginning of the new millennium, a majority of the countries in the Middle East have reached a critical stage in the evolution of their communication systems. As nations around the world privatize, restructure, and deregulate their national systems in order to compete globally, the Middle East remains impeded by old political divisions, static communication models, and poor performance. The introduction of digital technologies in the Middle East is at a very early stage of development, and while some countries have adopted the new electronic media, they remain limited to urban centers and elite communities. In the coming digital age, the major challenges for the region may be defined as follows: (1) to regain momentum by reexamining the structure of mass media and its relation to the international community, (2) to reorient the role of the mass media in Arab society away from its authoritarian model, (3) to acquaint people with the processes of privatization and democratization, and (4) to seek Arab institutional involvement in the process of globalization.

Digital age communication brings with it totally new concepts that should revolutionize media in the Middle East. The media forms that will be created will not be absolute monopolies, nor will they be under direct government control or supervision. In the near future, Arab governments will partner with the private sector and independent businesses to share ownership as well as operation of the digital broadcast entities. One of the many characteristics of the digital age is decentralization of media. A decentralized model is a challenge to governments in the Middle East, whose current broadcasting model reflects a desire for control and centralization in administration. Furthermore, the multichannel system will definitely confront the utilization of the broadcast media as a political and propaganda tool by these governments, as was the case throughout the 20th century. Eventually, the influence of digital communications on public opinion will become apparent. Increased availability and public accessibility to various national, regional, international, and transnational radio and television channels will be guaranteed by digital communications, and the audiences in the region will be exposed to a number of diverse opinions, which may even contradict government information services and political spin doctors.

The introduction of global satellite technology and the development of the Internet have given the news organizations more of a voice in international affairs than ever before. This, of course, has raised many concerns about information distribution and foreign influences of the media. These concerns are genuine, centering on issues of religion, politics, culture, and the social scene that will affect the civic discourse.

The promise that new digital communications brings can help Middle Eastern countries to leapfrog many of the barriers that block national development. The alternative is to fall even further behind in the creation of a First World economy, and to become an ever more marginal player in global affairs. Naturally, new media will increase the speed of information delivery, which will give Arab political leaders another tool in the processes of mobilizing the population and putting development into high gear. Within the region, however, there is an ongoing debate about the benefits of a communications revolution that challenges the old pillars of tradition and dominates the lives of Middle Eastern peoples every second of the day. At this very moment, professional and academic circles are debating the point-counterpoint issues of participating in the process of building a global culture, or resisting it. Among many intellectuals, the fear of cyberspace is real. The feeling is that access to this global network would somehow dilute the quality of Arab culture, would empower the public in affairs of state, and would create a forum of civic discourse for the people.

Moreover, the debate about media's role as an agent of cultural imperialism continues for several reasons. First, there is a belief that regional program production centers have not reached a mature state of development and cannot compete with media products coming almost exclusively from the West. And second, the recent multichannel television environment, a direct result of digital age media, shocked Middle Eastern audiences, creating a kind of civic hysteria that is well-documented in many parts of the region. The sudden appearance of numerous Western television channels conjured up the perception of cultural imperialism. Such communication services were not seen in a positive light, but the continuing process of social evolution should not be mistaken for cultural imperialism, which implies force and coercion, not choice. Just the opposite may be true. Digital communication systems may be a new hope for peace and diplomacy in the Middle East. Direct satellite television and networked personal computers, in fact, have empowered individuals, and have eliminated the control of information flow that Arab authoritarian governments have held in the past.

In reality, there is no turning back. It is on to cyberspace, where governments compete against international corporations and special interest groups for the attention of viewers. Digital communications technology is a wide-open field for freedom, a testament to human ingenuity to crash through the parameters of imagination. This book is a good example of digital media technology and the process of democratic consolidation of Middle Eastern civil society, functioning in a free environment.

Major changes are taking place every day in the Middle East. E-mail and networked computers are modifying traditional media settings and models of communication. Cyber cafés are gaining popularity and are creating a dialogue among groups that have not been traditionally interactive. Arab teens are making friends all over the world, and the once mysterious society that was often seen as off limits is no longer closed. The World Wide Web is used in every country of the Middle East, and each year hundreds of thousands of people acquire personal computers. Citizens link up with computer networks and communicate their ideas to their elected local, state, and national officials about the hot topics of the day.

Civic Discourse and Digital Age Communication in the Middle East is a book created for the express purpose of starting a dialogue among peoples of different nationalities and backgrounds. The most interesting development highlighted by the book is the way that computer networks are now being used to create new forms of a civil society; societies that are not national, but rather, transnational. The book is, in form, style and content, a nongovernmental organization (NGO), where local issues gain momentum and become transnational by nature. Obviously, this project was undertaken in the midst of a continuing process; therefore, it combines both promise and performance. It will leave you with a fresh perspective on the Middle East, not just in the technological arena, but also through the experience of transference of Arab sociocultural institutions and ideas, and their accompanying economic and political implications.

Discourse I
Diplomacy, Transnational Communications, and Mediated Discourse

TELEVISION AND CIVIC DISCOURSE IN POSTWAR LEBANON

Marwan M. Kraidy
University of North Dakota

INTRODUCTION

With its political variety, religious diversity, cultural pluralism and economic liberalism, Lebanon stands as an oddity in the Arab world. Numerous civic discourses are colorful threads in the fabric of Lebanese society, which is a blessing and a curse at the same time. It is a blessing because a multiplicity of discourses prevents authoritarianism and stimulates democratic political activity. It is a curse because changes in national, regional, or global politics can trigger upheavals ranging from economic instability to political tension to armed conflict. The adage that national electronic media reflect the political, cultural, and economic makeup of the country they operate in holds true for Lebanon. This was demonstrated by the wartime media explosion in Lebanon which, by 1994, had produced around 50 private television stations and more than 100 radio stations. This media proliferation called for legislation to regulate the broadcasting chaos, which created one of postwar Lebanon's most enduring controversies about media control, freedom, and the role of the mass media in society (Kraidy, 1998)

After only four television stations were granted licenses, a variety of political indicators pointed to a freezing of the broadcasting dossier, in other words to a television "monopoly of four." At that juncture, broadcasting issues took an increasingly economic turn. This chapter looks at the social role played by television in postwar Lebanon, focusing on how private television constructed a public space for civic discourse. The research into this area also indicates that a focus on commercial concerns in the television industry is not a setback for civil society and civic discourse in the country, but that under some circumstances competition between stations creates a public sphere that invigorates civic discourse and provides it with popular channels of expression.

A BRIEF PROFILE OF LEBANON: HISTORY, GEOGRAPHY, AND CULTURE

Located in western Asia, Lebanon is bordered by Syria to the north and east, Israel to the south, and the Mediterranean Sea to the west. The country's 4,015 square miles make it one of the world's smallest nation-states. Lebanon was a province of the Ottoman empire for four centuries, enjoying a relatively high degree of autonomy, until the Ottoman defeat in the First World War brought on the French mandate. Lebanon gained independence in 1943. A census conducted in 1996 with the assistance of the UN Population Fund found the population to be 3.1 million ("Il y a plus," 1998). A total of 18 religious groups are now officially recognized by the state, but the 1996 census avoided the sensitive issue of the sectarian composition of the Lebanese population.

Modern Lebanon's civil tensions began in 1958, when Arab nationalists, advocating Lebanese union with Egypt and Syria, fought a Lebanese nationalist administration that requested the help of the U.S. Sixth Fleet to preserve its authority over the country. The 1958 events brought to the surface Lebanon's fundamental identity dilemma: is Lebanon a unique country with Phoenician ascendance and Western affinities, distinct from its Arab environment, as Lebanese nationalists argued? Or is Lebanon an integral part of the Arab world, an inseparable part of a whole, sharing the history, cultural values, and national identity of its neighbors? This question ensnared Lebanon in a permanent identity crisis, which would lead to sporadic tensions culminating with the 1974–1990 war. It is important to note that ideological divisions crossed religious lines, and that both Christians and Muslims could be found on both Lebanese nationalist and Arab nationalist sides.

Constitutional Protection of Civic Discourse

According to the May 23, 1926 Lebanese constitution, Lebanon is a democratic republic, with legislative, executive, and judicial branches whose roles are sanctioned by law and whose prerogatives are stipulated. The chamber of deputies, a unicameral assembly elected for 4 years, represents the citizens of the republic and holds legislative power. The president of the republic, elected by the chamber of deputies and not by universal suffrage, is the head of the executive power, which he shares with the council of ministers. Judiciary power is represented by independent judges. The right to vote is extended to all citizens aged 21 and older, irrespective of gender or religious affiliation. The president of the republic governs for a nonrenewable 6-year tenure (Bustros, 1973).

The Lebanese constitution protected civic discourse in that it guaranteed civil liberties and freedom of creed. Article 8 declared that "individual liberty is guaranteed and protected" and Article 9 stated that "liberty of conscience is absolute" and that "the state respects all creeds and guarantees and protects their free exercise." Finally, Article 13 of the Lebanese constitution stipulated that "[F]reedom of expression by word or pen, freedom of thought, freedom of holding meetings and freedom of association are equally guaranteed within the framework of the law" (Bustros, 1973, p. 2).

The constitution laid the groundwork for a robust civil society as a framework for civic discourse: it guaranteed the rights of citizens to express their ideas and own private property, the rights of journalists to publish their opinions, and of labor unions to form and demonstrate. The constitution also recognized the right of Lebanon's numerous ethnic and religious groups; the judicial system is an obvious testimony to the strength of civil society in Lebanon, as only criminal cases are treated by state courts, whereas civil cases are the province of religious courts established by religious groups (Saadah, 1993). In Lebanon, civic discourse enjoys constitutional protection. The Lebanese media, with a long history of private ownership and relative freedom, provided a vital arena where a variety of civic discourses were voiced. In order for us to understand the role of television in facilitating civic discourse in contemporary Lebanon, we need to understand the development of the Lebanese mass media.

The Mass Media in Lebanon—The Press

Historically, the press in Lebanon has enjoyed relatively high levels of freedom and autonomy. Three years after the first newspaper was published in Lebanon in 1858, England, France, Austria, Prussia, Russia, and Turkey signed a protocol giving Lebanon special press freedom not seen in other parts of the Arab world. However, a new Ottoman administration persecuted the press to the point of publicly hanging 16 authors, intellectuals, and journalists in Beirut in 1916 (Dajani, 1992). Publications proliferated out of control after the 1943 independence. This prompted the Press Law of September 14, 1962, which limited the number of publication licenses to 25 political dailies and 20 weeklies, and reaffirmed press freedom but prohibited publishing material detrimental to national security (Abu-Laban, 1966). During the 1974–1990 war, the press went through economic and political difficulties. After the war, the Lebanese press regained momentum and held on to its relative independence. In the early 1990s, there were 53 dailies, 48 weeklies, and 4 monthly magazines, all licensed, in addition to more than 300 nonpolitical publications (Dajani, 1992), which indicates that press laws are hardly enforced.

Broadcasting in Lebanon

Radio began in 1937 as an anti-Nazi, French-operated station broadcasting propaganda against Arabic-language programs sponsored by the Germans and Italians (UNESCO, 1949). The station was renamed the Lebanese Broadcasting Station. Several short-lived clandestine radio services appeared during the 1958 war (Boyd, 1993) but radio boomed in the early 1980s when dozens of unlicensed, privately owned radio stations inundated the airwaves with a variety of musical genres and a diversity of viewpoints (Kraidy & Khalil, 1995).

A 1956 agreement between businessmen and the Lebanese government established La Compagnie Libanaise de Télévision, with two channels—one Arabic and one French and English—that went on the air in 1959 (Boulos, 1996; Boyd, 1993). Lebanese TV became the first Arab station. A second commercial station, the Television du Liban et du Proche-Orient, better known as Télé-Orient, started in 1962, partially financed by the American Broadcasting Corporation and later by British Thomson (Boyd, 1993). In 1977, the two stations merged to become Télé-Liban, a shareholding company, half private and half state owned (Boulos, 1996).

TELEVISION, CIVIL SOCIETY, AND CIVIC DISCOURSE IN WARTIME LEBANON

Broadcasting activities boomed in the mid-1980s with an unprecedented impetus, possibly a unique occurrence in modern history (Boulos, 1996; Boyd, 1991). This growth was symptomatic of a larger phenomenon in war-torn Lebanon: the emergence of a vibrant civil society that complemented or replaced government services. At the beginning designed to be direct instruments of political propaganda financed by militia-collected taxes, private stations became commercial corporations fueled by an audience preference for private broadcasting and a growing advertising market (Kraidy, 1998).

Civil Society in Wartime Lebanon

The emergence of a civil society in Lebanon during the war was a response to the failure of the government to provide social and economic services. In this context, it is important to note that civil society is understood as the "realm of organized social life that is voluntary . . . self-supporting . . . [and] autonomous from the state" (Diamond, 1994, p. 5). This clarification is necessary because the concept of civil society has been used in a variety of ways, referring to heterogeneous alliances of groups, organizations, businesses, and individuals, a fact that led Garcia-Canclini (1995) to refer to civil society as an "imagined community," a term he borrowed from Benedict Anderson's celebrated study of nationalism and media technologies.

Civil society involves a collective action by citizens who express interests and concerns, exchange information, and make demands on the state. As such, in Harik's words, "[I]n Lebanon . . . civil society is stronger than the government" (1994, p. 51). This was especially true during the 1974–1990 war, when the state apparatus suffered from complete disintegration. Financially able citizens enrolled their children in private schools. Militias and parties established networks of social services consisting of hospitals, schools, employment offices, public transportation, and cooperatives. Labor unions organized, religious authorities reinforced their authority, and an informal economic sector prospered. Entrepreneurs illegally provided services such as international phone lines, power supply, and others, replacing sporadic and unreliable government services. A vibrant culture of autonomy emerged in the country, and civic organization and private entrepreneurship replaced government services (Kraidy, 1998). The geopolitical reality of wartime Lebanon poses a paradox for the civil society perspective. On the one hand, the country witnessed a robust presence of civil society activity at a time when state military control, administrative authority, law enforcement, and political legitimacy all but disappeared. The resilient culture of autonomy on the structural level was reflected on the ideological and cultural levels by pluralism, diversity, and a variety of discourses from across the ideological spectrum. These were reflected by a plethora of private educational, social, and media institutions. Furthermore, the civil society framework fosters partialness, the concept that different groups represent different and partial segments of society. Herein lies the civil society paradox posed by the Lebanese situation.

The partialness, diversity, and pluralism manifested in Lebanon during the war were completely determined by the geopolitical status quo, whereby paramilitary formations assumed full control of portions of the national territory. Taken as a whole, Lebanese civil society appeared to be vibrant. Indeed, Lebanon witnessed myriad competing civic and noncivic discourses. The wide array of ideological, religious, political, and cultural discourses represented was remarkable when one keeps in mind the size of the country's population (equal to that of Minneapolis-St. Paul) and territory (four fifths of the size of the state of Connecticut).

However, a closer look at those territories held by militias revealed their reality as small authoritarian spaces where warlords imposed their ideology on the population. As such, Lebanon was a jigsaw puzzle of several authoritarian enclaves, in each of which civic discourses were muzzled and mobilized under one ideological "militia discourse" opposing several other militia discourses across the land. As such, these militia discourses failed to develop key markers of civil society such as pro-democratic attitudes, tolerance, and equality for all people regardless of ideological orientation. This reality was reflected in the media under militia control by biased news bulletins, partisan public affairs programming, and a general propensity to propaganda, most of the time subtle but occasionally direct.

Television and Civil Society in Wartime Lebanon

In spite of partisanship, private media, especially television stations, were highly successful in attracting viewers. Audience members abandoned unreliable state-run media and flocked to private media. The Ministries of Information and of the Interior have in the past scrutinized television programs to protect national security (Abu-Laban, 1966; Boulos, 1996; Browne, 1975). This was true during the 1974–1990 war when officials instructed television executives to minimize coverage of the war (Browne, 1975). This "sanitizing" of television news was intolerable for the audience during the war, because accurate information about ongoing events was crucial to basic survival. In search of more reliable information, citizens turned to foreign services in Arabic such as Radio Monte-Carlo Middle East, the British Broadcasting Corporation, and, to a lesser extent, the Voice of America (Boulos, 1996). The unreliability of official media largely explains the success of private broadcasting during the 1974–1990 war in Lebanon. Another symptom of the strength of civil society was the enormous amount of foreign programming in Lebanon. The Westernization of world television is a global phenomenon, but in Lebanon it reached unseen proportions. Many private radio stations had nearly exclusively Western programming. Some specialized in French pop, others in rock, jazz, blues, or heavy metal. English was the language most widely used, followed by French, then Armenian as a somewhat distant third; this extended even to talk shows or phone-in programs (Kraidy & Khalil, 1995). Television broadcasts were also largely foreign and pirated, or in a foreign language, such as local newscasts, talk shows, or variety shows in French and English. Stations broadcast Cable News Network (CNN); Antenne 2 and TF 1 (French networks) news; Euronews; numerous American situation comedies, soaps, and police series; British comedy; German documentaries; Egyptian soap operas; and Latin American *telenovelas*.

Foreign programming reflected Lebanon's pluralism and was partly due to low investments in local programming and widespread piracy. Another driving force behind the foreign, mainly Western, programming in Lebanon is the Western cultural identity and social taste of a sizable portion of the Lebanese population, especially among Christians. Unlike other countries in the Arab world with more homogenous populations and less democratic governments, Lebanon witnessed no protectionist measures against threats of Western cultural imperialism. The unregulated abundance of foreign programming undercut the government's aim to make television a shaper of a unified national culture, and demonstrated the strength of civil society's constituencies in having broadcast programs that suited their tastes.

Television, the Audience, and Civic Discourse in Postwar Lebanon

With the official end of the war in 1990, Lebanon was the scene of a media explosion that by 1995 had produced more than 50 television stations and more than 100 radio stations, in addition to more than 300 publications of different formats and frequencies. These media outlets were a reflection of the political anarchy of the war, and successive Lebanese governments failed to establish a regulatory framework for broadcasting (Kraidy, 1998). Finally, on October 19, 1994, the "Audio- Visual Law" was passed by the Lebanese Chamber of Deputies. It revoked Tele-Liban's monopoly on television in Lebanon, affirmed audio-visual freedom of information, and required Lebanese stations to produce more local programs. It stipulated that channels were the exclusive property of the state and included provisions for leasing channels to private broadcasters, who were given a set of conditions and a 2-month deadline to apply for licenses. Finally, the law established the National Council of Audio-Visual Media (NCOAVM) to lay down technical conditions and monitor programming to ensure abiding to the law ("An Audio-Visual Law," 1994). The law was criticized for ambiguously referring to the advertising industry and for enhancing state power over broadcasting (Kraidy, 1998).

From Broadcasting Chaos to Television Monopoly of Four

On February 2, 1996, the Lebanese council of ministers decided to slash private television and radio stations upon the recommendation of the NCOAVM. Only four private televisions were given licenses ("Lebanon to Slash," 1996). Although rumors had anticipated it, the Council's decision was met with strong objections culminating in a general uproar in which members of the chamber of deputies joined journalists, religious leaders, students, and labor unions. Stations were reduced from 60 to 4 in the case of television, and from 150 to 10 in the case of radio. All but one of the licensed stations belonged to people holding government positions. These were Future television, owned by Prime Minister al-Hariri; MTV (Murr Television), owned by the family of deputy prime minister Michel al-Murr; the Lebanese Broadcasting Corporation International (LBCI), saved by its capital increase and political cover; and finally NBN, a station that did not yet exist (thus punned No Broadcasting Network), owned by Speaker of the Chamber of Deputies Berri (Kraidy, 1998).

The Economic Turn in Lebanese Broadcasting

More than a year before the Lebanese council of ministers restructured private broadcasting, two events indicated that economics was becoming a major force in the Lebanese broadcasting industry. With the anarchy of the war over, piracy was no longer an option, and political pressures were applied on stations to adhere to the general policy of the regime, in line with Syria. Besides, in a consolidated market with a restricted group of television stations monopolizing the market, audience ratings and advertising revenues somewhat eclipsed political agendas. These factors explain the rise of commercial issues.

The advent of commercial competition at the expense of old political rivalries was first signaled on September 6, 1995, when LBC, renamed the Lebanese Broadcasting Corporation International (LBCI), announced a U.S.$34 million capital increase. Pierre al-Daher, LBCI's chief executive officer and principal shareholder, announced that the money injected by new shareholders raised LBCI's share capital to upgrade equipment and expand coverage. At the time, al-Daher said that the strengthening of the station (in terms of capital expansion and political cover) increased its chances to obtain a license. He was proven right in February 1996. Most of the new shareholders did not subscribe to the Christian-Lebanese Nationalist ideology of the Lebanese Forces, the militia that established LBC as its mouthpiece. In fact, these shareholders included members of the Hariri council of ministers and of the Lebanese chamber of deputies, in addition to other prominent Christian and Muslim politicians ("Lebanon's Top," 1995). From its inception in 1985, LBC has been run like a business with an ideological discourse to disseminate, rather than a fully subsidized mouthpiece. Despite its Christian Nationalist ideology, for instance, the station had high quality and considerable special programming during the Muslim holy month of Ramadan, which attracted substantial advertising dollars. The 1995 capital increase, however, signaled the rising importance of economic issues.

A second event pointed to the reaction of advertising executives to the 1994 Audio-Visual Law's treatment of their industry (Kraidy, 1998). Jean-Claude Boulos, a Lebanese television and advertising veteran, who is currently head of Tele-Liban, expressed the concerns of the advertising industry towards the Audio Visual Law. In his 1996 book *La Tele: Quelle Histoire! (Television What a History!)*, an autobiographical chronicle of Lebanese television, Boulos claimed that there were several contradictions in the text of the law. Article 40 stated that "all the matters related to the subject of advertisements that are not mentioned in this law are to be regulated by a special law" ("An Audio-Visual Law," 1994, p. 37). Advertising people feared that a future "advertising law" might restrict their freedom, and insisted on the independence of advertising from media regulation. They opposed an advertising law on the grounds that advertising is apolitical, and that Lebanon should maintain "a free advertising industry at the service of a free economy" (Boulos, 1996, p. 237). Instead, they favored a code of ethics and verification bureau (Boulos, 1996).

Rising economic concerns within the television industry also became manifest during a legal dispute between the LBCI and the government headed by Rafiq al-Hariri. After the live broadcast of an interview with an eminent Lebanese legal expert, who criticized the lack of freedom on information in the Arab world, LBCI was contacted by officials from the ministry of information requesting that the interview not be broadcast via satellite to the Arab world in order not to offend Arab regimes with whom Lebanon had good relations and economic interests. Although LBCI officials said they would comply with the ministry's directive, government forces stormed the site and disconnected the broadcast. In its complaint with Lebanon's Shura council, the equivalent of the U.S. Supreme Court, LBCI's legal argument was not politically based, but economically motivated, citing among others the station's future inability to realize news scoops and exclusive interviews because of censorship ("Censure: La LBCI," 1997). In addition to legal struggles between LBCI and MTV over the exclusive Lebanese rights to live broadcasts of the Formula One car racing world championship, these events marked the rise of economic concerns in the Lebanese television industry.

The Audience: Citizens or Consumers?

The economic turn in the Lebanese television industry has profound implications for how the television audience is regarded. The perspective, which holds that television viewers are citizens to be informed, was replaced by an understanding of audience members as consumers to be sold products and services. This new perspective looks at audience members not as citizens with rights and duties in the realm of civil society, but as consumers with capital and commodities in the realm of consumption society. On the surface, this reconceptualization of the audience appears to be a serious threat to public life and civic discourse in Lebanon. For if society is looked upon as a market rather than a community, what would protect civic discourse from being either weakened by market forces or co-opted altogether for commercial purposes? What would prevent the public sphere from shrinking to a size tailored by economic forces of production and consumption at the expense of the common social good?

The answer is not as obvious as it appears at first glance. Without a doubt, the primary motivation of capitalistic media is to realize financial profit, with the implication that the public is viewed as an audience to be lured, rather than a citizenry to be informed. However, in contexts of inefficient and unreliable state infrastructures, such as during a war, a social vacuum is created where grievances are not followed up, services are not delivered, and questions are not answered. In such situations, the electronic media channel citizen discontent with government and exploit it in a variety of talk shows and other programs.

In developing countries, the magnitude of the state's institutional failure often affects a large number of citizens, while a rich and powerful minority circumscribes institutional inefficiency by the way of bribery, connections, and intimidation. This leaves the majority of people in a state of resentment, a feeling readily exploited by the mass media, especially television. In the words of Garcia-Canclini (1995) "the televisual realm is fast and appears to be transparent; the institutional realm is slow and its forms are complicated to the level of opacity" (p. 23). This is why, in Garcia-Canclini's opinion, people go to the media to achieve some social gains that the state fails to deliver, such as basic services, justice, or even simple attention.

This recourse to the electronic media compels us to reexamine prevailing notions of consumption and citizenship as two separate realms. In fact, in a context of private media ownership such as Lebanon, the realm of citizenship begins to overlap the domain of consumption when citizens turn to the media for social gains. Therefore, television, citizenship, and consumption should be understood in terms of their interdependence.

Television, the Public Sphere, and Civic Discourse in Postwar Lebanon

One of the most popular television genre in postwar Lebanon was the political and social talk show. Motivated partly by the 1994 Audio-Visual Law's requirement for local productions, and partly by the popularity of this genre with the Lebanese audience, several television stations produced immensely popular talk shows, as demonstrated by the large amount of advertising played during these programs. Among the licensed television stations, the LBCI and MTV had the most popular shows. LBCI's *Al-Shaater Yenki* (*May The Brave Speak Up*), presented by Ziad Njaym, *Hadiith al-'Umr* (*Dialogues of a Lifetime*), presented by Gisele, and *Kalam al-Naass* (*People Talk*), presented by Marcel Ghanem, competed with MTV's *Al-Hakeh Baynaatnah* (*Words Between Us*), presented by Maguy Farah, and *Sajjil Mowkaf* (*Take a Stand*), presented by Elie Nakouzi.

Lebanese Television Talk Show Formats

The hallmark of these programs broadcast live on prime time television was a charismatic host challenging guests with provocative and often embarrassing questions. These programs had different formats. In some, like LBCI's *Hadiith al-'Umr* and MTV's *Al-Haki Baynaatna*, the host and guest had a face-to-face conversation while sitting comfortably, with short documentary material about the guest and excerpts from the guest's public life broadcast during the conversation. An equivalent to this genre in the United States would be CNN's Larry King Live. Others such as *Al-Shaater Yehki* followed the town hall meeting format. The host, Ziad Njaym, moved on the stage, surrounded first by a circle of experts on the topic and second by an audience that had not been preselected. Other variations on the town hall meeting format included *Sajjel Mowqaf*, where two groups of people debated the pros and cons of an issue in a mock trial set-up facilitated by the host.

Some of these programs were exclusively political, such as LBCI's *Kalaam al-Naass*; others included a mixed menu of political, economic, cultural, and social issues, featuring Lebanese and Arab politicians, intellectuals, and artists. Others, such as *Al-Shaater Yehki*, focused on controversial social issues. Most of these talk shows took live telephone calls and direct intervention from the studio audience. In the words of Elie Nakouzi, host of *Sajjel Mowqaf*, ". . . [t]hat's what we want—to give people the chance to have their say face to face" (Baradhi, 1997). Political controversy often resulted from these programs. Their live format allowed for unpredictable questions from the audience, whether in person at the studio or by telephone, which often resulted in embarrassment for the host. This most often happened with callers venting their frustration at politicians and cornering them with tough questions to be answered live. In such situations, the host rarely intervened to help the guest exit an embarrassing situation, but rather pressed on with the question. Although it was reported that some politicians declined to participate, the immense popularity of these programs made them attractive to politicians seeking public exposure.

Television Talk Shows and Public Controversy

Perhaps more significant than political controversy was the fact that several of these talk shows openly discussed issues considered taboo, at least officially, in Lebanese society. These issues included premarital sex, incest, rape, homosexuality, and co-habitation. In one show about homosexuality, *Al-Shaater Yehki* featured several gay men with masks hiding their faces and distorting their voices, discussing the issue with a panel of "experts" consisting of a Christian priest, a Muslim sheikh, a lawyer, a psychiatrist, and a highly active studio audience divided on the issue. With homosexuality illegal and socially condemned in Lebanon, the show violated one of the most taboo subjects in the Arab world.

Understandably, the episode generated headlines for days, triggering a large controversy in the country with public statements by religious, political, and social leaders. A flurry of controversial talk show episodes led to what is referred to in Lebanon as the "morality on television" affair in the last few months of 1997. Whereas religious leaders called for ad hoc civil committees to monitor television performance on the moral front, the Cabinet headed by al-Hariri threatened stations with heavy sanctions if they continued to cover the worst in society and gave the impression that issues marginal to the Lebanese are part of the society's primary concerns ("Le Ministre," 1997). A statement by Minister of Information Bassem al-Sabaa summarized the official perspective on the issue: "[F]ree competition does not give the media the right to overstep the boundaries of ethical and cultural values" (Darrous, 1997a). The tension between economic imperatives and social mores became evident when critics accused the prime minister of triggering the row over television morals because his own Future television station was losing in audience ratings (Darrous, 1997b).

Television Talk Shows As an Avenue for Civic Discourse

Beyond the controversy created by the tension between markets and morals, these programs constituted a medium of expression for civic discourse. In a postwar era dominated by widespread beliefs that government officials are incompetent, corrupt, and removed from the concerns of citizens, and where grandiose reconstruction projects were the government's declared priority at the expense of social issues, these shows were perhaps the only avenue for Lebanese citizens to participate in public discourse, their only point of entry to the public sphere. Served by the set-up of these shows favoring spontaneity, frank dialogue, and provocative questions and emboldened by an "anything goes" atmosphere, citizens criticized policy, chastised politicians, demanded redress, and vented their frustrations in front of a national audience.

In addition to encouraging civic discourse, these programs contributed to making political discourse more transparent by offering a platform for direct confrontations between "loyalist" and opposition politicians, between exiled opposition politicians connected via direct satellite links and members of the administration, and, finally, between politicians and the public. In December 1997, former President of the Republic Amin al-Gemayyel participated live in a talk show on MTV, in which he accused Prime Minister al-Hariri of offering him a bribe of several million dollars during his presidency to appoint al-Hariri prime minister. Accusations of this scope require a response, and al-Hariri and his allies turned to similar talk shows to defend themselves against the accusation. A couple of weeks after the incident, a government ban on a scheduled live MTV interview with former prime minister and exile leader Michel Aoun caused an outcry and several days of demonstrations, strikes, and systematic and widespread civic action ("L'etat Empeche," 1997). One week later, a virulent anti-government interview with Beirut deputy Najah Wakim prompted Minister of Finance Siniora to call in live to defend himself against accusations of incompetence, corruption, cronyism, and misuse of public funds. Thus television offered a platform for competing political discourses, making important issues public, and pushing toward more transparency in public affairs and government accountability.

These talk shows offer insights on the relationship between a station's perceived political identity and the number of talk shows it offers and its success with audiences. LBCI, the station furthest removed from the regime in political terms, had more talk shows than any other station in the country. MTV, somewhat connected to the regime, offered some of these programs, but fewer than LBCI. Finally, Tele-Liban, still regarded as a state-related public company, had few talk shows, whereas Future television, widely perceived as the prime minister's public relations apparatus, could not compete in this market niche.

CONCLUSION

Whether television stations are driven by purely commercial motivations is irrelevant. After all, the economic turn may be temporary and political considerations may return to dominate in the event of political instability. Television shows in postwar Lebanon grappled with controversial social, political, and cultural issues, forcing public officials to explain their policies to the public in a live, nonscripted format. As such, these programs were beneficial to civic discourse in Lebanon, because private television stations offered a platform for several civic and other discourses to come in contact, therefore contributing to democratic life in the country. Television talk shows in postwar Lebanon provided a space of expression for a variety of discourses, including:

■ Civic discourses of individual citizens and constituencies of civil society (women's rights, environmental, professional, intellectual, artistic, and civic groups);
■ Discourses of ruling politicians to communicate with the public, civil society, and other politicians;
■ Discourses of opposition politicians to communicate with the public, civil society and other politicians; and
■ Discourses of exiled opposition politicians to communicate with the public, civil society, and politicians in Lebanon.

Although political parties in Lebanon are formed along sectarian lines, studies have shown that the television audience is fragmented across sectarian lines (Chaoul, 1997), not along them, therefore mitigating traditional sectarian and political polarities. This is remarkable because the ownership of licensed television stations follows sectarian lines: LBCI is Maronite Christian, MTV is Greek Orthodox Christian, Future is Sunni Muslim, and NBN is Shii Muslim. The fact that audiences do not follow these lines is an extremely important sign of the potential of Lebanese private television to construct a public sphere in which civic discourse and civil society converse with government officials. Television in Lebanon demonstrates that in some exceptional situations, the tension between morals and markets and the dilemma between citizens and consumers produces an alternative public sphere and fosters civic discourse.

DISCUSSION QUESTIONS

1. What are the exceptional circumstances that allow for civic discourse to be part of a public sphere that emerges between (political) authoritarianism and (market) capitalism?
2. Can private, capitalistic media contribute to the public interest in developing countries? How do we address the dilemma between private and public interest in such cases?
3. Why is the concept of civil society so important in providing a framework for civic discourse in developing nations?
4. Lebanon leads the Arab world in Internet subscriptions and Lebanese satellite television stations are very popular across the Middle East. Will new tech-

nologies foster or hinder civic discourse? Will they inhibit or empower citizens to be more active in public life'?

5. Reflect on your television viewing and on your cultural consumption in general. Do you perceive yourselves as "citizens" or "consumers"? What are the differences between these two concepts and their implications for civic discourse?

REFERENCES

Abu-Laban, B. (1966). Factors in social control of the press in Lebanon. *Journalism Quarterly, 43*, 510–518.

An audio-visual law at last in Lebanon: But are key aspects still missing? (1994, December). *Arab Ad,* 37–41.

Baradhi, A. (1997, December 1). TV's Nakouzi wants to talk about it now [Online]. *Daily Star.* Available: http ://www.dailystar.com.lb/1 - 12-97/feature3 .htm

Boulos, J. C. (1996). *La Tele': Quelle histoire* [Television: What a story!] [Online]. Beirut: Fiches du Monde Arabe.

Boyd, D. A. (1991). Lebanese broadcasting: Unofficial electronic media during a prolonged civil war. *Journal of Broadcasting and Electronic Media, 35*(3), 269–287.

Boyd. D. A. (1993). *Broadcasting in the Arab world.* Ames, IA: Iowa State University Press.

Browne, D. R. (1975). Television and national stabilization: The Lebanese experience. *Journalism Quarterly, 52*(4), 692–698.

Bustros, G. M. (Trans.). (1973). The Lebanese constitution. London: Bureau of Lebanese and Arab documentation.

Censure: La LBCI en appelle au Conseil d'Etat [Censorship: LBCI appeals to the Shura Council]. (1997, March 28). *L 'Orient-Le Jour,* p. 2.

Chaoul, N. I. (1997*). Les enjeux de l'audio-visuel: Reel fictif ou fiction realiste?* [The stakes broadcasting: Fictive reality or realist fiction?]. In J. Bahout & C. Douayhi (Eds.), *La vie publique au Liban: Expressions et recompositions du politique.* Beirut: CERMOC.

Dajani, N. (1992). *Disoriented media in a fragmented society: The Lebanese experience.* Beirut: American University of Beirut Press.

Darrous, S. (1997, November 25). TV stations told to stay within bounds of taste [Online]. *Daily Star.* Available: http://www.dailystar.com.lb/25- 11 -97/artS.htm

Darrous, S. (1997, December 10). TV morals row a camouflage for ratings war. *Daily Star,* p. 1.

Diamond, L. (1994). Toward democratic consolidation. *Journal of Democracy, 5*(3), 4–17

Garcia-Canclini, N. (1995). *Consumidores y ciudadanos: Conflictos multiculturales de la globalización* [Consumers and citizens: Multicultural conflicts of globalization]. Mexico City: Grijalbo.

Harick, I. (1994). Pluralism in the Arab world. *Journal of Democracy, 5(3),* 43–56.

Il y a plus de femmes que d'hommes au Liban [There are more women than men in Lebanon] [Online]. (1998, July 13). *L 'Orient-Le Jour.* Available: http//: www.lorient-le-jour.dm.lb/htdocs/ 7-13-10.html

Kraidy, M., & Khalil, J. (1995, April). *Hello out there: Cultural politics and programming tactics on Lebanese radios*. Paper presented at the Popular Culture Association Annual Convention, Philadelphia.

Kraidy, M. M. (1998). Broadcasting regulation and civil society in postwar Lebanon. *Journal of Broadcasting and Electronic Media, 42*(3), 387–400.

Lebanon's top private TV raises $34 million capital. (1995, September 6). Beirut: Reuters.

Lebanon to slash private broadcasters. (1996, February 7). Beirut: Reuters.

L'Etat empeche la diffusion de l'interview de Aoun sur la MTV [The state prevents Aonn interview from airing on MTV]. (1997, December 12). [Online]. *L'Orient-Le Jour*. Available: http://www. Orient-lejour.dm.lb/htdocs/12-12- 11.

Le Ministre de l'Information rappelle a l'ordre les televisions [Minister of Information calls television stations back to order]. (1997, December 3). *L 'Orient-Le Jour*, p. 1.

Saadah, S. A. (1993). *The social structure of Lebanon: Democracy or servitude?* Beirut: Dar An-Nahar.

UNESCO. (1949). *Press, film, radio*. Paris, France: Author.

2

WHY KIDS WANT THEIR MTV: A CROSS-CULTURAL PERSPECTIVE

Rasha A. Abdulla
American University in Cairo

INTRODUCTION

On August 1, 1981, *Warner Amex Satellite Entertainment Company* (*Warner Communication* and the *American Express Company*) launched the famous 24-hours-a-day music station, Music Television, better known as MTV. Since then, entertainment, television production, and the music industries have never been the same.

Starting with initial capital of $20 million to reach 2 million cable homes in 1981, the station had already established a viewership of 22.6 million homes by 1984 (at least one quarter of all households with television then), making a profit of $60 million for that year (Brown & Campbell, 1986; Sherman & Dominick, 1986). In 1987, MTV was catering to more than 36 million homes (Kalis & Neuendorf, 1989). MTV now is owned by Viacom International Inc., which also owns VH-1 (Video Hits 1). In 1994, Viacom Inc.'s revenue exceeded $7.36 billion (*Broadcasting and Cable Yearbook*, 1994; Levinson, 1995). The channel now caters to more than 60 million households on 8,290 cable systems in the United States alone, with a worldwide audience estimated at over 250 million households. Tom Freston, chairman and chief executive officer (CEO) of MTV Networks, believes that about half of the estimated 600 million television homes in the world will soon have access to MTV.

Although most critics predicted that MTV would not last for long, it was so popular in the United States that it was introduced to Europe on its sixth birthday in 1987. Combining a global presence and a single global brand with a product designed for separate regional markets, MTV today has several international affiliates. Special MTV editions already exist for Europe, Asia, Australia, Brazil, Japan, Latin America, New Zealand, and most recently, Russia. MTV Russia was launched at midnight on September 25, 1998, marking the first time a Western television station had been adapted for a Russian audience.

As *MTV at Work* (1995) puts it, "The MTV concept has become a global institution of youth culture and its irreverent and innovative on-air presentation has left an indelible imprint on music, television advertising, movies, and fashion the world over."

Cable News Network (CNN) published a story on its official web page stating that "MTV changed the music industry on August 1, 1981," the date the channel was launched. The article contends that unlike the popular song in which "video killed the radio star," in the case of MTV, video actually "made" the radio star. The article cites celebrities that it believes MTV helped make famous, including big names such as Rod Stewart, Michael Jackson, Peter Gabriel, Boy George, Madonna, Dire Straits, Duran Duran, and, more recently, Nirvana and Pearl Jam ("Video," 1998).

MTV in Egypt

On May 1, 1993, MTV was introduced to Egypt in what the channel called the "Cairo Crash Out." The agreement to bring MTV to Egypt was negotiated through Cable Network Egypt (CNE), the company that brought CNN to Egypt in 1991. CNE signed an agreement with Star TV, the MTV licensee (F. Amer, personal communication, January 2, 1994). In late 1994, CNE handed over the management of its subscription business to another company, MultiChoice.

According to Farouk Amer, general manager of CNE, the introduction of MTV doubled the subscription rates for CNN in less than six months (1,400 MTV subscriptions). MTV and CNN were offered as one package in an effort to more widely market CNN. So while subscribers could subscribe to CNN without MTV, they could only subscribe to MTV if they had CNN (F. Amer, personal communication, January 2, 1994).

There is another way, however, for the audience to have access to MTV in Egypt; that is through a satellite dish. At least four of the channels that CNE provides are available through satellite dishes. However, while CNE provides MTV Europe, the signal available through a satellite dish is MTV Asia.

MTV's Target Audience

The target audience of MTV is primarily teenagers. Brown and Campbell (1986) report that 83 percent of the MTV audience falls within the age bracket of 12 to 34 years old. Those viewers are reported to watch for an average of one hour a day on weekdays, reaching up to an average of one-and-a-half hours a day on weekends. This same age group is what Brown and Schulze (1990) claim to be MTV's primary target audience. Levinson (1995) pointed out that MTV is running out of growing room in the United States, since "most of the 18- to 24-year-olds who might be induced to watch MTV already tune in." Illustrating the strong hold of the music station over teenagers are the words of Robert Pittman, MTV's vice president for programming. He says, "At MTV we don't shoot for the 14-year-olds. We own them" (Greeson, 1991, p. 1909).

Content of MTV

Words like Robert Pittman's are why researchers, mass communicators, and dedicated parents worry about what their children watch on MTV. The controversy about the content of music videos shown on MTV never cools off. Researchers argue that, among other things, a dangerous dose of sex and violence is presented to the target audience of MTV through their favorite music channel.

Programming on MTV relies heavily on music videos. They are considered the main ingredient of the station. Music videos are basically 3- to 5-minute films accompanying a song or a piece of popular music. The videos are set apart by interviews with pop and rock stars, features, news, short programs, commercials, and video disc jockey or veejay spots (Sherman & Dominick, 1986).

Music videos have been accused of containing an overdose of sex and violence, thus raising much criticism. Many researchers have argued that MTV presents too much aggression, drug use, sexual activity, and sex-role stereotyping (Greeson, 1991; Harvey, 1990; Kalis & Neuendorf, 1989; Sherman & Dominick, 1986; Tapper, Thorson, & Black, 1994). Greeson (1991) reports on his earlier study with Williams (1986), which suggested a causal relationship between watching violent and sexual music videos and adolescent attitudes towards conformity, aggression, and premarital sex (Greeson, 1991). Professional associations and organizations such as the American National Coalition on TV Violence (NCTV), the Parents' Music Research Center (PMRC), and the American Academy of Pediatricians (AAP) have often condemned rock music videos shown on MTV as "bad for teens" (Kellam, 1992). Hansen and Hansen (1991b) argue that rock music and rock music videos concentrate heavily on themes of violence, sexuality, antisocial behavior, Satanism, sexism, drug use, and suicide. The authors fear that exposure to an overdose of such themes may have a harmful effect on adolescent viewers (pp. 373–374).

However, whether this effect really exists or not, or just how serious it might be, is not the concern of this chapter. Rather, the focus is on the uses and the gratifications of MTV viewing among different age groups of adolescent viewers in Egypt. Our concern is not with how MTV uses its audiences, but rather, with how those audiences use their favorite music channel, and what needs they seek to gratify through watching.

Uses and Gratifications Approach

The uses and gratifications approach has recently become one of the most popular theories in the field of mass communication. It has developed as an alternative to the failure of a good deal of communication research to produce direct evidence of media effects on audience members. The theory, adopted by followers of the functions approach to mass communication, provides an explanation of media consumption through the uses to which audiences put a particular medium (or contents of a medium) and the gratifications they obtain from that medium (Blake & Haroldsen, 1982).

The theory of uses and gratifications concentrates on the receiver of the communication message and considers him or her an active agent in the process of communication. The theory argues that the audience is actively utilizing the media rather than being used or influenced by them. It therefore does not assume a direct relation between the communication message and the effects on the consumers, but rather argues that it is the consumer who puts the messages to use, and however he or she uses the messages is an intervening factor that influences the effects of those messages on him or her (Littlejohn, 1983).

As Katz and Foulkes (1962) put it, "This approach [of uses and gratifications] proceeds from the assumption that the social and psychological attributes of individuals and groups shape their use of the mass media rather than vice versa. This is the approach that asks the question, not 'What do the media do to people?' but, rather, 'What do people do with the media?'" (p. 378).

Uses and Gratifications of MTV

With MTV growing as an effective medium of music communication for adolescents, some studies have been conducted, especially in the United States, to try to investigate why children and adolescents watch MTV. Sun and Lull (1986) surveyed 603 students enrolled in grades 9 through 12 in an ethnically diverse high school in San Jose, California. Among the reasons reported for viewing the channel, music appreciation ranked the highest in importance, followed by entertainment/enjoyment (no mean scores were reported for those reasons). Reporting means on a scale of 1 (strongly disagree) to 5 (strongly agree), "Passes time when I'm bored" scored a high mean of 3.57, "Take my mind off things" scored 3.38, "Do with friends" scored 3.30, "Relieves tension" scored 3.14, and, "Nothing better to do" scored 3.05 (pp. 118–119).

In the same study, Sun and Lull report other reasons for watching MTV, including visual appreciation, information and social learning, emotional satisfaction, escape/mood, and social interaction. The authors conclude that "the reasons that adolescents most frequently gave for watching MTV had to do directly with some aspect of music . . . . MTV viewers know what to expect from MTV and specifically want to see and hear their preferred music" (pp. 119–121).

Tapper, Thorson, and Black (1994) report on a study by Brown and Campbell (1986), who found that 39.1 percent of MTV adolescent viewers used MTV to "learn about current trends" (p. 104).

RESEARCH DESIGN AND METHODOLOGY

Although many studies have been conducted involving MTV, and its uses and gratifications in the United States, no studies of that sort have been conducted in Egypt, perhaps because MTV has not been available in Egypt for very long. The study described in this chapter is the first of its kind to try to investigate the uses and gratifications of MTV among its primary target audience in Egypt, namely teenagers and adolescents of a certain socioeconomic background.

The study set out to examine the uses and gratifications of MTV in Egypt. That is, primarily, why school-age students and university-age students watch MTV, and what needs they seek to gratify and satisfy through watching their favorite music channel. Independent variables studied in relation to uses and gratifications were age, gender, and favorite music genre.

Measurement

The uses and gratifications of MTV viewing were measured through 25 statements (reasons) coded in a Likert scale. Respondents were asked whether they (a) strongly agree, (b) agree, (c) disagree, or (d) strongly disagree with each of the statements. The "neutral" choice was intentionally excluded to force the respondents to make up their minds whether they actually used MTV in that particular way or not. The 25 statements, comprising probable reasons for watching MTV, were compiled based on previous literature. Useful guidance was obtained from studies by East-man (1979), Greenberg (1974), Rubin (1977), Sun and Lull (1986), Wells (1990), and Wells and Hakanen (1991).

The data were collected through a self-administered survey. Three hundred questionnaires were distributed to school and university students. The researcher (or a trained class teacher) was available at all times while respondents filled out the questionnaires. A purposive sample of 300 school and university students constituted the subjects for this study. The sample was comprised of three different age groups, with each group consisting of 100 students who were MTV viewers. An MTV viewer was defined as someone who watches MTV for a total of one hour or more every week. Non-MTV viewers were not included in the sample.

FINDINGS AND DISCUSSION

The research problem was broken down to two parts. The first part of the problem looked generally at the uses and gratifications of MTV viewers in Egypt. It examined the reasons why school-age students (two age groups) and university-age students (one age group) watch MTV, and what needs they try to gratify through watching. Demographic characteristics, such as age and gender, were studied as independent variables, and their effect on uses and gratifications was determined.

Hypothesis 1. Subjects are (or at least claim to be) more likely to watch MTV because of their interest in some aspects of music, dance, style or fashion, or for emotional satisfaction and mood management, than because of their interest in sexually explicit or violent music videos.

The general objective behind this hypothesis was to prove that although much controversy is raised over the content of MTV, and the amount of sex and violence included in the music videos shown on the channel, neither sex nor violence was one of the more important reasons why MTV's audience watches the channel. In other words, subjects did not watch MTV to satisfy a need for sex or violence.

Results show a fair amount of support for the first hypothesis. Out of 25 reasons that respondents were given for watching MTV, "Because I like the violence in the music videos," and, "Because I like the sexually explicit music videos" ranked among the lowest in importance. With a mean score of 1.813 (out of 4.000) for violence, only 20 percent of the respondents across all ages agreed (or strongly agreed) that violence was a need they sought to gratify through watching MTV. Only 30 percent agreed (or strongly agreed) that sex was a reason, with sex scoring a mean of 2.057. More than half the sample strongly disagreed on violence as a reason for watching MTV, and 40 percent strongly disagreed on sex. (For a listing of reasons' agree percentages, mean scores, and standard deviations, see Table 2.1).

On the other hand, reasons that had to do with music information, such as "To be up-to-date with the latest music and videos," seemed highly important to respondents, with 83.66 percent agreeing on that reason (with a mean of 3.207). The most important reported use for MTV was "To see particular singers or bands," scoring the highest mean of 3.280, and an agree percentage of 87.33. The visual aspect of MTV also seems to attract viewers, scoring a mean of 2.533 (an agree percentage of 51.34).

Those results seem consistent with previous research. For example, they are consistent with Sun and Lull's (1986) survey of 603 students in the United States, described earlier.

Social interaction also seemed important to respondents in the current study. "Because it [MTV] is something to do with friends" scored a mean of 2.423 (an agree percentage of 46.00), and "So I can talk about it [MTV] with my friends" scored a mean of 2.220, with an agree percentage of 38.66.

Overall, results show strong support for this hypothesis. While respondents reported concern about learning music information, enjoying themselves, and being entertained, neither sex nor violence appears to be a basic reason why MTV viewers watch the music channel, at least not at the conscious level.

TABLE 2.1.
Agree Percentages, Mean Scores, and Standard Deviations for 25 Listed Reasons for Watching MTV

Reported Reason for Watching MTV by the Whole Sample (n = 300)	Agree %	Mean	SD
Because it relaxes me and relieves my tension	58.00	2.583	0.879
To be up-to-date with the latest music and videos	83.66	3.207	0.816
Because it makes me feel less lonely	29.67	2.083	0.923
Because it passes time away when I'm bored	88.67	3.247	0.775
As background noise	53.67	2.540	0.955
Because I like the violence in the music videos	20.00	1.813	1.037
Because I have a good time watching	76.00	2.940	0.820
So I can talk about it with my friends	38.66	2.220	0.917
Because it is a fantasy, like a dream world	20.00	1.800	0.918
Because I learn from news and other spots	46.67	2.383	0.920
Because it's a habit, just something I do	49.33	2.540	0.937
Because it is exciting and entertaining	85.00	3.123	0.746
Because I want to be like the music stars	13.33	1.653	0.881
Because it takes my mind off other things	72.67	2.883	0.795
Because I like sexually explicit music videos	30.00	2.057	1.100
To follow the latest fashion and styles	46.66	2.417	0.980
Because I like to sing and dance along	45.66	2.403	1.022
Because it cheers me up	67.66	2.777	0.888
To see particular singers or bands	87.33	3.280	0.777
Because I like the fancy videos	51.34	2.533	0.958
Because it is something to do with friends	46.00	2.423	0.938
Because it helps me learn about myself and others	18.00	1.820	0.874
Because it makes me wild	25.66	1.957	1.025
Because there's nothing better to do or watch	57.66	2.667	0.948
To learn new dances	25.00	1.963	0.976

The second hypothesis had to do with age.

Hypothesis 2.   Age is a significant factor in determining the uses and gratifications of viewing MTV.

A.   Middle school-age students are more likely to enjoy sexually explicit MTV videos than high school-age students and university-age students.

B.   Middle school-age students are more likely to enjoy violent MTV videos than high school-age students and university-age students.

To test this hypothesis, mean scores for all reasons were first compared for each age group. Consistent with past research, the results proved that there are minor differences in the way audiences of different ages use MTV, or the gratifications they seek to satisfy through watching. However, as the hypothesis proposed, in general, the younger the age, the more the identification with each of the uses or reasons for watching. This is shown by higher means for most reasons among the middle school-age group, with those means decreasing among the high school-age group, and decreasing even more among the university-age group.

These findings are consistent with those of Greenberg (1974). He surveyed 726 British schoolchildren in three age groups—9, 12, and 15 years. Greenberg reported a structural flow of motivations from 9 to 15 years of age, for which the 12-year-old data identify a transitional period. Greenberg concluded that, "The younger child shows more identification with each of the gratifications than does the older child" (p. 84).

The results of this study are also consistent with those of Rubin (1977), who surveyed 401 children of three age groups—9, 13, and 17 years—in American public schools. Rubin found that age related negatively to identification with television uses. The relative importance of each use was largely stable for all three age groups, with minor differences.

The current study concludes, therefore, that although it is true that younger children show more identification with the uses and gratifications of MTV, age does not seem to be a significant factor in determining what those uses and gratifications are.

Hypothesis 3.   Gender is a significant factor in determining the uses and gratifications of viewing MTV among different age groups of school and university students.

A.   Males are more likely than females to appreciate sex in MTV music videos.

B.   Males are more likely than females to appreciate violence in MTV music videos.

To test this hypothesis, first of all, mean scores for all reasons were compared for both genders (Table 2.2). Consistent with past research, the results showed that gender is a significant factor in determining the uses and gratifications of MTV viewing. As parts A and B of the hypothesis proposed, males were more likely than females to appreciate sex and violence on MTV music videos. While the mean score for males on sex was 2.497 (an agree percentage of 46.98), that for females was 1.623 (an agree percentage of only 13.24). Moreover, 57.62 percent of the females strongly disagreed that they watch MTV because they "like the sexually explicit music videos."

As for violence, the mean scored by males was 2.107 (an agree percentage of 30.87). Females scored a mean of 1.523 on violence, an agree percentage of only 9.27. Showing an even stronger rejection of violence than of sex, 63.58 percent of the females strongly disagreed that they watch MTV because they "like the violence

TABLE 2.2.
Mean Scores Calculated for 25 Listed Reasons for Watching MTV by Gender

Reported Reason for Watching MTV ("I watch MTV because . . .")	Mean Scores by Gender	
	Male	Female
Because it relaxes me and relieves my tension	2.651	2.517
To be up-to-date with the latest music and videos	3.094	3.318
Because it makes me feel less lonely	2.054	2.113
Because it passes time away when I'm bored	3.188	3.305
As background noise	2.416	2.662
Because I like the violence in the music videos	2.107	1.523
Because I have a good time watching	3.020	2.861
So I can talk about it with my friends	2.188	2.252
Because it is a fantasy, like a dream world	1.758	1.841
Because I learn from news and other spots	2.315	2.450
Because it's a habit, just something I do	2.497	2.583
Because it is exciting and entertaining	3.134	3.113
Because I want to be like the music stars	1.738	1.570
Because it takes my mind off other things	2.859	2.907
Because I like sexually explicit music videos	2.497	1.623
To follow the latest fashion and styles	2.215	2.616
Because I like to sing and dance along	2.208	2.596
Because it cheers me up	2.745	2.808
To see particular singers or bands	3.302	3.258
Because I like the fancy videos	2.544	2.523
Because it is something to do with friends	2.342	2.503
Because it helps me learn about myself and others	1.846	1.795
Because it makes me wild	2.000	1.914
Because there's nothing better to do or watch	2.591	2.742
To learn new dances	1.765	2.159

in the music videos." This means that males are more likely to watch MTV because they enjoy sex and violence than females.

These findings are consistent with those of Greeson (1991), who found that males are more likely to enjoy watching sexually explicit music videos on MTV than females, and that females rated the explicit videos significantly lower than males. The findings are also consistent with the research of Wells (1990), who argued that gender makes a difference in terms of the uses and gratifications of music. More males claim to be energized by songs, sometimes within a sexual context. Wells reports on a male who said, "The songs can get you up and make you wild with your girlfriend." Females, on the other hand, were more likely to use music to relax. One female wrote, "It makes me feel as if the world is just so beautiful and there are no troubles to worry about." Wells concludes that, in general, "Men may use music to 'wind up,' women to 'wind down'" (p. 112).

The second part of the research problem looks at respondents' favorite music genre, and examines how it relates, if it does, to their uses and gratifications of MTV. To investigate this part, the following hypothesis was formulated.

> **Hypothesis 4.**   Subjects who prefer hard rock and heavy metal music genres are more likely to enjoy violent and sexually explicit music videos than subjects who prefer other music genres.

To test this hypothesis, a simple calculation of the mean for enjoying MTV's violent music videos for hard rock/heavy metal fans was first obtained (Table 2.3). These fans scored a mean of 2.389 for violence, while non–hard rock/heavy metal fans scored a mean of 1.632. On another calculation of the mean for enjoying MTV's sexually explicit music videos, hard rock and heavy metal fans scored a mean of 2.486 for sex, while non-hard rock/heavy metal fans scored a mean of 1.921.

Next, a Pearson r correlation between hard rock/heavy metal fans and enjoyment of MTV's violent music videos was obtained, which proved that the more one tends to be a fan of hard rock and heavy metal, the more likely one is to enjoy violence on MTV videos. The same was indicated for enjoyment of MTV's sexually explicit music videos. The more one tends to be a hard rock/heavy metal fan, the more one is likely to enjoy MTV's sexually explicit music videos. This seems consistent with past research, which shows that there is a correlation between preference for hard rock/heavy metal music and an interest in violence and sex on music videos (Hansen & Hansen, 1991a, 1991b).

Running t-tests for all reasons, hard rock and heavy metal fans proved to have a statistically significant positive identification with some gratifications, namely, enjoying violence on MTV music videos, enjoying sex on MTV music videos, watching to have a good time, watching as a habit, and watching to go wild. They proved to have a statistically significant negative identification with watching to follow style and fashion.

However, further research indicated that music genre does not seem to be an important factor in determining the uses and gratifications of MTV. For example, reasons that scored high means across the whole sample, like those on music information, scored high means with both the fans and the non-fans of hard rock and heavy metal. "To be up to date with the latest music and videos" scored a mean of 3.208 with fans and 3.206 with non-fans. (The mean score for this reason across the whole sample was 3.207.) "To see particular singers or bands," which scored a mean of 3.280 across the whole sample, scored 3.306 with fans and 3.272 with nonfans. These results are also consistent with past research.

TABLE 2.3.
Mean Scores Calculated for 25 Listed Reasons for Watching MTV by Music Genre

Reported Reason for Watching MTV ("I watch MTV because . . .")	Mean Scores by Music Genre hard rock/heavy metal	
	Fans	Non-fans
Because it relaxes me and relieves my tension	2.694	2.548
To be up-to-date with the latest music and videos	3.208	3.206
Because it makes me feel less lonely	1.986	2.114
Because it passes time away when I'm bored	3.194	3.263
As background noise	2.611	2.518
Because I like the violence in the music videos	2.389	1.632
Because I have a good time watching	3.167	2.868
So I can talk about it with my friends	2.278	2.202
Because it is a fantasy, like a dream world	1.806	1.798
Because I learn from news and other spots	2.222	2.434
Because it's a habit, just something I do	2.819	2.452
Because it is exciting and entertaining	3.278	3.075
Because I want to be like the music stars	1.792	1.610
Because it takes my mind off other things	3.042	2.833
Because I like sexually explicit music videos	2.486	1.921
To follow the latest fashion and styles	2.139	2.504
Because I like to sing and dance along	2.528	2.364
Because it cheers me up	2.806	2.768
To see particular singers or bands	3.306	3.272
Because I like the fancy videos	2.444	2.561
Because it is something to do with friends	2.500	2.399
Because it helps me learn about myself and others	19.03	1.794
Because it makes me wild	2.333	1.838
Because there's nothing better to do or watch	2.681	2.662
To learn new dances	1.778	2.022

CONCLUSION

In general, subjects in Egypt are more interested in watching MTV to satisfy music information and mood management needs than to satisfy sexual or violent needs. Their interest in sex and violence in music videos is minimal compared to other reported interests pertaining to music information and mood management.

These results are consistent with, for example, the findings of Sun and Lull (1986), who found that music appreciation and entertainment/enjoyment are the most important reasons for watching MTV. This confirmation shows that, although much controversy has been raised over the amount of sex and violence presented to MTV viewers in music videos, those viewers are not primarily interested in sex and violence in music videos. Rather, they watch MTV mainly to satisfy needs related to getting updated information on their favorite music and singers or bands, and they also use the music channel as a means of managing their moods.

Gender is a significant factor in determining the uses and gratifications of MTV in Egypt. Males were found to enjoy sex and violence in music videos significantly more than females. Gender also proved significant for other reasons for watching MTV. While males were significantly more likely to enjoy sex and violence in music videos, females were significantly more likely to watch MTV to be up to date with music, to have background noise, to follow the latest fashion, to sing and dance along, and to learn new dances. Those results are also consistent with past research. See, for example, Greeson (1991), Wells (1990), and Wells and Hakanen (1991).

The final independent variable that this study examined was music genre. In particular, the study analyzed how being a hard rock/heavy metal fan affects the pattern of uses and gratifications of MTV. The sample characteristics showed that hard rock and heavy metal fans are predominantly males. Hard rock and heavy metal fans proved to be significantly more likely to enjoy sexually explicit and violent music videos than non-fans. In general, though, music genre does not seem to be an important factor in determining the uses and gratifications of MTV. Reasons that scored high means across the whole sample, such as those pertaining to music information, scored high means with both the fans and the non-fans of hard rock and heavy metal. Those results are consistent with past research (Hansen & Hansen, 1991a, 1991b).

So what does it all mean? First of all, concerned parents probably should not worry too much about what their children are exposed to on MTV. The good news is that children do not really care that much about sex or violence in music videos. If sex and violence are among MTV viewers' interests, they do not primarily seek to satisfy those interests through the music channel. Those children are primarily interested in watching their favorite artists perform the music they like. They are also interested in having a good time, being in a good mood, and knowing "what's hot and what's not" for the sake of fitting well within their social environments.

Knowing the uses of MTV that most concern MTV viewers in Egypt is useful to both local television and music video producers, as well as international and MTV producers for whom Egypt is a part of the global target market they are trying to reach. To those producers, the message is as follows: It is creativity in the production that is most important, rather than meaningless sexual or violent scenes. This message is especially relevant to local music video producers, who do not seem to have clear guidelines for what makes a good popular music video. Some good lessons can be learned from the productions on MTV, and how viewers evaluate and use those productions. Instead of cramming a lot of dancing girls into a music video in an attempt to make it popular, producers should look for a creative theme. New technology utilizing graphics, computer animation, and shots of virtual reality could make a music video much more stimulating and interesting for viewers than out-of-place shots of a sexual or violent nature. When making a music video, producers should also be aware that, in a sense, they are creating style and fashion, and setting trends for their audience by what they show on their production.

Of special interest is the fact that the findings of this study are strikingly similar to the findings of other studies of the same nature conducted in the West. A factor contributing to this phenomenon might be the nature of the sample used in this study, students of the American University in Cairo and the Cairo American College. Although it might be argued that this is a "Westernized" sample, it is one typical of MTV viewers and the MTV target audience in Egypt. This is because those represented by the sample speak English and are likely to be from a socioeconomic class that could afford to have access to MTV.

Another factor that I believe has more to do with those similarities is the effect of the communication revolution the world is witnessing. More and more satellites are being launched and new television channels are becoming available daily to world audiences. Some youth of a particular socioeconomic class in Egypt are no longer that different from youth in the West, thanks to a global village that is becoming more homogeneous every day. As shown by this study, those youth in Egypt listen to the same music that youth in the West do. They have similar preferences and similar uses and gratifications for entertainment.

Sounds like a danger of cultural imperialism? Well, it might very well be. But only if local producers do not do anything to counter it. One positive aspect of MTV is that the station tries to incorporate local productions of its regional affiliates into the regular programming. However, these local producers have to compete with high MTV standards of production. In Egypt, music video production has tremendously improved over the past few years, but there is still a long way to go. The launch of the NileSat and five new Egyptian specialized satellite channels, including an international entertainment channel, offers the chance for our voice and our music to be heard. What some call cultural imperialism is really nothing but survival of the fittest. This underlying concept has been there all along, but with the speedily falling communication barriers of today, it becomes more evident. If local productions are fit enough to compete, they will have their share of air time, and I think that studies like this one show that youth worldwide are open to whatever is creative, without prejudice.

DISCUSSION QUESTIONS

1. Why is there such a big debate over the content and popularity of MTV? Do you think it is justified?
2. How might being a fan of a particular music genre affect the way someone uses MTV?
3. Comparing age and gender as two independent variables in this study, how significant are they to the uses and gratifications of MTV?

4. How does the global village we live in today affect youth preferences in different parts of the world in terms of what they see on television?
5. How might the threat of cultural imperialism be turned into something positive?

REFERENCES

Blake, R. H., & Haroldsen, E. O. (1982). *A taxonomy of concepts in communication* (3rd ed.). New York: Hastings House.

Broadcasting and cable yearbook (Vol. 1, 1994). New Providence, NJ: Bowker.

Brown, J. D., & Campbell, K. (1986). Race and gender in music videos: The same beat but a different drummer. *Journal of Communication, 36*(1), 94–106.

Brown, J. D., & Schulze, L. (1990). The effects of race, gender, and fandom on audience interpretations of Madonna's music videos. *Journal of Communication, 40*(2), 88–102.

Eastman, S. T. (1979). Uses of television viewing and consumer life styles: A multivariate analysis. *Journal of Broadcasting, 23*(4), 491–500.

Greenberg, B. S. (1974). Gratifications of television viewing and their correlates for British children. In J. G. Blumler & E. Katz (Eds.), *The uses of mass communication: Current perspectives on gratifications research* (pp. 71–92). Beverly Hills, CA: Sage.

Greeson, L. E. (1991). Recognition and ratings of television music videos: Age, gender, and sociocultural effects. *Journal of Applied Social Psychology, 21*, 1908–1920.

Hansen, C. H., & Hansen, R. D. (1991a). Constructing personality and social reality through music: Individual differences among fans of punk and heavy metal music. *Journal of Broadcasting and Electronic Media, 35*(3), 335–351.

Hansen, C. H., & Hansen, R. D. (1991b, June). Schematic information processing of heavy metal lyrics. *Communication Research*, 373–411.

Harvey, L. S. (1990). Temporary insanity: fun, games, and transformational ritual in American music video. *Journal of Popular Culture, 24*(1), 39–64.

Kalis, P., & Neuendorf, K. A. (1989). Aggressive cue prominence and gender participation in MTV. *Journalism Quarterly, 66*(1), 148ff.

Katz, E., & Foulkes, D. (1962). On the use of the mass media as "Escape": Clarification of a concept. *Public Opinion Quarterly, 26*(3), 377–388.

Kellam, J. (1992, Fall). Decoding MTV: Values, views and videos. *Media and Values*, 31–32.

Levinson, M. (1995, April 24). It's an MTV world. *Newsweek*, 44–49.

Littlejohn, S. W. (1983). *Theories of human communication*. Belmont, CA: Wadsworth.

MTV at work (1995). London: MTV.

Rubin, A. M. (1977). Television usage, attitudes and viewing behaviors of children and adolescents. *Journal of Broadcasting, 21*(3), 355–369.

Sherman, B. L., & Dominick, J. R. (1986). Violence and sex in music videos: TV and rock 'n' roll. *Journal of Communication, 36*(1), 79–93.

Sun, Se-W., & Lull, J. (1986). The adolescent audience for music videos and why they watch. *Journal of Communication, 36*(1), 115–125.

Tapper, J., Thorson, E., & Black, D. (1994, Winter). Variations in music videos as a function of their musical genre. *Journal of Broadcasting and Electronic Media*, 103–113.

Video made the radio star [Online]. (1998, July 31). Available: http://www.cnn.com/SHOWBIZ/
     Music/9807/31/encore.mtv/index.html
Wells, A. (1990). Popular music: Emotional use and management. *Journal of Popular
     Culture, 24*(1), 105–117.
Wells, A., & Hakanen, E. A. (1991). The emotional use of popular music by adolescents.
     Journalism Quarterly, 68(3), 445–454.

3

INTERNET PORNOGRAPHY: BETWEEN CONSTITUTIONALITY AND MORALITY

Mohammed el-Nawawy
University of West Florida

INTRODUCTION

The Internet, one of the modern technologies distinguishing the information superhighway, has been criticized for its transmission of indecent pictures and sexually explicit writings and speech. Critics argue that this indecent material has serious negative effects, especially on children. Those critics call for government intervention to regulate the Net and curb the indecency problem; meanwhile, staunch U.S. First Amendment supporters are against government regulation of the Net on the basis that it opposes the freedom of expression protected by the First Amendment and is, therefore, unconstitutional. Legal categories of sexually explicit speech include obscenity, which is not protected and can be banned, and indecency, which can be restricted for children, but not for adults. These categories are determined partly by community standards. In the case of the Internet, which lacks geographically identifiable community standards, the distinctions between obscenity, pornography, and indecency are not clear. This chapter investigates the cases dealing with Internet pornography, especially *ACLU v. Reno* (1997), in which the Supreme Court, in its first venture into cyberspace law, invalidated a key provision of the 1996 Communications Decency Act. The chapter also investigates the issue of Internet pornography in the Middle East and how cyberporn has been used by several Middle Eastern governments as a justification for censoring this new medium.

The Internet is a giant international, cooperative "network of networks," which connects many types of users. It is based on a common telecommunications protocol, a standard connection that allows different systems to communicate with each other. The Internet is mainly used to send and receive electronic mail (e-mail), to access remote computers, and to transfer files. Information on the Internet can be accessed in several ways, of which Gopher and World Wide Web are the most popular. The Web includes graphics and allows users to link to other information sites by clicking on highlighted words (*Cyberporn*, 1995).

The Internet has experienced extraordinary growth in recent years. In January 1995, the Internet served approximately 4.9 million host computers in 90 different countries. Today, over 9,400,000 host computers worldwide, of which approximately 60 percent are located within the United States, are estimated to be linked to the Internet. As many as 40 million people around the world have access to the communication Internet medium. That figure was expected to grow to 200 million Internet users by the year 1999 (*American Civil Liberties Union v. Reno*, 1996).

A certain amount of Internet traffic is pornographic, although the exact amount is unknown. Pornography is transmitted on the Internet in different ways. Some mailing groups have pornographic themes varying from mild erotica to bestiality. The World Wide Web contains sites that have pornographic images. Although most pornography sent in the form of e-mail is exchanged between consenting partners, unsolicited pornographic text can be transmitted through this channel. Most pornographic sites have titles reflecting their content. A portion of the pornography available in digital form, however, is not on the Internet, but on private bulletin boards that require proof of age and charge fees for membership. This was a source of confusion in the recent U.S. debate about the amount of pornography on the Internet (*Cyberporn*, 1995, p. 11).

U.S. politicians supporting the restrictions on Internet pornography argue that finding pornographic text and images on the Internet is extremely easy, and that children surfing the Net are likely to come across them, either intentionally or accidentally. Some of this material, they point out, would be considered obscene and, therefore, illegal in printed form (*Cyberporn*, 1995, p. 11).

Those in the United States who oppose restrictions argue that although some Internet pornography may be classified as indecent, much of the material is easily available in bookstores, video rental stores, or even libraries. Civil libertarians raise First Amendment concerns about restrictions. In addition, some opponents of restrictions fear that any threat of liability will hurt the development of the Internet (*Cyberporn*, 1995, p. 11).

INTERNET REGULATION AND THE FIRST AMENDMENT

The First Amendment to the U.S. Constitution provides that: "Congress shall make no law respecting an establishment of religion, or prohibiting the free exercise thereof; or abridging the freedom of speech, or of the press, or the right of the people peaceably to assemble, and to petition the Government for a redress of grievances." To ensure that some federal statute prohibits indecency over networked communications, U.S. Senators Exon and Gorton introduced the Communications Decency Act of 1995, which was designed to amend §223 of the Communications Act of 1934 to include specifically transmittal by means of a telecommunications device. Senator Exon announced that the Internet indecency is "a danger to society" and that "barbarian pornographers are at the gate and they are using the Internet to gain access to the youth of America" (Jasper, 1996).

On February 8, 1996, President Bill Clinton signed into law the Communications Decency Act (CDA), which constitutes Title V of the Telecommunications Act of 1996 (§314, 1995). Provisions of §502 of the CDA, which amend 47 U.S.C. §223 (a) (1) and (d), are as follows. Section 223 (a) (1) (B) provides in part that:

> any person in interstate or foreign communications who, by means of a telecommunications device knowingly . . . makes, creates, or solicits and initiates the transmission of any comment, request, suggestion, proposal, image or other communication which is obscene or indecent, knowing that the recipient of the communication is under 18 years of age shall be criminally fined or imprisoned. (§314, 1995)

Section 223 (d) (1) (the patently offensive provision) makes it a crime to:

> use an interactive computer service to send or display in a manner available to a person under age 18, any comment, request, suggestion, proposal, image, or other communication that, in context, depicts, or describes, in terms patently offensive as measured by contemporary community standards, sexual or excretory activities or organs, regardless of whether the user of such service placed the call or initiated the communication. (§314, 1995)

The provisions in §223 (a) (2) and §223 (d) (2) make it a crime for anyone to "knowingly permit any telecommunications facility under [his or her] control to be used for any activity prohibited in §223 (a) (1) (B) and 223 (d) (1)." The challenged provisions impose a punishment of a fine, up to 2 years' imprisonment, or both for each offense (Communications Decency Act, 1996). The American Civil Liberties Union (ACLU) filed suit challenging the constitutionality of the CDA provisions on the basis of First Amendment violation, as these provisions effectively ban a substantial category of protected speech from most parts of the Internet (*ACLU v. Reno, 1996*).

In *ACLU v. Reno* (1996), the U.S. District Court for the Eastern District of Pennsylvania struck down § 223 (d) (1) and 223 (d) (2) of the CDA as "unconstitutional on their face." In this context, the court said that in order to "obtain a preliminary injunction, plaintiffs must establish that they are likely to prevail on the merits and that they will suffer irreparable harm if injunctive relief is not granted." The court noted that in a case where the alleged injury is a threat to First Amendment interests, "the finding of irreparable harm is often tied to the likelihood of success on the merits." The court emphasized that "the loss of First Amendment freedoms, for even minimal periods of time, unquestionably constitutes irreparable injury." In this context, the court said,

> Subjecting speakers to criminal penalties for speech that is constitutionally protected in itself raises the specter of irreparable harm. Even if a court were unwilling to draw that conclusion from the language of the statute itself, plaintiffs have introduced ample evidence that the challenged provisions, if not enjoined, will have a chilling effect on their face expression. Thus, this is not a case in which we are dealing with a mere incidental inhibition on speech, but with a regulation that directly penalizes speech.

The court highlighted the fact that the CDA is "patently a government-imposed content-based restriction on speech, and the speech at issue, whether denominated 'indecent' or 'patently offensive,' is entitled to constitutional protection . . . . As such, the regulation is subject to strict scrutiny, and will only be upheld if it is justified by a compelling government interest and if it is narrowly tailored to effectuate that interest." In this context, the court further stated,

> The government asserts that shielding minors from access to indecent materials is the compelling interest supporting the CDA. It cites in support the statements of the Supreme Court that "it is evident beyond the need for elaboration that a State's interest in safeguarding the physical and psychological well-being of a minor is compelling. . . ." But the government has made no showing that it has a compelling interest in preventing a seventeen-year-old minor from accessing obscene images. (*American Civil Liberties Union v. Reno*, 1996)

The court criticized the CDA because of its overbreadth, and said that the Congress did not use the least restrictive means to achieve a compelling government interest. "The extent of the abridgment of the protected speech of adults that it has been shown the CDA would effect is too intrusive to be outweighed by the government's asserted interest, whatever its strength in protecting minors from access to indecent material" (*American Civil Liberties Union v. Reno*, 1996). In her comment on the overbreadth of the CDA and the Internet regulation's unconstitu-tionality under the First Amendment, Debra Burke, associate professor of law at Western Carolina University, argued that networked communications hold great promise for the free exchange of information among millions of users. Setting restrictions on the Internet, Burke, says, will inhibit this decentralized public expression and affect "the health of the First Amendment" since without full participation unskewed by regulation, "the promise of the First Amendment is only imperfectly analyzed" (Burke, 1996).

In its opinion about the unconstitutionality of CDA, the U.S. Supreme Court in *ACLU v. Reno* (1997) ruled that "the CDA is a content-based regulation of speech. The vagueness of such a regulation raises special First Amendment concerns because of its obvious chilling effect on free speech." The Court said,

> The CDA threatens violators with penalties including up to two years in prison for each act of violation. The severity of criminal sanctions may well cause speakers to remain silent rather than communicate even arguably unlawful words, ideas, and images. As a practical matter, this increased deterrent effect, coupled with the "risk of discriminatory enforcement" of vague regulations, poses greater First Amendment concerns than those implicated by the civil regulation reviewed in *Denver Area Ed. Telecommunications Consortium, Inc. v. FCC* 116 S. Ct. 2374 (1996).

The Supreme Court agreed with the district court on the overbreadth of the CDA and ruled that:

> the CDA lacks the precision that the First Amendment requires when a statute regulates the content of speech. In order to deny minors access to potentially harmful speech, the CDA effectively suppresses a large amount of speech that adults have a constitutional right to receive and to address to one another. That burden on adult speech is unacceptable if less restrictive alternatives would be at least as effective in achieving the legitimate purpose that the statute was enacted to serve. (*American Civil Liberties Union v. Reno*, 1997)

The Supreme Court's decision was hailed by the online civil liberties community as "a resounding victory for First Amendment rights everywhere." The lead attorney for the plaintiffs praised the ruling as reflecting "an enormously sophisticated understanding of the Internet," and predicted that it would "guide all future courts in deciding a whole variety of issues that apply to the net" (Chin, 1997).

Obscenity, Pornography, and Indecency: Confusing Terms

Courts have always struggled in their attempts to distinguish between obscenity, pornography, and indecency (Chiu, 1995). In *Roth v. United States* (1957), the Supreme Court held that "obscenity is not within the area of constitutionally protected speech or press." The court in *Memoirs v. Massachusetts* (1966), defined obscenity as a coalescence of three elements as follows: (1) the dominant theme of the material taken as a whole appeals to a prurient interest in sex; (2) the material is patently offensive because it affronts contemporary community standards relating to the description or representation of sexual matters; and (3) the material is utterly without redeeming social value. In *Jacobellis v. Ohio* (1964), the Court held that there is no shorthand description or intelligible definition of obscenity. In this case, Justice Stewart said in his observation of obscenity, "I know it when I see it." In 1973, the Supreme Court, in *Miller v. California*, announced a new test for obscenity as follows:

> The basic guidelines for the trier of fact must be: (a) whether the average person, applying contemporary community standards, would find that the work, taken as a whole appeals to the prurient interest; (b) whether the work depicts or describes, in a patently offensive way, sexual conduct specifically defined by the applicable state law; and (c) whether the work, taken as a whole, lacks serious literary, artistic, political, or scientific value.

In applying obscenity to the Internet, there should be a distinction between "variable obscenity" and "constant obscenity." "Variable obscenity of a given material is determined only by the context of the method of distribution and the intended and actual audience for the material." Meanwhile, "constant obscenity requires looking at the material to determine obscenity regardless of the method or objects of distribution" (Hixson, 1996).

In *Ginzberg v. New York* (1968), the Court sanctioned the concept of variable obscenity, whereby the state can restrict a minor's access to indecent speech, which for adults is constitutionally protected. In restricting a minor's access to speech not considered obscene, however, the state must not unconstitutionally burden adults' protected speech. The Court characterized "one overly eager effort to shield juvenile innocence as an attempt to 'burn the house to roast the pig.'" The CDA, which was designed to protect minors from indecent material on the Internet, also affects adults' rights to free speech (Burke, 1996, p. 123).

An element related to obscenity is "scienter." The Supreme Court has emphasized the importance of this requirement in the criminalization of obscene speech. In *Mishkin v. New York* (1966), the Court said "the Constitution requires proof of scienter to avoid the hazard of self-censorship of constitutionally protected material and to compensate for the ambiguities inherent in the definition of obscenity."

The Court in *Hamling v. United States* (1974) refined the scienter by requiring only that the defendant have knowledge of the contents of the materials distributed and of the character and nature of the materials, not their exact legal status. This scienter requirement poses several problems in the regulation of Internet obscenity. For example, how can a recipient of cybersmut have knowledge of the content of the materials, along with their character and nature, prior to downloading (Burke, 1996, p. 115)?

In *FCC v. Pacifica Foundation* (1978), the Court held that prurient appeal is not a necessary element in determining indecency. Indecent speech is defined by the FCC (Federal Communications Commission) as "language that describes, in terms patently offensive as measured by contemporary community standards for the broadcast medium, sexual, or excretory activities and organs."

The Supreme Court has concluded that "each medium of expression . . . must be assessed for First Amendment purposes by standards suited to it, for each may present its own problems." The Internet may be analogized to existing forms of communications in an effort to answer the many legal questions this new medium will pose (Burke, 1996, p. 124).

Some of the justifications behind the broad restriction on speech in the areas of broadcast media and telephone communications may not be relevant to cyberspace. For example, with respect to the banning of indecent material, the intrusiveness and scarcity rationales used to restrict broadcast speech should not be applicable to cyberspace. Network communication is neither scarce nor limited, and like cable television and dial-a-porn, it is invited into the home and is not an intruder. Therefore, any means to regulate indecency on the Internet must be narrowly tailored so as not to unduly burden protected speech (Burke, 1996, p. 125).

While the government has a valid interest in protecting children from indecent material on the Net, it does not have the right to ban cybersmut from consenting adults. "Such subjectively based paternalistic regulations are contrary to realizing a free marketplace of ideas and evidence the need for a reevaluation of the current obscenity standard (Burke, 1996, p. 125).

In *ACLU v. Reno* (1996), District Judge Daizell said this case is not about obscenity or child pornography, but it is about "indecency." Based on this fact, "the Government may only regulate indecent speech for a compelling reason, and in the least restrictive manner. It is not enough to show that the Government's ends are compelling; the means must be carefully tailored to achieve those ends. This most exacting scrutiny requires the Government to demonstrate that the recited harms are real, not merely conjectural, and that the regulation will in fact alleviate these harms in a direct and material way."

The court referred to the government's argument that this case is about Internet pornography. In this context, Judge Daizell said,

> Apart from hardcore and child pornography, the word pornography does not have a fixed legal meaning. When I use the word pornography in my analysis, I refer to for-profit purveyors of sexually explicit, "adult" material. Pornography is normally either obscene or indecent . . . . I would avoid using such an imprecise (and overly broad) word, but I feel compelled to do so here, since Congress undoubtedly had such material in mind when it passed the CDA. (*American Civil Liberties Union v. Reno*, 1996)

The Supreme Court in the *Reno* case said the CDA failed to provide any definition of the term "indecency" as used in §223 (a) (1) and, "importantly, omits any requirement that the patently offensive material covered by §223 (d) lack serious literary, artistic, political, or scientific value" (*American Civil Liberties Union v. Reno*, 1997). In this context, the Court said,

> Regardless of whether the CDA is so vague that it violates the Fifth Amendment, the many ambiguities concerning the scope of its coverage render it problematic for purposes of the First Amendment. For instance, each of the two parts of the CDA uses a different linguistic form. The first uses the word "indecent," 47 USCA §223 (a), while the second speaks of material that "in context, depicts or describes, in terms patently offensive as measured by contemporary community standards, sexual or excretory activities or organs," §223 (d). Given the absence of a definition of either term, this difference in language will provoke uncertainty among speakers about how the two standards relate to each other and just what they mean.

In addition, the Court said, "the general, undefined terms 'indecent' and 'patently offensive' cover large amounts of non-pornographic material with serious educational or other value" (*ACLU v. Reno*, 1997).

Community Standards

Under the first prong of the *Miller* obscenity test, the jury in the United States is to apply "contemporary community standards." In *Miller,* the Court rejected the requirement of a national community standard. According to the Court, "it is neither realistic nor constitutionally sound to read the First Amendment as requiring that the people of Maine or Mississippi accept public depiction of conduct found tolerable in Las Vegas, or New York City" (*Miller v. California*, 1973).

The Court in *Miller* concluded that under U.S. federal law, the community could be defined as being that from which the jurors were selected (*Miller v. California,* 1973). *Miller* failed to take the next logical step and define "community." There are inherent dangers in using an undefined "community." One of these dangers is that the defense cannot determine the extent and scope of evidence to put forward on community standards when it does not know what community the jury has in mind. The prosecution faces a similar dilemma (Sordillo, 1990, p. 632).

Another inherent danger in using an undefined community is that the jury may see itself as a mirror of the community. With no extrinsic standards to rely upon, jurors may have no choice but to rely on their own. Therefore, current obscenity standards may "create a community of the twelve seated in the jury box and permit their standards to largely determine whether material is obscene" (Sordillo, 1990, p. 632). *Miller*'s vague obscenity test has proven to be problematic even when applied to traditional works. But the inadequacies inherent in the community standard test become even more apparent when the standard is employed in the Internet (Burke, 1996, p. 108). As community standards do not remain constant, inconsistencies may arise over time and across jurisdictions. Over time, the concept of community standards may change, usually as social mores become more liberal. In addition, because the definitions of patent offensiveness and prurient appeal are dependent upon a jury's application, the concept of community standards may vary from place to place, or even from case to case depending on how each jury applies the test (Burke, 1996, p. 108). Beyond the community standards argument, restricting access to persons living in geographical areas less tolerant of sexually explicit speech than the community in which the message originates may be technologically impossible. While restricting messages sent by mail and even recorded messages transmitted by phone to certain geographical areas may be economically feasible, restricting interactive online communications would present a tremendous economic burden (Burke, 1996, p. 112).

Modern communication technologies have affected local community standards because the Internet has the ability to change relationships of time and space, such that geographical barriers have less impact (Chiu, 1995, p. 203). If a court can pass the threshold question of which "community" is at issue, the next step is to determine what the term "standards" means in the context of obscenity. The answer to that question was provided by the Federal District Court in *United States v. Pryba* (1988). The court in this case observed that "community acceptance is the touchstone of admissibility. It's axiomatic that community tolerance or availability does not equate with acceptability."

United States v. Thomas (1996), provided the first opportunity to question whether the court's use of local community standards to define obscenity is still viable in the modern computer communication context. Robert and Carleen Thomas (the defendants) ran a private, adults-only computer bulletin board system in California, and they electronically transferred computer-generated sexual images to the Western District of Tennessee. The court acknowledged the general principle that "in cases involving interstate transportation of obscene material, juries are properly instructed to apply the community standards of the geographic area where the materials are sent." In this context, the court said,

> Venue for federal obscenity prosecutions lies in any district from, through, or into which the allegedly obscene material moves . . . . This may result in prosecutions of persons in a community to which they have sent material which is obscene under that community's standards though the community from which it is sent would tolerate that material."

Defendants in *Thomas* argued that "to impose the standards of Memphis, Tennessee on national communications networks would have a chilling effect on the free speech rights of members of other communities. These networks would be compelled to self-censor and impose on the entire nation the standards of the most restrictive community" (*United States v. Thomas*, 1996). The defendants centered their argument on the point that Memphis standards should not be used to set ground rules for all cyberspace. "Allowing the conviction to stand would fly in the face of

Miller by creating a single national, even global, standard based on the law of Tennessee" (*United States v. Thomas*, 1996).

In its response to this argument, the court said "obscenity is determined by the standards of the community where the trial takes place . . . . The federal courts have consistently recognized that it is not unconstitutional to subject interstate distributors of obscenity to varying community standards" (*United States v. Thomas*, 1996).

Minors' Access to Internet Pornography

In his comment on the effects of Internet pornography on minors, Senator James Exon, the CDA's chief sponsor, said, "It is no exaggeration to say that the most disgusting, repulsive pornography is only a few clicks away from any child with a computer. I am not talking just about *Playboy* and *Penthouse* magazines . . . . I am talking about most hardcore, perverse types of pornography, photos and stories featuring torture, child abuse and bestiality" (Katsh, 1997). The court said "even if credit card verification or adult password verification were implemented, the Government presented no testimony as to how such systems could ensure that the user of the password or credit card is in fact under 18. The burdens imposed by credit card verification and adult password verification systems make them effectively unavailable to a substantial number of Internet consumers" (Katsh, 1997).

Otto Larsen, a law professor at the University of Washington, said "it may turn out that obscenity cannot corrupt. Even if it can, we may conclude that the family is better suited than the law to insulate the young and, failing that, to inform them that pornography is not within the sphere of adult society's approval" (1994, p. 75).

CREATING A NATIONAL COMMUNITY STANDARD

The existence of local community standards has either become extinct or is about to enter extinction because of society's growing interconnectedness. These local standards are irrelevant to cyberspace, "a technological expanse which transcends provincial boundaries" (Chiu, 1995, p. 216). The appropriate community should be the "virtual" community that can be judged using a national standard. Computer technologies allow communities to be created by individuals who share similar interests and who come from global villages whose citizens are more connected to their electronic neighbors than to their geographical neighbors.

> The cyberspace community is as much a community as traditional geographic divisions. This community should have the right to articulate its standards on the issue of obscenity. A definition of community based on connections between people rather than one based on geographic location will ensure that all communities have the right to define protected speech. (p. 216)

With a local community standard, people such as the Thomases, discussed earlier, who operate in the modern telecommunications age, risk liberty and property without reasonable notice. A national standard will provide notice to every citizen in the country, because it is one standard that applies to the distributor's and the recipient's communities (Chiu, 1995, p. 216). Juries should use Justice Brennan's formulation in *Jacobellis,* where he noted that "juries' decisions should be based on views of the society at large and people in general." This is basically a national standard (*Jacobellis v. Ohio*, 1964).

Internet Pornography in the Middle East

Despite the fact that the Internet is accessible by less than 1 percent of any given population in the Arab world, the issue of censoring the Internet has been raised in many Arab countries. While industrialized countries rapidly establish the foundations of the 21st century's "information society," already identified with fifth-generation computers, many Middle Eastern countries still have an antagonistic approach toward the Western technology, and they still live by the 19th-century mentality that resists any technology from the West. Therefore, the new technologies, including the World Wide Web, widen the gap between those who have access to information and those who do not have the resources, the opportunity, or the freedom to make independent decisions (Gonzalez, 1988). This information gap between the haves and the have-nots is based not only on industrial capability and economic strength, but also on access to and control over information, political independence, and cultural ideology (Gonzalez, 1988).

The issue of Internet pornography in the Arab countries and the way these countries view the Internet raise the following questions:

1. What are the problems impeding Internet accessibility in the Middle East?
2. Should an Internet government or regulatory facility be created to be responsible for traffic flow and content?
3. Should there be an international standard for judging the Internet?
4. What kind of theoretical paradigm can be used to define the status and positionality of the Arab countries in the communication and information age?

Barriers to Internet Accessibility in the Middle East

The so-called informatization of society forms part of the current global agenda through which there is a one-way cultural and technological flow from the Western countries to the developing countries. This results in future shock for these developing countries that lack adequate means and appropriate social values to assimilate and cope with the Western technology (Gonzalez, 1988).

In the Middle Eastern countries, conservative religious groups have always associated the Internet with pornography and perceived it as similar to an X-rated movie. Thus, religious groups regard the Internet as taboo without even thinking of the advantages of this new technology. This resistance to the Internet is part of the Arab-Islamic suspicion toward all modern carriers of Western sources of information. "The more conservative guardians of the old Muslim traditions yearn for a return to the slow pace of pre-colonial information growth;" computer technology for those conservatives has gained the status of an unquestionably "bad thing" that disseminates sexual values and Western lifestyles (Haywood, 1995, p. 133). They tend to take it at face value that the Internet is harmful because it includes pornography without actually trying to study this new medium.

The increasing intolerance of many followers of Islam toward what they perceive as the "corrupt and materialistic foundation" of many Western sources of information has been strong in countries such as Egypt and Algeria, where Islam is a dominant creed and where the Islamic extremists have been arguing that the banning of Western technologies, including the Internet, is the only way to ensure religious and moral salvation for the Islamic societies (Haywood, 1995, p. 255). The Islamists' call for the suppression of Western information sources creates fear among Arab people toward using any technology from the West. Moreover, it puts pressure on the Arab governments to apply strict censorship to the information sources imported from the West. "Strident and uncompromising, the Islamists' messages convey confrontation rather than ecumenicism, a message of insistence rather than fraternity, the closing up and turning inward of a rich culture rather than an opening out of it as part of a community of learning and exploration" (Haywood, 1995, p. 142). In this context, the president of the Internet Society of Egypt has recently stated that government filtering would be a proper measure to censor the Websites and limit access to pornographic material. Censoring the Net would be easier in Egypt, where the server is government owned, than it would be in the United States.

The Internet is not the only Western source of information that is being censored in Egypt. The Egyptian government, under pressure from conservative Islamic groups, has also removed several controversial books by Arab writers from the market on the basis that they oppose Islamic values. In taking this step, the Egyptian authorities have sided with officials from Al-Azhar, the leading Sunni Islamic organization based in Cairo. Al-Azhar officials argued that these books disseminate ideas that are improper for an Islamic society (Haywood, 1995).

In their opposition to Western sources of information, the Islamic conservatives argue that these sources introduce English as a currency of communication and as the language of the West instead of the Arabic language of the Koran. They claim that this contributes to the "Western imperialism of informatics" (Gonzalez, 1988, p. 65). Informatics and censorship of Western information sources create previously unknown situations for which the vast majority of the Middle Eastern countries still have not adopted legislation.

Religious and ideological opposition is not the only barrier to Internet accessibility in the Arab world. The lack of human expertise and material resources, the inadequacy of production and management capabilities, the outdated telecommunications facilities, and the lack of scientific and technological infrastructures contribute to the complexity of the problem (Gonzalez, 1988, p. 3). All these barriers limit Internet accessibility in the Arab world to very few social elitists, especially university professors.

Accessing the Internet: An International Standard

In regulating the Internet and evaluating its pros and cons, should an international community standard be applied? The issue of international regulation was first introduced by UNESCO in the debates over a new international information order during the late 1970s. In the course of these debates, a report was first introduced by the McBride Commission, proposing the "formulation by all nations and particularly developing countries, of comprehensive communications policies linked to overall social, cultural, economic, and political goals" (Gonzalez, 1988, p. 38). The adoption of this international regulation failed because the United States and the Western countries regarded it as "nothing more than another UNESCO effort to promote state control over the press" (p. 37).

Merrill (1998) argues that international communications standards can be applied on equipment, but not on people. According to Merrill, different nations and different people have different cultures and different values. "It is indeed difficult, if not impossible, for an international communication system to adequately suit all these cultures" (p. 13).

In this context, it has been argued that technology is not neutral. It is a medium conceived of and oriented toward specific political, social, and cultural contexts, and, therefore, it cannot be subject to an international regulatory system (Gonzalez, 1988).

Who Should Control the Internet?

Governing access to the Internet and other "Western" sources of information will always be a provocative and controversial issue in the Middle East and other developing countries. The questions raised in this context are: Who should do the governing? and, How will they be selected? Many communication scholars argue that regulating children's access to the Internet should be the responsibility of social organizations, especially family and school. They say that the government, by setting strict controls over the information sources, increases the isolation, separateness, and "draconian seclusion" of the developing countries (Haywood, 1995, p. 138).

Those scholars oppose providing pornographic material to people under the age of 18. But, in the meantime, they argue that the responsibility of protecting children should be carried out by parents and school authorities through the use of filtering products, such as Cybersitter, Netnanny, and Safe Surf (Haywood, 1995).

COMMUNITARIANISM—A PARADIGM FOR INTERNET REGULATION IN THE MIDDLE EAST

The U.S. Supreme Court based its latest decision to strike down government regulation of the Internet on the freedom of expression provided by the First Amendment. Because Middle Eastern and other developing countries do not have a First Amendment, the issue of regulating the Internet in these countries can be approached from an authoritarian versus libertarian point of view. Authoritarianism gives governments the right to regulate the Internet and set limits on people's accessibility to the Websites. This is the case in all the Arab countries today, where freedom of the press is considered a "grant" from the government rather than the people's right.

In the meantime, libertarianism calls for a free marketplace of ideas, where there is no government intervention to regulate the media and where freedom is necessary for informational pluralism and diversity. However, there is some difficulty in applying the libertarian theory in the Arab countries, where competition and libertarian ideas are believed to be socially harmful, biased, greedy, and imperialist. According to Merrill (1998), the most suitable theoretical paradigm for media regulation in the developing countries in general and the Arab world in particular is the communitarian paradigm, which is described as "the cousin of social democracy in the West" and which is halfway between authoritarianism and libertarianism.

Clifford Christians, one of the founders of communitarianism (also called public/civic journalism) argued that "citizens are empowered for social transformation, not merely freed from external constraints as classical liberalism insisted" (Merrill, 1998, p. 13). The new theme raised by communitarianism is this: "Let the journalism sphere and the public sphere overlap. Let there be a symbiosis between journalists and people. . . . Let there be focus groups and more surveys and polls to guide the direction of journalism." In many ways, this new trend toward "peoples' journalism" is in keeping with the democratization principle of earlier days, but in other ways it flies in the face of the traditional American principle of owner-controlled journalism stemming from Enlightenment liberalism (Merrill, 1998, p. 11).

According to civic journalists, the people can provide better journalism (more reflective of national values) and they can help the journalists in ushering in a better, more socially responsible media system. "This is a step toward order, and it is being taken without throwing out many of the vestiges of libertarianism" (Merrill, 1998, p. 11).

The Role of Family and School in Internet Regulation

According to the communitarians, the family, as a social entity, plays a vital role in guiding children and internalizing social and moral values in their socialization.

Moreover, the public schools formulate the moral infrastructure for children, especially during their early years. Communitarians argue that the schools enhance the personality capabilities that enable people to act morally and civilly. Among these capabilities is the ability to control one's impulses. A mature person needs to recognize urges—sexual urges, for instance—and acquire ways to curb them or channel them toward socially constructive outlets (Etzioni, 1996). The communitarians, in highlighting the significant role of family and school in children's socialization, stress the argument made earlier that regulating the Internet is the responsibility of the family and school, not the government.

CONCLUSION

The U.S. Supreme Court's decision in the *Reno* case in June 1998, which struck down the 1996 Communications Decency Act, will not put an end to the conflict and controversy surrounding pornography over the Internet. The U.S. courts will continue to resist attempts to restrict freedom of speech and expression, and political pressure will continue to combat pornography and the dissemination of sexually explicit material.

The information superhighway is part of an information revolution in which millions of messages can be transmitted to anyone, anywhere, in a matter of seconds or even portions of seconds. In the information and technology age, many countries in the Middle East and elsewhere are still trying to censor the people's access to information sources, including the Internet. The governments of these countries cannot recognize that it is becoming virtually impossible to block the flow of information traveling electronically or to prevent the installation of devices for receiving it. They cannot recognize the ability of the modern telecommunications technology to cross borders. This ability makes it impossible for even the most closed countries to keep out information. All it takes is time. And time is definitely not on the side of the constraining or regulating forces whose efforts to interfere effectively with transborder information flows will fail to stop the globalization of this information.

DISCUSSION QUESTIONS

1. Outline the history of Internet regulations in the United States with reference to the 1996 Communications Decency Act.
2. How has the U.S. Supreme Court differentiated between obscenity, pornography, and indecency?
3. How do Internet regulations in the United States compare to those in the Middle East?

4. Can an international community standard be applied to regulate the Internet in the Middle East? Why or why not?
5. How might communitarianism be used to regulate the Internet in the Middle East?

REFERENCES

American Civil Liberties Union v. Reno, 929 F. Supp. 824-855 (E.D. Pa. 1996).
ACLU v. Reno, 117 S.Ct. 2329-2346 (1997).
American Civil Liberties Union v. Reno, 929 F. Supp. 824, 831 (E.D. Pa. 1996).
Burke, D. (1996, Winter). A call for a new obscenity standard. *Harvard Journal of Law and Technology, 9(1),* 124–131.
Chin, A. (1997). Making the World Wide Web safer for democracy. *Hastings Comin/Ent. Law Journal, 19,* 310–317.
Chiu, D. (1995). Obscenity on the Internet. *Santa Clara Law Review, 36,* 189–196.
Communications Decency Act, 502 USC §223, 56 (1996).
Cyberporn: Protecting our children from the back alleys of the Internet. Hearing before the Subcommittee on Basic Research and Technology, Committee on Science, U.S. House of Representatives, 104th Cong., 1st Session, 16 (1995).
Denver Area Ed. Telecommunications Consortium, Inc. v. FCC, 116 S.Ct. 2374 (1996).
Etzioni, A. (1996). *The new golden rule: Community and morality in a democratic society.* New York: Basic Books.
FCC v. Pacifica Foundation, 438 U.S. 726, 743 (1978).
Ginzberg v. New York, 390 U.S. 629 (1968).
Gonzalez, E. (1988). *The hidden war of information.* Norwood, NJ: Ablex.
Hamling v. United States, 418 U.S. 87, 123 (1974).
Haywood, T. (1995*). Info-rich -info-poor: Access and exchange in the global information society.* New Providence, NJ: Bowker.
Hixson, R. (1996). *Pornography and the justices.* Carbondale, IL: Southern Illinois University Press.
Jacobellis v. Ohio, 378 U.S. 184, 197 (1964).
Jasper, M. (1996). *The law of obscenity and pornography.* London: Ocean Publications.
Katsh, E. (1997). *Taking sides: clashing views on controversial legal issues.* Guilford, CT: Dushkin.
Larsen, O. (1994). *Voicing social concerns.* New York: University Press of America.
Memoirs v. Massachusetts, 383 U.S. 413, 418 (1966).
Merrill, J. (1998). *Culture, communication and control: A quest for order and social harmony.* London: Longman.
Miller v. California, 414 U.S. 881 (1973).
Mishkin v. New York, 383 U.S. 502, 511 (1966).
Paris Adult Theatre I v. Slaton, 413 U.S. 49 (1973).
Roth v. United States, 354 U.S. 476, 478 (1957).
Saliba v. State, 475 N.E. 2d 1181 (Ind.App.2 Dist. 1985).
Sordillo, D. (1990). Emasculating the defense in obscenity cases. *Loyola Entertainment Law Journal,* 10.

Telecommunications Act, 104th Congress, 1st Sess. §314 (1995).
United States v. Pryba, 678 F.Supp. 1225 (1988).
United States v. Thomas, 74 F.3d 701 (6th Cir.1996).

Discourse II
Western Cultural Invasion: Myth or Monster?

4

MEDIA IMAGES OF ARABS, MUSLIMS, AND THE MIDDLE EAST IN THE UNITED STATES

Yahya R. Kamalipour
Purdue University–Calumet

INTRODUCTION

"We live in a world of things seen," writes Arthur Asa Berger (1989), "a world that is visual, and we expend much of our physical and emotional energy on the act of seeing. Like fish we 'swim' in a sea of images, and these images help shape our perception of the world and of ourselves" (p. 1).

When I was in high school, my late father used to tell me a very simple, yet profound, anecdote that I still vividly remember and often share with my students whenever we discuss the impact of mass media on individuals and society. "Tell me," he would say, "if you were a fish, swimming in an ocean, could you really understand and appreciate all that surrounds you—your environment?" "Furthermore," he would continue, "if someone who could speak in fish language would ask you—the fish—the meaning of water, do you think you would be able to answer?" Of course, I did not have a clue as to how to answer his rhetorical questions. Upon seeing my puzzled facial impression, he would say, "Of course, you could not understand your complex environment clearly nor could you describe the meaning of water, unless one day a storm would somehow land you on the shores—the dry land. It is then, only then, that you would be able to answer those questions." The lesson that he was trying to convey to me was this: We are all born and raised in different environments, not according to our desires but by pure

55

chance. We are then gradually acculturated—learning to do what others in our cultures do, eat what they eat, wear what they wear, learn to speak in their language, think in the way they think, and so on. This is why a Russian baby grows up to be Russian in language, likes and dislikes, mode of dress, and world view. In a way our culture becomes like an invisible ocean that envelops us. Gradually we become immersed in a cultural environment that has been largely defined for us by others, including our parents, teachers, leaders, clergies, and increasingly by the mass media of communications (Lippmann, 1922).

For the most part we do not first see and then define, we define first and then see. In the great blooming, buzzing confusion of the outer world, we pick out what our culture has already defined for us, and we tend to perceive that which we have picked out in the form stereotyped for us by our culture (Lippmann, 1922). On the other hand, our culture is influenced, shaped, and reshaped by the mass media, particularly the visual media. In fact, we live in a media culture. This means that "Media no longer just influence our culture. They are our culture" (Silver, 1992, p. 2).

GLOBAL MEDIA AND THEIR IMPACT

Today, we swim in a media-induced cultural environment that is inundated by a barrage of mass-produced images. Images of all kinds are generally intended to serve a commercial purpose, from selling cigarettes and political candidates, to ideas and automobiles. Consequently, our worldview, or our perception of other peoples, events, and places, is largely defined—often in an unrealistic and stereo-typical manner—by the mass media that span the globe. For example, stereotyping is the process of typecasting, mentally, a cultural group (Arabs, Africans, Jews, Irish, Mexicans, Iranians, Native Americans), a religion (Islam, Judaism, Christianity, Buddhism, Hinduism), or a geographical region (Asia, the Middle East, Africa, Latin America, Europe), often in an oversimplified manner. Samovar and Porter (1995) write, "The reason for the pervasive nature of stereotypes is that human beings have a psychological need to categorize and classify. The world we confront is too big, too complex, and too transitory for us to know it in all its details. Hence, we classify and pigeonhole" (p. 290).

Although stereotyping exists in practically every culture, today it has become more pervasive than ever before, mainly as a result of the popularity, multiplicity, universality, and influence of the mass media that are owned and operated by a handful of transnational conglomerates, such as General Electric, Time Warner, Disney, and Westinghouse. It is through the mass media that stereotypical images of cultural groups are often manufactured and reinforced. George Gerbner argues that "While the world is changing, the obsolete and damaging image-bound media system is becoming increasingly rigid, commercialized, concentrated, and global-ized. Channels multiply but communication technologies converge, media merge, and merged media conglomerate" (1997, p. xiv). The owners of these conglomerates or "lords of the global village," as media critique Ben Bagdikian (1997) calls them, exert a homogenizing power over ideas, culture, and commerce that affects populations larger than any in history. It is often through media depictions and reports that we define the "outer world," learn about certain events, and form our perceptions of "others." In his 1922 classic book, *Public Opinion*, Walter Lippmann wrote: "Man . . . is learning to see with his mind vast portions of the world that he could never see, touch, smell, hear, or remember. Gradually he makes for himself a trustworthy picture inside his head of the world beyond his reach" (p. 181).

Mass Media and the Information War

According to Mary A. White, "Information is shifting from print to imagery . . . and the shift . . . is affecting deeply how we see our world, how we think about it, and how we solve its problems" (qtd. in Anderson, 1992, p. 16). In 1967, the late Canadian media critic, Marshall McLuhan, wrote that "Real, total war has become information war. It is being fought by subtle electric information media—under cold conditions, and constantly. The cold war is the real war front—a surround—involving everybody—all the time—everywhere" (McLuhan & Fiore, 1967, p. 138). In other words, he predicted that future wars will not be fought using conventional weapons on the battlegrounds, but rather through images portrayed by the mass media.

On the eve of the dawn of our third millennium, "the war of images" or "the information war" is in full swing, and image-makers are busily packaging everything from soaps, toys, and breakfast cereals to presidential candidates, nations, religions, and ideas. Unfortunately, wars produce casualties, and in the contemporary wars of images, the Middle East and everything associated with it, including religion, politics, language, climate, and custom has been under an unscrupulous attack by the Western media. Based on the prevailing Western media reports and perception studies, it is safe to state that the Middle East is perhaps the most misrepresented, misperceived, and stereotyped region of the world.

The contemporary global media—newspapers, magazines, books, music, motion pictures, radio, television, and the Internet—have undoubtedly affected almost every aspect of our lives (Kamalipour, 1997). Todd Gitlin writes, "Of all the institutions of daily life, the media specialize in orchestrating everyday consciousness—by virtue of their pervasiveness, their accessibility, their centralized symbolic capacity. They name the world's parts, they certify reality as reality—and when their certifications are doubted and opposed, as they surely are, it is those same certifications that limit the terms of effective opposition" (1980, pp. 1–2).

American High School Students' Perceptions of the Middle East

In 1997, I presented a series of one-day seminars entitled *The Middle East: Learning From the Persian Gulf War* to nearly 500 high school students in five cities throughout northern Indiana in the United States. In each city, a selected number of students from various high schools were brought together in an auditorium to participate in the seminars. This annual event, called "World Affairs Conference," has been sponsored by the Rotary Club International and School Corporations of Northern Indiana for more than 15 years. Its main purpose is to promote international understanding and awareness among American youth. To that end, the Fifteenth World Affairs Conference provided me an opportunity to illustrate the interplay of media-society-and politics in relation to image, war, censorship, and perception. It also offered me a unique opportunity to conduct an opinion poll, by using an information-gathering method called "word-association," to gauge students' perceptions of the Middle East. Hence, prior to my introductory remarks, I would ask the participants to pick up a blank sheet of paper and a pen and write anything that would come to their minds, without censoring themselves, immediately after I gave them a word or phrase. Also, to ensure anonymity and a relative degree of accuracy, I would ask them not to write their names on their response papers. Then, at the beginning of every seminar, I would state the following words in this same order: The Middle East, Arabs, Muslims, Iranians, Israelis. Table 4.1 shows the results of their responses. Although the results are not compiled in any particular order, only responses that were mentioned in various ways by at least 20 students are included.

Based on the students' responses, it is quite evident that their overall perceptions of the Middle East, Arabs, Muslims, and Iranians were overwhelming negative. However, their perceptions of Israelis tended to be generally neutral to positive. For instance, while the respondents referred to others (Muslims and Iranians) as "anti-American," they referred to Israelis as "American allies." Also, other stereotypical and prejudicial labels such as "dark skin," "rag-heads," "terrorists," or "dangerous" were only used to describe the non-Israelis.

At the end of each seminar, the results of the opinion polls were shared with the participants. Owing to the strikingly similar responses generated at every location, I had routinely to point out the participants' overwhelmingly negative perception of the Middle East and ask whether there was anything positive that they could have ascribed to Middle Easterners. While a few were surprised by the negative results, others admitted that they could not really think of anything positive about the Middle East. Also, some of the students commented that they could not recall having seen anything positive about the Middle East in the media. In fact, in his 1984 study, Jack Shaheen quotes a television producer who stated that "most of the things people learn to love or hate or mistrust or adore, they get from television" (p. 63). Furthermore, after interviewing a dozen television producers, writers, and directors, Shaheen (1984) discovered that none of them could even recall any positive images of Arabs in any past or present television series.

TABLE 4.1.

Middle East	Arabs	Muslims	Iranians	Israelis
War	Muslims	Strict religion	Ayatollahs	Jerusalem
Terrorism	Turbans	Mosques	Khomeini	Netanyahu
Dangerous	Rag-heads	Mohammad	Extremism	Arafat
Oil	Veils	Long robes	Hostages	PLO
Desert	Highjackers	Veiled women	Anti-American	Rabin
Hot	Terrorists	Always praying	War	American allies
Camels	Dark skins	Mecca	Oil	Hate Arabs
Sand	Wealth	Mecca	Mean people	Palestinians
Saddam Hussein	Poverty	Holy war	Iran-Contra	Holy land
Kuwait	Tents	Arabs	Dark skin	Jewish
The Gulf War	Sand	Violence	Mustaches	Religious
PLO	Oil	Terrorism	Terrorism	Star of David
Jews	Robes	No women's rights	Conflict	Hebrews
Arabs	Harems	Allah	Religious	Moses
Muslims	Religious	Koran	Poverty	Hanukkah
Hate	Sheik	Religious	Muslims	West Bank
Fanatics	Yasser Arafat	Poverty	Strict	Gaza Strip
Radical	Repression	Dark skin	Fanatical	Conflict
Destruction	Arabian	Harems	Sand	Fighting
Oppression	Horses	Sacrifice	Fighting	Death
Dark skin	Ali Baba	Inequality	Arabs	Secrecy
Dress funny	Alladin	Militant	Death	Peace process
Black veils	Rebels	War	Hated	Powerful
Cab drivers	Sandals	Middle East	Saddam Hussein	Bible
Oppressed women	Cab drivers	Anti-American	Missiles	Terrorism
OPEC	Mecca	Strong beliefs	Not Without my Daughter (movie)	Strict religion
Always in news	Saddam Hussein	Bombings		
	Mustaches			
	Belly dancing			

Middle East as a "Big Blob"

Having discussed the students' responses, I subsequently distributed a map of the Middle East and asked them to point out any distinction, in terms of culture, language, geography, history, or politics, between the countries of the Middle East. Once again, they generally appeared to think of the Middle East as a "big blob," devoid of any variation or diversity. And again, as illustrated in the earlier table, only Israel was mentioned as a country having a distinct religion, language, culture, and politics. The students generally failed to mention, for instance, that Iran and Afghanistan are two Middle Eastern countries whose inhabitants are historically and culturally different from the Arabs and whose language is Persian not Arabic. Nor did they mention the distinct cultural, geographical, and political variations that exist between and within the Arab nations such as Morocco, Egypt, and Saudi Arabia, or the differences between the two main Muslim sects, Shi'a and Sunni.

Negative Images of the Middle East

The term "image" refers to many manifestations, including printed materials, photographs, films, political cartoons, public persona, symbols, and so on. According to John Berger (1977), "An image is a sight which has been created or reproduced" (p. 9). Thus, our worldview, or our perception, of "others" is often based on what we have seen, read, or heard in the media. In other words, images are created and framed by the image-makers.

Arabic and Islamic stereotypes date back to the Middle Ages, when the expansion of Islam into Europe pitted Arab against European, leading to Western cultural and political efforts to discredit Arab/Islamic culture (Fuller, 1997). According to Allen Woll and Ronald Miller, "In songs and literature Westerners portrayed Islam and Arabs as heathenish and dangerous. The Crusaders provided further political and cultural reasons to implant anti-Arab images in the Western mind" (qtd. in Fuller, 1997, p. 188).

Today, the Middle East suffers from a grossly distorted image and is perhaps one of the most misperceived regions of the world. Hence, American students are not alone, nor should they be blamed, for their stereotypical images of the Middle East. Jack Shaheen (1984) discovered that even television executives do not know much about Arabs or their nations. Shaheen, who has interviewed TV executives and analyzed TV programs for several years, states that the stereotypical images of Arabs on television, or "The Instant TV Arab Kit" as he calls it, "consist[s] of a belly dancer's outfit, headdresses (which look like tablecloths, pinched from a restaurant), veils, sunglasses, flowing gowns and robes, oil wells, limousines and/or camels" (1984, p. 5). Regarding Islam, a notable scholar, Edward Said (1981), argues that ". . . there is a consensus on 'Islam' as a kind of scapegoat for everything we [the Americans] do not happen to like about the world's new political, social, and economic patterns. For the right, Islam represents barbarism; for the left, medieval theocracy; for the center, a kind of distasteful exoticism" (p. xv). Furthermore, in a *Chicago Tribune* piece, Khan and Levine (1998) observe that in the U.S. media, statements against Asians are deemed "xenophobic," those against African-Americans are "racist," and if targeted against Jews, they are "antisemitic" (p. 10). But obnoxious statements against Muslims are justified in the name of nationalism, freedom of expression, and national security. Muslims are the last group we can still make fun of and not be politically incorrect (Khan & Levine, 1998).

In other words, when violent acts are committed by Middle Easterners or Muslims, the U.S. media unabashedly use such labels as "Muslim terrorists," "Arab terrorists," or "Middle East terrorists," while they rarely make a similar religious, ethnic, or regional association when, for instance, Christians, Jews, Africans,

Indians, South Americans, Europeans, or others commit similar acts of violence (Kamalipour, 1996). As to why Hollywood and television producers have to resort to stereotyping, Harvey Bennett, producer of *The Bionic Woman* and *Six Million Dollar Man*, offers the following response: "I don't have any explanation for stereotyping other than it's easy . . . . It's sign language. It saves the writer the ultimate discomfort of having to think" (qtd. in Alliance for Children and Television, 1998, n.p.).

The Simultaneous Bombing of U.S. Embassies

It seems that whenever a disastrous terrorist attack occurs, such as the simultaneous bombing of the U.S. embassies in Nairobi, Kenya, and Dar el Salaam, Tanzania, in the summer of 1998, journalists and political experts are quick to point their fingers at the Middle East. For instance, talking about these senseless attacks, a U.S. government official said, "it is only 'natural' for us to conclude that there is a Middle Eastern connection in these bombings, but we have to avoid making assumptions at this early stage" ("All Things Considered," 1998). Within the same newscast, it was also reported that security forces in Kenya and Tanzania were rounding up any "Arab-looking" individuals in public places for questioning ("All Things Considered," 1998). In a *Chicago Tribune* front-page report, Stephen Hedges (1998) wrote that "The initial list of bombing suspects was speculative, centering on groups and individuals who had issued threats against U.S. interests, primarily in the Persian Gulf and the Middle East" (pp. 1, 11). Two "Islamic fundamentalists," one based in Afghanistan and the other in Egypt, Saddam Hussein of Iraq, and ". . . a previously unknown group called the Liberation of Army of the Islamic Sanctuaries" were also mentioned as possible suspects (Hedges, 1998, pp. 1, 11).

The Simultaneous U.S. Missile Attack on Afghanistan and Sudan

On August 7, 1998, the U.S. embassies in Kenya and Tanzania were bombed. Two weeks later, the United States attacked—by firing some 80 cruise missiles—two suspected targets, a camp in Afghanistan and a pharmaceutical plant in Sudan (Watson & Berry, 1998). Reportedly, the Saudi Arabian millionaire and Islamic extremist, Osaman bin Laden, living in exile in a heavily fortified camp in Afghanistan, was behind the embassy bombings and other terrorist incidents. It was also alleged that a pharmaceutical plant in Sudan, with connections to bin Laden, was in the process of producing dangerous chemical agents for warfare. However, according to *Newsweek*, a leader of "Afghanistan's Taliban movement, insisted bin Laden had clean hands" (Watson & Berry, 1998, p. 26). Likewise, "Sudanese officials," rejecting any connections with bin Laden, "insisted the plant made innocent medicines for both humans and animals" (p. 27).

Interestingly enough, during the Persian Gulf War, some critics argued that President George Bush used that war to cover up his internal problems and shed his "wimpy" image (Kellner, 1992). After the simultaneous attacks on Afghanistan and Sudan, many critics suggested that President Bill Clinton used the twin attacks on Afghanistan and Sudan to divert attention from his sex scandal involving Monica Lewinsky. According to *Newsweek* (Watson & Berry, 1998), in the Pentagon briefing room, only minutes after the president announced the strike, Defense Secretary Cohen was asked whether he had seen the film *Wag the Dog*. In this film, a fictional president creates a made-for-television war to divert attention from a sex scandal. Was our real president striking just at terrorism—or also at Independent Counsel Kenneth Starr and his superstar witness, Monica Lewinsky (Watson & Berry, 1998)?

At the same time, it seems that the allegations regarding the pharmaceutical plant in Sudan were baseless, while allegations against bin Laden still seem somewhat credible. Although an aura of uncertainty surrounds both attacks, it is quite certain that, once again, the terrorist image of the Middle East and the fanaticism of Islam were reinforced in the court of public opinion.

The following instances provide further illustrations as to the distorted images of the Middle East and its peoples. It should also be noted that another reason for the public's misperception of the Middle East in relation to terrorism is the ongoing conflict between the Israelis and Palestinians. These conflicts, routinely reported by the Western media, not only overshadow the entire region negatively, but also create the mistaken belief that the Middle East is, indeed, a constant battlefield—perceptually a dangerous place.

The Persian Gulf War

Prior to the Persian Gulf War, a highly orchestrated media campaign began to transform Saddam Hussein's Clark Gable image in the United States into that of a ruthless ruler, worse than Hitler. (Interestingly enough, just prior to Iraq's invasion and occupation of Kuwait in 1990, the U.S. government had vigorously supported Saddam's war against Iran for 8 years.) On the other hand, the American public relations firm of Hill & Knowlton was hired by Kuwait's ousted rulers to stage media events aimed at stirring up American public opinion in favor of military intervention. Hence, the Kuwaiti ambassador's 14-year-old daughter was trained by Hill & Knowlton tearfully to tell the U.S. Congress that she had personally witnessed Iraqi troops taking newborn babies out of hospital incubators in Kuwait and throwing them onto the floor to die. The reality was that she had not even been in Kuwait during Iraq's invasion, but her emotional eyewitness testimony was aired repeatedly on television networks in the United States and elsewhere around the world to stir up the public's sentiment in favor of the already orchestrated war. Of course, television viewers did not know, nor were they informed, that they were watching a concocted fictional story. In the process, public opinion was mobilized by her emotional testimony, and Americans were skillfully persuaded by the media and media handlers to support the war efforts. According to Douglas Kellner:

During the Gulf War, the mainstream media were cheerleaders and boosters for the Bush administration and Pentagon war policy, invariably putting the government "spin" on information and events concerning the war. By all accounts, the U.S. government was extremely successful in managing public opinion and engineering consent to their Gulf War policies. (1992, p. 1)

Furthermore, President Bush had successfully overshadowed his domestic political-economic problems, had helped the oil companies to boost their profits by increasing the price of petroleum, had illustrated the military might of the United States to the world as the only superpower, had gained the excuse to establish military bases in Saudi Arabia and Kuwait and increase the U.S. military presence in the Persian Gulf, and had gained support for his entire New World Order plan.

The Oklahoma City Bombing, the Olympic Bombing, and the Explosion of TWA Flight 800

The Oklahoma City bombing tragedy in 1995, the crash of a TWA Boeing 747 in 1996, and the bombing incident at the 1996 Olympic Games in Atlanta, provide further illustrations of a mindset that every terrorist act committed in the United States or abroad must somehow be linked to the Middle East. In a television report about the TWA Flight 800 explosion (which, based on conclusive findings, had been caused by an electrical problem), a man in the crowd with teary eyes and trembling voice spoke these words into the microphone: "I hope to God it was the work of people from the Middle East" (Semati, 1997). Even the respected *New York Times* alluded to a "Middle East connection" because, it argued, Oklahoma City is "home to at least three mosques," as if that were a necessary and sufficient condition for terrorist activity (Suleiman, 1996, pp. 16–17).

In practically every instance, assumptions and speculations by the media and government officials led the American public and, in turn, the world public, to believe that a Middle Eastern country, perhaps Iran, or Libya, or Syria, or Iraq, or perhaps a Muslim fundamentalist group, might have been behind those tragedies. In fact, such speculations and assumptions led U.S. security forces to detain and search a Jordanian-American who happened to be on a flight out of Oklahoma City on the day the bombing tragedy took place. Furthermore, the TWA crash was sufficient cause for President Clinton to sign a bill imposing strict economic sanctions against Iran and Libya in a meeting with many tearful mourners who had lost their loved ones in that crash. Of course, no journalist bothered to question the logic of that action. Were the two events (the TWA crash and the economic sanctions against Iran and Libya) connected?

Once again, America needed a scapegoat upon which to cast its ills. And the American media followed suit with such sensational headlines as "Who Wishes Us Ill? The CIA is casting a wide net for those who hate America, including groups from the Middle East" (*Time*, July 29, 1996). According to Fuller (1977), "The main point of Middle Eastern bashing, quite obviously, is framing that population as the enemy so that the United States emerges as the hero" (p. 191).

The Middle East and Islam as Post–Cold War Nemesis

The paradox is that in this post–Cold War era, when the Soviet communist nuclear threat against capitalism has vanished, most signs appear to demonstrate that the Middle East and Islam have replaced the "Red menace."

In his 1995 assessment of Arab Americans, Michael Suleiman (1996) makes the following observations:

> Arabs in America suffer from general anti-foreign and anti-immigrant sentiment, but they also feel the brunt of anti-Arab and anti-Muslim feelings. In 1995, such attitudes were often reflected in the mass media and popular culture as well as in the workplace. Also, a public television documentary, "Jihad in America," added to a climate of suspicion and mistrust of Arabs and Muslims in the United States. (p. 16)

Unfortunately, the prevailing public mindset, fostered largely by the Western mass media, the white Anglo-Saxon experts, and government officials or ex-officials, is such that the mere mention of the Middle East and Islam conjures fear, mistrust, hate, and terrorism. Hence, the general public unquestioningly accepts any accusations against Middle Easterners or Muslims for any act of violence, anywhere around the world.

According to Hamid Mowlana (1997), "The media images of the Middle East to a great extent have their roots in the media's image of Islam. Indeed, the Islamic identity and the media's understanding of this worldwide phenomenon determine the procedure through which events, policies, and actions are portrayed. Bosnia-Herzegovina with its large Muslim population in the heart of Europe provides an example of this image-making process that was also observed in the Persian Gulf War" (p. 4).

Even in daily conversations, writes Bud Khleif (1998), "The discourse of derogation belittles the Islamic 'other.' Now that communism is no longer the enemy of choice, Islam may be a substitute, particularly an Islam that may be associated with nationalism, the real enemy of American economic and security interests in the Middle East" (p. 277).

PORTRAYALS OF ARABS IN RADIO AND TELEVISION

In their study of media representation of Arabs, Rebecca Lind and James Danowski (1998) ". . . found very little coverage of Arabs and even less coverage of Arab culture in the U.S. electronic media" (p. 164). Based on their study, they also concluded that:

It appears reasonable to assume that if a people and their culture are ignored, this leaves a fertile field for negative stereotyping. The picture that emerges by the lack of attention to Arabs and Arab cultures is [that they are] neither significant nor important. If the American public counts on television for its news, it is not learning much about Arabs. Arabs and Arab culture thus are marginalized. (pp. 164–165)

Confirming the preceding observation about media coverage of the Arabs, Greta Little (1998) writes, "The predominant picture is that of the fanatical terrorist, driven by maniacal devotion to irrational causes. The image is underwritten by U.S. State Department profiles to protect American diplomats and airline passengers" (p. 257). Hence, the Western media are not alone. Western governments also fuel the existing stereotypical images of Arabs and the Middle East through their official statements and policies.

Portrayals of Arabs and Islam in Hollywood Movies

Hollywood's negative portrayals of the Middle East, Islam, and Arabs is not a recent phenomenon. In fact, according to Artz and Pollock (1997), "Depictions of Arabs in American popular culture have a long and colorful history, from *The Sheik* (1921), starring Rudolph Valentino, through Disney's blockbuster cartoon *Aladdin* (1991). American children grow up with stories about 'Ali Baba and the Forty Thieves' and 'Sinbad the Sailor'" (p. 123).

Since the silent era, perhaps with some minor exceptions, Hollywood producers have continued their relentless attack on the Middle East and Islam. Movie after movie and study after study have confirmed this phenomenon. "The movie Arabs, and now the television Arabs, have appeared as lustful, criminal, and exotic villains or foils to Western heroes and heroines. They represent a religion, Islam, supposedly at war with Judaism and Christianity and a region at war with Western concepts of political economy and order" (Fuller, 1997, p. 187).

Numerous Hollywood productions have depicted Arabs, Iranians, Palestinians, and Muslims in a highly derogatory and stereotypical manner, including *Hanna K* (1983), *Little Drummer* Girl (1984), *Children of Rage* (1975), *Honeybaby* (1974), *Rosebud* (1974), *Kidnapping of the President* (1980), *Death Before Dishonor* (1987), *Rescue Force* (1990), *Victory at Entebbe* (1976), *Raid on Entebbe* (1976), *Operation Thunderbolt* (1977), *Hours at Munich* (1976), *Prisoner in the Middle East* (1974), *Black Sunday* (1976), *Silver Bears* (1978), *Who Dares Win* (1982), *Terror Squad* (1987), *Three Days in Beirut* (1983), *Treasure of the Lost Desert* (1983), *Final Option* (1993), *Glory Boys* (1984), *Not Quite Jerusalem* (1984), *Threads* (1984), *Hell Squad* (1985), *Into the Night* (1985), *Iron Eagle* (1986), *Down and Out in Beverly Hills* (1986), *Iron Eagle II* (1988), *Counterforce* (1987), *Wanted Dead or Alive* (1987), *Trident Force* (1988), *The Naked Gun* (1988), *Cover Up* (1990), *Not Without My Daughter* (1990), *Madhouse* (1990), *Navy SEALS* (1990),

The Hitman (1992), *The Finest Hour* (1993), *Shield* (1992), *Hostage Flight* (1985), *The Delta Force* (1986), *The Taking of Flight 847* (1985), *Tragedy of Flight 103* (1988), *On the Wings of Eagles* (1986), *The Ambassador* (1984), *Deadline* (1984), *Killing Streets* (1991), *Held Hostage* (1991), *Executive Decision* (1996), *The Siege* (1998), and many more.

The Siege, a 20th Century Fox action film, portrays Arabs and Muslims as terrorists. It focuses on a U.S. government plan to round up all Muslims residing in the United States in order to counter a terrorist scheme to blow up the World Trade Center.

The movie *Executive Decision,* which premiered in 1996, is now available on video. It is perhaps an excellent testimonial to a concerted effort by Hollywood producers in their relentless and continuing attack on the Middle East, Arabs, and Muslims. The leader of a Middle Eastern terrorist group is captured and jailed. His followers hijack an American airliner and demand the release of their leader. In one scene, the lead hijacker, while holding a copy of the *Quran*, the Muslim holy book, tries to justify his terrorist act by making a vague reference to it. In another scene, he is shown performing his Islamic prayer. In another scene, upon learning that their leader has been ostensibly freed, the terrorists begin chanting *Allaho Akbar,* or "God is Great." In another scene, they claim to be the "soldiers of Allah" and "blessed by Allah." At some point, they refer to America as the "heart and belly of the infidels." Indeed, *Executive Decision* shamelessly fuels and reinforces the existing stereotypical images of Muslims, Arabs, and the Middle East. It is one of the latest lethal attacks by Hollywood.

Ethnocentric Media Coverage

In general, American journalists (as would, I suppose, journalists from other countries) tend to report world events in accordance with their own ethnocentrism, through their eyes, and largely in line with the views of their government, especially during conflicts and crises such as those mentioned earlier. Such ethnocentric reports coupled with the global reach of the American media, often tend to be more confusing than enlightening, entertaining than informative, sensational than factual, and biased than balanced. What is lacking in the American media coverage of the Middle East is precisely what the journalists should have learned in their journalism classes in colleges and universities—to be objective or impartial observers of events, and to report events in an accurate, balanced, and fair manner.

In 1997, according to the U.S. Department of State, there were 123 terrorist attacks against the United States, throughout the world, including 2 incidents in Africa, 3 in Eurasia, 4 in North America, 4 in the Middle East, 6 in Europe, and 7 in Latin America (Hedges, 1998). Furthermore, in his 1987 analysis of terrorism, Walter Laqueur revealed that most anti-American terrorism has primarily taken place in Latin America (369 incidents) and in Europe (458 incidents), not in the Middle East (84 incidents). He also argued that it is mistakenly believed that "terrorism is essentially a Middle Eastern problem, and most victims of terrorism are American" (Semati, 1997, p. 31). The evidence, according to the U.S. State Department and Laqueur, clearly confirms the inaccurate public perception of the Middle East with regard to terrorism.

According to Walter Lippmann (1922), the depictions by the mass media are often superficial and misleading, often creating completely false pictures in our heads for the "world outside." Our "mental pictures" are then largely based not only on *what* the media present to us, but also on *how* people or places are portrayed by the visual media. It is then no wonder that American opinion as well as world opinion concerning the Middle East has been highly negative. Allen Palmer (1997) writes:

> The mass media cannot be underestimated in terms of their power of perpetuating ethnic and racial bias; they are part of a cultural mechanism that promotes and exploits commercial stereotypes. Such images become dangerous when they materialize in the complex social narratives and foreign policies enacted simultaneously on the world stage and in the human mind and heart. (p. 139)

A Cradle of Civilization

Clearly, the current state of affairs is counterproductive to both the United States and the Middle East as a whole. Hence, the anti–Middle East rhetoric and the American mindset need to be changed in accordance with the realities of the Middle East—the cradle of Christianity, Judaism, Islam, and the birthplace of some of the earliest human civilizations, such as Egypt and Persia. As any historian would attest, few regions of the world can match the contributions in art, philosophy, science, medicine, language, and natural resources that the Middle East has made to the world and to humanity. Suffice it to say that even astronomy, the science that studies the universe, began in the Middle East over 5,000 years ago. Unfortunately, the American media tend to simplify, sensationalize, generalize, and, in the process, dehumanize an entire region by not only portraying the Middle East as a dangerous place, but also as a place where terrorists are born, raised, and trained. Today, writes Todd Gitlin (1980), "The media bring a manufactured public world into private space" (p. 1).

CONCLUSION

When it comes to the harmful portrayals of Arabs, Islam, or the Middle East in the U.S. mass media or in popular form such as Disney's cartoons, Shaheen argues that "although adults may be able to separate fact from stereotypes, to a child the world is simple. Once images of evil Arabs are embedded in their minds, they are almost impossible to eradicate. Unfortunately, tomorrow's filmmakers and animators will learn about Arabs primarily from these [Disney's] cartoons" (Yaqub, 1993, p.3). Still, there is no magic formula for changing the negative attitudes of people, mainly the Westerners, regarding the Middle East. What is clear is that creating a favorable image or impression requires knowledge about mass communication processes, public relations, interpersonal communication, intercultural communication, and nonverbal communication, coupled with careful research, planning, coordination, and implementation. Image, reality, or what others think of us, are social constructions, and the tools used to construct such an image are mainly the mass media (Anderson, 1990). It is, then, no wonder that today a huge industry exists in the United States and elsewhere whose job it is to transform unknowns into celebrities, build or enhance images, destroy images, package candidates for political offices, change appearances, and in the process change or modify public perception. In the final analysis, there is only one reality and that reality is perception—and the basis for perception comes from the mass media.

The events cited in this chapter, including the Persian Gulf War, the TWA explosion, the Oklahoma City bombing, the U.S. embassy bombings, and the 1996 Olympic bombing, provide many lessons, including mass media's dependency on government and vice versa, as well as propaganda techniques aimed at manipulating public opinion, reinforcing and globalizing stereotypical images of the Middle East, and manufacturing or altering public perception. Other lessons are that, in the final analysis, when it comes to politics and a nation's self-interest, ordinary citizens do not really matter—they can easily be sacrificed in battles for political and economic gains by lords of the global village and by those who own and control communication channels. Finally, despite the fact that the mass media's version of events usually differs from reality, it is the concocted media version or the manufactured reality that is internalized by people as reality. In other words, media portrayals of people, places, and events become perceptions, and perceptions become realities. These stereotypes or mindsets then become the basis for human interactions.

DISCUSSION QUESTIONS

1. What is acculturation?
2. What is an "information war" and how does it work?
3. What are some of the differences between various countries in the Middle East?
4. What is meant by ethnocentric media coverage?
5. Why should various cultural and ethnic groups be concerned about their negative media portrayals?

REFERENCES

Alliance for Children and Television. (1998). *Prime time parent kit*. Toronto, Canada: Author.
All things considered [Radio broadcast]. Chicago: WBEZ.

Anderson, N. (1992, Winter). Making a case for media literacy in the classroom. *Media & Values, 57*, 16.

Anderson, W. T. (1990). *Reality isn't what it used to be*. New York: Harper & Row.

Artz, L. W., & Pollock, M. A. (1997). Limiting the options: Anti-Arab images in U.S. media coverage of the Persian Gulf crisis. In Y.R. Kamalipour (Ed.), *The U.S. media and the Middle East: Image and perception* (pp. 119–135). Westport, CT: Praeger.

Bagdikian, B. H. (1997). *The media monopoly* (5th ed.). Boston: Beacon Press.

Berger, A. A. (1989). *Seeing is believing: An introduction to visual communication*. Mountain View, California: Mayfield.

Berger, J. (1977). *Ways of seeing*. New York: Penguin.

Fuller, L. (1997). Hollywood holding us hostage: Or, why are terrorists in the movies Middle Easterners? In Y.R. Kamalipour (Ed.), *The U.S. media and the Middle East: Image and perception* (pp. 187–197). Westport, CT: Praeger.

Gerbner, G. (1997). Foreword: What's wrong with this picture? In Y. R. Kamalipour (Ed.), *The U.S. media and the Middle East: Image and perception* (pp. xii–xv). Westport, CT: Praeger.

Gitlin, T. (1980). *The whole world is watching: Mass media in the making and unmaking of the new left*. Berkeley, CA: University of California Press.

Hedges, S. J. (1998, August 8). U.S. response: Clinton vows global hunt. *Chicago Tribune*, pp. 1, 11.

Kamalipour, Y. R. (1996). Media, cultures, and stereotypes. *Aljadid, 5*, pp. 16, 20.

Kamalipour, Y. R. (1997). Introduction. In Y. R. Kamalipour (Ed.), *The U.S. Media and the Middle East: Image and perception*. Westport, CT: Praeger.

Kellner, D. (1992). *The Persian Gulf TV war*. Boulder, CO: Westview Press.

Khan, M., & Levine, J. (1998, June 29). Anti-Muslim bias is intolerable. *Chicago Tribune*, p. 10.

Khleif, B.B. (1998). Distortion of "Islam" and "Muslims" in American academic discourse: Some observations on the sociology of vested enmity. In Y. R. Kamalipour & T. Carilli (Eds.), *Cultural diversity and the U.S. media* (pp. 275–287). Albany, NY: State University of New York Press.

Lind, R. A., & Danowski, J. A. (1998). The representation of Arabs in U.S. electronic media. In Y. R. Kamalipour & T. Carilli (Eds.), *Cultural diversity and the U.S. media* (pp. 155–165). Albany, NY: State University of New York Press.

Lippmann, W. (1922). *Public opinion*. New York: Free Press.

Little, G. D. (1998). Representing Arabs: Reliance on the past. In Y. R. Kamalipour & T. Carilli (Eds.), *Cultural diversity and the U.S. media* (pp. 257–268). Albany, NY: State University of New York Press.

McLuhan, M., & Fiore, Q. (1967). *The medium is the message: An inventory of effects*. New York: Bantam Books.

Mowlana, H. (1997). Images and the crisis of political legitimacy. In Y. R. Kamalipour (Ed.), *The U.S. media and the Middle East: Image and perception*. Westport, CT: Praeger.

Palmer, A. W. (1997). The Arab images in newspaper political cartoons. In Y. R. Kamalipour (Ed.), *The U.S. media and the Middle East: Image and perception* (pp. 139–150). Westport, CT: Praeger.

Said, E. W. (1981). *Covering Islam: How the media and the experts determine how we see the rest of the world*. New York: Pantheon Press.

Samovar, L. A., & Porter, R. E. (1995). *Communication between cultures* (2nd ed.). Belmont, CA: Wadsworth.

Semati, M. M. (1997, June). Terrorists, Moslems, fundamentalists, and other bad objects in the midst of 'us.' *The Journal of International Communication, 4*(1), 30–49.

Shaheen, J. G. (1984). *The TV Arab.* Bowling Green, OH: Bowling Green State University Popular Press.

Silver, R. (1992, Winter). Media culture: Why we can't "just say no." *Media & Values, 57,* 2.

Suleiman, M. W. (1996, October). Arab Americans in 1995: A view of the state of the community. *Aljadid, 12,* 16–17.

Watson, R., & Berry, J. (1998, August 31). Terror: Striking back at the embassy killers. *Newsweek,* 24–29.

Yaqub, R. M. (1993, November 12). Insult and injury: Harmful portrayals in cartoons are no laughing matter to Arabs. *Chicago Tribune,* section 5, p. 3.

5

ARAB/ISLAM PHOBIA: THE MAKING OF THE MEDIA IN THE WEST

Issam Suleiman Mousa
Yarmouk University

"When I see a Jew portrayed as a Shylock, I want to cry. So I know how an Arab
feels when he is described as a killer.
—Producer Alan Rafkin

INTRODUCTION

The Arab/Islamic stereotype in the West, as presented in the mass culture, has come
a long way from its inception in the 11th century A.D. to the present. It has witnessed
many shifts, which allowed it to be influenced by several factors, such as religion,
or romantic works, or the mass media. In the 20th century, and with the coming of
the electronic media, the image of Arabs and Islam wavered between romanticism
in the early years, and an extremely negative view, with religious overtones, by the
end of the century. Such portrayals undoubtedly affect the Arab character and
influence relations between the nations of the West and the Arab world.

Stereotypes are generalizations that are treated as if they were universally true.
People learn stereotypes from their culture, and they are reinforced through exposure to the media. Such stereotyping alienates and fosters hatred among nations,
instead of bringing about common understanding and cooperation. Research points
out that stereotypes leave a lasting impression on children's memories. Of greater
concern, these images play an important role in shaping foreign policy.

The objective of this chapter, therefore, is to briefly provide an overview of the development of the Arab/Islamic image over time, to highlight some of its potential effects, and finally, to raise questions about the moral role of communication managers in bringing about a desired change in this image.

THE ROOTS

Anti-Arab/Islamic feelings are not limited to Europe, alone. Arabs see the entire West as largely hostile to them. This attitude developed from the anti-Islamic polemic that began centuries ago, and was later enhanced as a result of colonialism. According to Daniel, an anti-Islam attitude was "formed in the two centuries or so after 1100" (1980, p. 1) and began as a religious bias. The anti-Islamic concepts astonishingly "were repetitions passed down over centuries" (p. 282). Defamation of the Prophet Mohammed was at the center of the polemic against Islam. Famous figures, such as Dante, Voltaire, and Gibbon fueled these old concepts in their writings.

In general, the anti-Arab/Islam attitudes that prevailed in the West had political and religious roots:

> In all the history of the West's political relationship with the Arabs, derived from the mixture of fear and distaste, there was a major preoccupation with sex. The roots of this go back to the earliest knowledge of Islam. . . . Western commentators thereafter tended to portray Muslims as sexually corrupt, "absorbed in the delights of lust" with the institutions of the harem, the veil and the eunuch attracting particular attention. The harem became the symbol of sexual license and the *Thousand and one Nights* only served to underline this picture. (Hopwood, 1980, pp. 10–12)

In Britain, for example, Hopwood finds that "a constituent part of the British political attitude towards the Arab, was a dislike which was especially felt for town dwellers rather than for the inhabitants of the desert." He adds that from "the earliest travelers, through dictionaries, to soldiers, the unfavorable picture continued . . . lexicons defined 'arab' as 'usurer' or (ironically) 'a Shylock', a 'street Arab' as 'an urchin'. . . 'Gyppo' or 'wog' were the terms [the soldiers] used. . . ." (1980, pp. 10–12).

The second anti-Arab/Islamic attitude, according to Hopwood, is romantic:

> . . . the Arab World [was viewed] as exotic and an escape from the oppressions of European society. The bringing of this image can probably be traced to the publication of the translation of the *Thousand and one Nights* and it has been perpetuated in countless films, books, operas and stories. . . . For many [Britons] romantic longings were fulfilled in the desert where they found the 'pure' Arab, the Bedouin, the proud, the dignified and the hospitable. The desert was clean, absolute and demanding. . . . Lawrence and his Bedu have been one of the most important cultural images of this

century, and Glubb could never have shown the same affection to Egyptian legion-naires. (1980, pp. 14–17)

On the American scene, around the end of the 19th century, the image was not much different from Europe. Arab image was highly influenced by the *Arabian Nights*. One historian suggested that the influences brought about by these tales, and Sunday schools, among other things, had "pigeonholed" the Arab as a stereotype in the American mind, to a "desert nomad surrounded by shifty sand dunes, camels, and harems" (DeNovo, 1963, p. 6). Another historian described how publicity about U.S.-based Middle Eastern archaeology, carried out by American universities in the period between the First and Second World Wars, helped somewhat to balance this more sensational image of the Arab by depicting the culture's sophisticated and powerful roots:

> Popularized in Sunday press supplements and less sensationally in books and magazine articles, archaeological discoveries contributed to an intelligent awareness of the Arab Lands within the American public, balancing somewhat the critical impressions derived from fictions such as *The Desert Song* of operetta and the silent film, *The Sheik.* (Stookey, 1975, pp. 47–48)

All this suggests a distorted Arab/Islamic image in the popular culture of the West.

THE IMAGE IN THE 20TH CENTURY

The Arab world, until very recently, was part of the colonial world that was dominated by France and Britain. Despite agreements reached with Sharif Hussein in 1916, this domination divided the Arab world into small helpless entities largely through the implementation of the Sykes-Picot Agreement, and the creation of the state of Israel. Although the United States was a latecomer, entering the region after the Suez Crisis in 1956, the anti-Arab/Islamic tradition continued in U.S. dealings, as well.

Research on the Arab image has revealed that Americans adopted some of the same stereotypes coined by the Europeans who had colonized the Arabs. Between 1916 and 1948 a content analysis of the *New York Times*, representing the prestigious segment of the U.S. press, showed that the European sources "reported more unfavorable attributions and relationships towards Arabs than favorable or neutral ones. The French and Jewish sources led in reporting" these negative attributions (Mousa, 1984, p. 162). Further, the research revealed that before 1944, the U.S. reports increasingly drew from "French, British, and Jewish sources" (pp. 164–165). Hence, the logical conclusion is that American stereotypes of Arabs were colored by the European view based on the mostly "French-British-Jewish view" that was formed in the 1940s or before (p. 165).

This situation can be illustrated by looking at the reporting of events in Palestine, as an example. The Palestinian armed men who fought for the liberation of their homeland were labeled prior to 1948 in the *New York Times* as "Arab terrorists or saboteurs." This stereotype was coined by the British in the 1940s and, unfortunately, survives today as the catchall phrase for any Palestinian effort at self-determination (Mousa, 1993). Worse still, these reports even stole the Palestinians' national identity. Over more than 30 years of press reports, the sampled reports showed that there was only one reference to an "Arab Palestinian." Instead, the indigenous people of that country were labeled Muslims, Christians, Arabs, Arab peasants, nomad Bedouins, Arab saboteurs, anti-Zionists, anti-Jewish, armed bands of Arabs, oriental Arabs, and "inferior" Arabs (compared to the Jews). Arabs who protested against U.S. Congressional decisions were reported by the paper as being "a few wealthy Arabs under British domination" or "the Arab minority," or even "Arab puppets," in the words of some U.S. senators.

THE IMAGE BEFORE 1948

Two conclusions can be drawn from this research:

1. A spillover effect from the European to the American press resulted in the adoption of stereotypes created by the Europeans.
2. The press played a significant role in propagating the stereotypes against Arabs and reinforcing them through other media channels (Mousa, 1998).

The Film Industry

Nassir (1979) discusses the portrayal of Arabs in American films between the turn of the 20th century and the late 1940s. He suggests that from its inception, the film industry in the United States showed an early interest in the Arabs. The early movies depicted Arabs as "entertainers and associated them with both guns and magic" (p. 142). The 1920s saw a highly romanticized portrayal of Arabs in movies such as *The Sheik* and *The Son of the Sheik.* The same period also witnessed the beginning of a new theme depicting Arabs as villains, the counterpart to French and British heroism. In Foreign Legion stories, the Arabs were presented as villains acting against the benevolent activities of the British and French in Arab countries. In addition to themes of mystery, adventure, and romance, the 1930s saw an emphasis on political and religio-political themes wherein Islam was presented as a religion set in opposition to Christianity. During World War II, a new theme appeared, depicting the Arabs as Nazi spies, and as blackmailers and kidnappers. By the end of the 1940s, a new political theme began to emerge, involving Arabs and Jews, in which the Arabs were presented as threatening the Jewish state (Nassir, 1979).

The Press

In a 1984 work, Mousa analyzed the cognitive and affective components of the Arab image in the *New York Times*, as representative of U.S. elitist press, between 1916 and 1948. The year 1916 was chosen as a starting point because it marked a very important event in modern Arab history: the Arab Revolt. For the first time in four centuries, the Arab character was divorced from the Ottoman-Turk; the Arab thus became an independent actor, whom the press would cover as such. The year 1948 was picked as an end point because it marked the first Arab-Israeli war, and because several existing studies dealt with the Arab image after 1948. However, all of these studies compared the Arab image to the Israeli one. Thus, the Arab image became a function of that comparison.

The findings provided answers to two main questions. The first question concerned how the news coverage reported the Arabs between 1916 and 1948. Coverage was found to be primarily event oriented (that is, the reports focused on Arabs associated with events and ignored others), conflict oriented (for half of the relationships), unfavorably oriented (except for the Arab-U.S. relationships before 1941, when the favorable outnumbered the unfavorable), and finally, coverage primarily focused on Arab relationships with western Europeans, the United States, the Jews, and other Arabs, while ignoring Arab dealings with the rest of the world. In the 1920s and early 1930s, coverage was more diversified than in later years, allowing for a more open image. Furthermore, coverage in the political and military contexts was characterized by high conflict and unfavorable treatment, whereas the economic was more balanced. Coverage allowed a European (French-British-Jewish) view to prevail until 1944, when it was replaced by an Arab-American-Jewish view, which provided for more balance, but not accuracy. Finally, coverage provided for a trace of romanticism of the Arabs in the early period, more so than in later years, when such traces occurred in isolated events. On that basis, Mousa (1984) concluded that the information reported on the Arabs (between 1916 and 1948) was limited, and, consequently, coverage was unbalanced.

My second question tackled the problem of the impressions this coverage left in readers' minds, and the type of image about Arabs they had formed. I suggested that limited information and unbalanced coverage had contributed to misconceptions, and possible distortions, about the Arabs prior to 1948. For example, the term "Arab" was used as a rubric to define only a small segment in some Arab societies. In addition, by accepting the European view of the situation in Palestine during the period between the world wars, journalists fell into the trap of defining Palestinian Arabs as "Arabs" and their acts as "Arab," leading to the introduction of more unfavorable terms, such as, "anti-Zionist Arabs" or "Arab terrorists" on a wider scale in later years than in the 1940s (Mousa, 1984, p. 175). More importantly, the term "Arab/Arabs" was constantly discussed in the context of conflict and unfavorable treatment. Conflict was found to be a constant feature in reporting of this referent. Further, the military, political, and religious contexts were most often discussed in conflict relationships. Finally, the sum of Arab relationships with the French, British, and Jews emphasized conflict over other relationships, thus aiding in creating a confrontational image of the Arabs as being anti-West (and possibly anticivilization) (Mousa, 1984). Undoubtedly, such coverage would aid in creating an image of conflict that is unfavorable to the Arabs in the minds of the readers, the recipients of such coverage.

In another study, Terry found that 1947 press coverage was overwhelmingly pro-Israel and was critical of the "unreasonable hostility" of the Arab nations (1971, pp. 96–97). Hopwood (1980) also provides us with an insight to the "prejudice engendered by the Zionist problem." He concludes that:

> . . . the collective guilt for the Jewish policy of Nazi Germany has to a certain extent changed into a hostility against the Arabs for their not allowing Europe to expatiate its crimes by quietly resettling the Jews in Palestine. There has been resentment that the Arabs have more and more drawn attention to *their* [*sic*] rights. The desire to placate the Jews at the expense of the Arabs can go to absurd lengths and editors and journalists rather than risk being thought anti-Semitic or anti-Zionist, will overcompensate in their coverage of and sympathy for the Jewish case. The age old image of the Arabs can easily be summoned up: the Jews are the bastion of Western democracy in the Middle East, the Arabs the fanatics intent on destruction, and the image is further confused by our biblical memories of the children of Israel's exile by the Nile. (p. 19)

THE IMAGE AFTER 1948

After 1948, the Arab image received more attention by communication researchers. It was analyzed in comparison to Israel's image and within the context of the Middle East conflict. In general, the Arabs were portrayed negatively, and the Israelis positively. Suleiman, who conducted several studies on the press image, summarized the image in the 1960s:

> The old romantic stereotype of an Arab as a wandering desert dweller has given way to that of a "dark, shifty-eyed schemer and coward." It is a stereotype that is reinforced by television and the movies. In contrast, the Israelis are pictured as "young, energetic, fun-loving, hard-working, brave, and deeply suntanned." (1970, pp. 141–142)

At the time of the 1967 war, the Arabs were frequently and almost indiscriminantly associated with the communist camp (Suleiman, 1970). Suleiman concluded that the Arab image at this point was dehumanized in the American press. This, he said, was accomplished by repeatedly reinforcing the stereotype, especially when presenting the bad qualities. However, the 1973 war brought about some changes.

Suleiman observes, ". . . a slight turn-away from such stereotypes came about as the Arab emerged as less bent on baiting Israel or seeking its destruction. Furthermore, the press displayed greater awareness of the Arab viewpoint by mentioning, relatively frequently, the Arab's desire for peace and by generally justifying their actions" (1974, pp. 116–117).

Reviewing his findings, Suleiman concluded that 1967 marked "the lowest ebb of impartial reporting . . . but that 1973 saw the beginning of a move toward balance" (1975, p. 35). Belkaoui also compared Arab and Israeli actors, as portrayed in the press. Her analysis yielded the following findings:

> . . . [in 1967] Israeli figures are cast as heroes . . . , as winners and splendid performers. Israeli political leaders are strong, decisive and confident; their military heroes are cool, calm, legendary and dashingly handsome; and their military forces are powerful, efficient, skillful and proud. . . . This image is not generally retained in the 1973 phase. The Israelis are increasingly described as angry, upset, worried, and gloomy. . . . While this indicates a shift toward a more negative image of the Israelis in the 1973 phase, some elements of the underdog are retained along with a feeling of betrayal. (1979, pp. 736–737)

As for the Arabs, Belkaoui concluded, "The Arab world in general also reflected the shift in image from loser to winner. Described as emotional, angrily chanting atomized mass in 1967, the Arab world emerged in the 1970's with a new spirit of achievement, unity, pride and honor" (p. 737)

In the late 1970s, the image of Anwar as-Sadat captured the press. His peace initiative of 1977 was highly credited. Although there was no greater support for the Arabs, there was increased criticism of Israel after the oil embargo of 1973 (Daugherty & Warden, 1979). Daugherty and Warden's findings confirmed those of Wagner (1973), the predominant theme being one of negotiating peace.

The Electronic Media

In his most famous work, *Orientalism,* Edward Said suggests that the electronic media had helped to reinforce the stereotypes by which the Orient is viewed:

> Television, the films, and all the media's resources have forced information into more and more standardized models. So far as the Orient is concerned, standardization and cultural stereotyping have intensified the hold of the 19th century academic and imaginative demonology of the "mysterious Orient." This is no where more true than in the ways by which the Near East is grasped. Three things have contributed to making even the simplest perception of the Arabs and Islam into a highly politicized . . . matter: one, the history of popular anti-Arab and anti-Islam prejudice in the West . . . ; two, the struggle between the Arabs and Israeli Zionism, and its effect upon American Jews as well as upon both the liberal culture and the population at large; three, the almost total absence of any cultural position making it possible either to identify with or dispassionately to discuss the Arabs or Islam. (1978, p. 26)

However, the impact of the electronic media on the Arab image is better explained by reviewing two articles that were published in the past decade. In 1989, the *Arab Business Report* published an article on "TV's Terrorists." It opens with the following statement: "one of the ideological assumptions found in the made-for-television, motion picture genre is that an Arab is a terrorist" (1989, p. 13). The article lists many names of films that were produced in the 1980s. In these pictures,

> Arabs are depicted as related to the likes of Hitler's SS and Attila's hordes. The Arab lurks in the shadows with an AK-47, bomb, or dagger in hand to reduce, beat, rape and murder innocents. Summing up these diabolic Others, a passenger in *Hostage Flight* says, "these bastards shot those people in cold blood. They think it's open season on Americans." The message to American viewers on whom to love and whom to hate is hardly subtle. (p. 13)

Similarly, in *Terrorist on Trial: The United States vs. Salim Ajami* (1988), a journalist in the film asserts that Arabs are more violent and more primitive than other people, "they are very clever, first thing they do is corrupt the language. They appeal to our sympathy by calling themselves guerillas or freedom fighters. They're not" ("TV's Terrorists," 1989, p. 13). The article notes that Ajami's own defense attorney asks the jury to view him as "someone who might as well have been from another planet." The film also includes scenes of "shabby Arab-Americans who demonstrate in favor of Ajami, leaving viewers with the impression that the Arab-American community sympathizes with terrorists" (p. 13).

Under Siege (1986) "conveys the warning that the Arabs are coming to terrorize the U.S. and the Arab-Americans are going to help them." Throughout the movie, "Iranians are interchangeable with Arabs, and the dialogue is racist" ("TV's Terrorists," 1989, p. 14).

According to the article, in *The Last Precinct*, Iraqi actor Nicolas Kadi says he did "little talking and a lot of threatening—threatening looks, threatening gestures, threatening actors. Every time we [he and other playing Arab heavies] said *America* we'd spit." In these movies and others,

> viewers see Arabs only as perpetrators of violence, never as victims. . . . There are no images of Arab arms being broken, Arab homes being blown up, Arab demonstrators shot dead. . . [, an] Arab mother singing to her child . . . [,] an Arab doctor tending the ill, an Arab teacher giving a lesson in algebra [which is an Arab invention], an Arab programmer working with a computer. An Arab man never embraces his wife. Families do not gather to go to mosque or church ("TV's Terrorists," 1989, p. 14).

In the second article, "Arabs in Film: Always The 'Bad Guy,'" Dima Hamdan (1998) says that Hollywood "never took such a hard attitude towards any ethnic group as it has towards the Arabs" (p. 7). She adds that "there has been a certain mode during the past two decades, which, at the very least, suggests a correlation between the changes in US political policies, and the ethnic stereotypes portrayed in Hollywood films." Hamdan believes that the Arabs'

> cinematic profile has changed over the past two decades in tandem with changes in the political sphere. Different stereotypes were displayed according to the desired image. During the 1980s, the dominant images were those of greasy oil-rich sheiks, oversexed men lusting after Western women, and abusive polygamists. Nowadays, however, not only has the Arab image changed to a characterization of the "Muslim terrorist," which is offensive to an even wider range of ethnic groups, but it is being stressed repeatedly through different forms which has made it an acceptable norm for the public. (p. 5)

Although this stereotype of terrorism, and equating of Arab with Muslim, was heavily implemented by the cinema and television industries, most recently *Time* magazine, spoke of "Islamic terror" in reporting the massacre of Luxor, while the *Paris March* wrote of "Allah's lunatics" (Fisk, 1997).

EQUATING ARABS AND MOSLEMS

One major outgrowth of such depiction by the media is mixing cards. An increasing trend in the West, and probably throughout the world, is to equate "all Middle East issues with Muslim issues. And, therefore, Arabs are being equated as Muslims" (Hanania, 1998). Thus, the varied ethnicity and religiosity of the population that inhabits the Middle East gives in to "intentional stereotyping" (Hanania, 1998). This serves the interests of those who want to obscure the view of events at a time when Arabs are moving toward a peaceful settlement of the conflict in Palestine. If in the past the Arabs were anti-West, in the present, Moslems and Arabs threaten the Western World. According to Jawad, "the media has always portrayed Islam and Muslims in a negative way: 'the Islamic threat,' 'West fears world-wide havoc from Muslim extremists,' and 'the Mosque militant.' Muslims are 'stealthy,' 'untrustworthy,' 'lazy,' and 'violent'" (1998, p. 33).

In present-day Spain, where marks of the Arab/Islamic civilization still exist, attitudes toward Arabs and Islam are exemplary—they are not different at all from those that exist in the United States or Europe, or in the rest of the world. The Arabs who live in present-day Spain "are considered inferior and then treated accordingly in working and social settings" or avoided in other settings (Velloso, 1998, p. 142). But for the rest of the Arabs, the image is dismal:

> . . . the Arab usually becomes the Muslim extremist. News on television and in newspapers often bring[s] . . . any of these two words together with any of the following ones: massacre, fundamentalism, blood, integrists [sic], assassination, jihad, bomb, Allah, and some others. None . . . includes words like love, family,

progress, joy, friendship, and hope. . . . violence is almost inevitably linked to the Islamic religion and culture" (p. 142).

THE PUBLIC AND THE MEDIA

Such depictions undoubtedly have grave consequences for the public. For example, when a Jordanian man, Eyad Ismail, aged 26, was sentenced to 240 years in prison, a fine of $250,000, and a $10 million payment for restitution, for his role in the February 26, 1993, World Trade Center bombing, Judge Kevin Duffy addressed Ismail in these words: "You were like Ramzi Youssef [alleged mastermind of the operation] because your God was evil. . . . I am not talking about an evil God. I am talking about the personification of Evil" (*Jordan Times*, April 4, 1998).

Once the "evil God" concept was invoked by this judge, in this context of a Middle Eastern Arab/Moslem, it would certainly invoke a stereotype of a merciless terrorist, with a different God, designed to create havoc and kill Americans. No doubt such words would also justify the defendant's conviction in many eyes. Such an image certainly exists, and we all remember that a dark Middle Eastern was immediately accused by the media of being behind the Oklahoma City terrorist explosion, before the real perpetrator, a white American, was brought to justice. In a 1997 letter to the editor of the *Jordan Times*, a European reader, Dr. Hendrick S. Weiler, viewed the situation as follows: ". . . the American public is increasingly Arabphobic and Islamphobic, this prejudice is being fuelled by America's popular press. Read only the last few issues of *Time, Newsweek* . . . and newspapers, to get the full impact of these phobias passing of as 'news' in the U.S. . . ." This view might be simplistic, but it is buttressed by research findings and still holds true today.

THE WEST IN THE EYES OF THE ARABS AND MOSLEMS

In recent years, following the failure to implement UN resolutions toward a peaceful settlement in the Middle East, the West was generally depicted by Arabs and Moslems as a group that applies "double standards" (Fisk, 1997, p. 7). When the Sykes-Picot agreement and the Balfour Declaration became well known, the stereotype of the West as infidels and hypocrites surfaced in Arabic countries. This allowed Westerners to be portrayed as dishonest, untrustworthy colonialists who implemented a policy of divide and rule, and as an enemy to Islam and to Arabs. There was also "a sense of admiration" (*Can Cultures Communicate?*, 1976, pp. 4–5), mainly because of the West's technological superiority.

A moderate Jordanian Islamic figure wrote in the Arab daily *Al-Rai* that this matter of double standards is a fact "that is clear not only to Arabs, Moslems, and Third World nations, but also to Westerners themselves." He refers in particular to the events that surrounded Iraq's destruction, the Islamic nuclear bomb, the Garoudi trial (a Frenchman tried because of his writings on Islam), and Salman Rushdi. He adds that such "standards do not serve the West . . . do not reflect true civilization, and do not reflect neither sound logic nor a just world order." He concludes by saying that "Moslems and Arabs condemn such policy of double standards . . . and for a productive dialogue to succeed . . . this policy should be dropped" (Emoush, 1998, p. 22).

IMPLICATIONS

Hamdan, in her 1998 article, refers to the studies carried out by Jack Shaheen, the author of *The TV Arab*, as suggesting that the American children "are exposed to negative images of Arabs on television every week." Such films, although fictitious, "can have a significant impact on young impressionable minds" (Hamdan, 1998). Devine suggests that "there is strong evidence that stereotypes are well established in children's memories before children develop the cognitive ability and flexibility to question or critically evaluate the stereotypes' validity or acceptability. . . ." (1989, p. 6).

More pertinent, still, such images play an important role in shaping foreign policy. Coplin suggests that images "orient" the behavior of foreign policy decision-makers. They provide "one of the basic rationales of any given policy," especially in relation to the initial images to which the policy-makers tend to cling, even after such images "become incorrect or irrelevant" (1980, p. 142). Anti-Arab interest groups play a significant role in influencing foreign policy decisions in the U.S. For example, in the wake of American missile strikes against Sudan and Afghanistan in August 1998, "the Washington Institute for Near East Policy, an influential think-tank that usually hosts Israeli officials and opinion makers, . . . circulated three, in-house articles on the week's events, one a compilation of Anti-American views in the Arab Press" (Hishmeh, 1998).

Further still, the rigidity of images, whether for Israelis or Arabs, can become counterproductive; it will not serve the cause of a peaceful settlement to the Middle East conflict at all (Mousa, 1991).

CONCLUSION

The Arab image has come a long way from its early romanticism to the present depiction. Clearly, the Arab occupies a negative value in the Western media. The media, particularly the electronic media, are waging an ugly war against Arabs and Moslems. American and Western stereotypes created by the electronic media are shown worldwide, allowing for the negative effect to spread out internationally. This is reflected in the attitudes of some decision-makers, who are willing, for example, to accept that a Middle Eastern could be behind the explosion in Oklahoma City. It is also reflected in daily political decisions, such as the bombing of a medical factory in Sudan. Worse still is the fact that the media teach children to hate others. To instill this attitude in the minds of young children worldwide is a grave and unforgivable mistake. Is this fair? Is this objective? Is this moral? What should we do about all of this? What is the role of communication educators and managers in coping with such an unhappy situation? How can they work together to improve the relations between the Western and Arabic nations? If these are legitimate questions, then we probably should join hands together in at least one thing: to fight those who teach our beloved children to hate others in their very early formative years.

DISCUSSION QUESTIONS

1. How do the mass media distort images of Arabs, Muslims, and the Middle East?
2. What is stereotyping? Why is it used? And how can it be avoided?
3. What is an image and what impact does it have upon perception?
4. How do the mass media influence our cultural environment?
5. How do our mental images affect our interpersonal and intercultural relations?
6. How does stereotyping affect international relations?

REFERENCES

Belkaoui, J. (1979). Images of Arabs and Israelis in the prestige press, 1966–1974. *Journalism Quarterly, 55*, 732–738.

Can cultures communicate? (1976). Washington, DC: The American Institute for Public Policy Research.

Coplin, W. D. (1980). *International policies*. Englewood Cliffs, NJ: Prentice Hall.

Daniel, N. (1980). *Islam and the West*. Edinburgh, Scotland: University of Edinbugh Press.

Daugherty, D., & Warden, M. (1979). Prestige press editorial treatment of the Middle East during 11 crisis years. *Journalism Quarterly, 56:* 776–782.

DeNovo, J. A. (1963). *American interests and policies in the Middle East: 1900–1939*. Minneapolis, MN: University of Minnesota Press.

Devine, P. G. (1989). Stereotypes and prejudice: Their automatic and controlled components. *Journal of Personality and Social Psychology, 56*, 5–18.

Emoush, B. (1998, January 26). The duality of the West. *Al Rai*, 22.

Fisk, R. (1997, December 17). Religion in the Middle East: The fundamental problem. *The Jordan Times*, p. 7.

Hamdan, D. (1998, April 28). Arabs in film: Always the bad guy. *The Jordan Times*, p. 7.

Hanania, R. (1998, August 25). Drift between Arab Muslims and Christians pleases outside forces. *The Jordan Times*, p. 6.

Hishmeh, G. (1998, August 26). U.S. attacks raises opposing analyses in American circles. *The Jordan Times*, p. 6.

Hopwood, D. (1980). *British images of the Arabs*. Khartoum, Sudan: Institute of African and Asian Studies.

Jawad, H. (1998). Islamic extremism and its impact on Western images of Islam. In J. Nielsen & S. Khasawnih (Eds.), *Arabs and the West: Mutual images* (pp. 29–43). Amman, Jordan: University of Jordan Press.

Jordanian man sentenced to 240 years for U.S. bombing. (1998, April 4). *The Jordan Times*, p. 1.

Mousa, I. (1984). *The Arab image in the U.S. press*. New York: Peter Lang.

Mousa, I. (1991). The Arab image in the U.S. press: Implications for peace. *Communication Research* (University of Cairo), *6*, 237–253.

Mousa, I. (1993). A case of inequality: The reporting of Palestine in the *New York Times* 1917–1947. *Dirassat* (University of Jordan), *20*, 20–30.

Mousa, I. (1998). Breaking down the stereotype (wogs, wops and what else?). In J. Nielsen & S. Khasawnih (Eds.), *Arabs and the West: Mutual images* (pp. 73–83). Amman, Jordan: University of Jordan Press.

Nassir, S. (1979). *The Arabs and the English* (2nd ed.). London: Longman.

Said, E. (1978). *Orientalism*. New York: Pantheon Books.

Stookey, R. (1975). *America and the Arab states*. New York: John Wiley.

Suleiman, M. (1970). American mass media and the June conflict. In I. Abu-Lughod (Ed.), *The Arab-Israeli confrontation of June 1967: An Arab perspective* (pp. 134–154). Evanston, IL: Northwestern University Press.

Suleiman, M. (1974). National stereotypes as weapons in the Arab-Israel conflict. *Journal of Palestine Studies*, *3*, 109–121.

Suleiman, M. (1975). Perceptions of the Middle East in American news magazines. In B. Abu Laban & F. Zeady (Eds.), *Arabs in America: Myths and realities* (pp. 28–44). Wilmette, IL: Medina University Press.

Terry, J. (1971). A content analysis of American newspapers. In A. Jabara & J. Terry (Eds.), *The Arab world from nationalism to revolution* (pp. 94–113). Wilmette, IL: Medina University Press.

TV's terrorists. (1989). *Arab Business Report, 10*, 13–14.

Velloso, A. (1998). Spanish attitudes towards the Arab world: From ignorance to mistrust. In J. Nielsen & S. Khasawnih (Eds.), *Arabs and the West: Mutual images* (pp. 139–145). Amman, Jordan: University of Jordan Press.

Wagner. C. (1973). Elite American newspapers opinion and the Middle East: Commitment vs. isolation. In W. Beling (Ed.), *The Middle East: Quest for an American policy* (pp. 306–335). Albany, NY: State University of New York Press.

Weiler, H. S. (1997, December 16). Letter to the editor. *The Jordan Times*.

Discourse III
Cyberspace Digital Technologies: An Overview

6

INFORMATION TECHNOLOGY,DEMOCRACY, AND DEVELOPMENT: AN OVERVIEW

Ali A. Attiga
Arab Thought Forum

Although democracy and development represent two distinctly different human endeavors, they both require, for success and sustainability, adequate levels of information and popular participation. Up-to-date information is essential in both cases. It is essential to establish facts on the ground, and disseminate their contents and significance with a specific purpose of mobilizing popular support or expanding market share or influencing social change toward an established goal. In the case of democracy, adequate and up-to-date political, economic, and social information and data are needed to establish common ground for informed judgments among the voters and their different pressure groups. Open competition for public posts among different candidates with their different platforms can become rather confusing and counterproductive unless the voting public has access to reliable sources of up-to-date information. Modem communication technology is neutral in this respect. It can be used or abused for achieving a given objective. It is efficient in both directions. What matters here is the content and purpose of the message conveyed. It is here that the objectivity and scope of information are of vital concern for the success and sustainability of democracy.

Democracy is a form of government and governance, whereas development is a process of social and economic change. Development, like democracy, needs an adequate level of reliable and up to date information regarding resources, markets, social values, and institutions. The same principle concerning objectivity and scope of information applies to both democracy and development. The more objective and the wider the scope of information conveyed, the more likely democracy and development will be more sustainable. As in the case of democracy, modern information technology is essential in the speed and efficiency with which data and news are processed and disseminated among different actors in the development process. Efficient market competition requires adequate knowledge among consumers and investors for rational decision making. This is rather similar to the need for a common information base among the voting public in the case of free, democratic elections. Thus, competition in both democracy and development requires an adequate level of objective and up-to-date information before it can produce efficient results.

Another common and related requirement for both democracy and development is an active level of public participation. In the case of democracy, participation is needed to establish and reinforce the legitimacy of public office and public authority. Without that sense of public legitimacy, any form of democracy would be only a frame without substance. Similarly, development needs active public participation to establish common goals and objectives for development and take the necessary actions to implement them in the best possible way.

While purely physical development of infrastructure, buildings, and even factories can take place without active popular participation, it is virtually impossible to do the same with comprehensive human development. Development in this sense cannot be accomplished without democracy, and democracy will not survive without this kind of development. Thus, popular participation and adequate information are common to both. But if that is the case, how can we explain the impressive development of Japan, Germany, Italy, and the Soviet Union when they were under repressive authoritarian requires? How did these countries manage to become formidable powers without democracy? Is China today managing to achieve rapid rates of development without having to change its political system? These are basic questions open for debate and discussion. I hope this roundtable will focus on their contents and significance as they relate to the complex relations between information technology, democracy, and development.

My own observation is that certain patterns of specific development can take place without democracy. Thus, economic growth, research and technological development, the spread of formal education, public health, and literacy can be attained and indeed have been accomplished under authoritarian regimes. In fact, there is a recognized school of thought that claims development of this scope requires a top-down approach in order to efficiently establish priorities, assign responsibilities, and control decisions through central authority. All dictatorships generally adhere to this form of governance.

In this pattern of development, all sources of information are centrally controlled and public participation is formally mobilized through official ideology and repressive authority. People are simply required to follow the official line and to show support and enthusiasm for their "gifted" leadership and its approach to development and even to life itself. This sort of development and its leadership gained wide acceptance in most developing countries during the cold war years. It was supported by both the Western and the Eastern blocs in their competition for influence and control in different parts of the world. We can all remember how quickly and enthusiastically *coup d'etat* were carried out in most emerging developing countries, shortly after their formal independence. It was rather depressing and yet interesting to note how this military takeover replaced traditional forms of governance that had the potential to develop democratic institutions and habits. Yet, despite this obvious destruction of the democratic evolution and normal political process, there was always a clear competition between the two superpowers centered on giving recognition and support to new and repressive authoritarian regimes.

In Latin America and the Caribbean, military regimes were in control of public and private lives for 200 years or more. In a country such as Bolivia, there were 180 *coup d'etat* in 157 years. It is certain that there was not much of a chance for any meaningful development to take place during that period. But fortunately, for the people of Latin America, most countries in the region at long last are experiencing a promising process of political and economic transformation. Democratic forms of government are replacing dictatorship. It will be most interesting to watch and study how the nature and approach to development will change as a result of the political transformation to democracy. How will information and popular participation change the development process? Will development be more real and sustainable than was the case in the past under oppressive regimes? I will venture to answer yes, but I recognize that there are others who would say no.

Democracy requires adequate economic growth, an acceptable level of social equity in the distribution of wealth, and opportunities for education, health, and employment. It requires the adherence to the rule of law. Above all, it requires able and dedicated leadership that is open to renewal and change through the political process. Democracy in this sense, cannot fail to induce genuine and comprehensive development. Similarly, the attainment of such real development will work to reconfirm and reinforce democracy. But any failure or distortion in either one of them will be reflected on the scope and function of the other. What is most difficult to do is the transformation from dictatorship to democracy and from centrally planned economy to market oriented economic and social process of development. No country has so far managed to make that transition without enormous sacrifice and hardship. Yet, there seems to be no viable escape from experiencing this kind of change. Some countries with sufficient natural resources and small population may afford to delay it for some time. But in the end, the process of globalism and the end of the Cold War are making it more difficult to avoid the change much longer.

The countries of Latin America and the Caribbean, except Cuba, have come a long way in their political and economic transformation. Most countries in Southeast Asia made the transformation some time before Latin America. We all know how these countries are now experiencing the pains and sacrifice associated with unbalanced market-oriented development. Russia and the countries of East and Central Europe are fully engaged with the process and problems of reform and transition. Most of them are faced with grave problems of having to depend on market economies, without modern public regulatory institutions designed to monitor, evaluate, and balance the prevailing trends and forces of market economies. At present, most of these countries are just not able to provide the majority of their people with the necessary goals and services for an acceptable standard of living. Unemployment, inflation, poverty, and social unrest have characterized and obstructed their transition to democracy and development through market economies.

China is undertaking its own type of transition. It is giving priority to economic reform in a gradual and experimental manner. At the same time, it is experimenting with administrative reform in terms of upgrading its efficiency and increasing its reliance on decentralization of public authorities. Undoubtedly, modern information technology is accelerating this process of reform. The big question for China is, when and how will political reform take place?

The same question may be raised in the case of most Arab countries. What will be the impact of information technology on political and economic reforms? Will it be an evolutionary process or take the form of revolutionary crisis? Will the transition take shape while the region is still coping with inherited and newly created bilateral and regional conflicts? Is it realistic to expect transition to democracy and comprehensive development while the region is still highly penetrated by external forces and influences? Although I have no answers to those difficult questions, I recommend that they receive adequate research and attention.

Experience shows that the countries of Southeast Asia and East and Central Europe, as well as those of Latin America and the Caribbean, were not able to begin the transition to democracy and market development until they ceased to be centers of Cold War conflicts and competition by the superpowers. This observation may help answer some of the questions regarding when and where the Arab countries will undertake sustainable political and economic reforms. Top priority must be given to peaceful conflict resolution within and between countries before transition to democracy and development can become real and sustainable. Priority should also be given to the promotion and mobility of qualified leadership, capable of implementing transitional reforms. Effective public education and viable civil society are essential for the transition to take place.

DISCUSSION QUESTIONS

1. Why is information needed for the achievement of democracy and development?
2. Why is public participation important to democracy and development?

3. Some scholars argue that democracy is a prerequisite for development. Do you agree with that argument? Why? Why not?
4. What are the requirements for achieving democracy and comprehensive development?
5. In your opinion, can the Arab countries achieve political reform and economic development? Explain your answer by referring to examples of other non-Arab countries.

7

ARAB COUNTRIES' GLOBAL TELEPHONE TRAFFIC NETWORKS

James A. Danowski
University of Illinois at Chicago

INTRODUCTION

The study described in this chapter, addresses the question of whether there is evidence from international telephone traffic networks for an "Arab Nation," a regional political entity often discussed among Arab intellectuals and political actors. NEGOPY (Richards, 1988), a computer program for network analysis whose name is derived from the physics term "negative entropy," was used to analyze intercountry telephone traffic among the world's nations using data complied by Telegeography from 1995–1996. Results showed that there is not one large global network, as Sun and Barnett (1994) previously found. Rather, there emerged a distinctively Arab-centered group, in addition to a larger group comprised of most of the remaining world nations. This differentiation of global communication networks is consistent with theoretical reasoning (Danowski, 1993a). In contrast to broadcast media, the network-based media carrying messages over telephone circuits may increasingly promote less unified global networks with regional subgroups of increasing variation. Future research can determine to what extent there is evidence for further development of a trend of this kind by using international telephone traffic data and network analysis as the years unfold.

PROBLEM STATEMENT

The Arab Nation is a concept frequently discussed in the Middle East region. There are numerous formal communication activities that articulate the Arab Nation. These include events such as conferences among religious and civil organizations across Arab countries, political communication among leaders, and participation of individuals in associations offering Arab news services, tourism councils, and cultural exchanges.

Given these organizational-level communication activities that make frequent references to the Arab Nation, one may assume that there are other levels of communication that are associated with this concept. In this research, interest is centered on communication that occurs via telephone, whether this medium is used for voice, Internet, video, or other modalities of communication. Social scientists do not often investigate telephone-based communication, even though there are statistical methods in network analysis to measure it. One reason appears to be that researchers are not yet widely aware that rich data on telephone traffic are available. At the same time, social science research on the Internet is at the beginning stages. Researchers of the Internet tend to think of more microlevels, such as individuals and groups, and are less likely to conceptualize research at the international level. Part of the reason for this is that intercultural communication research has tended to be based on qualitative case studies, not on empirical analysis using statistical techniques for qualitative analysis such as network analysis. Moreover, in English-language academic literature, there are few studies of any kind about communication in Arab contexts.

Attempting to address these gaps in the literature on communication, the goal of this chapter is to examine telephone communication patterns among Arab countries and others. My intent is to see what evidence there is for an Arab Nation based on these telephone call patterns at the global level. The research question is this: Does empirical evidence support existence of an Arab Nation based on telephone call patterns among Arab countries and others?

This question is important because there is increasing conceptualization of global phenomena in terms of information and communication. Global communication patterns have been of popular interest since the work of McLuhan in the 1960s. His concern, however, was primarily with broadcast television rather than telecommunications media that carry phone calls, data, Internet traffic, video, and audio in a nonbroadcast manner. As discussed more fully elsewhere (Danowski, 1993a), the broadcast media can be expected to foster a highly interconnected global network. This is because these media "glow" information widely, and satellite broadcast technology has enabled this glow to remove most of the world's information shadows. In contrast, telephone communication and its outgrowth, Internet communication, is primarily a network method of information distribution. Messages are "beamed" through switched, relatively narrow networks that emerge differently for different communication situations. This network model, as opposed to broadcast model of information distribution, is more likely to foster a differentiated global network, one with subgroups of varying structures connected together in different ways depending on content (Danowski, 1993a). Because of the increasing growth of network over broadcast information distribution, one is more likely to find evidence for the reconfiguration of global information systems from one large interconnected world system to one with more distinct subgroups.

In studying Arab globalization into the 21st century, the investigation of telephone traffic patterns is, therefore, significant. As Arab countries increase their domestic telephone penetration and use, one would expect more evidence of an Arab Nation as a distinct subset of the global system. Network analysis is an effective conceptual and methodological platform for investigating this prediction.

Communication Network Concepts

By "networks" I do not mean the physical telecommunications infrastructure. While at a particular time there is a relatively fixed hardware and software based network, my concern here is with the social networks that human actors produce and reproduce within this technological architecture. Technology both enables and constrains these social networks. Within these constraints, there is wide latitude for individuals, groups, organizations, and other social units to communicate in different patterns. These emergent and changing social networks are the focus of the research described here.

Accordingly, the constructs of network analysis developed in the social sciences are used here (Emirbayer & Goodwin, 1994). Researchers operating within these perspectives define a network as a pattern of links among nodes. Links can be any sort of relation defined by the researcher, such as gift giving, economic exchanges, friendship contacts, and so forth.

Communication social scientists, along with sociologists and anthropologists, have increasingly used network analysis over the past several decades. Nevertheless, the widely accepted origins of network analysis date back 65 years ago to the work of Moreno (1934), who developed sociogram analysis. After that time, social scientists made fruitful applications in the 1940s and 1950s (Jacobson & Seashore, 1951) and the 1960s and 1970s (Boissevain & Mitchell, 1973). In the 1980s and 1990s, network research blossomed. This is evidenced in research presented at the annual meetings of the International Networks of Social Network Analysts and American Sociological Association, and in the journal, *Social Networks*.

Network Nodes and Links

Network analysis is a method of representing the structure of relations among social units. The social units, called nodes, can be people, departments, organizations, nations, or message elements such as words. Links are the attributes defining the relations among nodes (Danowski, 1993b). Examples of the varying definitions of links and nodes in prior research include the following: communication through face-to-face conversations, telephone calls, or memos (links) among organizational members (nodes) (Danowski, 1980); electronic mail exchange (links) by individuals (nodes) (Danowski & Edison-Swift, 1983); co-occurrences (links) of actors (nodes) in Cicero's ancient letters (Alexander & Danowski, 1990); co-occurrence (links) of concepts (nodes) in pairs of computer bulletin board post and response messages (Danowski, 1982); co-occurrence (links) of words (nodes) within messages (Danowski, 1988, 1993b); co-membership in different divisions (links) of individuals (nodes) in an association (Barnett & Danowski, 1992); shared use of public relations and advertising firms (links) by organizations (nodes) (Danowski, Barnett, & Friedland, 1986); and telephone call frequencies (links) among nations (nodes) (Sun & Barnett, 1994). These examples show the richness of link and node possibilities. In this research, links are conceptually defined as telecommunications traffic between countries. In other words, a link is the occurrence of telephone calls between two countries. The greater the number of minutes of telephone calls, the stronger is the link. The nodes in the network studied are countries.

Network Analysis Methods

Communication network analysis, reviewed by Barnett, Danowski, and Richards (1993), has mainly used the approach embodied in the NEGOPY network analysis computer packages (Richards, 1988). Some research (Alexander & Danowski, 1990; Barnett & Danowski, 1992) has compared NEGOPY to methods more often used by sociologists: multidimensional scaling, block modeling, cluster analysis, correspondence analysis, and other matrix modeling methods (Wellman & Berkowitz, 1997). Results show NEGOPY to have concurrent validity, plus advantages in terms of the number of nodes that can be analyzed at once. This is because NEGOPY uses an adjacency list-processing algorithm instead of a matrix model. As a result, NEGOPY can process thousands of nodes, whereas matrix methods until recently were usually limited to several hundred nodes at best.

With increases in the central processing unit (CPU) size of desktop computers and software improvements in packages, particularly the University of California at Irvine Network Analysis Program, or UCINET (Everett, Borgatti, & Freeman, 1992a, 1992b), the gap in node size is closing. NEGOPY still has advantages over other methods particularly: (1) its explicit linkage-based approach to representing links among nodes, (2) its explicit definitions of network roles, and (3) its explicit group identification methods. These features allow less arbitrary representations of network structures than the other network analysis methods.

Operational Definitions of Network Roles for the Current Research

Definitions of network roles are operationalized in the NEGOPY network analysis computer program (Richards, 1988) and are illustrated in Figure 7.1. Groups are of interest in this research and are defined next.

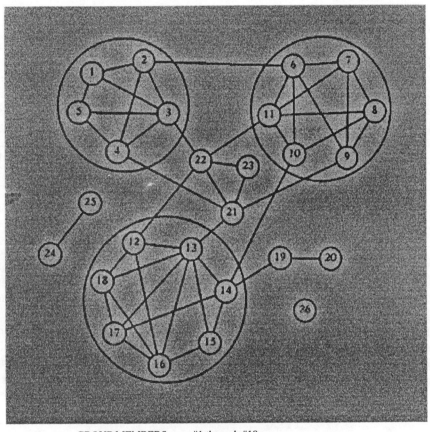

GROUP MEMBERS:	#1 through #18	
LIAISONS:	(DIRECT)	__#21 & #22
	(INDIRECT)	__#23
ISOLATES:	(TYPE 1)	__#26
	(TYPE 2)	__#20
	(DYAD)	__#24 & #25
	(TREE NODE)	__#19

FIGURE 7.1.   Role definitions used by NEGOPY.

Network Groups

A group is a set of at least three nodes that (1) have more than 50 percent of their links with one another, (2) are connected to each of the other members in the group by some path lying entirely within the group, and (3) remain so connected when up to 10 percent of the group is removed (there were no critical nodes that can cause the group to be decomposed into disconnected subgroups). A group member is a node that has more than 50 percent of its links with other members in the same group. Group members must have at least two links with other members.

Group Centrality

Within a group, NEGOPY computes centrality scores for members. A node that is more central has, on average, shorter paths connecting it to other members of the group. A path length is defined as the number of steps it takes to connect two nodes. For example, if nodes are directly connected, their distance score is 1. If they are connected through one intermediate node, their score is 2. If connected through two intermediate nodes, their score is 3, and so on. The centrality statistic first averages these shortest paths for a node across the nodes in a group. Then, to normalize the measure and remove the effects of group size so different groups can be compared, the Z statistic is computed for the average shortest path distance for each node. Smaller Z scores (more negative) indicate higher centrality for a node.

METHODS

This study analyzes data on the volume of telephone calls among countries around the world. Data were obtained on intercountry telephone traffic from the Telegeography annual reports for 1996–1997 (Staple, 1996). Telegeography is an independent research and publishing company cooperating with the International Institute of Communications, a London-based nonprofit educational and conference organization. For each country, the publication typically lists the top 20 nations with which they have telecommunications activity. Along with this, they report the millions of minutes of outgoing calls aggregated for a year for each pair of these nations. Given the yearly aggregation and the time needed to collect and publish data, there is a lag. For example, the 1996–1997 publication reports data for 1995 and 1996.

Data from these reports were coded into a record for each pair of countries. The records include sender country, receiver country, and millions of minutes of telephone traffic. These paired country data were input to the network analysis software, NEGOPY. Before presenting a network analysis of the intercountry data, nation-centric patterns are illustrated. For example, Jordan's 1995 outgoing call patterns with other nations are shown in Table 7.1.

For the main analysis, records were compiled for all pairs of nations for whom either outgoing or incoming traffic frequencies were available. Next, a network

TABLE 7.1.
Outgoing Telephone Traffic from Jordan, 1995

Receiving Country	Frequency (%)	Percentage
1. Israel	9.8	13.0
2. Saudi Arabia	8.6	12.0
3. Iraq	7.9	11.0
4. Egypt	6.4	9.0
5. Syria	6.4	9.0
6. United States	4.4	6.1
7. United Arab Emirates	4.1	5.7
8. United Kingdom	2.9	4.0
9. Kuwait	2.5	3.5
10. Lebanon	2.4	3.3
11. Germany	1.4	1.9
12. Italy	1.1	1.5
13. Qatar	1.0	1.4
14. France	1.0	1.4
15. Oman	0.8	1.1
16. Yemen	0.8	1.1
17. Turkey	0.7	1.0
18. Bahrain	0.7	1.0
19. Canada	0.6	0.8
20. Switzerland	0.5	0.6
Other	7.8	10.9

analysis was run to identify the overall structure of the network among countries. The default parameter settings for group detection and role identification in the NEGOPY network analysis program were used. Directional links of outgoing and incoming telephone minutes were made nondirectional. This means that a link from country A to country B was treated as also reflecting a link from country B to country A. This compensated for the fact that data were not available for some countries. For country-country links for which both directions were available, the program averaged the two values.

For link strengths, the raw values of millions of minutes were used. For countries with less than one million annual minutes, numbers were rounded up to 1 million because the program will not deal with decimals below 1.0 and other transformations would exceed the upper link strength the program could handle. To examine changes over time in the network, two comparison data sets were created; one set combined data from 1991 and 1992, the other, from 1995 and 1996.

Telephone traffic includes Internet activity. Internet data were also compiled separately to assess their relationship to raw telephone minutes. Numbers of Internet hosts in the Arab countries are shown in Table 7.3 on page 102. Web posting counts shown in Table 7.4, on page 104, were obtained by using the search engine, Lycos. Each country name was entered into the search engine and the count of total number of Web page hits tabulated. Each time the country name appears anywhere on a Web page, the count is incremented. This is a measure of the Web presence of each country.

For the estimates of the number of Internet hosts per country, data generated by the robot deployed by Net Wizards, Inc., were used. This company conducts a worldwide search of the Internet twice per year, counting the number of hosts encountered. Their searches began in the first half of 1995. These data do not include the number of users per host, which would be a much more accurate measure of Internet penetration in countries. For a detailed discussion of the Net Wizards methodology and limitations, see their Website at www.nw.com. Given the research interest in international communication, data on traditional media were also compiled, using ratings of press freedom on nations from Freedom House. Each year, they rate each nation on three aspects of broadcast freedom and three aspects of print media freedom. For discussion of their methodology, see their website at www.freedomhouse.org. This research used 1998 press freedom ratings (Sussman, 1998).

RESULTS

Basic telephone infrastructure data are shown in Table 7.2. These data were included in the Telegeography reports for 1998 (Staple, 1999). Future research will analyze the telecommunication network for 1997 and 1998 data. Table 7.3 on page 102 reports basic statistics on Internet variables for Arab countries. Figure 7.2 on page 103 shows the aggregated trend.

Because Internet packets travel over telephone circuits, they contribute to more telephone minutes between pairs of nations through whom Internet traffic passes. To assess the magnitude of the relationship between telephone traffic and Internet activity, the number of Internet hosts were correlated across 60 nations for which data on both incoming and outgoing telephone traffic and hosts were available. The correlation between total telephone traffic and number of Internet hosts in the last half of 1997 is .70 ($p < .01$) and with telephone traffic and number of Web page hits (see Table 7.4) is .67 ($p < .01$).

Global Telephone Network: 1991 and 1992 compared to 1995 and 1996

The network analysis of the 1991–1992 data showed one large group of nations across the world. Arab countries were in a peripheral position relative to the dominant core of Western industrialized nations.

In 1995 and 1996, two network groups were found. One contained most of the world's nations, with the United States and the United Kingdom most central. A sizable second group was evident. Most of these nations are Middle Eastern Arab nations. There are, however, some Arab countries that are in the larger global group,

TABLE 7.2.
Telephone Statistics for Arab Countries: 1998

	GDP US$ billions	Pop. (mills.)	Main Lines (Thous.)	Lines per 100 people	Cell Users (Thous.)	Outgoing TT[a] Mills. Mins.	Pct. Chg. from 1997	Incoming TT Mills. Mins.	Pct. Chg. from 1997
Algeria	48.4	30.1	1600	5.3	19	121.3	n.a.	n.a.	n.a.
Bahrain	5.3	0.6	158	24.6	92	124.4	16.7	102.1	19.6
Egypt	174.3	66	3972	6	91	127.3	6.7	475.3	5.3
Iran	100.3	65.8	7355	11.2	390	177	10.1	185.7	42.7
Jordan	7.4	6	403	6.7	70	122.6	33.4	176.9	22
Kuwait	43.7	1.8	412	22.7	250	160.5*	n.a.	n.a.	n.a.
Morocco	35.1	27.9	1515	5.4	116	158	5.4	460	26.4
Oman	15	2.4	220	9.2	103	92.9	25.1	74.2	5.4
Qatar	12	0.6	151	26	66	112.5	12.6	70	17.8
Saudi Arabia	125.8	20.2	2878	14.3	627	932.6	16.4	n.a.	n.a.
Sudan	31.2	28.3	162	162	9	18.4	24.5	88	103.7
Syria	16.3	15.3	1530	10	n.a.	103	15.3	173.9*	n.a.
Tunisia	8.9	63	0.5	0.3	6	69.9**	n.a.	n.a.	n.a.
UAE	47.2	2.4	915	38.9	493	874.8	18.5	n.a.	n.a.

[a]TT = Total telephone traffic
*1997
**1995

not the Arab-centered group. These exceptions are Iran, Tunisia, Algeria, and Morocco. Nations included in the emergent telephonic Arab Nation and their centrality scores appear in Table 7.5 on page 104.

This table shows the more central positions of Arab countries in this group. It also contains non-Arab, yet predominantly Muslim countries of Pakistan and Bangladesh as peripheral members. Because other Muslim countries are not included in this group, but instead are members of the larger global group, the emergent group cannot readily be considered an "Islam Nation." Given the centrality of Arab countries, at this time it appears most appropriate to view it as primarily an "Arab Nation." Into the 21st century, it will be useful to observe the evolution of this group. It may become more clearly "Arab," or perhaps more Muslim, or may change in other ways, such as integrating with the larger group of nations, or becoming part of some other new group.

Discriminators of Group Membership

To explore what differentiates membership in the Arab-centric group compared to the other group, multiple discriminant analysis was run using as possible discrimi-

TABLE 7.3.
Number of Internet Hosts Estimated by Country Semi-Annually

	Number of Internet Hosts										
	95a	95b	96a	96b	97a	97b		98a	98b[a]	99a	99b
Algeria	10	16	16	18	28	31		17	19	23	26
Bahrain	0	0	142	236	841	896		339	337	577	1110
Egypt	161	214	591	817	1,615	1,894		16,930	18,554	1908	1746
Iran	18	224	271	307	285	—		204	264	244	292
Iraq	0	0	0	0	0	0		0	0	0	0
Jordan	0	0	19	79	140	170		249	364	370	551
Kuwait	220	776	1,233	1,963	2,920	3,555		4,749	6,653	6231	4573
Lebanon	0	1	88	359	601	1,128		1,377	1,552	2358	2997
Libya	0	0	0	0	0	4		2	2	4	2
Morocco	0	0	234	351	477	888		463	511	548	801
Oman	0	0	0	0	0	0		671	667	664	673
Qatar	0	0	0	6	21	345		191	24	13	32
Saudi Arabia	2	18	27	275	0	293		37	42	319	2508
Sudan	0	0	0	0	0	2		0	0	0	0
Syria	0	0	0	0	0	0		0	0	1	1
Tunisia	57	65	82	40	39	15		69	57	67	53
UAE	0	11	365	469	1,802	1,994		1,995	13,765	17904	11103
Yemen	0	0	0	0	0	2		10	14	20	27

UAE, United Arab Emirates.

[a] Estimates are from Net Wizards, Inc.'s Web robot system, which sweeps the Internet in the first and second halves of each year beginning in 1995. Procedures were changed in January of 1998 to get around blocking that some sites performed. For this reason, Net Wizards suggests comparisons over time for some countries will be misleading. Unfortunately, we do not know specifically how, although by examining the data one can see anomalies for some countries. Both 1998 surveys were conducted using exactly the same procedure so results for these two time periods can be validly compared.

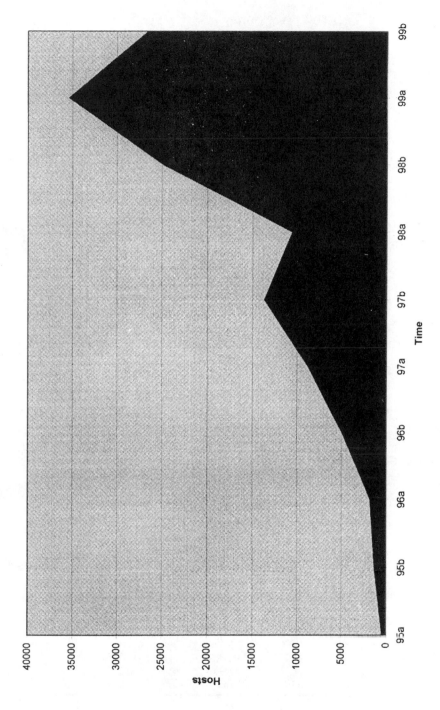

FIGURE 7.2.   Arab countries' aggregated Internet host growth.

TABLE 7.4.
Lycos World Wide Web Hits on Country Name

Jordan	48,643
Egypt	37,034
Lebanon	18,500
Iran Islamic Republic	17,836
Kuwait	13,965
Saudi Arabia	13,425
Oman	13,056
Iraq	12,589
Morocco	12,487
Syrian Arab Republic	9,744
United Arab Emirates	9,260
Bahrain	9,093
Sudan	8,759
Algeria	8,360
Tunisia	8,338
Qatar	6,692
Yemen	6,182
Libyan Arab Jamahiriya	6,025

TABLE 7.5.
"Arab Nation" Country Centrality

Standardized Group Average Distance	Country
−1.700	United Arab Emirates
−1.416	Saudi Arabia
−1.133	Kuwait
−0.850	Qatar
−0.567	Bahrain
−0.283	Jordan → Iraq
0.283	Egypt
0.283	Pakistan
0.283	Bangladesh
0.850	Syrian Arab Republic
0.850	Oman
0.850	Lebanon
1.133	Sudan
1.416	Yemen

nating variables a set of seven press freedom variables. Three measured broadcast freedom, three measured print media freedom, and one was a summary measure. The best predictor of membership in the two groups was the variable of press freedom. Countries in the Arab-centered group had significantly higher press freedom than those in the larger world group.

DISCUSSION

A limitation of this study is that Telegeography does not report the top 20 outgoing call recipient nations for all countries. For example, Libya and Iraq are among Arab countries with missing data for outgoing calls (see Table 7.2). This limitation is reduced by the fact that most of the countries with missing outgoing call data appear in other countries' lists. Because the study did not distinguish between outgoing and incoming call minutes in the network analysis, this limitation was adjusted for. Nevertheless, it would be best if all countries had outgoing call data reported. It is most often the case, however, in any sort of network analysis on message traffic that some data are missing on the direction of links. These adjustments to link directionality make for a robust aggregate network analysis. The data for 1995–1996, used in this study, are more complete than that from previous years. So this limitation of missing data is reducing.

SUMMARY

Analysis of nations' telephone call patterns gives an important perspective on the communication dynamics of Arab countries and of the Arab Nation in its global international context. The results show evidence for an Arab-centered group of nations, including, in order of centrality, the countries of United Arab Emirates, Saudi Arabia, Kuwait, Qatar, Bahrain, Jordan, Iraq, Egypt, Syria, Oman, Lebanon, Sudan, and Yemen. Pakistan and Bangladesh are also included but are the most peripheral nodes in the group. These latter two members are not considered Arab in contemporary terms, although historically these countries were converted to Islam by peoples from the Arab region.

The inclusion of Morocco, Tunisia, and Algeria in the larger global group and not the Arab group may be the result of their current economic relationships with the European Union. Iran's membership in the large global group and not the Arab-centered group may stem from two causes. First, it has more recent expatriates than other Arab countries as a result of the outward migration that took place after the Islamic revolution in Iran. Many of those who left Iran settled in the United States and other countries in the West. A second reason may relate to the historical and cultural differences between Iran and other Arab countries. Iran's traditional language is Farsi, not Arabic, and many Iranians consider themselves Persians, different from Arabs.

As telephone penetration in these countries increases in the future, one would expect more intra-Arab Nation telephone traffic. This is because, in the diffusion of telephones in most countries, the medium has been used first by elites, then middle classes, and then lower classes. The higher status groups, more likely to be educated in the West, may have more foreign ties. This may lead to more telephone communication with Western countries. As more middle- and lower-class groups increase their telephone use, one might expect proportionately more regional and less overseas telephone contact.

A related reason for such a change may be language. Higher social classes are more likely to be English speaking, while lower classes in the Arab countries are more likely exclusively Arab speaking. With greater downward diffusion of telephones in the social hierarchy, Arabic language commonality between nations may increase telephone traffic among them. On the other hand, the European Union is developing closer economic ties with Arab countries. As this occurs, the distinct Arab telephone group may fade, either as it merges with the larger world network, or as the world differentiates into other groups. For example, perhaps one group will center on the European Union nations and affiliates, and another group around the United States and other nations.

Another factor likely to influence future global international telephone networks is the Internet. Internet development is growing in Arab countries, as shown by Table 7.4. If Internet users in Arab countries create more telephone traffic between these countries, one would expect an even more distinct Arab Nation into the 21st century.

In the larger world context, there is evidence from this study to support the hypothesis that increasing use of *network* as opposed to broadcast media will be associated with the breakup of the one world group into subgroups reflecting increasing world diversification. Until this time, the most recent available network analysis of telephone traffic used only 1992–1993 data. Sun and Barnett (1994) found one large world group up through that time. Within only 2 years after that, a time when World Wide Web growth accelerated, this study found that the world nations had differentiated into two notable groups, the Arab Nation and the rest of the world. This difference, however, may stem from the less-than-complete data available for Arab countries before 1995–1996. In examining the network for 1991–1992, one finds that while there was one large world group of nations, the Arab nations that in 1995–1996 were a distinct group were positioned closely within the larger group. Missing data may account for the difference in the current network structure and that reported by Sun and Barnett (1994).

CONCLUSION

This study addressed the question of whether there is evidence from international telephone traffic networks for the existence of an "Arab Nation." Data from

1995–1996 do not show one large global network, as Sun and Barnett (1994) previously found. Rather, a distinctively Arab-centered group has emerged along with a larger group of other nations. This differentiation of global networks is consistent with theoretical reasoning (Danowski, 1993a). In contrast to broadcast media, the network-based media carrying messages over telephone circuits may increasingly promote less unified global networks with regional subgroups of increasing variation. Future research can determine to what extent there is evidence for further development of a trend of this kind by using international telephone traffic data and network analysis in subsequent years.

DISCUSSION QUESTIONS

1. How does the concept of an Arab Nation pertain to telephone traffic world-wide?
2. How does NEGOPY compare to other computer programs used to analyze communication and other social networks?
3. What is Telegeography, and how does it relate to intercountry telephone research?
4. Analyze the number of Internet hosts in the Arab world. What did you find?
5. To what extent is there evidence that further improvement of international telephone traffic data is possible? Is there a correlation between Internet and Web development and international telephone traffic?

REFERENCES

Alexander, M., & Danowski, J. (1990). Analysis of an ancient network. *Social Networks, 12,* 313–335.

Barnett, G., & Danowski, J. (1992). The structure of communication: A network analysis of the International Communication Association. *Human Communication Research, 19*(2), 264–285.

Barnett, G., Danowski, J., & Richards, W. (1993). Communication networks and network analysis: A current assessment. In G. Barnett & W. Richards (Eds.), *Progress in communication sciences XII* (pp. 1–20). Norwood, NJ: Ablex.

Boissevain, J., & Mitchell, J. C. (1973). *Network analysis: Studies in human interaction.* The Hague, Netherlands: Mouton.

Danowski, J. (1980). Group attitude conformity and connectivity of organizational communication networks for production, innovation, and maintenance content. *Human Communication Research, 6,* 299–308.

Danowski, J. (1982). A network-based content analysis methodology for computer-mediated communication. *Communication Yearbook, 6,* 904–925.

Danowski, J. (1988). Organizational infographics and automated auditing: Using computers to unobtrusively gather and analyze communication. In G. Goldhaber & G. Barnett (eds.) *Handbook of organizational communication* (pp. 335–384). Norwood, NJ: Ablex.

Danowski, J. (1993a). An emerging marco-level theory of organizational communication: Organizations as virtual reality management systems. In L. Thayer & G. Barnett (Eds.), *Emerging perspectives in organizational communication* (pp. 141–174). Norwood, NJ: Ablex.

Danowski, J. (1993b). Network analysis of message content. In G. Barnett & W. Richards (Eds.), *Progress in communication sciences XII* (pp. 197–222). Norwood, NJ: Ablex.

Danowski, J., Barnett, G., & Friedland, M. (1986). Interorganizational network position, media coverage, and publics' images. *Communication Yearbook, 10*, 808–830.

Danowski, J., & Edison-Swift, P. (1985). Crisis effects on intraorganizational computer-based communication. *Communication Research, 12*, 251–270.

Emirbayer, M., & Goodwin, J. (1994). Network analysis, culture, and the problem of agency. *American Journal of Sociology, 99*(6), 1411–1454.

Everett, M., Borgatti, S., & Freeman, L. (1992a). *UCINET IV*. Columbia, SC: Analytic Technologies.

Everett, M., Borgatti, S., & Freeman, L. (1992b). *UCINET X*. Columbia, SC: Analytic Technologies.

Jacobson, E., & Seashore, S. E. (1951). Communication practices in complex organizations. *Journal of Social Issues, 7*, 28–40.

Moreno, J. L. (1934). *Who shall survive?: A new approach to the problem of human interrelations*. Washington, DC: Nervous and Mental Disease Publishing.

Richards, W. (1988). The NEGOPY network analysis program. *Connections*, 76–83.

Staple, G. C. (1996). *Telegeography 1996/97: Global telecommunications traffic, statistics & commentary*. London: International Institute of Communications.

Staple, G. C. (1999). *Telegeography 2000: Global telecommunications traffic, statistics & commentary*. London: International Institute of Communications.

Sun, S., & Barnett, G. (1994). The international telephone network and democratization. *Journal of the American Society for Information Science, 45*(6), 411–421.

Sussman, L. (1998). *Press freedom 1998, global warning: Press controls fuel the Asian debacle*. New York: Freedom House.

Wellman, B., & Berkowitz, S. (1997). *Social structures: A network approach*. Greenwich, CT: JAI Press.

8

DIGITAL COMMUNICATIONS IN THE ARAB WORLD ENTERING THE 21ST CENTURY

Hussein Y. Amin
American University in Cairo

Leo A. Gher
Southern Illinois University

INTRODUCTION

In 1965 the first commercial satellite was launched into orbit. With the rollout of services, that initial geosynchronous satellite could handle only 240 voice circuits at a single time. Today, orbiting satellites carry about 33 percent of transnational voice traffic, and virtually all television exchange between countries. All that is about to change. In 1999 several new personal communications satellite systems will be launched utilizing low-earth orbits (LEOs), which will minimize transmission delay; still another system will be built principally to handle data streaming, such as linking to the Internet. According to *Scientific American* (Evans, 1998), in less than a decade three to five voice-type satellite systems and possibly a dozen data-oriented systems could begin operations. Global communications will once again reinvent itself, and industrialized nations and international business conglomerates will make the most of these planetary, cyberspace technologies. A critical question arises. How will emerging economies and Third World countries cope with the geometrically expanding technology gap between those who are prepared to take advantage of 21st century communications and those who are not? The nations of the Arab world are no exception and must begin the task of transforming their economies, communications infrastructures and educational systems to meet the demands of the new millennium. The purpose of this paper is to update previous research data centered on digital communications in the Arab world entering the 21st century, and to explore the economic and cultural impact of developments within the region.

It is difficult to define the boundaries of digital communications (the information superhighway) because such electronic media are changing moment by moment. For this paper, digital communications will be broadly defined, and will include modern technological developments such as compressed digital satellites, Internet connectivity and telephony, websites, direct-to-home (DTH) satellite radio and television, and interactive personal computer (PC)–based computing. These technologies distinguish new media from old, which usually includes newspapers, international newspapers, news agencies, publication houses, and magazines. The researchers recognize that some print publications reproduce their newspaper or magazine as a Website on the Internet. This, however, does not place such information sources in the same camp with the cyberspace technologies of the information superhighway.

Research Questions

The following questions are addressed in this study:

1. What is the current status of digital communications in the Arab world?
2. What are the perspectives for developing cyberspace infrastructures and technologies that support digital communications in the region?
3. What are the economic and cultural ramifications of a new electronic media on Arabic societies in the coming millennium?
4. What are the current developments in digital communications worldwide?

Methodology

Research question 1 was answered using traditional historical research methods. Data were compiled from the following sources: (1) *Statistical Yearbook 1996*, UNESCO, Paris, France; (2) *Europa Yearbook 1997*, Europa Publications Limited, England; (3) *World Development Report 1996*, The World Bank, Oxford University, England, 1998; (4) *Human Development Report 1995*, UNDP, Oxford University Press; (5) *Status Report 1998*, the Internet Society; and (6) MEID country statistics, *Middle East Internet Directory, 1999*.

Research questions 2 and 3 were explored using information collected through field studies and interviews. All question 2 and 3 research was conducted on-ground by the authors or by assistants under direct supervision, using only primary sources. Research information was gathered over a 3-year period in the following Middle

Eastern countries: Saudi Arabia, Egypt, Jordan, Lebanon, Morocco, and Tunisia. Three interviews were conducted outside the region in England and the United States. Some ancillary information was gathered in Italy and Germany. For example, one primary researcher conducted two on-site visits to Telespacio, Europe's premier satellite facility at Fucino, Italy, where most Arab world satellite operations and some live studio facilities are located. Originally a questionnaire was employed as a research tool, but statistical applications were found to be uninformative and even misleading because of a preponderance of self-serving responses. However, the questionnaire was found to be worthwhile as an organizational tool for interviewing; also, anecdotal reports were utilized to compile general information, which when cross-referenced with empirical data proved to be appropriate for developing broad conclusions.

Limitations

Descriptive field investigations, as Stephen Isaac (1987) points out, are investigations intended to systematically describe the facts and characteristics of a unique subject. Working with emerging Second and Third World governments has hidden complications. Because of the challenge of political sensitivities, or the reluctance to disclose financial information, or regional competitiveness, or privacy issues, ascertaining reliable data is difficult at best, and often impossible. In this study, Likert-style surveys were constructed to test attitudes about new electronic media in the Arab world. It was hoped that the collected data could be subjected to correctional protocols in order to compare and contrast Western data with Middle Eastern information. But the results of the pilot instrument were unacceptable. The subjects marked nothing but the most flattering evaluations of their superiors. Thus, the research is limited to descriptive analyses only; no other research methodology is applicable. New electronic media research (MEID, 1999) is updated annually.

Another area of concern for this research is the reliability of Internet connectivity data. During personal communications and oral interviews, several subjects questioned the numbers reported as being underestimated. However, the data must be verifiable to future researchers, and therefore only verifiable sources are reported herein.

STATUS OF RADIO AND TELEVISION INDUSTRIES IN THE ARAB WORLD

Over the past 7 years, the Middle East has witnessed the development of a number of national, regional and international, Arabic telecommunication services. This wave began with the launching of the Egyptian Space Channel (ESC), which was soon followed by the creation of the Saudi Middle East Broadcasting Center (MBC), the Kuwaiti Space Channel (KSC), the Jordanian Arab Space Channel

(JASC), the Space Network of Dubai, Tunisia TV7, Moroccan Satellite Channel, Oman TV, and United Arab Emirates TV. Other channels, such as Saudi national television and Egypt national television, were later placed on Arabsat for direct-to-home reception. The Arab world has also witnessed the birth of two private international services, Arab Radio and television (ART), which carries seven specialized Arabic channels, and Orbit, which consists of 16 channels containing both Arabic and English programming (Gher & Amin, 1999).

Generally speaking, communications systems in Arab states are absolute monopolies, under direct government supervision. Most Arab governments operate their own broadcasting institutions. These sovereign states embrace the broadcast media as a political and propaganda tool, and are keenly interested in keeping these technologies out of hostile hands. Another reason for centralized control of media is the relatively low literacy throughout the area. Radio and television can surmount the problem of illiteracy, and are frequently used as an arm of the government to guide and control the public. (Amin & Boyd, 1993) Almost all Arab radio and television systems are subsidized by the state, and only partially financed by advertising revenues.

Regardless of the fact that most Middle Eastern broadcast systems are under the direct control of Arab governments, there are some significant differences among them. Most consequential are the political rules by which they play. Arab radio and television systems can be divided into two groups. The first group operates under a national mobilization philosophy, a type of broadcasting system observed in Algeria, Egypt, Iraq, Libya, Sudan, Syria, and Yemen. These countries have exercised total control over broadcasting. Egypt, which is the most influential state in terms of television development, is somewhat the exception. Egypt's long theater tradition and well-established film business have provided the talent for a stable entertainment industry that not only has enabled Egypt to produce most of its own television programming, but has also provided products and talent for other Arab countries (Amin & Boyd, 1993).

The second major group operates under a bureaucratic, *laissez faire* philosophy, and includes all other Arab states except Morocco and Lebanon. These states exercise control over radio and television broadcasting, but are more relaxed in the sense that they do not manipulate their media in a controlled manner.

STATUS OF TELECOMMUNICATIONS IN THE ARAB WORLD

Arab states have an average of four telephone lines per 100 inhabitants, which is approximately one tenth the number in industrialized countries. This ratio varies in the region from a high of 30 in the United Arab Emirates (UAE) to less than one in the Sudan. Telecommunication long-lines grew around 10 percent per year over the past decade, with the highest growth in Egypt and Oman. (F. Y. Amer, personal communication, October 10, 1990) Around 80 percent of the capacity of the local telephone networks in the Arab world are already being occupied; telephone networks are 95 percent automatic with an average of 50 percent using digital switchers. The number of telex subscribers, however, has been declining. The international traffic of telegrams and telexes has declined 50 percent and 40 percent, respectively over the past 10 years. On the other hand, international telephone traffic has increased 150 percent, mostly outgoing traffic with non-Arab countries. Saudi Arabia and the UAE are among the busiest countries in the world in this respect.

New telecommunications services are being introduced in most Arab countries. Mobile phones are common in the Gulf States; packet-switched networks are available in Egypt and the Gulf States as well as in three Maghreb countries. Telecommunications staff in the Arab world has average growth rate of 2 percent per year during the past 10 years, while productivity (number of lines per employee) improved 9 percent per year. In 1991, revenues generated from this sector exceeded U.S. $4.5 billion, while investment surpassed U.S. $1 billion (Jubaili, 1994).

STATUS OF SATELLITE COMMUNICATIONS IN THE ARAB WORLD

The 1967 war with Israel precipitated many changes among Middle Eastern countries, and a reexamination of the role of Arab media. In 1969 the Arab States Broadcasting Union (ASBU), emerged as a specialized agency of the Arab League, created to coordinate radio and television activities and to train personnel (Boyd, 1982). Arabsat was created at about the same time. Arabsat member nations invested according to their means, and currently there are 22 members: Algeria, Bahrain, Djibouti, Iraq, Jordan, Kuwait, Lebanon, Libya, Mauritania, Morocco, Oman, Qatar, Somalia, Sudan, Syria, the UAE, Yemen, the Palestine Liberation Organization, South Yemen, Saudi Arabia, and Egypt (Arab League, 1995).

Initially COMSAT served as Arabsat technical advisor. Aerospatiale of France was selected for the U.S. $134 million contract to produce three satellites with Ford Aerospace. A French Ariane rocket launched the first satellite, 1-A, in 1985, but it deviated from its planned orbit due to stabilizing gyroscope failure soon after launch. The second satellite, 1-B, was successfully activated from the American space shuttle, *Discovery*, in 1985. In 1991 Arianespace of Paris won a U.S. $35 million contract to launch the third downlink, 1-C, in early 1992. ("Arianespace Issues," 1991) Arabsat serves regional, national, and international customers, point to point, two way with direct broadcasting (Abu-Argoub, 1988). Each satellite has 26 transponders, 8,000 telephone circuits, seven television channels, and one large channel for community broadcasting. Yet after a year, the first two satellites used less than 5 percent of their capacity (Turkistane, 1988). However, attitudes toward media use changed, especially with the introduction of new compressed digital technology, and because of recent unexpected demand to lease transponders, a Saudi group bought a fourth satellite, 1-D, adding to the fleet of Arabsatdownlinks.

Despite difficulties confronting Arabsat, the Arab states are proceeding with growth plans, which include the rollout of a second-generation of Arabsat (Arab League, 1995). On April 17, 1993, Arabsat signed a contract with Aerospatiale to manufacture and launch second-generation satellites. The contract was for U.S. $258 million, and the launch of the first satellite was conducted in 1996; a second satellite will be ground-stored for 5 years. Each satellite contains 34 transponders, 22 of them are C-band and 12 are Ku-band. Expected life span is 12 years with an operational life expectancy of 16 years. These second-generation birds are designed according to the latest technology and will support the needs of direct-to-home broadcasting (Amin, 1995).

Several other satellite projects are breaking new ground in the region. The Egyptian government's plan for development calls for the expansion of radio, television, and information services. The new satellite, Nilesat, was placed in service in 1998. Other regional projects include ETISALAT, a communications satellite with DBS transponders for the UAE, and Saudsat, a downlink with similar capabilities (Amin, 1995).

DEVELOPMENT OF DIRECT-TO-HOME
TELEVISION SERVICES

Television, especially Egyptian programming, pervades much of Arabic society. Although Egypt's economy has its weaknesses, its powerful diplomatic contacts, rich television tradition, and longtime involvement in program exchanges set the stage for the development of Egyptian Space Net when Egypt returned to the Arab League in 1988. On November 6, 1990, the Egyptian Radio and Television Union (ERTU) signed an agreement with Arabsat to lease the bulk capacity of 1-A's transponder 26, the direct television downlink. The contract began on December 1, 1990, and continued for 3 years. At the time, neither the League nor any other Arab state used this transponder intended for community service broadcasting (ERTU, 1990). One week later, Egyptian Space Net commenced transmission with an average of 13 hours of daily programming, which included news, sports, entertainment, religious, educational, and cultural programs. The satellite's footprint covered the Middle East, North Africa, Europe, and a small portion of Asia. In a related development, the Saudi Middle East Broadcasting Centre (MBC) leased the S-band transponder on Arabsat. Five years later, ERTU switched the Space Net transmission to Intelsat to exploit the advantages of a more powerful transmitter and increased coverage (Abdulsalam Khallil, personal communication, January 5, 1992).

Nile TV is another Egyptian network. It began official broadcasting in 1993 on the European satellite Eutelsat II F3, covering Europe and North Africa. Egyptian Space Net plans to broadcast African programs to African countries in their native

TABLE 8.1.
Egypt

National Data

Population	60,300,000	Principal Cities	27
Gross National Product (per capita)	U.S. $1,180	Land Area (sq km)	1,001,499
Population Density (per square km)	62	Principal Language	Arabic
Literacy Rate	51%	Political System	presidential

Print Media

Daily Newspaper Circulation	2,600,000	Newspapers (dailies—14; Weeklies—35)	49
International Newspapers (*Al Ahram*)	1	News Agencies (MENA)	1
Number of Magazines	(unavailable)	Publication Houses	27

Electronic Media

TV Broadcast Hours (stations—7)	14,040	Number of TV Receivers	6,850,000
DTH Transmissions (households)	800,000	International TV Networks	2
Radio Broadcast Hours	73,236	Number of Radio Receivers	19,400,000
Cable Operators (CNE)	1	Telephone Lines (per 100 inhabitants)	4.99

Cyberspace Media

Internet Access Providers	35	E-mail-only providers	5
WWW—Websites	190	Governmental Restrictions	none

languages. Nile TV's broadcasting schedule incorporates English and French programs, and the main objective is to promote the image of Egypt in Europe and attract tourism.

In Saudi Arabia, unofficial broadcasting services were initiated in 1955 when EGLTV went on the air in Dhahran, the eastern province of the Kingdom. EGLTV was operated by the United States Air Force. A second station, HZ-22-TV, started in Dhahran in 1957, broadcasting from the ARAMCO compound, which served that company's American employees. Television was subject to considerable opposition in the early years, and earned the antagonism of many conservative religious groups. Saudi Arabia is the heart of the Islamic world, and thus, religious programming plays a major role in Saudi television.

On September 18, 1991, after 2 years of concentrated effort, the MBC was launched as the first independent Arabic language satellite channel. The aim of

MBC is to provide a communication link with home and culture for Arabs who live or work in Europe. Since its first transmission, MBC has offered a pro-Western sentiment, which reflects the Saudi regime's point of view. Abdullah el-Masry, executive director of MBC's Board stated, "Through MBC we hope to prepare for reconciliation in the Middle East . . . to be a bridge of understanding" (qtd. in Ibrahim, 1992). MBC aspires to become the Arab version of a major American network (Ibrahim, 1992). Arab investors own MBC, chiefly Walid Ibrahim, the brother-in-law of King Fahd of Saudi Arabia. The company was capitalized by the World Space Corporation, based in Washington, D.C. (MBC, 1992), and was granted permission by the U.S. Federal Communications Commission to launch a satellite capable of transmitting to the Middle East and Africa (Marlow, 1992).

MBC began telecasting to Europe and North Africa via the Eutelsat II Fl satellite, and to the Middle East by way of Arabsat 1-B. From its London studios, MBC's

TABLE 8.2.
Saudi Arabia

National Data

Population	20,100,000	Principal Cities	14
Gross National Product (per capita)	U.S. $7,040	Land Area (sq km)	2,240,000
Population Density (per square km)	8	Principal Language	Arabic
Literacy Rate	63%	Political System	monarchy

Print Media

Daily Newspaper Circulation	1,060,000	Newspapers (dailies—13; weeklies—9)	51
International Newspapers	2	News Agencies (IPA, SPA)	22
Number of Magazines	58	Publication Houses	10

Electronic Media

TV Broadcast Hours	(unavailable)	Number of TV Receivers	4,700,000
DTH Transmission (households)	banned	International TV Networks (ANA)	1
Radio Broadcast Hours	63,969	Number of Radio Receivers	5,320,000
Cable Operators (MMDS, Global Satellite)	2	Telephone Lines (per 100 inhabitants)	10.64

Cyberspace Media

Internet Access Providers	2	E-mail-only providers	(unavailable)
WWW—Websites	50	Governmental Restrictions	controls

TABLE 8.3.
Kuwait

National Data	1,691,000	Principal Cities	7
Population			
Gross National Product (per capita)	$19,040	Land Area (sq km)	17,818
Population Density (per square km)	95	Principle Language	Arabic
Literacy Rate	79%	Political System	monarchy
Print Media			
Daily Newspaper Circulation	655,000	Newspapers (dailies—9; weeklies—9)	18
International Newspapers	(unavailable)	News Agencies (KUNA)	1
Number of Magazines	(unavailable)	Publication Houses	6
Electronic Media			
TV Broadcast Hours	7,365	Number of TV Receivers	625,000
DTH Transmissions	permitted	International TV Networks (KSC)	1
Radio Broadcast Hours	23,256	Number of Radio Receivers	800,000
Cable Operators (MMDS)	1	Telephone Lines (per 100 inhabitants)	35.8
Cyberspace Media			
Internet Access Providers	3	E-mail-only Providers	3
WWW—Websites	100	Governmental Restrictions	controls

transmissions are uplinked to the Eutelsat II Fl satellite for DTH and cable coverage through the British Telecommunication International Docklands teleport. MBC is now unencrypted, using the PAL standard. Coverage extends from Scandinavia to North Africa and from Ireland to eastern Europe, reaching all major population centers of Europe. Saudi Arabia's national television channels are on Arabsat as well. The first channel is primarily in Arabic and is mostly conservative in terms of religious programming. The second channel, with programs in English, is designed to serve foreign expatriates (Gher & Amin, 1999).

In 1994, Arab states witnessed a new trend in television broadcasting—specialization. ART was the first Arab satellite network to establish niche services. Entrepreneur and international businessman Sheikh Saleh Kamel, a media tycoon who broke from the MBC partnership, and started his own satellite television channels heads, ART. Arab Media Corporation (AMC), incorporated in the Cayman Islands–British West Indies, wholly owns ART. The latter company has been established through investments of the Dallah Al Baraka Group, chaired by Kamel. The initial capital investment for AMC amounts to U.S. $300 million, while the total business volume of Dallah Al Baraka amounts to U.S. $6 billion, covering 43

TABLE 8.4.
Jerdan

National Data

Population	4,400,000	Principal Cities	8
Gross National Product (per capita)	U.S. $1,570	Land Area (sq km)	91,860
Population Density (per square km)	55	Principal Language	Arabic
Literacy Rate	87%	Political System	monarchy

Print Media

Daily Newspaper Circulation	250,000	Newspapers (dailies—4; weeklies—6)	10
International Newspapers	(unavailable)	News Agencies (TETRA)	1
Number of Magazines	(unavailable)	Publication Houses	2

Electronic Media

TV Broadcast Hours (stations—7)	5,380	Number of TV Receivers	430,000
DTH Transmissions (households)	permitted	International TV Networks (Jordan Satellite)	1
Radio Broadcast Hours	36,264	Number of Radio Receivers	430,000
Cable Operators (MMDS in progress)	1	Telephone Lines (per 100 inhabitants)	7.29

Cyberspace Media

Internet Access Providers	5	E-mail-only Providers	(unavailable)
WWW—Websites	110	Governmental Restrictions	none

countries all over the world (Gher, Amin, & Hashem, 1996). At present, the seven ART channels broadcast 24 hours a day, which amounts to 168 hours of television programming per week and 8,736 hours per year, a huge commitment of broadcast origination for any enterprise (S. Kamel, oral interview, August 18, 1995). The headquarters of production is in Cairo with subsidiary offices in Riyadh, Tunis, Kuwait, and Oman, and contacts are being made with many other Arab countries, including Qatar. ART transmission covers all parts of the Arab world. Programs are transmitted from Fucino, Italy, to Arabsat 1-D ("Editorial," 1994).

On May 25, 1994, Orbit initiated its television package for the Middle East. The company was headed by Prince Khaled bin Abdel Rahman Al Saud, a well-known figure in the business world. The Orbit package consists of 16 television channels and 4 radio networks. The 16 channels include Egyptian Television Channel 1, Egyptian Television Channel 2, All-News Network Channel, CNNI, BBC Television Arabic Service, the Fun Channel, ESPN-Orbit Channel, Hollywood Channel, the Discovery Channel, America Plus, C-Span, Music Now, the Super Movies Channel, Orbit 1

TABLE 8.5.
Algeria

National Data

Population	29,300,000	Principal Cities	48
Gross National Product (per capita)	U.S. $1,490	Land Area (sq km)	2,381,741
Population Density (per square km)	12	Principal Language	Arabic
Literacy Rate	62%	Political System	presidential

Print Media

Daily Newspaper Circulation	1,440,000	Newspapers (dailies—6; weeklies—4)	10
International Newspapers	(unavailable)	News Agencies (APS)	1
Number of Magazines	(unavailable)	Publication Houses	2

Electronic Media

TV Broadcast Hours	(unavailable0	Number of TV Receivers	2,500,000
DTH Transmissions	permitted	International TV Networks (ATV)	1
Radio Broadcast Hours	(unavailable)	Number of Radio Receivers	6,700,000
Cable Operators (SEA-ME-WE-2)	3	Telephone Lines (per 100 inhabitants)	4.38

Cyberspace Media

Internet Access Providers	2	E-mail-only providers	2
WWW—Websites	4	Governmental Restrictions	controls

(Arabic movies), Orbit 2 (variety channel), and Orbit News. Orbit News incorporates news and news programs from ABC, NBC, CBS, and the *Wall Street Journal*.

In the wake of the Gulf War, Kuwait found it necessary to establish its own television network, the Kuwaiti Space Network. Badr Mohammed el-Modaf, head of Kuwaiti Television, stated that "the Kuwaiti network will transmit valuable messages and broadcast in different languages" (KUNA, 1992), referring to Kuwaiti prisoners of war and pressuring the Iraqi government for their release. *Public Opinion*, a Kuwaiti newspaper, announced the network's experimental transmission in 1991. The following year, the Ministry of Information reported the initiation of the Kuwait Space Network via Arabsat 1-C, C-band (26 degrees east). Hours of transmission are from 17:00 to 22:00 GMT, and reception is acquired at 4051.75 megahertz with accompanying voice at 6.2 megahertz.

Because it transmits solely on the Arabsat 1-C, a C-band transponder with low signal power, Kuwait's coverage area is limited to the Middle East, Southern Europe, and East Asia. Kuwait is attempting to increase its power so that transmissions can reach countries in western Europe. The annual operating cost of the network has been estimated at U.S. $1 million, or 700 Kuwaiti dinars per day.

TABLE 8.6.
Tunisia

National Data			
Population	9,300,000	Principal Cities	10
Gross National Product (per capita)	U.S. $2,090	Land Area (sq km)	164,150
Population Density (per square km)	55	Principal Languages	French/Arabic
Literacy Rate	67%	Political System	presidential
Print Media			
Daily Newspaper Circulation	400,000	Newspapers (dailies—7; weeklies—15)	22
International Newspapers	(unavailable)	News Agencies (TAP)	1
Number of Magazines	(unavailable)	Publication Houses	15
Electronic Media			
TV Broadcast Hours	(unavailable)	Number of TV Receivers	800,000
DTH Transmissions	permitted	International TV Networks	(unavailable)
Radio Broadcast Hours	(unavailable)	Number of Radio Receivers	1,800,000
Cable Operators (submarine cable)	5	Telephone Lines (per 100 inhabitants)	6.43
Cyberspace Media			
Internet Access Providers	6	E-mail-only Providers	(unavailable)
WWW—Websites	16	Governmental Restrictions	none

The Jordanian Radio and Television Corporation started broadcasting the Jordanian Arab Space Channel on February 1, 1993, utilizing Channel 24 on Arabsat 1-C, which blankets most of the Arab world and parts of Europe. After 11 months, the Jordanian Arab Space Channel began a daily schedule of 16 hours of programming (8:00 to 24:00 GMT), which does not include the Arabic teletext service. New plans for the Jordanian international television channel encompass utilization of the second generation of Arabsat 2-A, engaged by a Ku-band transponder (Zayd, 1994). Future expansion of the Jordanian Arab Space Channel includes a transmission of the service to Europe, Canada, and the United States.

Television made its entry into Morocco in March 1962. RTM-TV, the main channel, reaches most of the population in Morocco. In 1989, the first private television station, 2M International, was introduced as a mixture of Arabic, French, and English programs with emphasis on entertainment. In 1992, the Moroccan

TABLE 8.7.
United Arab Emirates

National Data			
Population	2,600,000	Principal Cities	7
Gross National Product (per capita)	U.S.$17,400	Land Area (sq km)	90,559
Population Density (per square km)	26	Principal Language	Arabic
Literacy Rate	79%	Political System	presidential
Print Media			
Daily Newspaper Circulation	300,000	Newspapers (dailies—18; weeklies—6)	24
International Newspapers	(unavailable)	News Agencies (ENA)	1
Number of Magazines	(unavailable)	Publication Houses	3
Electronic Media			
TV Broadcast Hours	5,763	Number of TV Receivers	230,000
DTH Transmissions	permitted	International TV Networks (Dubai and UAE)	2
Radio Broadcast Hours	(unavailable)	Number of Radio Receivers	600,000
Cable Operators (Dubai Cablevision)	1	Telephone Lines (per 100 inhabitants)	32.66
Cyberspace Media			
Internet Access Providers	1	E-mail-only Providers	(unavailable)
WWW—Websites	240	Governmental Restrictions	none

national service was placed on Arabsat for transmission of its programs to the rest of the Arab world (Amin, 1996).

Algerian television started in 1956, relying chiefly on broadcasts from Europe, especially from France. After the revolution, the Algerian government began the task of making its channel more Arabic in character. Radio and Television in Algiers (RTA) telecasts one channel throughout the country through microwave links and one channel through satellite distribution on Intelsat. Network programs are a blend of entertainment and news designed to promote policies of the current political regime (Qandiil, 1989).

Television was introduced into Tunisia on May 31, 1966, Tunisia's national day. Broadcasting in French and Arabic, the programs were similar to Tunisia's radio services, which focused great attention on national development issues. On November 7, 1992, Tunisia inaugurated its own international television network, TV7. TV7

TABLE 8.8.
Oman

National Data

Population	2,300,000	Principal Cities	8
Gross National Product (per capita)	U.S. $5,200	Land Area (sq km)	212,457
Population Density (per square km)	10	Principal Language	Arabic
Literacy Rate	20%	Political System	monarchy

Print Media

Daily Newspaper Circulation	63,000	Newspapers (dailies—4; weeklies—6)	10
International Newspapers	(unavailable)	News Agencies (ONA)	1
Number of Magazines	(unavailable)	Publication Houses	6

Electronic Media

TV Broadcast Hours	4,770	Number of TV Receivers	1,450,000
DTH Transmissions	liberal	International TV Networks (Oman TV)	1
Radio Broadcast Hours	12,853	Number of Radio Receivers	1,280,000
Cable Operators	(unavailable)	Telephone Lines (per 100 inhabitants)	8.59

Cyberspace Media

Internet Access Providers	1	E-mail-only Providers	1
WWW—Websites	60	Governmental Restrictions	none

utilizes one of the Ku-bands on the Eutelsat II F3 satellite. Communication between Tunisian expatriates in Europe and the home country was the main objective for launching the Tunisian television service.

In Abu Dhabi, television was launched under the leadership of the Sheikhdom, and telecasting began in August 1969 before the formation of the UAE federation. Much of the UAE's television time is dedicated to religious programming and materials dealing with the Koran, specifically *hadith*, the sayings of the Prophet Mohammed (Amin, 1996). By the mid-1980s, the UAE added a second national television channel heavily dependent on English programs. The Space Network of Dubai is part of the Arabsat system. It initiated operation on October 24, 1992, and covers the entire Arab world, southern Europe, Turkey, Pakistan, India, Africa, and the Islamic republics of the Commonwealth of Independent States (CIS). This satellite footprint covers nearly one third of the world's population. The main programming of the Space Network of Dubai consists of news services (six Arabic news bulletins and four in English), cultural documentaries, variety programs, and drama (Arabic and English films). The Space Network of Dubai broadcasts 24 hours a day, and at the conclusion of any broadcast period channel, viewers are automat-

TABLE 8.9.
Lebanon

National Data			
Population	4,200,000	Principal Cities	5
Gross National Product (per capita)	U.S. $3,350	Land Area (sq km)	10,452
Population Density (per square km)	289	Principal Languages	Arabic/French
Literacy Rate	92%	Political System	presidential
Print Media			
Daily Newspaper Circulation	330,000	Newspapers (dailies—14; weeklies—28)	42
International Newspapers	(unavailable)	News Agencies (MENA)	1
Number of Magazines	(unavailable)	Publication Houses	18
Electronic Media			
TV Broadcast Hours	(unavailable)	Number of TV Receivers	1,100,000
DTH Transmissions	permitted	International TV Networks	(unavailable)
Radio Broadcast Hours	(unavailable)	Number of Radio Receivers	2,680,000
Cable Operators (LBCSAT satellite)	1	Telephone Lines (per 100 inhabitants)	14.93
Cyberspace Media			
Internet Access Providers	12	E-mail-only Providers	1
WWW—Websites	280	Governmental Restrictions	none

ically connected to the space network, enabling them to access Dubai programming without a satellite dish.

Omani TV started in the capital city, Muscat, on November 17, 1974. In 1975, a second station was opened in Salalah to cover the southern part of the Sultanate. In 1979, both channels were integrated into one national channel, and were positioned on Arabsat 1-C to telecast to the rest of the Arab world (Via Satellite, 1996). In Lebanon, traditionally the most liberalized state in the Arab world, television was initiated in May 1959. Tele-Orient was the first television operation and was owned jointly by Lebanese interests and the ABC, which later sold its shares to the British Thompson Corporation.

One unique development in the Middle East was the introduction of pirate telecasting during the Lebanese civil war. After the war, more than 40 commercially owned television stations set up operation. Rafik el-Hariri, the Lebanese prime minister and media entrepreneur, started an international television service called

TABLE 8.10.
Bahrain

National Data

Population	620,000	Principal Cities	5
Gross National Product (per capita)	U.S. $7,500	Land Area (sq km)	676
Population Density (per square km)	822	Principal Language	Arabic
Literacy Rate	85%	Political System	monarchy

Print Media

Daily Newspaper Circulation	70,000	Newspapers (dailies—3; weeklies—7)	10
International Newspapers	(unavailable)	News Agencies (KNA)	1
Number of Magazines	(unavailable)	Publication Houses	7

Electronic Media

TV Broadcast Hour	(unavailable)	Number of TV Receivers	262,000
DTH Transmissions	Permitted	International TV Networks (BSM)	1
Radio Broadcast Hours	(unavailable)	Number of Radio Receivers	320,000
Cable Operators (MMDS, SCC)	2	Telephone Lines (per 100 inhabitants)	24.11

Cyberspace Media

Internet Access Providers	3	E-mail-only Providers	(unavailable)
WWW—Websites	110	Governmental Restrictions	none

Future. The station provided a mixture of foreign programs from the United States, Europe, and Egypt, and was extremely popular throughout the Middle East, even in Saudi Arabia the most conservative Arab state. However, the Lebanese Cabinet eliminated the channel in 1994. The reason for its elimination, according to government sources, was to allow for the nationwide reorganization of the radio and television industry in Lebanon (Nusseir, 1995).

By the beginning of the decade of the 1990s, Bahraini TV had two channels offering viewers a variety of programs; the most popular of which were Arabic soap operas from Egypt. In 1993, Bahrain's main channel was secured on Arabsat for direct broadcast transmission throughout the region (Amin, 1996). Color telecasting was established in Bahrain in 1973 as a part of that nation's first broadcasts.

In 1970, Qatar television was introduced in monochrome; color broadcasting was implemented 4 years later. The Arabic main channel was placed on Arabsat in 1993, utilizing a C-band transponder. The intent of this national service was to showcase Qatar to the rest of the Arab world (Amin, 1996).

TABLE 8.11.
Qatar

National Data			
Population	680,000	Principal Cities	4
Gross National Product (per capita)	U.S. $11,600	Land Area (sq km)	11,437
Population Density (per square km)	50	Principal Languages	Arabic/English
Literacy Rate	79%	Political System	monarchy
Print Media			
Daily Newspaper Circulation	80,000	Newspapers (dailies—4; weeklies—6)	10
International Newspapers	(unavailable)	News Agencies (QNA)	1
Number of Magazines	(unavailable)	Publication Houses	5
Electronic Media			
TV Broadcast Hours	6,121	Number of TV Receivers	220,000
DTH Transmissions	banned	International TV Networks	(unavailable)
Radio Broadcast Hours	16,995	Number of Radio Receivers	240,000
Cable Operators (Qatar Cable)	1	Telephone Lines (per 100 inhabitants)	23.93
Cyberspace Media			
Internet Access Providers	6	E-mail-only Providers	(unavailable)
WWW—Websites	50	Governmental Restrictions	(unavailable)

DEVELOPMENT OF COMPUTERS IN THE ARAB WORLD

Computers were introduced in Arab states in the mid-1960s and flourished through-out the 1980s. By the beginning of the 1990s, several multinational corporations had offered Arabic software suitable to local markets that were user friendly. As computers became more available, Arab governments encouraged foreign compa-nies to invest in local industry. Macintosh managed to produce software for the Arabic consumer, and International Business Machines (IBM) started to invest in Arab markets as well. However, computer usage was not common, and only began to develop slowly at national universities and top business organizations within the Arab world. Oil industry money in Saudi Arabia and other Gulf States was the driving force that widened computer usage throughout the region. Sales of imported computers as well as software reached their peak in the mid-1980s, but slow development of Arabic software has hindered continued progress (Alam el-Din, 1994).

Needless to say, the Arab states as a whole represent a growing market for PCs. As for mainframes and supercomputers, the needs are limited mainly to governmental institutions. Recently, some Arab states such as Egypt, the UAE, Algeria, Saudi Arabia, and Libya have started industries to assemble personal computers, but local production has not kept up with local demand (Alam el-Din, 1994).

The Arab Gulf States are considered the most developed region with regard to computer manufacturing. In the UAE alone, revenues exceed U.S.$300 million. Produced and assembled in the Al Sharka emirate, the UAE marketed its first PC in 1989, and by end of 1993 the UAE was assembling 10,000 PCs annually. The nation's demand for computers has surpassed 20,000 PCs a year, and thus the UAE plans to increase local component production in the coming years. Meanwhile, the price of computers within the UAE has fallen by as much as 30 percent as a result of the open market policies of the government, and in Gebel Ali, the country's tax-free zone, investors do not face the usual import difficulties found in the rest of the Arab world.

Saudi Arabia represents the most lucrative market for electronics in the Middle East. The government invested substantial amounts of money to upgrade its telecommunication institutions as well as its computing capabilities for the Saudi oil sector. It was the increased demand for computing power that created substantial business opportunities in the Kingdom. Furthermore, the new Saudi computer education policies resulted in an extended demand for PCs, and in 1989, a modern telephony network was established in King Fahd City for computer information services in the field of science and technology. This network accommodates almost 6,000 subscribers in 19 cities within the Kingdom and is interconnected with many other nations around the world. The National Information Center and the Saudi University network offer similar services, while the ARAMCO network deals with the oil business exclusively (Aref, 1995).

Egypt's provincial computer industry was launched in 1988 when three factories began assembling component parts for PCs. In 1981, state law No. 627 was passed. It required all government institutions to use computers. As a result, many computer information centers were established throughout the country, including the Information Decision Support Center (IDSC), which studies ways to create a positive economic environment to encourage investments in high-tech industries in Egypt (I. Attia, personal communication, December 14, 1990). One of the IDSC's major projects, according to a 1995 *Business Monthly* report, is the Pyramids Technology Valley, which is modeled on such ventures as Silicon Valley in California and Bangalore Valley in India. As an affiliated project, the IDSC created a sister institution, the Regional Information Technology and Software Engineering Center (RITSEC) that deals with software technology. Sales volume for computers in Egypt was estimated at U.S. $3.3 million in 1985; U.S. $54.7 million in 1988, and by 1992, it had increased to U.S. $161.8 million. The annual growth rate for the Egyptian market is now estimated at 16 percent (Gher & Amin, 1999).

DEVELOPMENT OF THE INTERNET IN THE ARAB WORLD

Today, attempts to systematically gauge the size and status of the Internet are difficult—the mere act of "stopping to measure" causes inaccuracies in the measurement. In one 12-month period, for example, websites sextupled as recorded by the Internet Society (1996). Anything growing at such a geometric pace is, to say the least, a challenge.

Through the years, the growth of the Internet was estimated at a somewhat steady 10 percent per month. But in 1994, Internet growth erupted (Kline, 1995). The Internet Domain-Name Database reported in 1996 that the World Wide Web included 325,444 registered servers, with 190,255 websites. Given a comparable sustained growth rate, aggregate worldwide online users of the Internet should exceed 700 million by 2005 (NUA, 1999).

In the United States and Canada alone, the total number of users who have direct online access is almost 100 million, as reported by the NUA Internet Survey of 1999, in the most current research of Internet users. Out of approximately 100 million U.S. households, virtually all (99 percent) have a telephone connection, and by the close of the 20th century, forecasts estimate the number of U.S. households with home computers will surpass 70 million, with 65 million having access to the Internet (MIDS, 1996). With the implementation of personal communication system (PCS) technology in 1997, the penetration of telephone and television services, along with conversion technology for computers, the U.S. market will become the first fully integrated cyberspace, telecommunication market in the world.

The picture for the Arab world is far different, but no less challenging. The investment in communication infrastructure is considerably slower, and the development of essential components (computer accessibility, telephony networks, cyberspace technology, and Internet connectivity) to give the region access to the global information superhighway is far behind First World nations, as shown in Figure 8.1.

Central Arab Region

This subregion consists of six countries: Egypt, Israel (Palestine), Jordan, Lebanon, Sudan, and Syria (Kamel & Baki, 1995).

Egypt

Egypt has 35 online servers (MEID, 1999) such as EgyptNet, which is connected to the Internet and the global public data network. The total number of Websites is 190, mostly related to tourism, travel, or government information. The Egyptian University Network (EUN) is a server utilized by faculty, staff, and students, and is interconnected with Bitnet and Internet. A recent link-up introduced in Egypt is the Egyptian National Scientific and Technical Information Network, Enstinet, which provides services to researchers (Aref, 1995).

The Arab Republic of Egypt National Telecommunications Organization (AR-ENTO) has constructed many telephone networks in the country; its goal is to have one line for each 10 inhabitants by the year 2000. Approximately 95 percent of the lines are connected with digital transformers where fiber optic networks are utilized. Dial-up access telephone numbers in Cairo can always be achieved from any other Egyptian city provided one has a long-distance connection, and access to major providers such as America Online and Compuserve is possible through some Egyptian Web servers. At present time, the total number of Internet users in Egypt

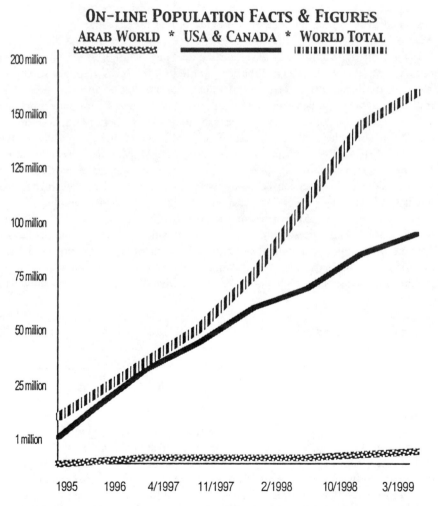

On-line Population Facts & Figures
Arab World * USA & Canada * World Total

FIGURE 8.1.   Online population facts and figures. (From NUA Internet Surveys, March 1999.)

exceeds 2,000, with 70 percent in the academic sector. But because the growth rate (148 percent) in Internet usage in Egypt is one of the fastest in the world, information provided through these links changes rapidly (Ashmawy, 1996).

Israel (Palestine)

Currently, Arabic online servers number eight, with more than 30 Websites available to users (MEID, 1999). Israel has 19 online servers available, mostly located in university settings such as Ben-Gurion University, Hebrew University, Weizmann Institute of Science, and Bar-Ilan University; all are linked to the Internet. Total websites presently employed in the county are 101, with most used for education services.

Jordan

The Internet came to the Hashemite Kingdom of Jordan in October 1995 (J. Fisher, personal communication, November 2, 1996), with the establishment of a node at the National Information Centre (NIC). The Kingdom has embarked on a program to establish a National Information System (NIS), which aims to develop information resources to ensure the flow of information to users, both public and private. At present, Jordan lacks a digital network that is capable of high-speed data transmission. This, in turn, hinders the ability to transfer data or even have remote access to data in an efficient and cost-effective way. Telephone availability in Jordan is 335,000 (65 percent in Amman) with the number of subscribers exceeding 287,000; the number of cities and towns served is 434. Approximately 2,200 telex and 1,500 mobile telephone subscribers are also being supported. Moreover, there are 17 exchanges in Jordan combined with one national and one international exchange. However, 21 new exchanges and 80 branch exchanges are to be activated with 86 optical fiber links and 17 microwave links (Nusseir, 1995).

Lebanon

Lebanon has 12 online servers (MEID, 1999) available for its citizens such as Cyberia and T-net, which are linked with the Internet. The total number of Websites currently functional in the country is 280, mostly references to tourism and travel, government information and business.

Sudan and Syria

Unfortunately, very little telecommunication information is available concerning the Sudan. Syria, however, is a different matter. Syria recently initiated the conversion to fiber-optics networks, and the government is presently aiming to secure telephone service for 1 million users. The latest computer network introduced in Syria is called Syria Pack; it is used by many different government sectors, including science and technology, trade and industry, education, human resources, tourism, and banking. Syria Pack network is also available for public use. The Higher Institute for Applied Sciences and Technology is the state training facility that provides programs in computing, testing, monitoring, and evaluation (Aref, 1995).

Gulf Region

This subregion has special characteristics owing to the wealth from oil production and other natural resources. The telecommunication infrastructure in the countries is significantly superior to other subregions of the Arab world. The Gulf region consists of a mixture of nations such as Bahrain, Kuwait, Oman, Qatar, Saudi Arabia, the UAE, and Yemen (Kamel & Baki, 1995).

Bahrain

"Bahrain will be connected to the Internet through a service provider in the United States or to the nearest Internet node," according to Nader Nasry, nodes administrator and VAX systems manager, University of Bahrain. Currently the University

TABLE 8.12.
Sudan

National Data			
Population	27,900,000	Principal Cities	5
Gross National Product (per capita)	U.S. $280	Land Area (sq km)	2,505,813
Population Density (per square km)	11	Principal Language	Arabic
Literacy Rate	46%	Political System	presidential
Print Media			
Daily Newspaper Circulation	650,000	Newspapers (dailies—5; weeklies—1)	6
International Newspapers	(unavailable)	News Agencies (SUNA)	1
Number of Magazines	(unavailable)	Publication Houses	6
Electronic Media			
TV Broadcast Hours	2,544	Number of TV Receivers	2,240,000
DTH Transmissions	(unavailable)	International TV Networks (Sudan TV)	1
Radio Broadcast Hours	6,357	Number of Radio Receivers	7,200,000
Cable Operators	none	Telephone Lines (per 100 inhabitants)	0.27
Cyberspace Media			
Internet Access Providers	(unavailable)	E-mail-only Providers	(unavailable)
WWW—Websites	21	Governmental Restrictions	(unavailable)

TABLE 8.13.
Syria

National Data			
Population	14,900,000	Principal Cities	8
Gross National Product (per capita)	U.S. $1,150	Land Area (sq km)	185,180
Population Density (per square km)	77	Principal Language	Arabic
Literacy Rate	71%	Political System	presidential
Print Media			
Daily Newspaper Circulation	274,000	Newspapers (dailies—8; weeklies—14)	22
International Newspapers	(unavailable)	News Agencies (AASI)	1
Number of Magazines	(unavailable)	Publication Houses	6
Electronic Media			
TV Broadcast Hours	(unavailable)	Number of TV Receivers	950,000
DTH	(unavailable)	International TV Networks	(unavailable)
Radio Broadcast Hours	(unavailable)	Number of Radio Receivers	3,750,000
Cable Operators (submarine)	17	Telephone Lines (per 100 inhabitants)	8.15
Cyberspace Media			
Internet Access Providers	1	E-mail-only Providers	(unavailable)
WWW—Websites	30	Governmental Restrictions	none

of Bahrain's Computer Centre, has a Bitnet connection through Gulfnet. The country's Ministry of Education is linked similarly.

Kuwait

Kuwait has three online servers (MEID, 1999) available for its citizens, which are linked with the Internet. The number of functional Websites currently in use in the country is estimated at 100. Kuwait public data network uses the X.25 protocol and provides its customers with local and international services. In Kuwait, another way to gain access to the Internet is through shell accounts on the Gulfnet Kuwait server (Badr el-Modaf, personal communication, December 21, 1994). With a shell account, one is buying access on Gulfnet Kuwait. This process supports the use of

SLIP (serial line internet protocol) and PPP (point-to-point protocol) services. Using a normal telephone line or a dedicated leased line and a high-speed modem, a computer can directly access the Internet through one connection or the other; speeds are up to 64 kbps and are of digital quality. Gulfnet Kuwait has created Kuwait.net as an open domain for all Kuwaiti users (Kamel & Baki, 1995)

Oman

Sultan Qaboos University in Oman is using a gateway located in the United States (California), squ.edu—an alias for squ.uu.holonet.net, for Internet e-mail processing. All university mail is sent and received through the Holonet gateway on a daily dial-up basis. A U.S. address is required for Holonet gateway administrative purposes.

United Arab Emirates

The UAE has established the most up-to-date cyberspace infrastructure in the region through its public and private shared PTT Etisalat, including 600,000

TABLE 8.14.
Yemen

National Data			
Population	16,300,000	Principal Cities	8
Gross National Product (per capita)	U.S. $270	Land Area (sq km)	8
Population Density (per square km)	28	Principal Language	Arabic
Literacy Rate	87%	Political System	presidential
Print Media			
Daily Newspaper Circulation	230,000	Newspapers (dailies—3; weeklies—12)	15
International Newspapers	(unavailable)	News Agencies (SABA and ANA)	2
Number of Magazines	(unavailable)	Publication Houses	4
Electronic Media			
TV Broadcast Hours	3,286	Number of TV Receivers	420,000
DTH Transmissions	Permitted	International TV Networks	(unavailable)
Radio Broadcast Hours	6,570	Number of Radio Receivers	650,000
Cable Operators	None	Telephone Lines (per 100 inhabitants)	1.29
Cyberspace Media			
Internet Access Providers	1	E-mail-only Providers	(unavailable)
WWW—Websites	20	Governmental Restrictions	control

telephone lines and a full-fledged fiber-optic network covering the entire country (Kamel & Baki, 1995). The network started with the traditional X.25 system with dedicated PAD (X.28) access via dial-up service with speeds from 50 bps to 64 kbps. The UAE's Etisalat is a general organization, established in 1976 for computer networks by means of telephony link-ups. The UAE government owns 60 percent of Etisalat, while 40 percent is publically owned. Services provided by Etisalat include e-mail, telex and fax services, and telephone exchange (cellular and other phone systems), in addition to offerings for specialized data in different fields. One access provider supplies UAE with more than 240 operational websites (MEID, 1999).

Maghreb Region

The Maghreb countries include Algeria, Morocco, and Tunisia; Libya is included here as a geographical partner. The telecommunication infrastructure in these countries includes a number of advanced services varying from normal phone lines

TABLE 8.15.
Libya

National Data			
Population	5,300,000	Principal Cities	7
Gross National Product (per capita)	U.S. $5,310	Land Area (sq km)	1,761,132
Population Density (per square km)	3	Principal Language	Arabic
Literacy Rate	86%	Political System	presidential
Print Media			
Daily Newspaper Circulation	71,000	Newspapers (dailies—4; weeklies—5)	9
International Newspapers	(unavailable)	News Agencies (JANA)	1
Number of Magazines	(unavailable)	Publication Houses	4
Electronic Media			
TV Broadcast Hours	(unavailable)	Number of TV Receivers	550,000
DTH Transmissions	(unavailable)	International TV Networks (LTV)	1
Radio Broadcast Hours	(unavailable)	Number of Radio Receivers	1,250,000
Cable Operators	(unavailable)	Telephone Lines (per 100 inhabitants)	5.88
Cyberspace Media			
Internet Access Providers	(unavailable)	E-mail-only Providers	(unavailable)
WWW—Websites	15	Governmental Restrictions	(unavailable)

TABLE 8.16.
Morocco

National Data

Population	27,500,000	Principal Cities	13
Gross National Product (per capita)	U.S. $1,250	Land Area (sq km)	711,000
Population Density (per square km)	59	Principal Language	Arabic
Literacy Rate	44%	Political System	monarchy

Print Media

Daily Newspaper Circulation	390,000	Newspapers (dailies—13; weeklies—11)	24
International Newspapers	(unavailable)	News Agencies (WMA)	1
Number of Magazines	(unavailable)	Publication Houses	4

Electronic Media

TV Broadcast Hours	(unavailable)	Number of TV Receivers	2,500,000
DTH Transmissions	(unavailable)	International TV Networks	(unavailable)
Radio Broadcast Hours	(unavailable)	Number of Radio Receivers	6,000,000
Cable Operators	(unavailable)	Telephone Lines (per 100 inhabitants)	4.53

Cyberspace Media

Internet Access Providers	11	E-mail-only Providers	2
WWW—Websites	(unavailable)	Governmental Restrictions	none

to leased analog lines, mobile phones, and X.25 (Evans, 1995). Morocco and Tunisia are even offering numeric and fiber-optic leased lines with speeds up to 2 Mb/s. The services offered in all countries are government-owned monopolies: Itissalat Al-Maghrib is the telecommunication authority in Morocco, the Direction Generale des Telecommunication (DGT) in the Ministry of Telecommunication is the Tunisian telecommunication authority, and the Algerian Ministry of Post and telecommunication is the authority in Algeria. No telecommunication information is available for Libya.

Algeria

The Algerian X.25 network called Dz-pack is composed of four main switching exchanges located in Algiers, Oran, Constantine, and Ourgla. It serves most urban regions of Algeria. The total capacity of this network is around 4,000 lines and it is connected to international networks such as Euronet, Telenet, and Europac.

TABLE 8.17.
Iran[a]

National Data			
Population	61,000,000	Principal Cities	23
Gross National Product (per capita)	U.S. $1,780	Land Area (sq km)	1,648,000
Population Density (per square km)	42	Principal Language	Iranian
Literacy Rate	72%	Political System	presidential
Print Media			
Daily Newspaper Circulation	1,150	Newspapers (dailies—3; weeklies—7)	10
International Newspapers	(unavailable)	News Agencies (KNA)	1
Number of Magazines	(unavailable)	Publication Houses	10
Electronic Media			
TV Broadcast Hours	(unavailable)	Number of TV Receivers	4,300,000
DTH Transmissions	(unavailable)	International TV Networks	12
Radio Broadcast Hours	(unavailable)	Number of Radio Receivers	15,580,000
Cable Operators (CNE)	1	Telephone Lines (per 100 inhabitants)	39.53
Cyberspace Media			
Internet Access Providers	6	E-mail-only Providers	(unavailable)
WWW—Websites	50	Governmental Restrictions	(unavailable)

[a]Iran is usually not considered within the Arab world, but is included in this study because of its economic and geographic proximity to the region.

Morocco

In Morocco, Shabaket El Maghreb (Maghreb network—CHAMA) provides e-mail services as well as specialized news services. The network has five nodes; officials plan to connect CHAMA with the Internet. Two Brothers University started leasing lines with the Euronet to serve research purposes for faculty and students (Alaoui, 1995). The Moroccan X.25 network, MAGHRIPACK, is composed of four switching exchanges installed in Casablanca, Rabat, Fes, and Marrakech, which are connected by 64 kb/s numeric lines.

Tunisia

Information networking in Tunisia was introduced in 1987 through EARN/Bitnet. In 1990, Tunis had the French Bitnet node hosted in that country and in 1991, it started to interface with the Internet. The Tunisian X.25 network, TUNIPAC, is composed of 22 switching exchanges with four principal exchanges, two in Tunis, one in Sousse, and one in Sfax, and two secondary exchanges in Nabeul and Gabes. In 1993, the Tunisian government established the National Network for Research and Technology (NNRT); it was interconnected to the French INRII network in Paris, and was instituted to supply a database for e-mail, teleconferencing, and technical information in Tunis. This network has the ability to deal with Telnet, which allows for file transfer and retrieval of information. Tunisia has its own gopher server that connects it with the rest of the world (Aref, 1995).

Iran

The Institute for Studies in Theoretical Physics and Mathematics (IPM), under the direction of Dr. Mohammed Javad Larijani, spearheaded Iran's entrance into the worldwide data communication network in 1992. The link was at first through Bitnet and Iran's membership in the Trans-European Research and Educational Networking Association. It later developed into a full-fledged Internet link with the assignment of 500 IP addresses as a Class C node. Tens of thousands of users are being served via a few slow 9,600-baud links. A variety of protocols for satellite channels at T1 speeds of 1.544 Mb/s were tested by the Data Communication Company of Iran. The Iranian academic link is through two 9,600-baud lines from IPM's MicroVAX 3100/20E to the University of Vienna in Austria. The Iranian academic network consists of a series of mostly leased (some dial-up) 9,600-baud lines. There are presently only two 64-kb links in this star-patterned network, between two of IPM's Teheran buildings, and IPM and Guilan University (Gher & Amin, 1999).

DISCUSSION

The entire Arab world has an estimated online population of 780,000. In other words, while 30 percent of the American population is online, less than 3 percent of the Arabic population is online. Additionally, the growth rate of online users is stagnant. NUA surveys project that online planetary users will double to 320 million by the end of the year 2000, and will continue to explode to 720 million by 2005. However, current estimates for Arab world expansion remain stagnant throughout this term.

There are three limiting factors for the growth of digital communications in the Arab world: (1) the techno-connectivity problem, (2) the English literacy problem, and (3) the oral culture of Arabic civilization, which has existed for more than 1,500 years. The Arab world is not hard-wired for business, unlike North America and Europe where telephone penetration exceeds 95 percent. Answers, however, may be available in the future. In the coming years, data-type satellite systems such as Cyberstar, Spaceway, and Teledesic may be the solution to overcome the problem of laying hundreds of thousand of kilometers of fiber-optic wire across the Sahara, Arabian, or Nubian Deserts.

The issue of English literacy, the preeminent language of the information super-highway, is also a significant impediment to a mass penetration of Internet services in the Arab world. Literacy in the Middle East is placed at 60 percent, while literacy in English does not exceed 6 percent. Obviously, this means that even if the technical connectivity problem were solved, more than 90 percent of the population would not be able to communicate because of language deficiencies.

And lastly, Arabic cultural heritage must be considered when trying to evaluate the impact of digital communications in the Arab world. Primary among many cultural issues is the fact that the oral tradition is the preferred mode of communication among Arabic peoples. Western civilization has been molded by a written culture for about as long as the oral tradition in the Arab world, but too often Western eyes are oblivious to such facts which will have a powerful affect on the development of Internet services in the region.

ECONOMIC IMPACT

In his seminal thesis on 21st century economics, Lester Thurow (1996) states, "Today the world is in a period of punctuated equilibrium—which is being caused by the simultaneous movements of five economic plates." These tectonic forces are identified as (1) the end of communism, (2) an era dominated by man-made brainpower industries, (3) changing demographics, (4) a global economy, and (5) no dominant political or military power. For the most part, the energy driving these forces is the fuel of the communications revolution.

Arabic nations are now confronted by inexorable, planetary dynamics. The Middle East's passage from feudal economics to free enterprise capitalism is an absolute necessity for the ultimate survival of the Arab world. According to current statistics, the average per capita income of the region (including Iran) is $1,942, less than one fourth the average of the Asian Tigers, which are usually classified as emerging Second World economies. Antiquated government policies such as import substitution and quasisocialism must be abandoned, and a large investment by the rich states of the region in education and communications infrastructure must be made. The development of the Arabic man-made brainpower industries and global economic strategies is almost entirely dependent upon literacy, especially in English. Literacy rates range from 20 percent in Oman to 92 percent in Lebanon, and the ability to use English by the general population is extremely low, estimated at less than 5 percent. These research data place the region squarely in the Third World category, and are testimony to meaningful deficiencies. Without considerable investments in education, economic rectification, and communication infrastructure, the Arab world will remain rooted in 19th-century economics.

With time, however, change may be possible, and the potential for improvement is truly great. Imagine, for a moment, peace in the region—with 50 million low-wage workers in Egypt, a literate population, a modern communications infrastructure, and wealthy investors in the Gulf States. A golden age of economics and development for the Arab world is possible with time and commitment.

DISCUSSION QUESTIONS

1. Given the difference in online growth between the Arab world and the Western world, what digital technologies need to be developed in the countries of the Middle East to compete economically in the 21st century?
2. Compare and contrast the current status of digital infrastructure in the Middle East with other developing regions of the world.
3. Given the political atmosphere in the region, what are the perspectives for acquiring modern telecommunication technologies that support digital communications in the next decade?
4. What are the cultural and religious repercussions of acquiring new electronic media in Arabic societies?
5. Given the oral tradition of Arabic peoples and the English literacy rate in the Middle East, outline the steps needed to implement a contemporary communications system in the next millennium.

REFERENCES

Abu-Argoub, I. A. (1988). Historical, political and technical development of Arabsat. (Doctoral dissertation, Northwestern University, 1988). *Dissertation Abstracts International, 52,* 3118A.

Alam el-Din, M. (1994). Communication technologies in the Arab world. *Alam El Fikr* (The Insight World), *23*(1&2), 9–133.

Alaoui, M. A. (1995). *Moroccan networks.* Paper presented at the Regional Workshop on Communication and Networking in the Arab Region, Cairo, Egypt.

Amin, H. Y. (1995). Egypt and the Arab world in the satellite age. In J. Sinclair, E. Jacka, & S. Cunningham (Eds.), *New patterns in global television: Peripheral vision* (pp. 101–124). New York: Oxford University Press.

Amin, H. Y. (1996). The Middle East and North Africa. In A. Wells (Ed.), *World broadcasting: A comparative view* (pp. 121–143). London: General Hall Press.

Amin, H.Y., & Boyd, D. A. (1993). The impact of home video cassette recorders on the Egyptian film and television consumption patterns. *The European Journal of Communications, 18*(1), 2–7.

Arab League. (1995, January 9). *The ongoing committee for Arab Communication, Term 57. Study on the information superhighway.* Cairo, Egypt: Author.

Aref, R. (1995). Information and telecommunications networks in the Arab states. *PC World Middle East, 88,* 66–69.

Arianespace and ArabSat sign new launch contract. (1992, May 15). *PR Newswire*.

Arianespace issues launch manifest. (1991, September 19). *PR Newswire*.

Ashmawy, A. K. (1996, September). *Internet access in Egypt* [Online]. Available: ashmawy@geosystems.gatech.edu

Boyd, D. (1982). *Broadcasting in the Arab world*. Philadelphia: Temple University Press.

Editorial. (1994, April 3). *Al-Ahram*, p. 3.

Egyptian Radio and Television Union (ERTU). (1990). Contract with ArabSat. Cairo, Egypt: Ministry of Information.

Evans, B. T. (1995). United Kingdom of Great Britain. In L. S. Gross (Ed.), *The international world of electronic media* (pp. 42–46). New York: McGraw-Hill.

Evans, J. V. (1998, April), New satellites for personal communications. *Scientific American*, 70.

Gher, L. A., & Amin, H. Y. (1999) New and old media access and ownership in the Arab world. *Gazette, 61*(1), 59–88.

Gher, L. A., Amin, H. Y., & Hashem, W. A. (1996). *History and development of private direct-to-home broadcast services in the Arab World: The case of Arab Radio & TV.* Paper presented at the annual Broadcast Education Association Convention, Las Vegas, NV.

Ibrahim, Y. M. (1992). *Arab world tunes into Westernized TV channels*. New York Times Service, Cairo.

Internet Society. (1996). *Status report: Web sites sextuple* [Online]. Available: http://www.isoc.org

Isaac, S. (1987). *Handbook in research and evaluation*. San Diego, CA: EdITS.

Jubaili, Y. (1994). *The activities of the ITU regional office in the Arab region*. Paper presented at the regional workshop on communication and networking in the Arab region, Cairo, Egypt.

Kamel, T., & Baki, A. N. (1995). The communication infrastructure and Internet services as a base for a regional information highway [Online]. Available: http://www.tkamel@ritsec.com.eg

Kline, D. (1995, August 3). The day the web exploded. *Mercury News*, pp. 1–2.

KUNA. (1992). Kuwaiti National News Agency press release.

Marlow, L. (1992, June 22). The new Saudi press barons. *New York Times*.

MBC Middle East Broadcasting Center [Document]. (1992). London.

MEID. (1999, October). *Country statistics, Middle East Internet directory* [Online]. Available: http://www.middleeastdirectory.com

MIDS. (1996, March). Internet demographic survey. *Matrix Information and Directory Services, 6*, 3.

NUA Surveys [Online]. (1999, October). Available: http:/www.nua.ie/surveys/

Nusseir, Y. (1995, April 18). *Jordan's national information system* [Online]. Available: http://www.j_nic@ritsec.com.eg

Qandiil, H. (1989). *Arabsat: Al-Shabakah Al-Fadaa'iyyah Al-'Arabiyya*. Cairo: Al-Haya Al-Misria Al-Ama Lil Ketab.

Thurow, L. C. (1996). *The future of capitalism: How today's economic forces shape tomorrow's world*. New York: William Morrow.

Turkistane, A. S. (1988). News exchange via Arabsat and news values of Arab television news people (Doctoral dissertation, Indiana University, 1988). *Dissertation Abstracts International, 52,* 3126A.

Via Satellite. (1996, July). Via Satellite's global satellite survey. *Phillips Business Information, XI*(7), 16–26.

Zayd, F. (1994). *Arab Jordanian Space Channel* [Brochure]. Amman, Jordan: Jordanian Radio and Television.

9

BUILDING SECOND-LANGUAGE SKILLS FOR JOURNALISM STUDENTS: USING THE WORLD WIDE WEB TO EDIT STUDENT STORIES LONG DISTANCE

Roger Gafke
Ronald Naeger
University of Missouri–Columbia

INTRODUCTION

There is wide recognition among Arab and U.S. journalism educators that in a world in which information and the economy are global, students need more than their birth language to gather and deliver the news. However, setting an academic goal of second-language competence is one thing. Achieving the goal is another. In the United States, the problem is particularly severe. First, many students arrive at college or university with little or no second-language skill. Second-language instruction in elementary schools is considered an expensive luxury, often offered as an optional before- or after-school elective to a handful of students. In secondary schools, the instruction is only slightly more available. Few colleges or universities require foreign language for admission. For example, only two of eight public universities in Missouri do. At the University of Missouri, the requirement is two courses. Many U.S. journalism programs require their English-speaking American students to take two or three college or university courses in a second language. The requirement stops short of competence for most students.

Second, the University of Missouri, like many other U.S. schools, provides little opportunity in the journalism curriculum for students to practice their second-language skills. There are no second-language reporting, writing, or editing courses. Thus, these able students suffer from the paradigm of "use it or lose it."

Journalism educators in the Arabic-speaking world face similar problems. A team of journalism faculty representing Birzeit University (West Bank) and the University of Missouri conducted a study tour of journalism programs in Egypt, Lebanon, and Jordan in June 1998. A universal issue at all of the universities the team visited—both those teaching primarily in English and those teaching primarily in Arabic—was to find ways to help students function in a second language for gathering news and for news writing and editing. Journalism faculty at several Middle Eastern universities complained they must teach basic English rather than journalism to some of their students because of the low level of English competence the students bring to the university. One of those schools is considering making a third required English course elective because it is now such a severe barrier to graduation for students with poor English skills. Faculties actively seek partnerships with English-speaking university faculty to expand resources for teaching in English. Universities in which the language of instruction is English are exploring ways to expand opportunities for students to practice Arabic beyond their Arabic language electives. One institution requires students to have an internship in Arabic.

Several factors limit the ability of journalism faculty to achieve the goal of second-language competence for their students. Many of the solutions are beyond the scope of the journalism faculty to address. The quality and availability of pre-college or pre-university instruction and the general support within a nation for second-language programs are two examples. Departments themselves often lack faculty capable of coaching reporters and editing student work in a second language. Those faculty who are capable often carry full teaching loads within the current course of study and are unable to take on additional responsibilities. Competition within universities for faculty positions prevents many departments from attracting additional faculty for these assignments. Curriculum committees find resistance to adding additional courses or dropping current courses to devote more effort to this goal. Faculty debate is the better approach to second-language initiatives: devoting scarce resources to develop a basic level of skills for all students or directing those resources to enrich the experiences of students who already possess a sound foundation in a second language.

This chapter proposes a small step to build second-language journalism skills among students in the latter group with the resources currently available in many journalism programs or that can be secured through academic partnerships with other institutions. The proposal is based on work by the faculty at the University of Missouri over the past several years to develop techniques to teach news writing using the Internet as the means of publishing stories and providing feedback to students about their news writing. This chapter shows how this technology of distance education can enable faculty at one university to edit the work of students at another distant university, and in that way, provide second-language help to students that is not available at the student's own university.

PRINCIPLES OF DISTANCE EDUCATION

Distance education enables students in one location to benefit from faculty located elsewhere. Educators have been using aspects of distance education for decades. Textbooks have brought the work of distant scholars to the hands of students. Libraries, films, videotapes, telephone, radio, and television all have been used to bring the ideas and insights of scholars in one part of the world to students in other parts of the world.

In recent years, scholars have added computer-based activities to the inventory. Computer-based simulations make it possible for students to practice activities in which the cost or consequences of live practice is too great. They are useful for giving large groups of students extensive practice on repetitious tasks or on subject matter of stable content. Computer-based instruction provides consistent, immediate feedback to students.

The distance between teachers and students has been reduced substantially in recent years with the development of computer-based text, graphic, voice, and video communications. These developments enable educators to have live, immediate, and interactive relationships with students in distant locations (Kamper, 1991). The use of the World Wide Web and e-mail communications have increased the frequency, timeliness, and the personalization of teacher responses to student work (Sandell, Stewart, & Stewart, 1996). These technologies have increased student responsibility and autonomy in their learning (McCombs, 1994). These technologies also enhance other important elements of sound education practice—making student's study time more productive, clarifying course expectations, and accommodating different learning styles (Chickering & Ehrmann, 1996). The effects of computer-based instruction on students are generally positive (Kulik & Kulik, 1991). Students at the University of Missouri are eager to call their parents and friends to tell them when their work has been published on the Web. They add links to their stories on their personal home pages.

There is no attempt here to suggest that computer-based course activities replace face-to-face classroom activities between teacher and students. Nor are these computer-based activities problem free (Gillespie, 1997). The e-mail feedback from teachers is subject to misunderstanding as neither party can read the body language or hear speech inflections that are valuable parts of face-to-face communication. The absence of face-to-face communication also increases the possibility of students submitting another's work as their own. Just as some students fail to complete reading assignments before their on-campus classes, some overlook or choose not to read the help files, story examples, and other instructional help provided at the website.

Also, merely using this technology to deliver a course does not ensure learning (Najjar, 1996). Its effective use requires that faculty develop a systematic education plan that takes into account the weaknesses as well as the strengths of the technology (Welsh, 1997). The plan must include the following elements: assignments, expectations, instruction, application, examples and help, feedback, and testing.

Faculty who have begun to use this interactive technology to support their courses believe it enhances their relationships with their students, improves their teaching, and increases student participation in class activities (Benoit, Borcherding, & Holt, 1997). The long-distance capability also brings resources into the course that otherwise would not be as easily available to students.

The World Wide Web is predominantly an English-language medium; however, the techniques outlined here can be adapted to use by Arabic writers and editors using the Arabic version of Microsoft Word and an Arabic-enabled Web browser; for example, Internet Explorer for Arabic. Students submitting work and the distant editor and teachers will both need these systems to adapt this model for Arabic.

ONE APPLICATION

The University of Missouri faculty has developed a beginning news reporting and writing course that uses the World Wide Web, with an individual e-mail and an e-mail class discussion group for making news assignments, submitting and editing student work, and discussing themes and trends. The technology makes it possible for the faculty editors to make assignments, set expectations, provide instruction and help, review student work, and communicate with individual students or with the entire class outside of the scheduled class meetings. The URL for the course is http://www.missouri.edu/~jourrag/j105. The assignments, instructional elements including help files, and story examples are available to the public. Students must use a class identification and password to access the work they and their classmates submit: story drafts, quizzes, and in-class writing. When the final editing and grading is complete, the stories are shifted to the public portion of the site or transferred to the students' own Websites so that the public can read the stories.

The course is one section of a beginning news reporting and news writing course required of all students seeking admission to the School of Journalism at the University of Missouri. The 3-hour, one-semester course meets twice a week for 110 minutes each time. The online elements of the course supplement those in-class activities.

Just-in-Time Teaching

An online calendar is the central organizing element for the activities in the course. Selecting a specific date takes students to a list of activities, assignments, and discussion topics for that day. From there, students may select whatever they need to accomplish the activities for the day:

- Instructional materials for the day,
- Descriptions of reporting or writing assignments,
- Lists of textbook and other reading assignments,
- Quizzes used as tests of their understanding of the material, and
- Help files, examples, and critiques of previous assignments.

Assembling the materials in this fashion is part of our "just-in-time" approach to teaching, giving the students the assignments, instruction, opportunities for practice, and feedback at the time they need them to accomplish the work of the class.

Practice and Feedback

Rapid, often immediate, feedback for student work is a second major advantage of using this technology. When students submit their answers to a quiz, the computer provides a copy of the instructor's answers immediately. In practice sessions, students receive feedback and, if necessary, additional instruction based on the answers they select. The instructor's e-mail address is posted at the course home page and students, whose Web browsers are set up to send e-mail, can ask questions immediately. In those cases in which the browsers are not set up for e-mail, a student signs on to his or her university e-mail account to compose a message to the instructor. The instructor can respond at his or her first opportunity. In practice, students' questions posted during the day are often answered within an hour or so. Those posted by students late at night are answered early the following morning, often before the student has awakened. The process has virtually eliminated the need for routine office hours.

Feedback also comes from the writing and revising process. Many of the stories go through multiple drafts, usually three, before a grade is attached. Each draft is reviewed by the instructor or by other students in the class, functioning as peer editors, or by both. The peer editors' comments are sent to the instructor, testing the students' understanding of the writing assignment and, in a second way, their understanding of the role of editor. Each of the drafts is also posted on the Web and accessible to all students in the class to compare their work with others, thus providing a form of self-evaluation not easily available when stories are submitted on paper. The instructor provides commentary on the assignments to individual students by e-mail and to the class discussion group. In addition, he or she can provide additional instruction by posting on the Website examples of good and poor work from the stories with commentary.

Student Use of and Reaction to the Technology

Students in this class are in their second year at the university. Most use e-mail at least occasionally. A few have extensive experience in computer activities; however, for most, this class is the most extensive use they have made of computers.

Students report feeling initially overwhelmed by the technology, but value it highly as their skills and confidence in using the technology increases. It is essential in introducing new technology to give students risk-free periods to learn to use the equipment, to understand the assignments and the structure of the website (Sandell, Stewart, & Stewart, 1996) Thus, the initial assignments are easy and nongraded. Students are asked to send an e-mail message to the class discussion list introducing themselves and a personal message to the instructor indicating they are aware of how to find the Website and the list of course activities. The initial quizzes and exercises are nongraded. In their end-of-semester critiques, students routinely say the extensive use of computers was one of the best parts of the course.

Students are unaccustomed to relying entirely on the computer to provide information about course activities. Early in the semester, especially, they print the course schedule and many of the assignments, help files, and examples. They also are not familiar with or confident in editing stories online. They often print and revise stories with pen and paper and post the changes later. As the semester progresses, most make greater use of the computer and less use of printed material.

How Stories Are Posted

Students write the news stories from their reporting assignments for the course on whatever word processor is available to them. They use the cut-and-paste technique to submit the various drafts of their stories on templates provided at the course Website. These templates also require the students to type their name, e-mail address, headline, and brief summary of their story. When students press the "submit" button on the template, the stories are automatically posted on the class Website and students can check the display of their work immediately. The instructor or other students can click on the student's name in the by-line of the story to send an e-mail message to the writer about his or her work.

Other Applications for This Technology

The online elements of this course support an on-campus course in which the instructor meets with students twice each week. However, the instructor also developed this Website as part of the School of Journalism's plan to offer a beginning reporting class to incoming graduate students before they arrive at the university, thus reducing the time they will spend in residence for their graduate work. The online elements were also developed as a step in internationalizing the curriculum to enable students in several parts of the world to work simultaneously on common reporting projects or journalism issues.

There are additional applications in journalism education for which these techniques can be adapted. As the title of this chapter suggests, these techniques appear particularly useful as a means of enabling students with a good foundation in a second language to obtain additional practice in writing and editing in that language, even when faculty editors are not available at the student's location. Here are some possibilities:

■ Joint teaching of an international journalism class with students in different countries working on related issues.
■ Specialized reporting (for example, health, science, education, politics) from different locations.
■ Translation practice with distant editor/teachers to help students build their skills in acquiring information for stories in a second language.
■ Second-language copyediting skills with distant editor/teachers.
■ Second-language news writing with distant editor/teachers.
■ Recognizing cultural biases in news writing by using second-culture editor/teachers.

All of these applications can be accomplished with text-only technology. Adding graphics and photographs would extend the process to print and advertising design and photojournalism courses. The use of a streaming audio technology, such as Real Audio, by both student and editor or teacher would open the possibility of extending the process to radio news performance, and to speaking and reading in second languages.

What Experience Has Taught About Using these Technologies

The experience at the University of Missouri over the past several years in developing this distance education course leads us to recommend the following approach:

1. Take small steps in implementing these strategies. Identify specific educational issues and develop a plan to address that issue. One need not have an ultimate system designed before beginning.
2. Use these technologies to support current instructional methods, not to replace them. These techniques should appear to complement, not compete with current activities.
3. Design a test or pilot project and expand and adapt from that experience.

4. Use the least amount of technology possible to accomplish the task. The University of Missouri site uses text, primarily, although the university has resources for audio and video transmission, advanced graphics, and so on. None of those advanced techniques is required to accomplish the teaching at this stage. Keep the procedures as simple as possible.
5. Think of and act as if this technology is an extension of face-to-face classroom activities.
6. Begin with faculty who are early adopters. Learn from their experience.
7. As the technology appears productive, others will adopt it.
8. Provide administrative, technical, and training support to faculty who express interest in trying these techniques.
9. Supplement the online editing and critiques with telephone and, when possible, occasional in-person appearances of the distant editor/teacher to ensure that he or she will be perceived as part of the resident team.
10. Provide students risk-free opportunities to practice with the technology. Make clear to faculty, students and the distant editor/teacher what roles the distant ditor/teacher will play in grading student work and enforcing deadlines.
11. For institutions with limited computer resources to support e-mail, consider using a Web-accessible bulletin board system for the class discussion group rather than an e-mail–based system.
12. For institutions without e-mail systems, establish student identification and print critiques from the editor/teacher to students or ask students to sign up for commercial e-mail accounts from Web-based e-mail services such as Hotmail.com.
13. Develop procedures to ensure that students submit their own work. Compare submitted work with occasional in-class exercises. Provide proctors to monitor quiz or test taking if it is to be part of the grade.
14. Establish a formal exchange agreement between participating institutions to govern faculty workload and compensation, use of computing resources, and other relevant issues.
15. Ensure through periodic campus visits and other communication that the distant editor/teacher understands local news values, course objectives, and the general levels of performance expected of students at the home university.

Next Steps for the University of Missouri

The University of Missouri journalism faculty is planning three steps in the next short term to advance our use of these online techniques in news reporting and writing. For the semester beginning in January 1999, the Missouri faculty has sought a long-distance partner to undertake a pilot program in cultural awareness for students in the beginning news writing course.

We will use the "issue story" assignment in the course as the vehicle for this exercise. The distant editor or teacher will provide commentary on the difference in news values from his or her location and those implied in this assignment. The editor/teacher will review the students' story proposals and provide a commentary to the class discussion group about the news values implied in the proposals. When the stories are submitted, we will ask the editor/teacher to provide whatever comments he or she wishes to make to individual students and to provide a commentary on the quality of the stories as they would be evaluated in the second culture.

For the summer of 1999, the faculty have offered a version of this course with substantially more copyediting content to graduate students who will be enrolling in the masters program that fall. The online activities probably will precede a week-long, on-campus newsroom orientation in the week before the start of the fall semester. Based on our experience in the summer of 1999, the university may offer the reporting and copyediting course to students who want it alone, not as part of a University of Missouri degree program.

Based on what we learned about second-language capability from the June 1998 study tour with our Birzeit University colleagues, the University of Missouri faculty also is considering how best to add second-language news writing, copyediting, translation, speaking, and reading experiences for its students who have a good foundation in a second language. During the coming year, the university may seek exchange relationships with faculty who could assist the University of Missouri students as our faculty could assist their students.

DISCUSSION QUESTIONS

1. What are the factors that limit the ability of journalism faculty in the Arab countries to achieve the goal of second language competence for their students?
2. What is distance education and how does it benefit both faculty and students?
3. What is the impact of the World Wide Web and e-mail communications on students' learning process?
4. Can computer-based course activities replace face-to-face interactions between teachers and students? Explain.
5. Explain and describe the general characteristics and techniques of the Internet news writing course developed by the faculty at the University of Missouri. How might this type of course be utilized in a Middle Eastern university?

REFERENCES

Benoit, P., Borcherding, S., & Holt, D. (1997). *Promises, pitfalls, and challenges of teaching with technology at MU* [Online]. Available: http://www.missouri.edu/~muiit/html/challenge.html

Chickering, A. W., & Ehrmann, S. C. (1996 October). Implementing the seven principles: Technology as lever. *AAHE Bulletin, 49*(2), 3–6.

Gillespie, F. (1997). *Teaching and learning with technology: Promises, pitfalls, and challenges* [Online]. Available: http://www.isd.uga.edu/frank/pod97/ppcl.html#top

Kamper, R. J. (1991, November). Computer mediated communications: Conquest of time and space or just another technological seduction, *Education Technology, 31*(6), 20–25.

Kulik, C.-L. C., & Kulik, J. A. (1991). Effectiveness of computer-based instruction: An updated analysis. *Computers in Human Behavior, 2,* 75–94.

McCombs, M. (1994). Benefits of computer-mediated communication in college courses. *Communication Education, 43,* 159–170.

Najjar, L. J. (1996) Multimedia information and learning. *Journal of Educational Multimedia and Hypermedia, 5*(2), 129–150.

Sandell, K. L., Stewart, R. K., & Stewart, C. K. (1996). Computer-mediated communication in the classroom: Model for enhanced student learning. In L. Richlin (Ed.), *To improve the academy* (pp. 59–74). Stillwater, OK: New Forums Press.

Welsh, T. (1997, January-February). From multimedia to multiple-media: Designing computer-based course materials for the information age. *TECHTRENDS, 43*(1), 17–28.

10

NEW ELECTRONIC ARAB NEWSPAPERS: TECHNIQUES AND DISTRIBUTION

Shems Friedlander
American University in Cairo

INTRODUCTION

In what seems like a blink of an eye, we have emerged from Gutenberg's 15th-century invention of moveable type and subsequently the printing press to CD-ROM and the Internet. Quickly jumping over the other major communications breakthroughs such as radio, film, television, and video, let us look at the introduction of Arab newspapers on the Internet, their purpose, their appearance, and their effectiveness.

A number of Arabic electronic newspapers have been developed and implemented through the World Wide Web, marking the introduction of a new era in the Arab world. Although on the surface this trend promises developments, there are many barriers and obstacles facing the development of electronic journalism in this part of the world (Amin, 1995). These new developments are only initial and often tentative steps. The number of online Arabic newspapers is very small if compared with the number of electronic newspapers in the West, as is the number of websites.

This chapter proposes to examine the different obstacles to electronic journalism in the Arab world from a cultural and scientific perspective. The discussion in this chapter includes problems with utilization of advanced information technologies and describes a number of problems that affect electronic journalism from a visual dimension.

LITERACY IN THE MIDDLE EAST

A traditional problem that has affected the development of print media in the Arab world from the very beginning is the problem of illiteracy as most Arab countries have a very high illiteracy rate. Literacy rates range from 20 percent in Oman to 92 percent in Lebanon; Egypt, a big Arab country in terms of population, has a rate of 51 percent. This high illiteracy has had an impact on the circulation of the newspaper and therefore on its development (Labib, Qandiil, & Baker, 1983). Even those defined as literate can be segmented into different groups related to their age, socioeconomic class, and education, and therefore their exposure to and perception of newspaper text and pictures will definitely vary. From elementary education on, students are not exposed to audio-visual materials as learning tools, and therefore do not develop the ability to use pictures as sources of information. In addition, Arab newspapers generally use only a few monochromatic photos, and the result is a culture that is largely visually illiterate.

This visual illiteracy relates as well to a religious belief held by some Muslims that pictures create a distance between the believer and God, as pictures draw attention to themselves and thus away from the Divine. Religious fanatics fought the introduction of television in Saudi Arabia, and this culture also objects to the Internet for related but different reasons. English illiteracy is also extremely high in the entire Arab world, and raises many questions not only about the development of electronic journalism, but also about Internet progress and development generally speaking in this area.

Despite the fact that this region has a rich written tradition, embodied in the beauty of Islamic calligraphy, the Arabic printed page is not adorned by beautiful, elegant, or dignified typography. But English, the main language on the Internet, offers a plethora of typefaces that can enhance every mode of communication, thus giving English the advantage over Arabic.

The literate Arab, even if bilingual and able to read English newspapers, will most likely get his or her news from the Arabic newspapers (for the adult Egyptian, this was a tradition and a sign of the intellectual), and prefers to turn a page rather than scroll a screen. But tradition may change with the new generation, as the computer will come to define the intellectual.

Problems of Content

For generations, newspapers in the Arab world have been the tongue of the government (Rugh, 1979). Certainly, local information controlled by a government is not interesting material for the World Wide Web. Perhaps this is one of the reasons for the birth of a number of independent new and thoughtful newspapers that present a clearer look into news, politics, and economics. There are two kinds of press systems in the Arab world. One is the mobilization press, a system in which the government uses the press to mobilize the public's political thoughts and ideas; this system is found in Egypt, Iraq, Algeria, and Sudan.

The other system is the governmental press, found in the Gulf States, Lebanon, and Morocco. This system allows more freedom than the mobilization press, but both systems are classified under the authoritarian theory of the press, under which the main function of the press is to serve the political leadership and government. Severe rules of censorship are exercised in both, with a strong line of gatekeepers who make certain that what is written will not offend the government, especially the leaders of the state. Why would these systems enter or encourage the development of an open-forum page on the World Wide Web? Why should Arab governments, working under these press systems, encourage worldwide readership and the building of a new media habit by entrance to the Internet?

Problems of Training

Probably the foremost problem in the design and presentation of Websites, newspapers, and magazines in the Arab world rests in the fact that there is little or no training available for those interested in pursuing a career in graphic design. Without the availability of a solid program behind them, who is it that finally decides what is good or bad or whether a design is well done? Typography in the form of linotype, or metal type, has been used in European and English languages for some 500 years, but it has been only a century or so since Arabic letters were first carved into shapes and made into metal forms and used as linotype.

There is a significant relationship between the culture and its Websites. In Arab countries, there is little training and a good deal of illiteracy. Theirs is a verbal culture, one in which education has always been conveyed through an oral tradition. Technology cannot stand independent of the culture. Most of the journalism and mass communications programs in the Arab world pay more attention to theory than to practice. Very few programs are concerned with professional training. Most cannot update their programs with the rapid change in technology, and therefore remain primitive.

In 1994, the American University in Cairo offered no training in desktop publishing and visual editing. Nor did any other institution in Egypt. But by 1994, every major magazine and most newspapers in the United States were prepared both visually and editorially on the computer. They used desktop publishing programs with built-in typefaces, which basically eliminated graphic businesses such as typesetters and photo retouchers. The problem facing the Arab world is to provide complex, multifaceted training that develops an understanding of typography, photography, and layout design. And, more importantly, the task is to develop the creative mind.

Problems of Technology

High technology is available in some Arab countries, such as Egypt, but is limited to only a few. Instructors do not use audio-visual elements or computers, so in most cases students are not exposed to this method of teaching. There is an under-standable barrier against computers in a country where 54% of the population is illiterate. The Minister of Education in Egypt recently began an ambitious plan to connect Egypt's schools to the Internet. Two thousand public schools were linked in 1995–1996, and another 2,000 linkages were planned by 1998. Why the rush to link schoolchildren to the Net when most are not literate in English, the Net's primary language?

When technology is available, there often is little or no training and maintenance. As E. F. Schumacher so clearly put it in *Small Is Beautiful* (1989), it is not enough to give someone a fishing rod, you must also teach him to fish, and if you give a Third World farmer a tractor you must also teach him to maintain it, or you will soon find fields dotted with rusted tractors. The same principle applies to computer technology. Without proper training, the Arab world could be sent even farther back on the superhighway of global visual information.

At the moment, Internet technology in the Arab world is riddled with poor resolution and home pages designed and produced by people with no graphic training and little understanding of typography or the cropping of photographs. Of what use is it to put an Arabic newspaper which is selling over a million copies daily on the Web if it receives just a handful of visits a day on the site—probably just to make it seem it is a player in the game of cyberspace. No one really knows if this superhighway is paved with sand or gold, or just with the dreams of advertisers.

Problems of Budget and Finance

Per capita income is low in most of the Arab world. This only enhances the usefulness of the traditional print media. The availability of computers is limited, and the ratio of computers to inhabitants is extremely low. The limited introduction of Internet cafés in this region allows only a very few people access to cyberspace, and the expense of a personal home computer serves to distance people from the Internet. Purchasing a personal computer for the home is still an extravagance (Schleifer, 1992). More than 37 years after its introduction, there are still some houses without a television. Unlike television, with which one pays only for electricity, while the Internet users pay for electricity, telephone, and the service.

In the Arab countries, subscription rates for Internet service are relatively expensive compared with those in developed countries. The rates suit only the rich and have a tremendously negative impact on other users. It is thus extremely unlikely that most in the region will have the experience of "surfing the Net."

Problems of Telecommunications

Public telecommunication services in most Arab states are provided through government agencies. The Arab states have an average of four telephone lines per 100 inhabitants. Except for Saudi Arabia (which introduced the Internet only recently) and the Gulf States, the infrastructure of the telecommunications networks is below average. Most are not fiber-optic networks. In large countries such as Sudan, where the population is scattered, a major problem will be to develop and upgrade the telecommunications network. Traffic jams as a result of the infrastructure make it difficult to access the World Wide Web, even when it is affordable. A user might spend a long time trying to connect, and once in, faces the probability of being cut off because of poor connections. So even for those who can afford a computer and the service, using them can be frustrating and time consuming.

Problems of Visual Perceptions

Young Arabs who read fewer newspapers and fewer books than their elders are more comfortable with the on-screen word, although like their elders they may still find it difficult to decipher a screened page that is expressed in both Arabic and English, as are the current home pages. In terms of preference in words, people will read their native language more easily. The page becomes even more confusing by the addition of photographs that do not adjust to the S curve. (Arabic is expressed with the S curve, from right to left, whereas English is written on the Z curve, from left to right.) Placement of the Z and S curve together on the same page causes confusion.

The problem is that when one sees English one thinks in English, and the same with Arabic. This has more to do with the manner of one's formative education than with the fact that one is bilingual. For example, an Egyptian educated in an Arabic primary school, although bilingual, will most likely count in Arabic, whereas an Egyptian educated in the British system will probably count in English. Mixing languages on the Web is a distraction to users, no matter how bilingual or how educated.

POLITICAL ISSUES

Whenever revolutionary forces in the Arab world want to overthrow a government, the first thing they go after is the radio and television stations. This happened in the time of Sadat in Egypt and in the Sudan, and as a result tanks and soldiers with machine guns guard all radio and television buildings. Is it possible for governments to allow a bypass of this system with electronic journalism, or is it better for them to block the World Wide Web and introduce their own system of electronic journalism to the people?

CONCLUSION

The problems facing the Arab world in its quest to compete in the communications blitz center around technology, training, distribution, and an age-old cultural difference in presenting information; that is, the verbal culture versus the visual culture. Although our era is being called the Age of Information, it is probably more correct to refer to it as the Age of Visual Information, one in which pictures compete with text as information sources. Again, culture enters the picture. Many educated Arabs are interested in creating a fully Arabized Net, thus controlling what is available both in words and pictures. We are left with the following questions: Will the next generation of intellectuals in the Arab world, defined by their use of computers, create an even wider gap of wealth and intellect between themselves and the nonreader? And will Arabs find a site on the Net or be caught in the Web? In summary, what the Arab world is left with is the illusion of access to the Internet.

DISCUSSION QUESTIONS

1. What is "visual illiteracy" and why does it exist in the Arab world?
2. Describe the types of press systems in the Arab world. What are some of their characteristics?
3. How does culture affect technology in the Arab world? Give examples.
4. What are the problems facing technological development in the Arab world?
5. Why is purchasing a personal computer for the home considered to be a problem in the Arab world?

REFERENCES

Amin, H. Y. (1995). Arab global television. In J. Sinclair (Ed.), *Peripheral vision: Satellite television in the third world*. New York: Oxford University Press.

Labib, S., Qandiil, H., & Baker, Y. A. (1983). *Development of communication in the Arab states: Needs and priorities* (Publication No. 95). Paris, France: UNESCO.

Rugh, W. (1979). *The Arab press*. Syracuse, NY: Syracuse University Press.

Schleifer, S. A. (1992). Global media, the new world order—and the significance of failure. In R. E. Weisenborn (Ed.), *Media in the midst of war* (pp. 95–104). Cairo, Egypt: The Adham Center Press.

Schumacher, E. F. (1989). *Small is beautiful: Economics as if people mattered*. New York: Harper.

Discourse IV
Privatization of Media in the Middle East

11

SINGING THE ARAB MARKET ECONOMY'S NOTES

Jihad Fakhreddine
Pan Arab Research Center

INTRODUCTION

A conference on the Arab economies held in London in August 1998 and sponsored by *MEED* magazine, echoed some comforting news about the performance of the Arab economies. It was suggested that the relatively tight-lid approach to privatization, backed by a policy of shielding the Arab economies from the international capital markets, had saved them from the repercussions of the downfall of the Asian economies.

Put within the perspective of the economic cataclysm unfolding across Asia and Russia, such views bring certain consolation to Arab policy makers. But reviewing the Arab economic panorama from the perspective of the expectations since the final triumph of capitalism over communism, in 1989, we are set for some discomforting news. The conveyer of such news is none other than the World Bank. Basing his analysis on information reported by the World Bank, the Arab-American scholar, Fuad Ajami, conveys to us a very bleak preview of the sociopolitical and economic state of the Arab countries. In the autumn 1997 issue of *Foreign Affairs*, Ajami (1997) sums up this preview as follows:

> The balance of skills and the terms of trade have turned against the lands of the Middle East and North Africa. The World Bank report sounded the alarm: the economies of the lands of the Middle East and North Africa have stagnated. Some 260 million people in that region, we are told, export fewer manufactured goods than Finland's five million people. The average labourer was earning no more in

real terms in the mid-1990s than in 1970s. A mere one percent of the private capital flowing into the developing world finds its way into these lands. And the crisis is endemic: since 1986, per capita income has fallen by two percent a year, the largest decline in any developing region. Not even the oil-rich economies have been spared: the GDP per capita in these countries declined by four percent a year between 1980 and 1991. These Arab states of the Gulf have run down their foreign reserves, and their populations have doubled over the last two decades. Poverty had not come to the oil lands, but the ability of these states to maintain the entitlements of the past and absorb the surplus labour of their neighbours has come to an end. (pp. 42–43)

In short, Ajami states that the anachronistic elements of the political economy— protected markets, the strong public sector, and the bias against agriculture and a top-down educational system—must be adjusted to the modern world. For many Arab academics, Fuad Ajami remains the "black sheep" when it comes to making any statements on the political economies of the Arab world. I neither intend to refute, nor wholly subscribe to his theses. But I have found that my arguments in this chapter are largely in support of his observations, particularly with respect to the antiquated Arab university system, where plans have yet to be considered for restructuring it to meet the requirements of the future market economy.

To my knowledge, none of the hundreds of Arab universities has a fully fledged marketing department, bar one university or two in Lebanon. I believe that before Arab policy-makers can hope to experience functional market economies in the modern sense, they must begin to think about who is going to manage and market the products and services these market economies will produce.

The economic concept that demand creates its own supply holds some truth. For decades, the Arab economic-political systems bred static educational systems, where marketing and marketing communication were not needed. They had been economies that required salespersons, not marketers. In today's world, "marketing" has become a common-currency word, but is still easily exchanged for what the term "sales" stands for. It is, indeed, a situation where a marketing culture needs to be created virtually from scratch.

Nowhere in the Arab markets has the need for marketing activities become so pronounced as in the affluent Gulf markets, where local competitive businesses and multinationals cannot wait for the local educational reserves to be built up. Nor does the local build-up in marketing knowledge appear forthcoming. Hence, even if the transformation toward market economies across the various Arab states is to be shifted to second gear, they are bound to find themselves a hostage of their own incompetent university system. As things now stand, it is a system that fails to support the curriculum of an entering student majoring in marketing or marketing communications.

In my quest to acquire books on marketing in the Arabic language, I have yet to come across even a handful of them. One typical introductory marketing textbook written by an instructor at the University of Kuwait and being used in many Arab Gulf Counsil Countries (AGCC) universities contains the following physical features:

- It contains 450 pages.
- An average page contains an average of 250 words, which in the total adds up to about 113,500 words for the entire book.
- It consists of 12 chapters.
- Each chapter has a glossary of English marketing terms with their corresponding Arabic equivalents; no definitions are given.
- It has half a page for references in the Arabic language.
- It has two-and-a-half pages for references in the English language.

Alternatively, let us take a glance at the typical marketing textbook a first-year student at a U.S. university is exposed to:

- It contains about 800 pages.
- An average page contains an average of 480 words, which add up to about 380,000 words for the entire book.
- It consist of about 25 chapters.
- Each chapter has its own references, case studies, exercises and questions, outline of what a student is expected to learn, and one case study or more per chapter.
- It usually includes several of the following components: index of subjects, index of authors, recommended readings, index of important concepts, knowledgeable contributors, glossary with definitions of terms, instructor's course manual, instructor's course planning system, test item file for instructors, and course guide for students.

A marketing student at a U.S. university is expected to cover all or most of this material within one semester. His or her counterpart at an Arab university covers the assigned material in a full 8-month academic year. A student at a U.S. university will have most of the recommended reading material at his or her fingertips at the library and on the Internet. His or her Arab counterpart is not likely to have access to any of the recommended references, particularly those in English. The latter references are usually the private possession of the author, who would have acquired them while preparing for his or her doctoral dissertation at a Western university.

A student at a U.S. university is likely to attend a class of no more than 50 students. His or her Arab counterpart is likely to attend a class of 100 to 200 students. A student at a U.S. university could interact with his or her instructor in every class session. Often his or her Arab counterpart may not even attend one single class session, apart from that set for the final examination. A student at a U.S. university would be required to take a dozen pop-quizzes, as well as mid-term and final exams, and complete term papers, group work, and oral presentations. In most cases, his or her Arab counterpart may have to settle for one final examination.

Most marketing students at Arab universities do not master the basics of the English language, hence, shutting them off from the meager additional reading material that the university library might have. Consequently, this renders listing the basic terms and concepts of marketing in English of little value. This is compounded by the fact that while some of the Arabic equivalents of the English marketing terms are correct, many others are either somewhat vague, or totally incorrect. Arab linguists and academics in marketing have yet to attend to the need of creating a unified glossary of the hundreds of marketing terms currently used in the English language.

The lack of such an Arabic glossary is resulting in a state of anarchy in terms of assigning Arabic equivalents to marketing terms available in the English language. In this situation, one marketing term or concept for a student in Egypt may mean something very different to his or her counterpart in Kuwait, the United Arab Emirates (UAE), or Jordan. More alarming, it is likely that none of these marketing students at the different Arab universities would have common-currency knowledge in marketing with their counterpart at, for instance, the American University in Cairo or Beirut. Similarly, an Arab student at an Arab-American university would not know the Arabic equivalents of most, if not all, of the marketing terms he or she learns in English textbooks. Nor is the student likely to learn them, or to have a need to do so.

In no way are the preceding illustrations meant to discredit Arab university instructors and professors. Their limitations are simply dictated by the incompetence of the Arab university itself. Academics I know in marketing and advertising are extremely frustrated by having to teach with skeletal resources. They are neutralized by having to hand out photocopies of articles from marketing journals and chapters of books they brought with them from U.S. or British universities, where they did their graduate studies. Seasonal journals in Arabic, which are meant to act as an updated local reservoir of knowledge on marketing and marketing communication, do not exist. The meager local reset papers on consumer behavior find their way into the less-than-a-handful of psychological and sociological quarterlies published in Egypt or the GCC.

The main victims of this university system are the students. The private sector in a number of GCC markets is bluntly vetoing the recruitment of fresh graduates who have obtained their degrees from local or other Arab universities. In many job announcements the "U.S./U.K. educated" criterion is placed prominently, bluntly telling those who have graduated from Arab universities not to bother applying. This job application criterion is not limited to those in the marketing field, but also applies to other job openings. Incidentally, some think that such a job application criteria even exclude Arabs who have studied at U.S. or British universities. The implications of such a recurring phenomenon are many and serious indeed. They amount to a loud declaration by many quarters in the private sector in the GCC markets about the incompetence of the Arab university system to keep up with the requirements of the modern world.

This is an educational system designed originally to serve the old established sociopolitical-economic system. Now, with the same educational tools, the same system is expected to cater to the needs of an economy waiting to undergo a drastic shift into a market economy. There is a growing debate about whether the Arabic language is proving itself to be invariably less capable of expanding the scope of both marketing as an activity, as well as marketing communication. Perhaps this statement should be qualified to, instead, also blame the users and guardians of the Arabic language for conspiring with the cultural sluggishness of the Arab world to discredit the Arabic language from currency in the modern world.

Recently, much has been written about the pre-launch of the latest edition of the *Oxford Dictionary* and the rivalry between the main English dictionaries. The headlines read something along these lines: "Wars in the World of Words"; "Dictionaries Turn Best Sellers As Controversies Make Them Popular"; and "Dictionaries in World Wars." I have not seen the new *Oxford Dictionary*, but among its touted new features is the addition of about 2,000 new words.

Compared to the active battleground involving the half-a-dozen or so of the main English language dictionaries, the market for Arabic-Arabic dictionaries is a dormant one. The more prominent Arabic-Arabic dictionary is *Al-Munjed,* followed by *Al-Muheet.* I am most certain that results of a mini-survey for measuring the recall level of the top two Arabic-Arabic dictionaries among Arab professionals will be disappointing; more disturbing yet will be the ownership level of these dictionaries.

I have always felt the need to own one Arabic-Arabic dictionary. But I am simply not willing to invest money in a dictionary that was completed in the first decade of this century. In 1960, a list of a few hundred words was added to *Al-Munjed* in an addendum. In 1973, an updated introduction promised that this list would eventually be incorporated within the dictionary. The last printing of *Al-Munjed* was in 1994; it still could not deliver what it had promised to do in 1960.

Arab publishers of both dictionaries and books have mastered a publishing gimmick that seems to have worked well on the general public. Since the more recent the book is, the more impressive it is perceived to be, publishers print on the cover page in a large and bold typeface the year of print. Publishers are well aware that the general public is oblivious to the fact that there is a difference between a "new printing" and a "new edition" of a book. This appears to be an intricate part of the cultural drowsiness to which Arabs have become accustomed. More frighteningly, this gimmick is perpetuated by the supposed guardians of the culture.

No book typifies this publishing stunt more than the best-selling English-Arabic dictionary *Al-Mawrid,* as well as most of the academic books in Arabic. The font size of the "1998 print" on the hard cover of *Al-Mawrid* is practically larger than the font size of its title. Indeed, Munir Balbakie completed a mammoth job in compiling *Al-Mawrid* in 1967. But for the publisher of this dictionary, the English language has stood still since the mid-1960s. When communicating with Arab consumers, advertisers encounter a general public whose classical Arabic vocabulary is dwindling, or at best remaining static. Reference is made here to the everyday use of the Arabic vocabulary, as opposed to technical or scientific terms, which have grown considerably as a result of efforts by Arab linguists who work in a number of linguistic conventions.

At the crux of this cultural jeopardy is the fact that when Arabs communicate in classical Arabic, they process and verbally articulate their thoughts in a vocabulary that is somewhat, if not totally, different from what is stated in classical Arabic. There is almost always a discrepancy between what is communicated in classical Arabic and the same idea that is communicated verbally. This occurs practically with all the thoughts and ideas Arabs communicate, be they simple or complex ideas, and irrespective of whether the communicator is highly literate, moderately literate, or illiterate.

In this situation, the receivers of any sort of communication presented in classical Arabic will almost certainly process it in their own colloquial Arabic, and communicate it to others in their respective colloquial languages. Multinational companies think of the Arab world as a one massive, 260-million-person market. When it comes to marketing communication of any sort, this assumption loses much of its validity. In terms of mass communication, Arabs are fragmented by the nature of their respective colloquial dialects.

Because classical Arabic is not used in everyday verbal communication, it is a form of communication that is losing favor when it comes to advertising. Arab marketing communicators are increasingly finding it difficult to tame the classical Arabic language in order to ensure the creation of effective and appealing advertising messages.

This inflexibility in the classical language is due, in part, to the relative lack of mastery over the Arabic language of Arab copywriters in advertising agencies. Equally important, if not more serious, is that the Arab mind at the general public level is becoming less prone to, and even less willing, to process marketing communication messages in classical Arabic.

This marketing communication predicament becomes even more frustrating when communication kits are imported into the Arab markets along with the imported product itself. The flexibility in the English language in terms of coining or phrasing sentences or statements for advertising, positioning, or selecting brand names, outmatches that available in the Arabic language. Often, Arab translators find themselves stuttering when it comes to translating even the most basic but still catchy phrases, such as "Just Do It."

This does not deny the fact that many Arab advertising agencies have produced international award-winning advertising. But again, such award-winning advertising is in English and not in Arabic. The lack of flexibility the Arabic language for modern-day marketing communication can also be linked to the limited vocabulary Arabs use in their daily lives, or are exposed to in the print or audio-visual media and in different sorts of books, other than scientific and technical texts.

Although I do not have an estimate of the size of the pool of Arabic words used by the Arab, I am confident in claiming that it is at least stagnant, if not shrinking in size. The addition of new names for various objects and services is offered by modern-day life, however, this shrinkage in the pool of Arabic vocabulary, particularly the classical Arabic, is giving way to the adoption of English words, instead. Moreover, colloquial Arabic is being disseminated through television or other modes of interaction.

Most of these colloquial Arabic and English words are finding their way into advertising in Arabic, because the flexibility they allow in phrasing catchy communication is not always available in classical Arabic. This is not to claim that classical Arabic is lacking in vocabulary that could perform this task. But many of its flowery and more expressive words are found mostly in ancient literary works.

With such literary works in mind, it is safe to assume that even in the pre-Islamic Arab era, the vocabulary of an average illiterate Arab was much larger than that of an Arab with a high-school education today. Of course, this excludes all references to objects, services, and facilities available to modern-day Arabs. To illustrate this point, simply ask an Arab university student to decipher one poem written by a pre-Islamic poet. Bear in mind that the same poem would have been understood and enjoyed in its time by an audience of which only a marginal proportion could read or write.

As the Arab market economies steer the rudders of their boats into the waters of the market economy, educators, advertisers, communicators, and consumers find themselves in one boat: all stuttering when communicating in Arabic. Steering this boat is bound to become more difficult as the Western culture current, manifested by U.S. culture, becomes stronger. For good or for bad, more and more Arabs are abandoning the Arabic-boat language for the one where English is widely spoken; others are readying themselves to do so, or hoping that their children will one day be able to switch boats.

The concern is that members of the socioeconomic class who can afford to obtain the required education in marketing or marketing communication are among the first to abandon the Arabic boat. All the top Arab marketing communicators are products of the U.S. or British university systems. Such an education has become an international passport for a life in an unpromising world. The American ship cruising by at full speed is creating a massive cultural current of which the English language is only one manifestation. Many of these Western cultural manifestations are already rocking the Arab boat. The way in which some of these cultural currents are impacting Arab culture requires careful research and analysis.

As market researchers, we are just beginning to explore the depth of this cultural transformation. As Arab educators and linguists, we face a need to draw and implement plans for the language or languages in which the rhymes to celebrate the induction into the market economy will be written.

DISCUSSION QUESTIONS

1. Explain the anachronistic elements of the political economy and protected markets in the Arab world. How does this model compare with the Western models?
2. In the Arab educational system, marketing and marketing communications are not part of the business school curriculum. What are the implications of this omission?
3. How do U.S. library and Internet access compare with their Arab counterparts, particularly those in English?
4. What is meant by my assumption that the Arab private sector in several of GCC markets is bluntly vetoing fresh graduates who have obtained their degrees from local or other Arab universities?
5. How might classical Arabic and colloquial Arabic be modified to improve marketing communication in terms of mass communication for the Arab world?

REFERENCES

Ajami, F. (1997). Al-khobaraa hawl al-Amsal lil al-rabiyya. *Foreign Affairs*, 76(2), 22–23.

12

TELECOMMUNICATIONS MANAGEMENT IN THE ARAB WORLD: THE CASE HISTORY OF ARAB RADIO AND TELEVISION

Leo A. Gher
Southern Illinois University

Walid Arab Hashem
Arab Media Corporation

INTRODUCTION

During the second half of the 20th century, traditional broadcasting networks have dominated the electronic infrastructure of most sovereign states. CBS was the model in the United States; the BBC in the United Kingdom; Gostelradio in the USSR; and in such countries as China, India, Finland, and Egypt, networks were ruled and regulated by governmental institutions. All that has now changed.

The Disney/ABC merger is the millennium's prototype for a transglobal, corporate new world order—a production company joining forces with a distribution business. The newly created company is able to monopolize all aspects of an industry: from creation to production, from production to distribution, and from distribution to exhibition. This kind of power play is similar to the old Hollywood system of the 1930s and 1940s. But unprecedented superplayers have suddenly emerged on the international scene: telephone companies, entertainment conglomerates, cable operators, satellite distributors, and many more are now venturing onto a worldwide field. Coming to global broadcasting only recently, Arab telecommunications companies have made up for lost time with great energy, drive, and a huge amount of money.

In the past 6 years, the Middle East has witnessed the development of many national and regional television services. This wave began with the launching of the Egyptian Space Channel (ESC), which was soon followed by the creation of the Saudi Middle East Broadcasting Centre (MBC), the Kuwaiti Space Channel (KSC), the Jordanian Arab Space Channel (JASC), the Space Network of Dubai, Tunisia TV7, Moroccan Satellite Channel, Oman TV, and United Arab Emirates TV. Other television channels, such as Saudi national television services and Egypt national television services, were later placed on Arabsat for direct-to-home reception in the Middle East region. The Arab world has also witnessed the birth of private international television services, such as Arab Radio and Television (ART), which carries five specialized Arabic television channels, and Orbit, which consists of 16 television channels containing both Arabic and English programming.

As Radi al-Khas, managing technical director of Arab Radio and Television, stated (personal interview, August 16, 1994):

> As we looked at the world picture, the developments of international telecommunications, we found most nations and ethnicities were developing global television networks, and so the principals of our company decided that we should do likewise. The purpose for creating ART was threefold: first, to construct an international television network designed exclusively for the peoples of Arabic descent; [second,] to maintain and promote the values of Islam around the entire planet; and [third,] to create a company for the economic well being of the region and for the financial benefit of its owners and employees.

The purpose of this chapter is to examine the creation and development of ART. In addition, this case study of a telecommunications conglomerate will attempt to compare and contrast traditional Arab business practices with current, Western corporate structures, as both advance onto the playing field of the 21st century.

RESEARCH QUESTIONS

The following questions are addressed in this study:

1. What is the historical and cultural impetus for the creation of ART?
2. What are the current operational and managerial structures of ART?
3. What future developments are planned to implement the global vision of the parent company?

4. How do the corporate business structures of ART compare or contrast to equivalent Western telecommunication companies?

METHODOLOGY

All research questions conducted in this case study are answered by employing traditional historical research methods. Data were complied from the following sources: (1) *Statistical Yearbook 1995*, UNESCO, Paris, France; (2) *Europa Yearbook* (1994), Europa Publications Limited, England; (3) *World Development Report 1995*, The World Bank, Oxford University, England; (4) *Human Development Report 1994*, UNDP, Oxford University Press; and (5) *Status Report, July 1996*, the Internet Society.

This onground research was compiled over a 3-year duration in the following countries: Saudi Arabia, Egypt, Jordan, Lebanon, Morocco, Tunisia, England, Italy, Germany, Israel, and the United States. All field interviews were single communications to the researchers and were conducted in the field by the authors or by personnel under their direct supervision. Only primary sources were brought to bear in the report. Research questions 1, 2, and 3 were examined using information collected in field studies and personal interviews.

Initially, a questionnaire was utilized as a research tool, but statistical applications were found to be unreliable, and even misleading because of a preponderance of self-serving responses. However, the questionnaire was found to be beneficial as an organizational mechanism for interviews. Anecdotal reports were also used to compile general information, which, when cross-referenced with empirical data, proved to be pertinent for developing broad conclusions.

LIMITATIONS

In this research, a Likert-style survey was completed to test general attitudes toward management. It was hoped that the collected data could be subjected to correlational protocols in order to compare and contrast Western models with Middle Eastern data. But the results of the pilot instrument were unacceptable. The subjects marked nothing but the most favorable evaluations of their superiors. As a consequence, this research is limited to descriptive analyses only; no other research methodology is applicable. As Rubin, Rubin, and Piele (1996) point out, descriptive field research is an investigation intended to systematically describe the facts and characteristics of a unique subject. Working with emerging Second and Third World governments or corporations has hidden complications. Because of the challenge of political consciousness, the hesitation to disclose financial information, regional competitiveness, or privacy issues, ascertaining reliable data is difficult at best, and often impossible to obtain.

DEVELOPMENT OF TELEVISION IN THE ARAB WORLD

The Arab world occupies a large geographical area estimated at 13,738,000 square kilometers. It extends from the shores of the Atlantic Ocean in the west to the Persian Gulf in the east. The population of the Arab world was estimated at 200 million in 1990. Often, the Arab world is defined by its primary language, Arabic, or its dominant religion, Islam. But great varieties exist within these cultural boundaries.

Television is a very important medium throughout the Middle East; the only countries where television is not used by large numbers of people are Yemen and the Sudan, countries that are less developed economically. It was the desire of Arab governments, motivated mainly by political, cultural, and social factors, to support the development of a strong television industry (S. El-Sherif, personal communication, January 2, 1992). And with few exceptions, Arabic television is a government-operated activity. The function of the media in the Arab world may be defined as follows: conveying news and information, interpreting and commenting on events, reinforcing social norms and cultural awareness, providing specialized data for commercial promotion, and, finally, entertainment (Rugh, 1979).

Historically, Arab governments have set the media agenda and have viewed television as an effective means to promote their political goals. Also, television has proven to be an efficient tool for communication, because Arab households are closely knit units—mostly self-contained—where entertaining is done in the home (Amin & Boyd, 1993).

Television broadcasting began in the Arab world in the 1950s. It was established in Morocco in 1954, and in Algeria, Iraq, and Lebanon in 1956. The introduction of television broadcasting progressed to other Arab nations during the 1960s and 1970s and was inaugurated in Egypt and Syria in 1960, Kuwait in 1961, Sudan in 1962, Democratic Yemen in 1964, and Saudi Arabia in 1965. All networks were launched as terrestrial broadcasting operations.

HISTORY AND DEVELOPMENT OF ART

ART is a seven-channel satellite television network broadcasting to the Arab world, Europe, and North America. Each channel covers a specialized area of interest that appeals to different tastes within Arabic society (Figure 12.1). ART 1, the variety channel, broadcasts 24 hours a day, and provides entertainment programming, talk shows, leisure time documentaries, and television serials (ART, 1995). In an interview with Mohammed Naguib, a public relations official for ART channels, the issues of content, mandate and purpose of the variety channel were discussed:

> The variety channel specializes in providing programs for viewers of all interests, all age groups and people of different classes within the Arabic society. It broadcasts comedy, business, the most popular Arabic TV serials, and movies with social themes,

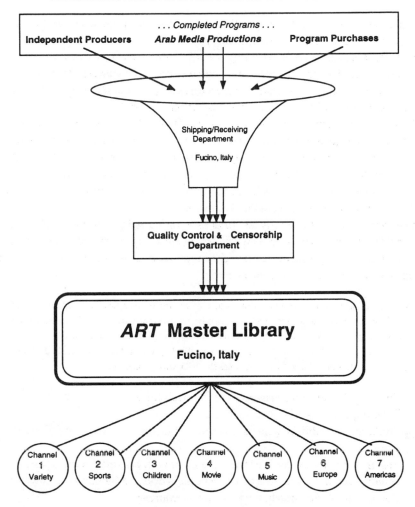

... *Completed Programs* ...

Independent Producers   *Arab Media Productions*   **Program Purchases**

Shipping/Receiving
Department

Fucino, Italy

**Quality Control &   Censorship
Department**

ART **Master Library**

Fucino, Italy

| Channel 1 Variety | Channel 2 Sports | Channel 3 Children | Channel 4 Movie | Channel 5 Music | Channel 6 Europe | Channel 7 Americas |

FIGURE 12.1.   ART Library: Catalog and censorship control.

intrigue and science fiction. ART 1 aims at accomplishing media coordination and cooperation among the Arab peoples. It also strives to bridge the cultural gap of the different countries of the world.

Its first priority is to attract the interest of the Arab viewer. This is accomplished by developing programs that can compete with the international media now invading our borders. It is hoped Arab viewers will choose ART 1 over the other non-Arab channels. Also, it is hoped that these viewers will find a genuine interest in the Arab world; its arts, culture, history, civilization, heritage, and values. The channel therefore strives for originality and modernity in the Arab world, and is committed to its roots and cultural identity.

To accomplish these goals, planning for the general channel was comprehensive and purposeful. A conscious effort was made to consider viewers' demands in all fields: cultural, religious, scientific, entertainment, political literature and artistic. (M. Naguib, personal communication, November 12, 1994)

ART 2 is dedicated to sports. It is, as Ali Dawoud, the head of the channel, reported (personal communication, May 5, 1995), "A permanent seat in the stadium for our viewers . . . with live coverage, commentary, and analysis of the world's major sporting events." The channel also offers instructional programming to teach different games, provides schooling in the rules of play, and furnishes interviews with famous sports figures from the Arab world.

The channel dedicated totally to children is called ART 3. It presents cartoons and children's shows for 14 hours a day, which are always intended to be prosocial and are designed to preserve traditional Arabic values as well as entertain. As Mr. Naguib divulged in a personal interview:

> As children are the future, television is one of the influential devices that can affect their lives. It is an educational and entertaining device that works to help bring up the future generation. The channel broadcasts 14 hours a day and is planning for 16 hours later in the year. ART 3 feels a great responsibility being the first Arab children specialized channel. Therefore, it has set the following objectives:

1. Ensuring the religious principles of the Arab child.
2. Ensuring good morals.
3. Working on establishing social and cultural linkage for Arabic children of the world.
4. Ensuring the involvement of the Arab child with his small society: family or country, and the wider Arabic and Islamic world and humanity as a whole.
5. Continuing of the Arab history as a good example.
6. Caring about the Arabic heritage.
7. Making children ready to take part in the real world.
8. Encouraging the child to develop hobbies.
9. Building up the child's imagination.
10. Increasing the use and ability of Arabic language.
11. Encouraging sports activities and creating team spirit.
12. Developing a suitable atmosphere between normal and abnormal children. (M. Naguib, personal communication, November 12, 1994)

The next channel, ART 4, is dedicated to movies 24 hours a day. Arabic, Indian, and Western films are shown, in all types and forms, including modern, old classics, recent theatricals, and blockbusters. The movie channel specializes in broadcasting the most up-to-date Arabic and Western movies. At present, the channel broadcasts 12 films a day, 7 Arabic and 5 Western.

The channel is also interested in the arts of the theater, and has telecast nearly 30 plays from the most prominent Arabic collection. ART 4 uses an innovative style—presenting Arabic and Western movies through the use of a distinguished cinema critic who analyzes the artistic and subjective sides of the film. The Cineclub provides in-depth criticism of the films through interviews with actors, directors, and producers. As Mr. Naguib elaborated in later personal communications (November 16, 1994):

> ART 4 is considered the leader in block broadcasting of films for Arab movie stars. Until today, the channel has broadcast movies featuring the following actors: Farid Shawky, Adel Emam, Kamel el-Shenawy, Faten Hamama, Ismael Yassin, Nour el-Sharif, Sabah Shadia, Shoukry Sarhan, Salah Abu Seif.
>
> Moreover, ART 4 has covered all the international and Arab cinema festivals and has interviewed some of the most celebrated movie stars and directors worldwide. It has also participated in the TV film festival on the international and Arab level.

The film channel gives particular attention and heed to special periods during the year. For example, during Ramadan the channel presents many religious shows that feature competitions and audience participation. The movie channel is also keen on providing films that feature important human values, and the heritage of the Arabic and Islamic world. Worth noting is the fact that all films are put under the eye of the censor. Until a suitable censor was hired, this task was performed by Sheikh Saleh Kamel himself. As he so vigilantly explained it (personal communication, August 19, 1995), "As the person in charge, I have a great moral and ethical responsibility to the audience. It is my personal duty to make sure that ART television programming is suitable for viewing in the eyes of the Islamic world" (refer to Figure 12.1).

ART 5 is the music channel, dedicated to Middle Eastern style and culture. The director of musical programming is the Saudi Imir, Waleed Ben Talal. Traditional Arab songs and modern musical videos fill the programming schedule. The music selection as well as its rotation is filled with an unlimited Arabic genre that is both classical and contemporary (ERTU, 1997). ART 6 and ART 7 are cultural modifications of the variety channel targeted for the European and North American markets, respectively. EuroART was launched in July 1995, and ArtAmerica kicked off its programming schedule in March 1996 through EchoStar Satellite Services. The ART transmitting facilities are located in Fucino, Italy, at the renowned satellite uplink center, Telespazio, which is considered the best in Europe. The original five channels are transmitted to Arabsat in a geosynchronous orbit that creates a telecasting footprint that covers southern Europe, northern Africa, and the Middle East. The European ART channel transmits its signal to the Hotbird satellite, which blankets the rest of the European continent. The North American ART channel transmits its signal to the Orion satellite, which overlays the North American continent through the distribution system of EchoStar Satellite Services.

ART revenue strategies include varying subscription schemes, pay-per-view, and advertising. For the present, the five ART channels covering the Middle East are free over-the-air telecasts for those who own satellite dishes that can receive the Arabsat C-band signal. The first channel transmission was launched in mid-October 1993 from Arabsat 1-D. ART channels are engaged by dishes ranging in diameter from 1.5 to 2.4 meters within the Gulf region or northwest Africa and from 1.2 to 1.5 meters within the Near East. Currently, 2.5 million dishes are able to acquire ART signals throughout the Arab world.

Moreover, it is possible to receive ART transmissions through cable operators in Tunisia, Jordan, Kuwait, and Bahrain. Plans call for scrambling these signals as soon as ART channels are combined with approximately 23 foreign signals to form a full-service television distribution operation called Multichoice, which is modeled on the PrimeStar, DirecTV, and USSB services in the United States. This satellite service will then compete head-to-head with Orbit, the region's current, Arabic/English full-service satellite provider (Amin, 1995). Other than program content, the real difference between these competitors will be the purchase price of consumer dishes and decoders. For Orbit, the initial retail price of this equipment exceeds $10,000, whereas the projected costs for a complete downlink setup for ART customers will be less than $1,000.

In the interim, Arab Media Corporation (AMC) has joined forces with the Kirch Television Group of Germany, the Saudi Imir, Waleed Ben Talal (owner of EuroDisney), and the Richardson Broadcasting Consortium of South Africa to provide capital for the venture. The group's first act was to purchase a majority interest in the media properties of Silvio Berlusconi, the film and television mogul and President of Italy (al-Mashat, 1996).

ART is wholly owned by AMC, incorporated in the Cayman Islands–British West Indies. The latter company has been established through investments of the Dallah Al Baraka Group, chaired by the eminent Saudi investor, Sheikh Saleh Kamel. The initial capital investment for AMC amounts to U.S.$300 million, while the total business volume of Dallah Al Baraka amounts to U.S.$6 billion dollars, covering 43 countries all over the world (Gher, Amin, & Hashem, 1996).

Currently, seven channels broadcast 24 hours per day, which amounts to 168 hours of television programming per week and 8,736 hours yearly, a huge commitment of origination for any enterprise. To sustain and nurture this commitment, the parent company, AMC, has created a global support systems (Figure 12.2).

The formal corporate support system for the ART networks includes six companies created under the umbrella of AMC. They include: Sunnyland Films, Ltd. and ROTANA (AMQ), Arab Media Production (AMD), Arab Media Distribution (AMO), Arab Reach Media (ARM), and Arab Media Advertising (AMA). (Fareed Felemban, personal communication, August 18, 1995).

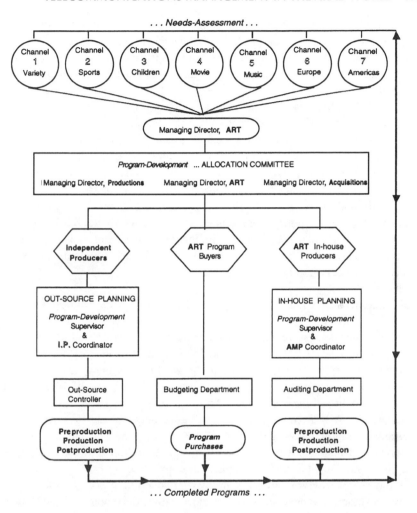

... Needs-Assessment ...

| Channel 1 Variety | Channel 2 Sports | Channel 3 Children | Channel 4 Movie | Channel 5 Music | Channel 6 Europe | Channel 7 Americas |

Managing Director, **ART**

Program-Development ... ALLOCATION COMMITTEE

Managing Director, **Productions**   Managing Director, **ART**   Managing Director, **Acquisitions**

Independent Producers   **ART** Program Buyers   **ART** In-house Producers

OUT-SOURCE PLANNING

Program-Development Supervisor & **I.P.** Coordinator

IN-HOUSE PLANNING

Program-Development Supervisor & **AMP** Coordinator

Out-Source Controller   Budgeting Department   Auditing Department

Preproduction Production Postproduction   *Program Purchases*   **Preproduction Production Postproduction**

... Completed Programs ...

FIGURE 12.2. Arab media productions and support.

AMC/ART Management Structure

There are basic structures (or divisions) for the AMC (see Figure 2); they comprise (1) the programming division, (2) the technology division, (3) the acquisition division, (4) the creative division, (5) the distribution division, (6) the marketing division, (7) the administration division, and (8) the external affairs division.

AMC is certainly unique in many ways; however, these structures conform to standard organizational models in the entertainment industry. Each division is headed by the *modir* (managing director), a top professional in his or her field, who has both authority and responsibility for the day-to-day operations. For the present, each *modir* reports to the *modir cabir* (chief executive officer [CEO], Sheikh Saleh Kamel). The CEO is the final authority and, of course, has veto power over any decision made within the company (S. Kamel, personal communication, August 21, 1995).

Plans call for the creation of an Executive Committee. The Executive Committee will be composed of four *ries* (executive directors) and the CEO, who will chair this committee. The duties and responsibilities of this senior group are to develop long-range plans (corporate aims), formulate tactics for global strategies, establish and evaluate annual targets (goals) for each division, and finally, to approve budgets. Once the top management team is in place, the CEO will interfere with operations reluctantly and rarely. The chief financial officer (CFO, Walid A. Hashem) is the de facto second-in-command, and acts in the absence of Sheikh Saleh Kamel. This group will not normally be involved with the daily operations, but will oversee the global vision of the company and will coordinate the divisional operations so that everything runs smoothly (see Figure 12.2).

ART Creative Division

ART has one major advantage over other Middle Eastern broadcasters—its vast library of films, music videos, plays, and dramas. The decision to acquire this library was wise. Every other major player on the world scene is cornering its share of entertainment properties: Turner has purchased the library of MGM Studios; Viacom bought out the Paramount library; Disney owns its library and has now purchased the ABC network (Mohammed Yassin, personal interview, May 5, 1995). Corporate conglomerates worldwide are now seeking vertical and horizontal integration of all related business activities in order to dominate the market, or at the very least, not be controlled by suppliers or competitors.

Today, ART program purchases are driving scheduling policy within the company. The practice of needs-assessment and program-development must come from two key business concerns: what sells and what attracts a large audience or subscriber base (H. Kandil, personal communication, August 17, 1995). But because of its newness, communication among ART personnel within the creative division (Figure 12.3) is unstable.

People are scattered throughout different cities and countries. For example, at the Sports Channel, the *modir* is based in Jeddah, a program buyer is based in Amman, and a channel coordinator is found in Fucino, Italy. At the Movie Channel, there are joint channel heads, one in Cairo and the other located in Beirut, with the coordinator in Fucino. To solve this problem, the company has instituted the first phase of a global e-mail communications system for corporate operations.

Scheduling tactics for ART networks will be developed as a group process in the future, using established American entertainment strategies combined with expert

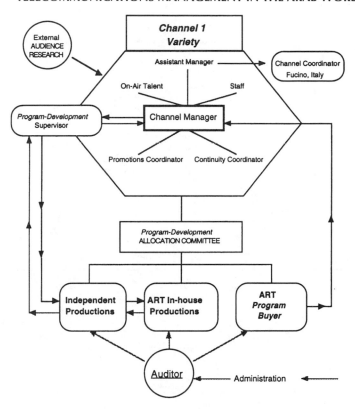

FIGURE 12.3.   ART creative programming.

Arabic knowledge of the products and shows. Programming strategies for the channels of ART use both the cable and the broadcast paradigms.

ART Acquisition Division

As a branch of administration, this small department serves three primary functions: (1) allocating budgets for in-house productions, (2) auditing independent producers, and (3) acting as a buying service for the channels. The acquisition division (Figure 12.4) controls and allocates all program acquisition budgets.

This division is crucial to the operation of the ART networks in order to control costs, while maintaining quality for the channels. The process of acquisition begins from within, after needs-assessments have been completed by each channel's program department. A follow-up request is then routed to the managing director of the ART networks (M. Laibi, personal communication, July 7, 1994). Next, the managing directors of networks, productions and acquisitions meet to recommend one of three options: (1) assigning the program-development project to an in-house

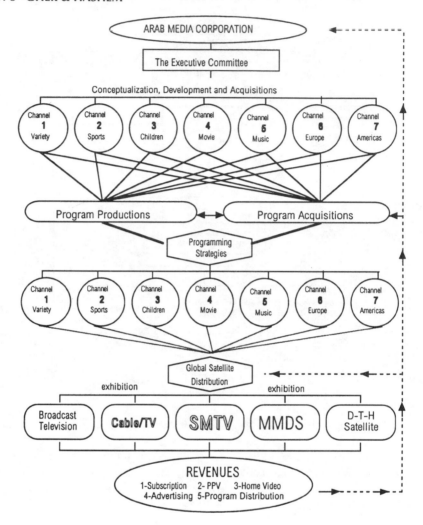

FIGURE 12.4.   ART acquisitions functions.

producer, (2) awarding the project to an established independent producer, or (3) assigning the program-development project to an in-house buyer, who will seek the requested program or series at markets such as MIP-TV or NATPE.

In this manner, the company keeps very tight controls on costs, while producing programs specifically designed for marketing on ART channels. The only purpose for having in-house production facilities is to guarantee on-time delivery of shows for the network, and to "own the rights" for future syndication sales, programs saleable on the worldwide, open market.

ART Production Division

Because ART is rapidly becoming an international broadcaster, it is in need of two types of program production facilities: ART in-house facilities, and independent resources (see Appendix). In-house facilities are divided between those offering large-scale services (Comprehensive Production Operations or CPO) and those providing limited services (Limited Production Operations or LPO).

CPOs are or will be located at strategic geographical centers: Jeddah, Saudi Arabia; Cairo, Egypt; Fucino, Italy; and Chicago, Illinois, USA. These tactical placements establish the CPOs on four continents, with Jeddah servicing the Gulf region, Cairo catering to the African zone, Fucino accommodating Europe, and Chicago serving North America.

Production equipment available at CPOs includes electronic field production (EFP) units, remote production vehicles, studio facilities, and postproduction editing, all serviced by on-site technical personnel. The basic purpose of the CPOs is to generate ART programs; however, the facilities are rented out when not in use by ART producers.

LPOs support single EFP units and one off-line editing system. Each LPO is sustained by a two-man production unit and one remote vehicle, which is used to create an on-site studio when needed. For the ART facilities to work at maximum capacity, plans are being developed for each CPO to produce a network franchise, a television show, or a serial that anchors the channel's daily schedule.

ART Technology Division

The technology division (see Appendix) is and will always be a support service to broadcast operations, especially to the creative and production divisions. In the specific case of the ART networks, however, the technical division is required to maintain its role as a self-contained functional operation in addition to its supporting role.

Obviously, the transmission site at Fucino is primarily a technical or engineering application, and is supervised under the guidance of the director of technology. Four duties are currently being performed at Fucino: uplink transmitting, program producing (both live and videotape), library cataloging and storage, and channel programming (F. Lubbadeh, personal communication, July 20, 1995).

SUMMARY

Overall, the network channels of ART seem to be targeted to several different audiences. In an unpublished research report (Amin, 1994), which investigated the original four channels of ART, several results appear to be significant.

First, for the variety channel viewership is up 89 percent across the board; 48 percent of the total viewing audience is male, compared to a 52 percent female. ART 1 appeals most to educated people and housewives. Second, the sportsviewership channel attracts viewers ranging in age from 20 to 30 years. It reaches 63 percent of those who watch television from 5 to 7 days per week. Third, the children's channel has a 60 percent share of its target audience. Fourth, ART 4, the movie channel, has a 90 percent appeal to those in managerial positions. Residents of Riyadh, Saudi Arabia, are believed to make up 16 percent of the target audience of this channel. And finally, the music channel appeals, as would be expected, to youth ranging in age from 11 years old to the late 30s.

Future plans for the ART networks include services to Asia, especially to the Muslim populations of Indochina, and to South America, where Arab-Americans live in greater numbers than in the United States.

ARABIC AND WESTERN DIFFERENCES AFFECTING CORPORATE CULTURE

To draw comparisons between Arabic and Western business cultures is not easy, nor is it straightforward. On paper, there seem to be many similarities, but such an assessment would be misleading. The differences are not found in accounting procedures, nor in corporate flow charts describing the company's structure. The dissimilarities are deeply rooted and philosophical. Corporate organizational patterns, moreover, are tied closely to family, politics, religion, and culture.

Language differences may be used as a prime example. English, now becoming the universal vocabulary of business, trade, and the Internet, is intrinsically different from Arabic, the authorized and lawful language of the *Koran*. Besides the obvious Semitic and Germanic alphabetic and structural distinctions, Arabic is fundamentally an oral language, whereas English derives authority in written forms. In Western corporations, the memorandum is the official document that initiates action. In Arab companies, it is the verbal command. While this may seem trivial, it can be a major problem for business communications.

In 1995, at the suggestion of a Western management consultant, AMC instituted a company-wide Intranet for communications using e-mail via the World Wide Web. In Western minds, this is a practical application of modern technologies that saves money, gives explicit command and control to one central authority, and overcomes time zone problems for an international business. For an Arab company, it is not so straightforward.

Islamic beliefs and religious practices often result in a diminished reliance on media. Fundamentalist groups object to their members using the communications media, specifically television. The view has been expressed at times that the media have a negative, corrupting, and immoral influence on Muslims. Public fear of these negative influences is documented in every Arab state (Schleifer, 1992). In numerous instances, AMC employees simply refused to use e-mail on religious grounds, and company *modirs* (this Arabic word does not translate well because it embodies religious connotations—the English word, "boss," comes closest to the correct meaning) declined to demand cooperation from these employees for the same reason.

Traditional Western management research tools are not useful for investigating Arabic institutions. In the ART case study, employees, supervisors, and managers alike found the written questionnaire to be confusing, offensive, and incomprehensible. Many refused to participate. When Arab oral interpreters were used as mediators, most *AMC* employees eagerly responded to the questions. However, an overwhelming majority of the responses were at the extreme positive end of the Likert scale. Employees were simply not willing to evaluate or criticize their bosses (*modirs*). Even in Egypt, where complaining is the national pastime, AMC and ART personnel rejected management commentary in any meaningful way.

But the roots of these differences with the West are more than linguistic, cultural, and religious; they are also unquestionably anchored in family ties and obligations. As a people, Arabs are even today divided along clan and family lines. For example, in Jordan jobs in banking are usually reserved for Christians, while Muslims hold control over military operations. Segregation by sector is often complicated by regionalism as well as tribalism. Certain seats in the Jordanian parliament are traditionally understood to be reserved for specific families. Within the corporate structure of ART, each network *ries* (president) has an important family, clan, or political relationship to Sheikh Saleh Kamel, the *modir cabir* (big boss). In Arab corporations, outsiders (*hawagas*) are used primarily as consultants when required for political expedience or when special knowledge is mandated.

CONCLUSION

The introduction of new communication technologies in the Arab world is very recent. Arab computer, broadcasting, telecommunications, and satellites systems have been vastly underutilized since their introduction. Although on the surface it appears that Arabs share a common language, culture, religion, and geography, there are many social differences and diverse political ideologies. With this in mind, whatever is defined as Arab corporate culture is now challenged by the information superhighway, and the results of this communication revolution will come with great speed throughout the Arab world. But this is true for businesses worldwide, not just within the Arab sphere of influence.

Transworld consortia like AMC are currently forming alliances with other global companies to create worldnets (Gher, 1996), which have no statutory responsibility to sovereign nations. Crucial social and self-regulatory issues are raised, involving political editorials, public inspection files, advertising requirements, indecency and obscenity rules, and programming diversity—areas which will no longer be addressed. What are the consequences brought about by worldnets? The answers, of course, are not immediately known. Such answers are being formulated and cultivated as a global industry remakes itself for the new millennium ahead.

DISCUSSION QUESTIONS

1. Explain the evolution of satellite television in the Arab world. In particular, how does this evolution support the notion of cultural invasion?
2. Describe Arab management organization in terms of personnel structures. How do training and promotion protocols in the Middle East compare with those of Western corporations?
3. In what ways are Western organizational strategies similar or dissimilar to management systems found in the Arab world?
4. How does the one-way flow of information pertain to Middle Eastern nations? How is this flow changing as we enter the 21st century?
5. What economic growth patterns and communication infrastructure support can you identify within the different regions of the Middle East?

APPENDIX

ORGANIZATIONAL CHART

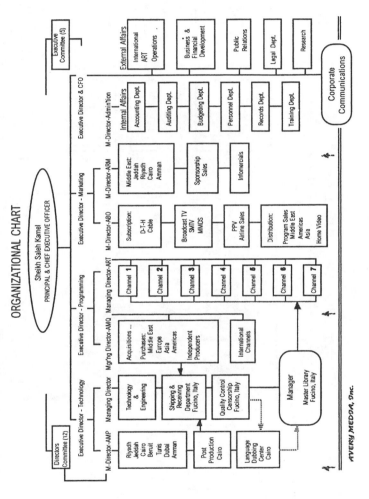

FIGURE 12.5.

AVERY MEDIA, Inc.

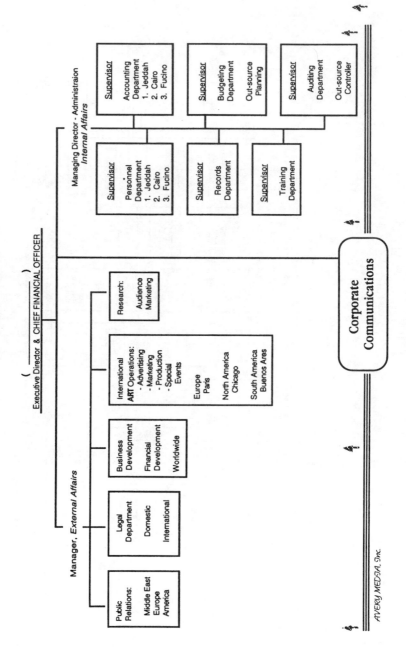

ADMINISTRATION DIVISION

Executive Director & CHIEF FINANCIAL OFFICER

Manager, *External Affairs*

Public Relations:
Middle East
Europe
America

Legal Department
Domestic
International

Business Development
Financial Development
Worldwide

International ART Operations:
- Advertising
- Marketing
- Production
- Special Events

Europe
Paris

North America
Chicago

South America
Buenos Ares

Research:
Audience
Marketing

Managing Director - Administraion
Internal Affairs

Supervisor
Personnel Department
1. Jeddah
2. Cairo
3. Fucino

Supervisor
Accounting Department
1. Jeddah
2. Cairo
3. Fucino

Supervisor
Records Department

Supervisor
Budgeting Department
Out-source Planning

Supervisor
Training Department

Supervisor
Auditing Department
Out-source Controller

Corporate Communications

FIGURE 12.6.

AVERY MEDIA, Inc.

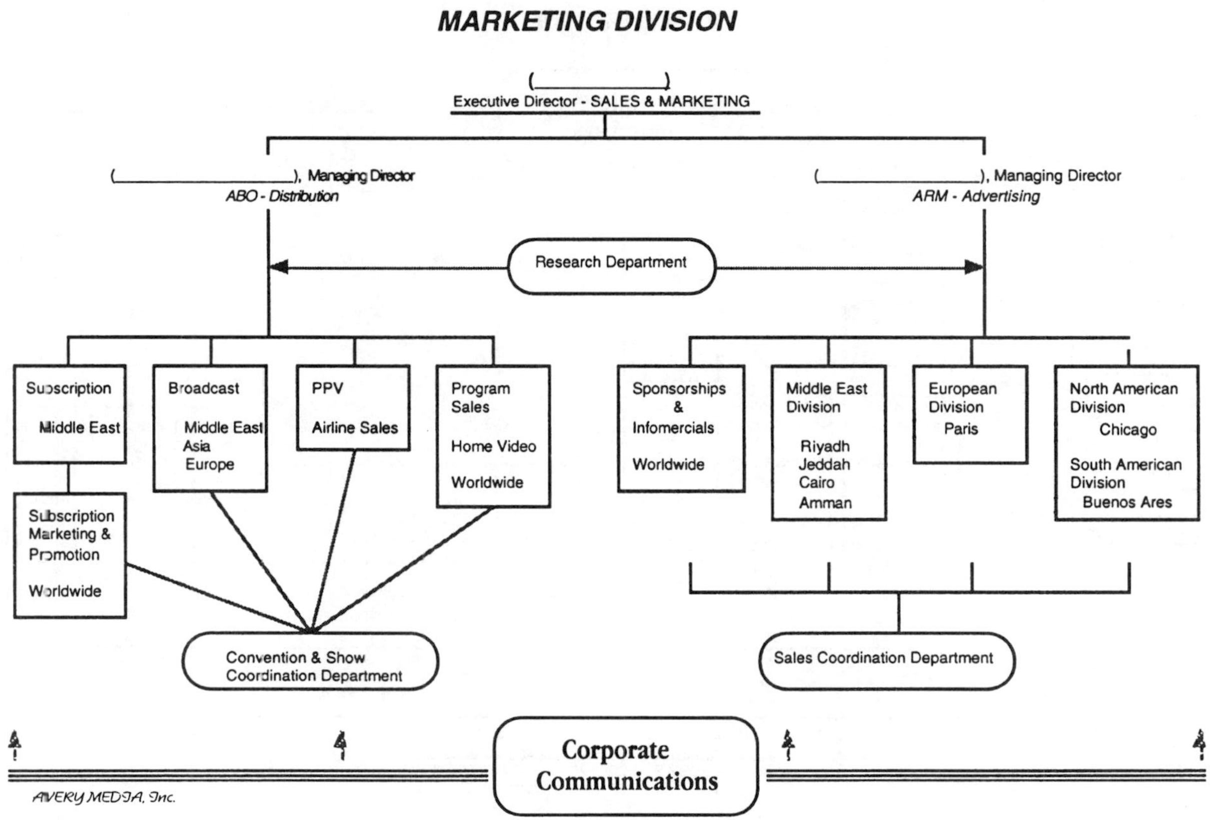

MARKETING DIVISION

Executive Director - SALES & MARKETING

(_____). Managing Director
ABO - Distribution

(_____). Managing Director
ARM - Advertising

Research Department

Distribution (ABO):
- Subscription — Middle East
- Subscription Marketing & Promotion — Worldwide
- Broadcast — Middle East, Asia, Europe
- PPV — Airline Sales
- Program Sales — Home Video — Worldwide
- Convention & Show Coordination Department

Advertising (ARM):
- Sponsorships & Infomercials — Worldwide
- Middle East Division — Riyadh, Jeddah, Cairo, Amman
- European Division — Paris
- North American Division — Chicago, South American Division — Buenos Ares
- Sales Coordination Department

Corporate Communications

FIGURE 12.7.

AVERY MEDIA, Inc.

185

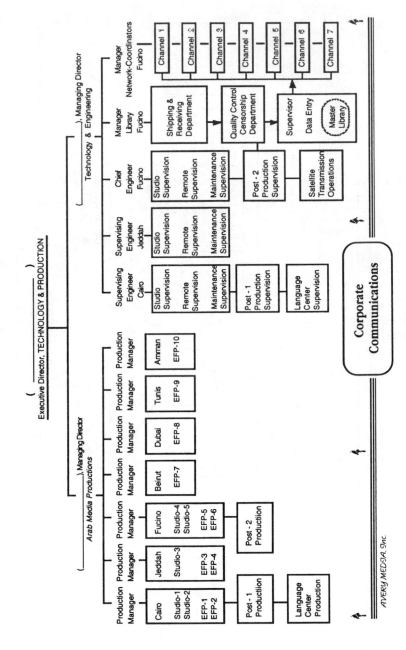

TECHNOLOGY DIVISION

FIGURE 12.8.

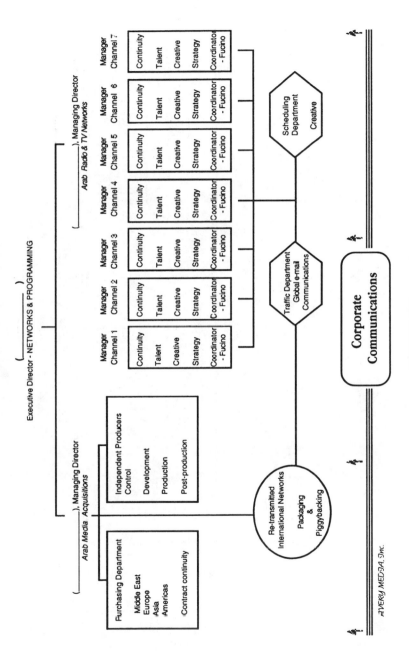

FIGURE 12.9.

187

Arab Media Productions - Equipment & Facilities

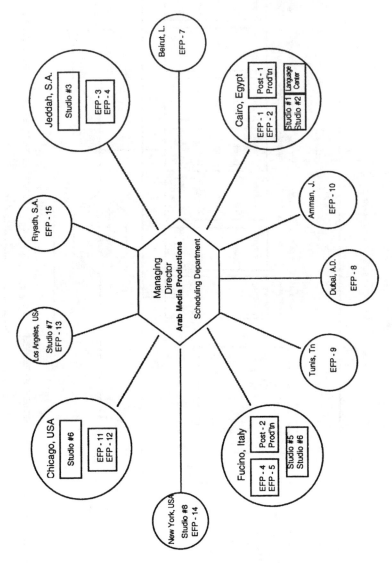

FIGURE 12.10.

REFERENCES

Al-Mashat, A. (1996). *Al-Shabakah al-Arabiyya lil itisalat al-fadaa'iyyah wa imkanitha.* Riyadh, Saudi Arabia: Gulf Television.

Amin, H. Y. (1994, April). *Viewers evaluative assessment.* Cairo, Egypt: Pan Arab Research Corporation.

Amin, H. Y. (1995). Egypt and the Arab world in the satellite age. In J. Sinclair, E. Jacka, & S. Cunningham (Eds.), *New patterns in global television: Peripheral vision* (pp. 101–124). New York: Oxford University Press.

Amin, H. Y., & Boyd, D. A. (1993). The impact of home video cassette recorders on the Egyptian film and television consumption patterns. *The European Journal of Communications, 18*(1), 2–7.

ART. (1995, October). Press release. Jeddah, Saudi Arabia: Press Office of *ART.*

ERTU. (1997). Egyptian Radio and Television Union [Printout]. Cairo, Egypt: Ministry of Information.

Gher, L. A. (1996). WORLDNETS—*New electronic distribution systems: The effects and issues of transnational programming and production.* Paper presented at the Broadcast Education Association Conference. Las Vegas, NV.

Gher, L. A., Amin, H. Y., & Hashem, W. A. (1996). *History and development of private direct-to-home broadcast services in the Arab world: The case of Arab radio & TV.* Paper presented at the annual Broadcast Education Association Convention, Las Vegas, NV.

Rubin, R. B., Rubin, A. M., & Piele, L. J. (1996). *Communication research: Strategies and sources* (4th ed.). Belmont, CA: Wadsworth.

Rugh, W. (1979). *The Arab press.* Syracuse University Press.

Schleifer, S. A. (1992). *Global media, the new world order—and the significance of failure: Media in the midst of war.* Cairo, Egypt: The Adham Center Press.

13

A Q STUDY OF REACTIONS TO DIRECT BROADCAST SATELLITE TELEVISION PROGRAMMING IN SAUDI ARABIA

Safran S. al-Makaty
Umm al-Quara University

Douglas A. Boyd
G. Norman Van Tubergen
University of Kentucky

INTRODUCTION

The on-again, off-again debate about cultural and media imperialism during the 1970s and 1980s has become less intense for several reasons, including the fact that regional production centers, such as those in Hong Kong, Cairo, Bombay, and several Latin American states, are now supplying some of the film and television offerings that once came almost exclusively from the West. Regional productions have an obvious language advantage: films in Spanish, Arabic, Indian languages, or one of the Chinese dialects can be shown to audiences without dubbing or subtitling. This, of course, does not mean that some states, including European Union members, are no longer concerned about an invasion of cultural and informational programming from English-speaking Western countries, primarily the United States.

There have been some technical developments during the past 15 years that have altered the traditional debate over cultural invasion via film and television. First, the enthusiasm for videocassette recorders (VCRs) (and the usually associated pirated material in the developing world) showed that there is a market for nonindigenous programming that is not found in local cinemas or on terrestrial television. Second, direct satellite broadcasting (DBS)[1] has made it possible for viewers in many parts of the world to see entertainment material without having to visit local VCR rental stores or watch local television. News via DBS could be thought of as similar to that from international shortwave radio broadcasting. Depending on the consumer's perception of the supplier's credibility, news from satellite broadcasting received in the developing world circumvents the government-influenced news in some Asian, African, and Middle Eastern countries.

This research concerns DBS in the Kingdom of Saudi Arabia, the largest country on the Arabian Peninsula that continues to figure prominently in world economic and political developments. Saudi Arabia is the home of Islam's two holiest cities and is wealthy because of its enormous oil reserves.

The electronic media in the Arab world are government-operated through a ministry of information. Saudi television started in 1965 in Jeddah and Riyadh, the two largest urban areas. By using microwave and satellite connections, the two Saudi national television channels, one in Arabic, the other in English, provide nationwide service.

The kingdom is the only country we know of that does not permit public cinemas. The government remains concerned about large groups of people gathering for entertainment, especially to see films from the West or from other Arab states that depict cultures and religions that are not in keeping with the kingdom's conservative Islamic tradition. Thus, television—a medium easily controlled by the government—was seen as ideal for a home-centered society. However, in the late 1970s the VCR was introduced, and by the mid-1980s, ownership had reached more than 80 percent among those with television receivers.[2] Like the earlier introduction of the audiocassette, the VCR boom virtually eliminated control of imported visual material, despite the fact that the government enacted laws restricting the distribution of certain video material (Boyd, Straubhaar, & Lent, 1989).

Although a few wealthy Saudi businessmen and members of the royal family owned satellite dishes in the 1980s, the government officially discouraged the practice. It was the 1990 Iraqi invasion of Kuwait that provided a strong motivation to acquire a dish to watch news from CNN and other Western sources. Egypt found it necessary to transmit its domestic television programming via satellite for terrestrial rebroadcast on portable transmitters to Egyptian troops stationed in the eastern part of the Arabian peninsula. More importantly, the war started a rush of both private and government efforts to reach Arabs with television from satellites operated by Arabsat, an Arab League–backed consortium to supply up- and downlink facilities to members.

Several satellite television offerings are available to residents of Saudi Arabia. In the eastern part of the country, one can view Hong Kong–based Star TV's five channels (including a music video channel and the British Broadcasting Corporation [BBC] World Service Television News). Other offerings are CNN International and several Arab government–run satellite services from Egypt, Kuwait, and Dubai (Amin & Boyd, 1995). However, the services that have made DBS part of the Middle Eastern landscape in the 1990s are specifically targeted to the area, broadcast in Arabic, advertiser or subscription supported, and owned by members of the Saudi Arabian royal family. The London-based Middle East Broadcasting Centre (MBC) started telecasting on September 18, 1991, and provides a daily 12-hour unencrypted entertainment and news channel. Arab Radio and Television (ART)—operating from Jeddah, Saudi Arabia, and Cairo, Egypt, and owned by Saudi investor Saleh Kamel, who helped start MBC—provides four channels of films, music, sports, and children's programming that are uplinked to an Arabsat transponder from Italy. The newest DBS entry is Orbit Communications, which started service in May 1994. Headquartered in Rome, Italy, Orbit operates 17 separate Arabic- and English-language television channels for those able to purchase a dish and decoder (at a cost of U.S. $2,500) and pay a monthly fee for the multichannel service. It is only on Orbit that subscribers can watch the BBC's London-based World Service Television in Arabic (Hansen, 1995; Khalaf, 1994).

The future of DBS in the area is somewhat complicated by the fact that at least two states, Qatar and Saudi Arabia, have banned satellite dish ownership. Although dissimilar to the satellite dish ban in Than, where the government mandated that existing dishes be taken down (Saudi Ministers Council, 1994), as of March 10, 1994, in Saudi Arabia dish ownership is against the law. This research took place before ART and Orbit went on the air and just prior to Saudi government decree No. 128 banning private satellite dish ownership (Saudi Ministers Council, 1994).

This study examines the attitudes of Saudi Arabians toward the use of DBS news and entertainment programming. Information about audience reactions to DBS could be a first step toward enriching our knowledge about how both Arab government and privately owned satellite-delivered programming is perceived and utilized in this conservative Islamic state.

Audience research in the Arab world has a very short history. Previous work in this regard has been largely exploratory and descriptive in nature. It must be recognized at the outset that, compared to research activities in the United States, a study such as this is limited by many social, political, and religious restrictions. Conducting mass media research in Saudi Arabia is difficult. Citizens and public officials are usually unwilling to give researchers information. This obstacle has been faced by many media researchers. Najai (1982) stated that:

> Audience research is highly sensitive to the long-standing traditions and culture of the country. Saudi Arabia has experienced an extensive period of isolation and self-contained discipline which generally predisposed the individual to subordinate his needs and opinion to the collective interests of family, tribe, and the community at large. (p. 10)

Kheraigi (1990) indicated that people were hesitant to state their opinions, even with guarantees of confidentiality and promises that the results would be used only for academic purposes. He described his experience as a challenging exercise in patience, and often disappointment and frustration.

Women were excluded from the study described in this chapter because men are not allowed to interview women, and skilled female interviewers are scarce. The genders are separated at all educational levels and in most workplaces for cultural and religious reasons. In this male-dominated society, it is the male head-of-household who makes the final decision about acquiring a dish.

Q methodology is a form of quantitative inquiry that is identified with single-subject or small sample research designs, phenomenological analysis, and topological analysis. This study examined sociocultural perceptions of DBS among Saudi men. Such perceptions are actually considered subjective behaviors and are expected to vary from one person to another. The Q sort has not been widely used in the Third World, but it has been employed successfully with Arab respondents who indicate a high degree of involvement in the task, and its greater appeal over conventional questionnaires has been noted (al-Makaty, Boyd, & Van Tubergen, 1994; Boyd, 1978).

METHODOLOGY

Q technique and its methodology were proposed in 1935 and developed over the next 20 years primarily by William Stephenson to assist in the orderly examination of human subjectivity. Q-methodology examines the phenomenological nature of the individual or small numbers of individuals without losing the strength of statistical analysis. In Q technique, a sample of objects is placed in an order that is significant to the individual. In its most typical form, the sample involves statements of opinion (Q sample).

Q is a way to identify and describe different subjectively held belief systems through examination of the significance orderings provided by different people. It emphasizes meaning and the way we see our world rather than forcing a fit to constructs devised by researchers (Stephenson, 1953). Moreover, with a small number of individuals selected for their possible subjective diversity, Q can identify these differences very clearly. Hence, Q supplies a rich understanding of multifaceted subjectivity. Q sampling does not usually concentrate on people, but rather on the universe of discourse that is likely to function as explored attitudes. Population samples (variables) for Q methodology studies are usually small, with individuals selected intentionally to ensure inclusion of various points of view. Further, Q methodology findings are not used to make generalizations about specific populations, because people in Q are used as variables. Also, Q is inductive in nature; thus, no hypotheses are posed at the outset of the research, beyond the expectation that diverse patterns of value perceptions exist and are discoverable.

In this investigation, the researchers sought to identify Saudis' possible prevailing attitudes and beliefs about DBS utilization and then to draw a representative sample from that domain. Based on the researchers' previous experience in constructing Q items (al-Makaty, Boyd, & Van Tubergen, 1994; Boyd, 1978, 1986) and consultation with experts and individuals, the 38 items in Table 13.1 were reviewed. The statements did not focus on a particular dimension, but covered important cultural, social, and political issues. The 38 statements were originally written in English, translated into Arabic, and validated by back-translating into English independently by two native speakers. This process was employed to ensure close correspondence between idiomatic subtleties in English and the meaning conveyed in Arabic. The final versions of the Arabic statements were also scrutinized by the translation center at a Saudi Arabian university. The final instrument consisted of 38 index cards, each bearing one of the attitude statements in Arabic. One of the researchers conducted data collection in the Saudi capital, Riyadh, during December 1993.

Data collection for the study involved two steps. First, each participant was asked to sort the attitude statements further into three piles: those he agreed with; those of which he was not sure; and those he did not agree with. Second, each participant was asked to sort the attitude statements into an 11-rank, quasinormal, forced distribution to indicate relative agreement or disagreement with each statement. A questionnaire about media use and demographics was then administered orally in Arabic.

Participants were 50 male Saudi nationals that formed a convenience sample. All 50 participants in this study were residents of Riyadh. Ages ranged from 18 to 48 years: one was 18 years old; three were 20; two were 23; one was 24; two were 25; one was 26; three were 27; one was 28; one was 29; six were 30; one was 31; two were 32; two were 33; three were 34; three were 35; three were 36; one was 37; two were 38; two were 39; five were 40; two were 42; two were 46; and one was 48 years old. Most participants had large families (average of five members) and lived in their family houses. Fifty-eight percent (29) were men who owned the houses they lived in, but the remaining 42 percent (21) rented. Participants worked a daily average of 7.56 hours.

Formal education ranged from 1 to 26 years: 14 participants had earned high school diplomas; 21 had B.A. degrees; 9 had M.A. degrees; and 6 were Ph.D. holders who were university professors. Respondents also included 33 government employees, 8 students, and 3 businessmen. Nearly 38 percent (19) reported annual income between U.S.$20,000 and 24,999; 34 percent (17), U.S.$25,000 or more; 16 percent (8), less than U.S.$10,000; and 12 percent (6), between U.S.$15,000 and 19,000. Forty-seven respondents (94 percent) owned television receivers, with an average of three television sets per person. Seventy-eight percent (39) possessed VCRs, with a weekly average usage of 1.74 hours. All participants listened to radio an average of 8.82 hours weekly, and watched television an average of 15.18 hours weekly. Sixty-four percent (32) reported they had satellite dishes. Only two participants indicated that they had bought their satellite dishes before the 1990–1991

Gulf War, but the rest, almost 94 percent (30), bought them after 1991. Sixty-nine percent (22) got their satellite dishes from local electronic stores in Riyadh, but 31 percent (10) got them on the black market. During the time of this study (December 1993), the average cost of a satellite dish in Riyadh was about 6,000 Saudi riyals (U.S.$1,600). The average weekly hours spent watching DBS channels was 15.94.

ANALYSIS

Each respondent's Q sort was correlated with every other's sort, and a principal axis factor analysis was conducted, using the QUANAL computer package with squared multiple correlation (SMC) utilized as commonality estimates. The Scree test and Humphery's test indicated a three-factor solution, accounting for 39 percent of total variance or 97 percent of trace variance, suggesting three distinct groups (or types) of Saudi men, each holding a set of perceptions of DBS that contrasted explicitly with the perceptions held by the other two groups (or types). Factors were rotated to oblique single structure.

For each type of man, a weighted average response to each of the 38 attitude statements was computed, representing the typical pattern of sorting response for the men in the group. Each pattern was then expressed in standard (z) score form to facilitate comparisons. Attitudes with z score exceeding $+1-1.0$ were strongly agreed or disagreed with, and were usually placed in the highest two or three ranks by participants in the type. Attitudes that differed in z score by 1.0 or more between types differentiated the types and were typically placed at least four or five ranks apart by the men in each type. The complete English text of all 38 attitude statements is provided in Table 13.1, along with each statement's z score for each of the three types of Saudi men.

RESULTS

Consensus

Although the three types of men ranked most of the attitude statements somewhat differently, 10 of the 38 attitudes were ranked similarly by all respondents; Table 13.2 contains these statements with their average z scores.

Most prominent among these was the strongest agreement (1.53 average z score) among all types that parents should teach their children how to make better use of DBS (item 5 in Table 13.1). This statement is nonjudgmental, and examination of the types suggests that some respondents may be expressing concerns for DBS's impact on children, while others may have believed that the statement is simply good advice for those who have satellite dishes. The next strongest statement represents all types' perceptions of the nature of DBS as a fact of life so the

TABLE 13.1.
Z Score Responses of Three Types of Saudi Men

	Typal Z		
Item Descriptions	1	2	3
1. DBS programs encourage people to imitate the way people live and behave in the countries where these programs originate.	−0.7	0.6	−0.6
2. DBS is a new cultural invasion in the Middle East.	−0.1	1.0	0.5
3. Most DBS programs are not in compliance with Islamic principles.	−0.1	1.3	−0.3
4. DBS will undermine Saudi censorship.	1.0	0.2	−0.5
5. Parents should help their children make better use of DBS.	1.7	1.3	1.6
6. Saudi television may be the first casualty of DBS.	1.0	0.5	−0.5
7. DBS is our window to the world.	1.0	−1.1	0.9
8. DBS helps promote mutual understanding and respect among people and nations.	−0.1	−1.3	0.8
9. DBS is a true fact, therefore, we should utilize it to advance the Islamic cause.	−0.9	0.5	1.6
10. The United Nations must take responsibility and regulate DBS for the benefit of mankind.	−1.7	1.5	1.4
11. It is offensive to Saudis to see references to other religions on DBS networks.	−1.0	−0.3	−1.2
12. DBS is a great service to the people in the Third World because it can become a watch dog on government activities.	0.5	−1.1	0.6
13. Thanks to DBS, authoritarian regimes will not be able to stop the flow of information to their people.	1.1	0.2	0.9
14. Am not bothered by the information and news on DBS, but I am very troubled by DBS entertainment programs.	−0.7	0.8	−0.2
15. DBS will have a strong negative impact on viewers.	−0.8	0.3	−1.0
16. DBS will be another source of international conflict.	−0.9	−0.8	−1.6
17. DBS will force Saudi television to offer better quality news and entertainment programs.	0.4	0.8	1.1
18. We must learn to adapt to changes in our society, because people's exposure to advances in communication technologies will make it impossible to prevent those changes.	1.1	−1.0	1.3
19. DBS can significantly improve the security and social stability of the Arab world.	−1.7	−2.1	−0.8
20. DBS networks will only serve the ideological, political, and economic interests of originating nations.	1.1	−0.2	−0.8
21. It is offensive to Saudis to see unveiled women on DBS networks.	−0.8	0.5	−1.4
22. DBS presents unfair competition to Saudi television because Saudi media can only reflect Saudi society, while DBS can show the diversity of life in the world.	−0.2	−0.8	0.1
23. DBS will take audiences away from Saudi television channels.	1.5	0.1	0.4
24. The introduction of foreign ideas through DBS will undermine Islamic values.	0.7	0.4	−0.2
25. DBS will encourage Saudi women to become more westernized.	−0.5	0.3	−1.0
26. DBS will not change our social fabric because our cultural values are very strong.	−0.5	−2.1	−0.4
27. The Saudi government should ban the use of satellite dishes.	−2.2	1.0	−2.1
28. Because of DBS, students will have less study time, thereby reducing their academic achievements.	0.4	0.1	−1.3
29. DBS can have a negative impact on our children.	0.7	1.5	−0.1

TABLE 13.1.
(Continued)

		Typal Z		
	Item Descriptions	1	2	3
30.	Through DBS, the advanced nations will set the agenda of the world priorities and determine its lifestyles.	−0.5	−1.2	−0.7
31.	DBS is the natural development of modern society.	0.6	−1.2	1.3
32.	DBS will promote the Middle East peace agreement between Arabs and Israel.	−1.3	−1.6	−0.7
33.	DBS will promote more international interaction and understanding.	−0.4	−1.3	0.9
34.	The advanced countries will utilize DBS to dominate the world culturally and economically.	−0.0	0.7	−0.7
35.	DBS will make the Arab world more dependent on the West intellectually and economically.	−1.0	0.4	−0.6
36.	The United Nations should put restrictions on developed countries so they do not misuse DBS to harm other nations' values and cultures.	−1.2	1.0	1.3
37.	DBS will transform the world into a small village.	1.1	−0.4	1.1
38.	Education systems have primary responsibility for minimizing the negative effects of DBS.	1.5	1.3	0.9

Note: Number of participants for each type is as follows: type 1, 22; type 2, 11; type 3, 17.

TABLE 13.2.
Ten Concensus Items and Average Z Scores

	Item Descriptions	Average Z Score
5.	Parents should help their children make better use of DBS.	1.526
38.	Education systems have primary responsibility for minimizing the negative effects of DBS.	1.253
17.	DBS will force Saudi television to offer better quality news and entertainment programs.	0.760
13.	Thanks to DBS, authoritarian regimes will not be able to stop the flow of information to their people.	0.731
24.	The introduction of foreign ideas through DBS will undermine Islamic values.	0.321
22.	DBS presents unfair competition to Saudi TV because Saudi media can only reflect Saudi society, while DBS can show the diversity of life in the world.	−0.281
30.	Through DBS, the advanced nations will set the agenda of the world's priorities and determine its lifestyles.	−0.816
11.	It is offensive to Saudis to see references to other religions on DBS networks.	−0.839
16.	DBS will be another source of international conflict.	−1.104
32.	DBS will promote the Middle East peace agreement between Arabs and Israel.	−1.204

Note: Criterion is 1,000.

education system should have another function, that of teaching society how to deal with the DBS challenge (item 38, z average = 1.25).

All participants strongly disagreed (item 32, z average = −1.20) with the statement that DBS would promote the Middle East peace agreement between Arabs and Israel, and with the statement that DBS would be another source of news about the next international conflict (item 16, z average = −1.10). Also, they more moderately disagreed with the statement that DBS would enable advanced nations to set the agenda of the world's priorities and determine its lifestyle (item 30, z average = −0.82). They moderately agreed that DBS would force Saudi Arabian television to change its programming style to meet the DBS challenge (item 17, z average = 0.76). DBS is seen, therefore, as a neutral force in international politics, but as possibly having a modest impact on domestic broadcasting, and as imposing additional educational responsibilities on Saudi society.

Type 1

The 22 men associated with this group saw DBS as a threat to the political and economic interest of Saudi society in general, and specifically, to the national broadcast media. They wanted schools to provide educational measures to help minimize the possible negative effects of DBS (item 38, z average = 1.54). They particularly believed that new satellite channels would take audiences away from Saudi Arabian television channels (item 23, z average = 1.47), and they believed this much more strongly than did men in the other two types (difference between type 1 z and average of types 2 and 3 = 1.19). More than the other types, they were likely to believe that DBS would only serve the political and economic interests of the originating countries (item 20, z average = 1.14, z difference = 1.62) and, that DBS would undermine Saudi censorship (item 4, z average = 0.97, z difference = 1.12). They felt more strongly than did the others that Saudi television would be the first casualty of DBS (item 6, z average = 1.04, z difference = 1.03). Type 1 respondents did not feel Saudi government should ban the use of satellite dishes (item 27, z average = −2.24). They did not see that DBS would significantly improve the security and social stability of the Arab world (item 19, z average = −1.73) or promote the Middle East peace agreement (item 32, z average = −1.25). In addition, they believed that regulating DBS for the benefit of mankind is beyond the United Nations' responsibility (item 10, z average = −1.70).

The 22 type 1 males were demographically diverse, exhibiting few notable differences from the characteristics of the overall sample. These participants had the highest average age (34 years) and education (19 years) among the three types. Sixty-eight percent (15) of these men were government employees; 18 percent (4) were university faculty members; 9 percent (2) were students; and only one was a businessman. Fifty percent (11) of the men had annual incomes of $25,000 or more; 27 percent (6) earned yearly incomes between U.S. $20,000 and 24,999; and only 9 percent (2) had annual incomes of less than U.S. $10,000.

Type 1 men owned an average of 2.8 television sets (same as type 2 men). Twenty-seven percent (6) had two television sets, and 27 percent (6) had three television sets; 14 percent (3) reported owning five sets, and also 14 percent (3) had one set; only 9 percent (2) had four television sets. Seventy-seven percent (17) of the subjects had VCRs, with an average weekly use of 2.13 hours. Type 1 men listened to radio for an average of 9.82 hours weekly and watched television for an average of 12.41 hours weekly. Sixty-eight percent (15) of type 1 participants owned satellite dishes, with a weekly average of 15.73 hours of watching satellite channels. Forty-five percent (12) owned their homes.

Type 2

The 11 men of this type took the strongest position among the study types against the introduction of DBS in Saudi Arabia. They saw DBS as a serious cultural threat that could have a negative impact, especially on children (item 29, z average = 1.46). Unlike type 1 men, type 2 respondents believed strongly that regulating DBS for the benefit of all human beings is one of the responsibilities of the United Nations (item 10, z average = 1.53). They also saw the educational systems in the kingdom as having responsibility for discussing the possible effects of DBS (item 38, z average = 1.29). They felt that if a family has access to satellite channels, parents should help their children make better choices of DBS programming (item 5, z average = 1.27) because most DBS programs are not in compliance with Islamic teaching (item 3, z average = 1.26). These respondents regarded DBS as a new cultural invasion in the Middle East (item 2, z average = 1.02).

More than the other types, type 2 men strongly wanted the Saudi government to ban the use of satellite dishes (item 27, z average = 0.97, z difference = 3.13) and believed that the United Nations should take immediate action to regulate DBS technology for the interests of all mankind (item 10, z average = 1.53, z difference = 1.66). They strongly felt that it is offensive to Saudis to see unveiled women on DBS channels (item 21, z average = 0.54, z difference = 1.61).

Type 2 participants strongly rejected the idea that DBS could improve the security and social stability of the Arab world (item 19, z average = −2.06) and at the same time felt it would not promote the Middle East peace process (item 32, z average = 1.63). They also strongly perceived that in the long run, DBS would change the Saudi social fabric for the worse (item 26, z average = −2.05). On the international level, type 2 men believed that DBS would promote neither international interaction and understanding (item 33, z average = −1.30) nor mutual understanding and respect among people and nations (item 8, z average = −1.26). The 11 men in type 2 were demographically similar; they had the lowest average age (30 years) among the types, and the same years of education as type 3 (average 17). Fifty-five percent (6) were government employees; 36 percent (4) were students. Type 2 included only one university faculty member. Forty-six percent (5) had yearly incomes between U.S. $20,000 and 24,999; 36 percent (4) had less than U.S. $10,000; and only 18 percent (2) had annual incomes of U.S.$25,000 or more. Type 2 men had an average of 2.8 television sets. Thirty-six percent (4) owned two television sets; 27 percent (3) had three television sets; 18 percent (2) had five television sets; and only one participant reported owning one television set. Eighty-two percent (9) possessed VCRs, with an average use of 1.33 hours weekly. Type 2 participants listened to radio for an average of 7.55 hours weekly and watched television for an average of 17.64 hours weekly. The majority, 73 percent (8), of type 2 men did not possess satellite dishes. Twenty-seven percent (3) who owned satellite dishes watched satellite channels for an average of 9.67 hours weekly. Sixty-three percent (7) owned their homes.

Type 3

The 17 men affiliated with this type tended to accept DBS. They strongly believed that the Saudi government ought to use DBS to advance the Islamic cause world-wide (item 9, z average = 1.63). They considered DBS to be an international matter; therefore, the United Nations should regulate it for the benefit of mankind (item 10, z average = 1.44). They believed that it is impossible to prevent social changes as a result of introducing new communication technologies and Saudis should accept at least minor changes (item 18, z average = 1.33). They saw DBS as a normal development of modern society (item 31, z average = 1.28) that would transform the world into a small village (item 37, z average = 1.13). More than the other types, type 3 subjects strongly believed that DBS would promote more international interaction and understanding (item 33, z average = 0.89, z difference = 1.75). They also believed that DBS helps promote mutual understanding and respect among people and nations (item 8, z average = 0.83, z difference = 1.50) and did not believe that DBS will reduce students' academic achievement (item 26, z average = 1.31, z difference = -1.56) or that DBS would harm Saudi television (item 6, z average = -0.52, z difference = -1.31). They believed it is no problem for Saudis to see unveiled women on satellite television channels (item 1, z average = 1.36, z difference = -1.24). Type 3 respondents strongly rejected the idea of officially banning the use of satellite dishes (item 27, z average = -2.16), and thought DBS would not provoke any international conflict (item 16, z average = -1.61).

The 17 men connected with type 3 had the same average years of education as type 2 men (average 17 years) and almost the same average age as type 1 (average 33 years). Seventy percent (12) were government employees; 11 percent (2) were students; 11 percent (2) were businessmen; and one was a university professor. Forty-seven percent (8) had yearly incomes between U.S. $20,000 and 24,999; 24 percent (4) had yearly incomes of U.S. $25,000 or more; and only three men (18 percent) had between U.S. $15,000 and 19,999 annual incomes. Type 3 respondents had an average of 3.35 television sets, 82 percent (14) owned VCRs and used them for an average of 1.57 hours weekly. They listened to radio for a weekly average of 8.35 hours and watched television for a weekly average of 17.18 hours. Eighty-two percent (14) owned satellite dishes, with a weekly average of 17.5 hours of watching satellite channels. Fifty-nine percent (10) owned their homes.

DISCUSSION

The three types of respondents in this study can be described in the following way. Type 1 Saudis believed that DBS represents an economic threat to Saudi society, particularly to the Saudi broadcast media, and type 2 strongly believed that DBS represents a critical threat to Islamic culture. Further, it seems that type 1 subjects based their attitudes toward DBS on secular-societal, political, and economic concerns, but type 2 attitudes were based on sacred-religious and cultural concerns. Type 3 subjects, however, saw no serious threat from DBS and, in fact, may have seen it as helping to promote more international interaction and understanding; likewise, they believed that it would convert the world into a small global village. It is possible to label the men of each type as follows: Type 1 are moderately protectionist, type 2 are highly protectionist, and type 3 are cautious acceptors or adopters.

As occurred when radio, television, and VCRs were first introduced into the kingdom, Saudis overall have mixed reactions to DBS. It is quite possible that perceptions held by the study types toward DBS are part of the long-time perceptions these respondents have held toward electronic media in general. Saudis who rejected foreign influence (types 1 and 2). particularly Western influence, saw DBS as the strongest foreign cultural forces directly affecting and altering Saudi basic values. However, Saudis who advocated changes (type 3) saw DBS as one of several ways to help modernize Saudi Arabia and establish it as a positive partner in the world community.

The more television sets the respondents owned, the more positive their attitude toward DBS. Types 1 and 2 had the same average television set ownership (2.8), and type 3 had the highest average television set ownership (3.35). This difference is even more apparent in the case of satellite dish ownership: Type 3 had the highest percentage, 82 percent, followed by type 1 with 68 percent and type 2 with the lowest percentage (27 percent). A similar pattern is seen in VCR ownership: Type 3 had the highest percentage (82 percent).

In terms of radio listening, the pattern varied slightly: Type 1 had the highest weekly average (9.82 hours), and type 2 had the lowest average (7.55 hours weekly), but type 3 was in the middle (8.35 hours weekly). Television viewing patterns were interesting: Types 2 and 3 had the highest averages, approximately 17 hours weekly, and type 1 had the lowest average, approximately 12 hours weekly. Logically, the data indicate that type 3 had the highest weekly average hours (17.5) of satellite channel viewing, followed by type 1, with an average of 15.73 hours weekly, and type 2 with the lowest average, 9.67 hours weekly. The data indicate that type 2 men had larger families than type 1 and type 3 men, who had the same family size.

Finally, age, years of education, and income do not seem to have a significant relationship with how participants perceived DBS.

DISCUSSION QUESTIONS

1. What are the three types of respondents in this study, and how does each relate to audience viewership patterns in Saudi Arabia?
2. What technical developments during the past 15 years have altered the traditional debate over cultural invasion via film and television in the Gulf States?
3. The kingdom of Saudi Arabia is the only country known today that does not permit public cinemas. What concerns might explain the government's position about large groups of people gathering for entertainment, especially to see films from the West or from other Arab states?
4. How do the mass media influence the cultural environment in Saudi Arabia?
5. How do the long-time perceptions respondents in this study have held toward electronic media relate to perceptions of Saudis who rejected foreign influence in general?

NOTES

[1] We are using the better known term DBS to mean residence-based reception of television programming directly from satellites, rather than other terms such as direct-to-home (DTH) television reception.

[2] The 17.9 million residents of Saudi Arabia are well-equipped to receive radio and television broadcasts and to watch videocassette material. UBC statistics indicate that there are 6 million radio receivers, 5 million television sets, and 3 million videocassette recorders in the kingdom (British Broadcasting Corporation, 1994). There are no known estimates of the number of households in the kingdom. For a detailed history of the electronic media in Saudi Arabia and other Middle Eastern Arab states, see Boyd (1993).

REFERENCES

al-Makaty, S. S., Boyd, D. A., & Van Tubergen, N. G. (1994). Source credibility during the Gulf War: A Q study of rural and urban Saudi Arabian citizens. *Journalism Quarterly, 71*(1), 55–63.

Amin, H. Y., & Boyd, D. A. (1995). The development of direct broadcast television to and within the Middle East. *Journal of South Asian and Middle Eastern Studies, 17*(2), 37–49.

Boyd, D. (1978). A Q-analysis of mass media usage by Egyptian elites. *Journalism Quarterly, 55*(3), 501–507, 539.

Boyd, D. A. (1993). *Broadcasting in the Arab World: A survey of the electronic media in the Middle East.* Ames, IA: Iowa State University Press.

Boyd, D. A., Straubhaar, J. D., & Lent, J. A. (1989). *Videocassette recorders in the Third World.* New York: Longman.

British Broadcasting Corporation. (1996). *World radio and television receivers.* London: International Broadcasting and Audience Research Library.

Hansen, J. (1995, April 26). Relaunching a bid for Arab viewers. *International Herald Tribune,* p. 16.

Khalaf, R. (1994, November 16). Saudi businessmen reach for the media stars. *Financial Times,* p. 4.

Kheraigi, A. S. (1990). *Press freedom in a Muslim state: A critique with reference to freedom of expression in Islam.* Unpublished doctoral dissertation, University of Wisconsin - Madison.

Najai, A. M. (1982). *Television and youth in the Kingdom of Saudi Arabia: An analysis of the uses of television among young Saudi Arabian viewers.* Unpublished doctoral dissertation, University of Wisconsin, Madison.

Saudi Ministers Council. (1994, March 11). Authorization for cable TV and ban for satellite dishes. *Asharq Al-Awsat,* pp. 1, 4.

Stephenson, W. (1953). *The study of behavior.* Chicago: University of Chicago Press.

Discourse V
New Journalism: The Online Environment and Law

14

WITHIN THE LIMITS OF THE LAW: PRESS LAW 1995–ARAFAT'S ANSWER TO FREEDOM OF THE PRESS

Carolyn Crimmins
Georgia State University

The 1996 Palestinian Council elections brought a certain "democratic legitimacy" to Yasir Arafat's leadership over the self-ruled Palestinian territories. Yet the same reviewers who claimed a "new dawn for Palestinians," also spoke of Arafat's "patchy record on civil rights," and of his "previously unchallenged and frequently abused authority" (Schmemann, 1996, p. 14). Arafat's relationship with the Palestinian press has been one area in which his record on civil rights and his alleged abuse of authority have been called into question.

A critical analysis of Press Law 1995, adopted by the Palestinian National Authority (PNA) and signed into law by Arafat on July 27, 1995, revealed the flaws and inherent contradictions of the new legislation. Six case studies of American and Middle Eastern media coverage of Arafat's interference with the press both before and after the new law supported the conclusion that the law's declarations of press freedom were made in vain, and that Arafat intended to continue to control the press through censorship, arrests, and closures.

Media criticism of Arafat's order to arrest Maher Alami, an editor of the Palestinian newspaper *Al-Ouds* (The Holy or Jerusalem), in late December 1995, focused on the increasing intolerance of the PNA toward the press. Critics cried foul, protesting Alami's detention and Arafat's former praise of press autonomy.

The reason Alami was being held in "preventive security" had little to do with what he had printed. Alami's blunder was running a story on page eight instead of page one, where PNA officials ordered it (Schmemann, 1995, p. 5). The press was correct in pointing out the irony: a leader with a message of peace and tolerance punished a journalist for failing to give the message proper prominence. But, while the critics focused on Alami's fate, they paid little attention to the story itself—a story replete with symbolic historical significance, identifying modern-day leaders with seventh-century conquerors.

The story that cost Maher Alami his freedom told of a Christmas Eve reception between Arafat and the Greek Orthodox patriarch, Theodoras I, who compared the meeting of himself and the PNA leader to that of a seventh-century predecessor and his guest. The predecessor received the Muslim caliph from Arabia, Umas ibn Abdal-Khattab, who, with his warriors, conquered Jerusalem and according to local lore, ". . . gave an Islamic and Arab stamp lasting until now to all of Syria (including Palestine), the Fertile Crescent, and much of North Africa" (Kimmerling & Joel, 1993, p. 4). By ordering the story to appear on page one, Arafat intended to broadcast to the world the comparison of himself to this great ancestor.

Arafat's censoring of the *Al-Ouds* editor emphasized a disturbing reality of press management and control that has been directly related to issues of freedom, state authority, and nationalism. In the conflict between nation building and partisan opposition in the press, the former was clearly more important than the latter. The Palestinian leader has demanded that the press act to further the nation-building process through support of state policies against external and internal enemies. In the absence of press support, Arafat and his officials have argued they were justified in censoring, muzzling, and suppressing editors and journalists whom they viewed as a threat to the national welfare.

Now, as in the past, state authorities recognized very early that the press was one of the most powerful tools for building community allegiance toward the government, thus advancing the officially adopted policies and political programs. In an authoritarian model, government is deemed immune from criticism; individual and press freedoms are subjected to the supremacy of governmental authority (Ayalon, 1995, p. 116). The press is not given the right to criticize the government, discredit the state, undermine the official authority, or threaten the political or economic stability of the nation. Any acceptance of the concept of freedom of the press would necessarily have to be compatible with these stated limitations: Press freedom would only be as extensive as the law would allow. Through the centuries, ruling authorities required assent to the prevailing orthodoxy; likewise, Arafat's desire to create a united front shaped the current Press Law 1995.

In the Arab world, legislation affecting the press dated to the 1857 Ottoman Law of Printing and Publications, which required prepublication approval from the Council of Education and the Ministry of Police. The following year, the Penal Code of 1858 prohibited printing material "harmful to the Sultanate, its government, and its subject peoples," under penalty of closures and fines (Ayalon, 1995,

p. 111). By 1865, the Ottoman empire introduced its first press law, the Ottoman Law of Journalistic Publications, which espoused the same principles and penalties for offending the Sultan or members of his family: 6 months to 3 years imprisonment and a fine of 25 to 150 golden pounds (Ayalon, 1995, p. 112). From the beginning of press control, the government employed the three-fold strategy of licensing, prepublication approval, and prescribed punishments that would surface over and over again throughout the history of government-press relations, foreshadowing the current press law under discussion and its promulgation of press freedom "within the limits of the law."

In more modern times, Arab governments continued their efforts to marshal the media behind their causes, attempting to stem the tide of harmful public debate and opposition. In this regard, they were no different than leaders of 20th-century democracies who justified control over the media to protect the national interest when their countries were at war. Since World War II, the Arab-Israeli conflict has provided the single most important reason to control and influence the press in order to minimize public dissent. "Because of the degree to which the Arab-Israeli dispute has become the central issue and a matter of Arab patriotism, this justification is difficult to oppose" (Rugh, 1979, p. 8).

In the face of recent developments involving peace accords and initiatives between individual Arab countries and Israel, one can only begin to imagine the difficulty inherent in attempts to reverse a line of argument that was the driving force for nearly half a century. This has been acutely evident within the autonomous areas now controlled by the PNA. The test of patriotism that once required unity of purpose to fend off the enemy has now demanded the collective embracing of a "friend." The authorities, who exacted allegiance to fight against a hostile force, now sought that same allegiance to build peace with the former enemy. To Arafat and the PNA, this new peace agenda made it imperative to have the press behind their accords with the Israeli government, and, conversely, justified severe measures to silence the opposition press resistance to them. Because of the magnitude and gravity of the policy reversal, there was zero tolerance for public debate: Mobilizing support behind the new policies justified an absolute control of the press, but not without its price. Arafat has found himself in the compromising position of speaking with forked tongue, promising press freedom and democratic policies for the new Palestine, while at the same time continuing to censor and punish journalists and individuals who speak out against him.

Both historically, and in the present time, mobilization of the press has taken both overt and subtle forms of management. In addition to legislative and regulatory laws, there are less direct ways of exerting pressure and influence. Governments have operated their own press agencies that channeled news consistent with the party line to compliant editors, who reluctantly practiced self-censorship in order to remain in their positions and keep their papers operating. Frequently, the state subsidized the press, appointed personnel who actually ran the press, or outright owned the papers. Likewise, officials stayed in direct contact with editors to make requests, clarify positions, and give directions (Rugh, 1979). These same tactics from the past used to manage the media were also being used by contemporary leaders who recognized the significance of subtle methods of press influence over more austere measures. Press management through voluntary compliance became the acceptable way to persuade editors to behave, giving them the appearance of autonomy and independence and permitting the authorities to claim the same. When all else failed, however, officials did not hesitate to censure, arrest, and fine or close down the guilty party.

The historical precedents governing the relationship between the press and the state in the Arab world became more complicated as Arab journalists learned about Western concepts of press freedom, independence, and autonomy. Respect for authority on the part of subjects, long held as sacred in Arab culture, coupled with authority's need to mobilize the press behind the regime's political programs, clashed head on with journalists' struggles to practice Western-style independence. Repeated press interference also clashed with political leaders' desire to show the world they, unlike their intolerant predecessors, were committed to democratic principles. As it was impossible to have it both ways, criticism came from home and from abroad.

The success of the 1991 peace talks leading to the implementation of Palestinian autonomy placed Arafat in the vortex of this struggle. The eventual cession of the occupied territories to the PNA raised expectations on the part of Palestinian journalists, stemming from the removal of Israeli military censorship and the statements from Arafat claiming his openness to diverse views. Since the establishment of the PNA, however, Arafat's commitment to openness repeatedly has come under fire. Multiple instances of press interference by the PNA over a period of 18 months confirmed suspicions that the new authority would be as repressive as the old—even after the creation of Press Law 1995.

Case studies of newspaper interference beginning in July of 1994 through December 1995, defined Arafat's ambivalent attitude toward press openness and exposed the problematic actions taken against offenders. Media criticism of Arafat and the PNA came from around the world as well as from Palestinian journalists. Of particular concern was the fact that the incidents occurred immediately before and after Press Law 1995, raising critical questions about the law's real meaning and significance for the operation of an independent press.

The first warning signal came from the closing of *Al-Nahar* (The Morning), a Palestinian newspaper in East Jerusalem, leaving only one major daily Palestinian newspaper, *Al-Ouds*, which is known for its pro-PLO stance. Headlines in two American newspapers shouted "Palestinians Press Arafat on Issue of Press Freedom" (Ford, 1994, p. 6) and "Mr. Arafat Tarnishes a Vision" (1994, p. 24). According to the newspaper accounts, police banned the distribution of *Al-Nahar* in Gaza and Jericho for failing to renew its circulation license with the PNA. In protest, 37 Palestinian journalists signed a petition arguing that the ban was "contrary to the democratic basis that we hope to build for our society. Hanan

Ashrawi, former member of the Palestinian delegation to Middle East peace talks and present head of an independent human rights monitoring commission for the autonomous areas, stated that the ban was a clear violation of freedom of speech and freedom of the press" (Ford, 1994, p. 6). The information minister of the PNA, Yasser Abd Rabbo, also spoke out against the ban, denying it came from his office. Daoud Kuttab, one organizer of the protest, referred to the ban as an act of a "police state, rather than one where the rule of law applies," and claimed that, since no other paper has had to file for a license, "it is so blatant that this is an attempt to stifle one particular paper" (Ford, 1994, p. 7). Protestors argued that the PNA closed *Al-Nahar* because of its pro-Jordanian stance. The paper, subsidized by the Jordanian government, reported favorably on the agreement between King Hussein of Jordan and Prime Minister Yitzhak Rabin of Israel. One month before the shutdown of *Al-Nahar*, Arafat addressed a group of journalists in Gaza, and, according to the news article, "he expected them to defend 'Palestinian national interests' in their articles" (Ford, 1994, pp. 6–7).

Shortly after raising journalists' fears of an impending rule of censorship over the *Al-Nahar* incident, Arafat attempted to win back their support by granting licenses for two new dailies: *Falastin* (Palestine), under Taher Shriteh, and *Al-Watan* (The Nation), with Imad Falouji as editor. Arafat's critics viewed licensing the two papers as a political move. The first paper claimed to be politically independent; the second, an opposition paper. Shriteh had been arrested repeatedly by Israeli military police, and had received the National Press Club's 1993 Freedom of the Press Award; Falouji, also arrested by the Israeli authorities and jailed in 1991, was a leader of Hamas, the Muslim fundamentalist movement. By giving his support to two papers with opposite viewpoints, Arafat was able to proclaim his adherence to public debate and press freedom. He was quoted as saying: "I gave Hamas a license for this paper because they are part of the Palestinian nation and have the right, within the law, to express their views. We are not afraid of the opposition. We want a lively political scene" (Parks, 1994, p. 3). One American article pointed out Arafat's public relations ploy. The article, "Full-Court Press: Newspapers Multiply as Self-Rule Transforms Gaza," belied the general impact of the story, giving as much attention to the July shutdown of *Al-Nahar*. *Al-Nahar* did not reopen until the publisher, Othman Hallaq, promised to change his pro-Jordanian support, fired his managing editor, and printed an apology to Arafat praising him as "the brother, leader and symbol of Palestinian nationalism" (Parks, 1994, p. 3). Daoud Kuttab, who led a protest against the paper's censure, lost his position on *Al-Ouds*. The same article that provided Arafat's quote supporting diverse viewpoints also printed the following two quotes, the first by Arafat and the second by his justice minister, Freih abu Medeen: "I cannot accept that our press be fed by imported ideas . . . or be bought by Arab, Western or Asian countries"; "We are not saying no to criticism or no to opposition. Our demand is that the media operate within the broad national consensus, not outside of it" (Parks, 1994, p. 3).

While the headline and reporting on *Falastin* and *Al-Watan* had a positive ring to them, the framing of the message with an introduction and a conclusion that reported on press penalties turned an apparent good-news story into negative press for Arafat and the PNA. Arafat's authoritarian actions against editors and journalists who did not follow the PNA line generated skepticism and criticism from the West as well as from his fellow Palestinians.

By April 1995, just 7 months after its creation, *Al-Watan* was in the news again along with a series of reports of crackdowns on mosques and newspapers with fundamentalist perspectives. The newspaper that Arafat previously welcomed as part of the Palestinian nation with an inherent right to express its views now saw its chief editor, Saiyed Abu Musameh, and his deputy, Ghazi Hamad, detained for an editorial comparing Arafat's harassment of "Arab militants to Israeli repression and sweeps against Hamas and Islamic Jihad before the start of Palestinian self rule in May of last year [1994]" ("Latest from Arafat's Authority," 1995). The PNA even censured the loyal *Al-Ouds* when, in August, it reported that a Hamas rally had attracted a larger group than one organized by the PLO. The paper was closed for a day, suffering the loss of its printing plates. And yet again, the PNA banned distribution of *Al-Ouds* for a week for running a paid advertisement by an Islamic group criticizing the morality of an event sponsored by the Palestinian Minister of Culture in Nablus ("Latest," 1995; see also Zima, 1995, p. 4).

Such incidents were the topic of discussion in May 1995 at a United Nations seminar for Palestinian journalists held in Madrid. The journalists told of the closing of struggling newspapers, jailing of reporters with no charges, and pressuring of editors to present news in certain ways. One journalist even claimed that press restrictions under the PNA were no less frequent than when under the Israelis (Moseley, 1995). In defense of these violations of press freedom, an editor and a director from two pro-Arafat publications, *Al-Ouds* and *Wafa*, argued that "Palestinians shouldn't ask for democracy 'in absolute terms' in their present complex circumstances" (Moseley, 1995, p. 6). These two newspapermen echoed the exact sentiments expressed by Arafat's press coordinator, Mohammed Adwan at a seminar in Atlanta, Georgia. Adwan stressed that the PNA must develop a new democracy for the peculiar circumstances of the Palestinians. He also expressed fear that giving journalists too much freedom might upset the peace process, and that it was not a bad thing to put journalists in jail for a short while to teach them a lesson (M. Adwan, personal interview, October 1995). Adwan's statement was made in October, when Press Law 1995 was 3 months old. These sentiments evidenced the immense gap that existed among journalists who sought an independent press and those who viewed the press as part of the PNA. The latter defined democracy and freedom within the limits expressed by the ruling authority, while the former espoused concepts that permit criticism and challenges to that authority without fear of reprisal.

At the time of the Madrid conference, the PNA was in the process of writing the press law that it subsequently enacted in July 1995, and which was viewed as liberal for the Middle East. Within 2 months, the media were once again reporting on press restrictions and closures. A September 1995 article in the *Middle East Times*, "Palestinian Authority Keeps Tight Reign on Press," focused on a new crisis in the Palestinian press situation, especially in Gaza. *Al Watan* was once again closed down, as were other Islamic papers, this time by an "illegal" administrative order, since the new press law permitted closures by court order only (Zima, 1995). Press Law 1995 did not seem to make a noticeable difference in the operation and function of the Palestinian press in the months immediately following its adoption, nor was there any indication that it would at any time in the future.

Press Law 1995, adopted by the Palestinian Council of Ministers on July 17 and signed by Arafat on July 25, 1995, extended "absolute" freedom to the press and all Palestinians (Press Law, 1995). Article 2 read:

> Press and Printing are free. Furthermore, the freedom of opinion should be entitled to every Palestinian individual who attains the absolute right to express his opinion in a free manner either verbally, in writing, [in] photography or [in] drawing as different means of expression and information. (Press Law, 1995)

Articles 3 and 4, however, quickly stipulated that the press would carry out all of its functions; disseminating ideas and analyzing, publishing, and commenting on them, "within the limits of the law." The following 46 articles specified regulations for personnel qualifications, ownership, licensing, and content, along with penalties for violations.

Personnel guidelines addressed the editor-in-chief or owner of a newspaper, or the director of a publication house. Editors of newspapers must be journalists, residing in Palestine and possessing a command of the paper's language; editors of a specialized press or directors of a publication house must be Palestinian or non-Palestinian nationals who served with the Palestinian Liberation Organization (PLO). Both positions stipulated degrees related to each publication's specialty, with the latter requiring a university degree. The most lenient provision was for owners of a periodical, who must be Palestinian or otherwise seek prior approval. All positions were closed to anyone convicted of a felony or misdemeanor "pertinent to immorality or dishonesty" (Articles 11, 13, 14, 16).

Licenses for newspapers, daily, nondaily, and specialized, were granted to journalists, duly registered press corporations, and political parties. The Director-General of Publishing and Printing retained the authority to license a Palestinian news agency or a foreign news agency "in accordance with the principle of reciprocity and provided that the responsible editor-in-chief is a Palestinian journalist" (Article 17). With the exception of political party papers, the license for a daily and nondaily paper required the owner to posses minimum "registered capital" of 25 or 10 thousand Jordanian dinars respectively.

By far the most critical aspects of Press Law 1995 were the lists of subject matter prohibited from publication variously distributed among many Articles, but especially mentioned in Articles 7, 8, 10, and 37; two articles, 7 and 39, dealt specifically with content aimed at children. Article 37 encompassed the most complete list of prohibited topics:

1. Secret information about police and security forces;
2. Material harmful to religion and doctrines guaranteed by law;
3. Articles which may harm national security or cite [the] committing [of] crimes or planting seed of hatred, dissension and disunity, or instigate hostilities and sectarianism among the members of society;
4. Minutes of the secret sessions of the Palestinian National Council, the Council of Ministers and the PNA;
5. Articles and news which aim at shaking belief in the national currency;
6. Material harmful to an individual's dignity, personal convictions and liberties or personal reputation;
7. Material inconsistent with morals;
8. Advertisements of drugs, medicine, or cigarettes without prior approval.

Article 37 also forbade the import of any publications from abroad if they contained prohibited materials for publishing by virtue of Press Law 1995 (Press Law, 1995). Article 7 specifically prohibited the publication of any material addressed to children and teenagers "that could hamper the morals, values and Palestinian traditions" (Press Law, 1995).

Other prohibitions not listed in Article 37, but affecting the regulation of content were the prohibitions against publishing (1) court proceedings from lawsuits prior to the final verdict or of lawsuits involving children under 16 years of age (Press Law, 1995), and (2) material that contradicts the principle of freedom, national responsibilities, human rights, and respect of truth (Press Law, 1995).

Although most of the law declared what may not be published, five articles, 25 to 29, influenced content by addressing steps editors must follow to rectify mistakes or misinformation printed in their publications. Of particular interest was Article 26, which mentioned "inaccurate information pertinent to public interest." In such cases, the editor-in-chief must publish a correction free of charge (Press Law, 1995).

Finally, several articles indirectly influenced content through the regulation of potential foreign influence. Article 9 cited a prohibition that outlawed material support or instructions from any foreign country without prior approval from the Minister of Information (Press Law, 1995). In addition, Article 10 prohibited journalists from "establishing a business-like relationship with any foreign body, unless it has been established by the rules of the foreign information media correspondence system issued by virtue of this law" (Press Law, 1995).

Corresponding penalties to all violations involved either imprisonment or fines, or both, or the seizure or confiscation of all printed publications. Article 45, the severest, stipulated that anyone found in violation of Article 9 (assistance from foreign countries without prior approval) would receive punishment in the form of

4 to 6 months in jail or a fine of not less than 4,000 or more than 6,000 Jordanian dinars (Press Law, 1995). Penalties for all other violations fell between 1 and 2 months in jail or 500 to 2000 Jordanian dinars (Press Law, 1995). In addition to fines and imprisonment, Article 47 provided for the more drastic punishments of confiscation and temporary suspension of offending newspapers. These measures were reserved solely for violations against the prohibition against publishing the matters listed in Article 37 (material harmful to national interests, religion, economic stability, and so on). It is significant that the article empowered the "competent authority" to confiscate newspapers by administrative rule, only, as opposed to by court order, thus giving the authority direct and immediate power to act quickly against violators (Press Law, 1995). The law lacked a certain clarity regarding issues of due process; however, Articles 42 and 43 indicated that a public right lawsuit would be lodged against those deemed in violation of the law's provisions, and that the "competent court" would be responsible for determining this and the public prosecutor would then "investigate the validity of powers and procedures prescribed by [the] applicable penalty codes" (Press Law, 1995).

Unfortunately, little examination or analysis of Press Law 1995 existed at the time of this research. Although the English translation, supplied by the Minister of Information's Translation Office, was official, it did not have accompanying notes or clarifications to assist in determining exact meanings. In spite of this constraint, the intentions of the law were conclusive—to manage and control all forms of publication and the circumstances surrounding their operation. Thus, Press Law 1995 dictated that:

- Top press personnel were to be former supporters of the PLO;
- Owners of newspapers must possess needed capitol;
- Foreign investment and assistance in newspapers would require preapproval from the PNA;
- Content would be subject to an extensive list of material prohibited for publication; and
- Severe penalties would be attached to violations.

The restrictive nature of the law confirmed any doubts that Arafat and the PNA intended strong controlling measures in order to safeguard their political policies and programs, to oblige the press to function as their promoter, and to ensure the press's compliance through fear of fines, imprisonment, confiscation, and closure.

The disturbing consequence of Press Law 1995 was that it completely undermined the generous statement of freedom of the press and of opinion for the Palestinian people stated in Article 2. By defining freedom "within the limits of the law" proclaiming it, Press Law 1995 delivered freedom to the Palestinians bound in shackles. There was little difference between this law and other earlier versions that, in the guise of national interests, put absolute allegiance to authority over individual and press freedoms. That the law did not deliver more was disappointing.

Arafat had a worthy political agenda, namely peace accords with Israel; he needed credibility for his efforts to build national unity among the Palestinian Arabs around this agenda: A liberalizing press law would have brought him closer to the image of himself as a new democratic Arab leader he projected to the world. Instead, he chose to achieve support by suppressing dissent and by equating criticism with criminality. Arafat's acts of press intolerance, as well as the adoption of Press Law 1995, showed that he cannot have it both ways. Although Article 2 of the law extended freedom of the press and public opinion, Articles 7, 8, 10, 37, and 39 provided severe restraints, which Arafat was only too willing to impose.

DISCUSSION QUESTIONS

1.   What are the consequences of Press Law 1995 for the Palestinian region? Explain your answer.
2.   How does Press Law 1995 undermine the statement of freedom of the press and of opinion for the Palestinian people?
3.   Which articles of the new law have indirectly influenced content through the regulation of potential foreign influence? Explain.
4.   The success of the 1991 peace talks led to the implementation of Palestinian autonomy, and placed Arafat in the vortex of struggle. How did the cession of the occupied territories to the PNA lead to raised expectations on the part of Palestinian journalists for openness and diverse views?
5.   How does Arafat use the Palestinian press to further PNA control?

REFERENCES

Ayalon, A. (1995). *The press in the Arab Middle East: A history.* New York and Oxford: Oxford University Press.
Ford, P. (1994, August 4). Palestinians press Arafat on issue of press freedom. *Christian Science Monitor,* p. 6.
Kimmerling, B., & Joel, S. M. (1993). *Palestinians: The making of a people.* New York: Free Press.
Latest from Arafat's Authority. (1995, April 10-12). *Al-Akhbar,* IPA News [Online]. Available: iap@io.org
Mr. Arafat tarnishes a vision. (1994, August 5). *New York Times,* p. 24.
Moseley, R. (1995, May 28). Arafat in no rush to embrace freedom of the press. *Chicago Tribune,* p. 6.
Parks, M. (1994, September 20). A full-court press: Newspapers multiply as self-rule transforms Gaza. *New York Times,* p. 3.
Press Law. (1995). Articles 2–47, pp. 2–13. Palestinian National Authority, Ministry of Information, Translation Department, Directorate of External Media and Relations, Ministry of Information.

Rugh,W. A. (1979). *The Arab press: News media and political process in the Arab World.* Syracuse, NY: Syracuse University Press.

Schmemann, S. (1996, January 22). Elections: A dawn for Palestinians, legitimacy for Arafat. *New York Times*, pp. 3, 14.

Schmemann, S. (1995, December 31). Palestinian Christians feeling like a minority. *New York Times,* The Week in Review section, p. 5.

Zima, S. (1995, September 24-30). Palestinian authority keeps tight rein on press. *Middle East Times,* p. 4.

15

EGYPTIAN PRESS JOURNALISTS' PROFESSIONAL STANDARDS AND THE CHALLENGE OF PRIVATIZATION*

Yorck von Korff

INTRODUCTION

The Egyptian newspaper market is shifting, if only slightly. Even though the reprivatization of the domineering national papers is ruled out by government officials, a very partial privatization of the market is taking place through the introduction of a new private press. The new element is still rather small compared to the political party and the national press. However small, the private press has the chance to distinguish itself from the politically dependent papers by more balanced, objective, accurate, and therefore trustworthy reporting. At a first glance, the new papers do not seem to meet the challenge. In the intra-Egyptian debate about the "yellow press" at the beginning of 1998, the private press, in particular, was attacked for violating these standards. However, semiofficial and party newspapers such as *Rûz al-Yûsuf* and *al-Sha^cb* also were criticized.[1]

This chapter investigates whether professional ethics are, indeed, flagging in Egypt and what journalists can do by themselves to improve their standards. Many journalists and editors in the fledgling private press are and will be drawn from the

*Research for this article was supported by a grant of the German Academic Exchange Service.

existing newspaper infrastructure; that is, the national and the party press. Therefore, the professional standards of these journalists will be considered. Through surveys of Egyptian journalists, this chapter attempts to estimate to what extent problems exist and what can be done to overcome these problems. In subsequent chapters, other authors will briefly analyze the performance of the new private press. Before professional standards can be discussed, however, the working environment of Egyptian journalists shall be depicted as well as the development that has led to the growth of the private press.

DEVELOPMENT OF THE EGYPTIAN PRESS

President Nasser nationalized the Egyptian press in 1960. Before the revolution in 1952, there had been private party and semiofficial publications. Marina Stagh wrote in 1986 about this period: "In spite of intermittent censorship and harassment of the press, the debate has never been as intense and the freedom of expression never as wide as in these years . . . ." (p. 76). However, as Ami Ayalon notes, the professional heritage of that period is not necessarily one of consistently high standards. While some papers such as *al-Ahrâm* and *al-Muqattam* guaranteed high-quality reporting by remaining aloof from the muddy waters of central domestic issues, other papers became involved and showed much less restraint. "Whenever they were allowed to, journalists would criticize, attack, and offend, using colorful language and passionate expression . . . . Some journalists regularly lashed out at leaders of rival parties or at high state officials in columns carrying such titles as 'Facts and Rubbish,' or 'From a Filthy Well'. . . . 'You Whore' [is] a typical instance of the unrestrained style often employed by the press in the verbal battles of that period" (Ayalon, 1995, p. 26).

Freedom of expression was drastically curbed after the revolution and the nationalized press started to write "all the news that fits the president" as Munir K. Nasser put it (1982, p. 189). After the failure of Nasser's socialist nationalism in 1967 with the disastrous Arab defeat against Israel, President Sadat, who succeeded Nasser in 1970, opened the economy and the political system to a certain extent. As part of this policy, he added some pluralism to the monolithic national press when he reintroduced opposition parties and consequently granted them their own papers in 1977. However, strict press laws, such as imprisonment for publication offenses, remained. Equally problematic was the fact that it was nearly impossible for private individuals to open a newspaper.

Nevertheless, journalists began to enjoy an ambiguous freedom under Sadat. They could criticize, but a sword was dangling over their heads and they never knew exactly when it would descend. For the party press, this sword consisted mostly of the harsh penal laws; for the journalists in the national[2] press, the loss of career opportunities and other benefits loomed. Consequently, most journalists in the national press conformed to rallying the population behind the policies of the regime. There were, however, also important critical voices in these papers. The party press was less shy and started to attack the government relatively unabashedly. Topics were the normalization with Israel, economic policies, and freedom of expression (Nasser, 1990). Although Sadat preferred for the most part to ignore these and other attacks, he finally lost patience in September 1981, and 1 month before his assassination, he imprisoned more than 3,000 opposition figures, among them many journalists.

Under Sadat's successor, Mubarak, the number of party papers continued to grow. But the new president did not ease legal and political constraints on parties, professional syndicates, nongovernmental organizations (NGOs), and the press. The government also kept its control over the national press by appointing editors-in-chief. Thus, the ambiguous freedom of journalists endures. In February 1998, the private paper, al-Dustûr, was closed down for printing an alleged statement of an Islamic militant group. Shortly thereafter, an editor-in-chief and his deputy of a national magazine lost their jobs after they printed the same statement. In the first half of 1998, four journalists were imprisoned for publication offenses.

Despite the political freeze, changes happened in the national economy. Pushed since 1991 by the International Monetary Fund (IMF), the government began to privatize big national companies. As of 1998, more than 100 companies have been sold. And while television and radio remain firmly in the hands of the state, a new category of newspapers, described as private papers, started to become more prominent. Two main categories have to be distinguished here: private papers licensed in Egypt, and Egyptian-based papers with a foreign license.

Private Papers Licensed in Egypt

Until 1996, it was legally very difficult to open a private Egyptian newspaper. A license could only be obtained through a private shareholder company.[3] In this company, no shareholder had the right to hold more than 0.2 percent of the capital. The company also had to obtain approval of at least eight government authorities. From 1952 until 1996, no such paper was ever created (Ibrahîm, 1996). However, things started to change in 1996. The law was eased, and so far five new private papers have been issued.[4] Four of them are weeklies and concerned with general topics, including politics; one is a monthly sports magazine.[5] However, whether this trend to Egyptian-licensed papers will continue is doubtful: At the beginning of 1998, the government again raised the hurdles for obtaining a license by legally requiring the approval of the cabinet for the new paper.

Egyptian-based Papers with a Foreign License (the "Cyprus Press")

One loophole in the restrictive Egyptian publication laws for private publishers was the option to have the paper licensed abroad, in London, Athens, or Nicosia. After printing two or three issues abroad, the paper would normally apply at the Ministry

TABLE 15.1.
Daily Egyptian Papers

	National Press	Party Press	Private Press
Number	7	2	1
Distribution	3,000,000	200,000	5,000[a]

Sources: State Information Service (Internet) and *World Media Handbook* (1995), pp. 90–91.
[a]Exists since 1996.

of Information for the permission to print it in Egypt, and in many cases the Ministry would grant this license. The advantage for the authorities as compared to the Egyptian-licensed papers is the legal option of applying an import-censorship or of withdrawing the printing permission.

Even though these papers are legally foreign, they have to be considered Egyptian. The headquarters of the papers would normally be in Cairo, most articles deal with Egypt, and the staff consist of Egyptians, or in case of English-language papers, at least of journalists who live in Egypt. There are no official figures about the development of the so-called Cyprus press,[6] but there is some evidence that it has been a growing phenomenon in the 1990s.[7] However, even so, the private press can account for only a small share of the newspaper market. This is especially true for the dailies, as Table 15.1 shows. Among the weeklies, the showing of the private press is stronger. Their numbers are reported to have risen at least above 40 (*Cairo Times*, April 16–27, 1998).[8]

PROBLEMS OF EGYPTIAN JOURNALISTS' PROFESSIONAL STANDARDS

As the preceding discussion illustrates, it can be shown that the private press is slowly growing into an environment of ambiguity. The question now involves how journalists use this freedom. Are they trying to earn respect and influence for their profession by applying high ethical standards? Or do they waste the leeway they have by squandering their professional credibility? Three problem areas of professional standards can be distinguished: (1) conflicts of personal interests and professional standards, (2) critical attitudes, and (3) work performance.

Conflicts of Personal Interests and Professional Standards

Conflicts of interests occur when personal interests of journalists or corporate interests of the newspaper clash with professional standards. Two main problems can be distinguished: the admittance of advertiser influence on news content, and the acceptance of "presents" or personal favors for positive news coverage.

The Admittance of Advertiser Influence on News Content

Egyptian journalists are well aware of the problem of advertiser influence. Their code of ethics, as proposed by the Egyptian press syndicate in 1996, states that, "It is not permitted for the journalist to acquire or edit advertisements, neither to receive any direct or indirect payment for the review, editing or publication of advertisements. Besides, he must not sign any advertisement with his name" (Niqâba al-Suhufîyîn, 1996). How widespread is the problem? The Higher Press Council, a government-controlled supervisory board of the press, counted the instances in which Egyptian papers did not distinguish advertisements from news (Table 15.2). If advertisements are not labeled as such, advertisers naturally increase their influence over the readers of the newspapers. Thus, readers will not always be able to distinguish between an ad and a piece of news, and might be misled.

As evidenced in Table 15.2, sloppy advertisement practices seem to occur rather frequently among the papers that run many advertisements.[9] The recurrent negligence in the separation of news from advertisements also nourishes the suspicion that advertisers wield undue influence over the editors of the Egyptian press. This

TABLE 15.2.
Number of Cases in Which a Publication Did Not Distinguish from Advertisements

Type of Publication	Name (Number of Cases)
National dailies	al-Ahrâm (95)
	al-Ahrâm, al-Masâ'i (13)
	al-Akhbâr (34)
	al-Jumhûrîya (6)
	al-Masâ (8)
Party weeklies	Mâyû (18)
	al-Shaᶜb (2)
	al-Ahâlî (2)
	al-Ahrâr (5)
	al-Wafd (8)
National weekly magazines	al-Musawwar (74)
	Âkhir Sâᶜa (23)
	Rûz al Yûsuf (27)
	Hurrîyatî (8)
	Uktûbar (8)
	Sabâh al-Khair (3)

Source: Higher Press Council, *Annual Report* (1992) (latest available figures).
Note: al-Wafd is a daily, al-Shaᶜb, biweekly.

TABLE 15.3.
Survey Results Regarding Extent of Advertiser Influence

The Egyptian press hesitates to publish news that could hurt some advertisers	Strongly agree	Agree	Agree somewhat	Disagree	Strongly disagree
Percent (n = 20)	30%	35%	20%	10%	5%

Source: Bakhît (1996), annex p. 41.

suspicion is further confirmed by the fact that in some newspapers, among them *al-Ahrâm*, *al-Akhbâr*, and *al-Jumhûrîya*, the business and the editorial chief executive posts are not separated but, on the contrary, are united in one person.[10] The Egyptian journalists' code of ethics is thus already violated in the basic and important structural arrangements of some newspapers.[11] In a survey, 20 editors-in-chief and leading journalists said that the Egyptian press would hesitate to publish news that could hurt the interests of some advertisers (Table 15.3).[12]

In light of these results, it seems justified to assume a worrisome degree of advertiser influence on at least some leading Egyptian papers and magazines. However, the problematic influence of business interests on Egyptian journalism does not stop here.

The Acceptance of Presents or Personal Favors

One problem most Egyptian journalists mention is that their salaries are too low to provide for a decent middle-class life. Less than 17 percent of the 125 journalists questioned by Bakhit in 1991 relied solely on their first salary (Bakhît, 1996). One solution to this problem for many journalists is to work for a second or third newspaper or in a totally different job. Another "solution" is the acceptance of bribes and personal favors for favorable news coverage. In a 1995 survey, El Nawawy questioned 34 experts on the Egyptian media, mostly Egyptian scholars and distinguished journalists, regarding their impression about the occurrence of these practices. As Table 15.4 shows, most of the experts strongly believed in the existence of corrupting habits. Journalists themselves in another survey confirmed this impression, albeit to a lesser degree, as Table 15.5 shows.

Even if the extent of bribing cannot be known exactly, with the available data it seems fair to state that bribes constitute a noticeable phenomenon of journalists' culture in Egypt.

Critical Attitudes

Among the tasks of journalists—besides reporting facts—are to question the performance of decision makers; to analyze the political, economic, social, and cultural status quo; to expose problems; and to propose solutions. These activities

TABLE 15.4.

Survey Results of 34 Experts on the Egyptian Media

Accepting gifts and special favors by Egyptian journalists and considering these gifts part of the benefit of their job make journalists lose their social respect and dignity	Strongly agree	Agree	Disagree	Strongly disagree	Don't know
n = 34	24	9	0	0	1

Source: El Nawawy (1995), p. 111.

can be understood as constructive criticism that is an essential ingredient of successful progress and development for any social entity. In order to be able to utter constructive criticism, journalists have to develop critical attitudes.

To gain an idea about critical attitudes of Egyptian journalists, one has to look at their stance towards the role of the media and journalism. The available data give a somewhat ambiguous impression. It seems that the majority of Egyptian journalists are well aware of the importance of a critical attitude. Questioned by Bakhît about their ideal roles as journalists, more than three quarters of those surveyed said it was "important" or "very important" to analyze and explain difficult problems to readers and to scrutinize policies announced by the government (Bakhît, 1996, annex p. 20). However, when asked more directly about their ideal role concerning the treatment of news, only a minority of journalists, opposition and national journalists alike, depicted critical stances, as Table 15.6 shows.

A similarly ambiguous picture was the result of a 1995 random survey of 48 Egyptian journalists who were asked about the importance of news media. Most of the sample said it was important to create an informed electorate, help build democratic institutions, expose corruption in government, and expose all points of views on public issues. However, the majority of these journalists also said that it was important to support government policy, mobilize the public for economic development, support the stability of the current regime, and refrain from criticizing

TABLE 15.5.

Survey Results of 118 Journalists

The low income of journalists leads to their acceptance of presents and the publication of news flattering the donors	Agree	Agree somewhat	No opinion	Disagree
Percent (n = 118)	31.4	49.2	2.5	16.9

Source: Bakhît (1996), p. 26.

TABLE 15.6.
Survey Results Regarding Proper Role of Journalists

The role of the journalist should be confined to (n = 125[a])	Yes		No		
	National	Party	National	Party	Total
Presenting news	29.6%	33.6%	23.2%	13.6%	100%
Selecting news	15.2%	8.8%	37.6%	38.4%	100%
Analyzing the news	9.6%	14.4%	43.2%	32.8%	100%
Commenting on the news	7.2%	6.4%	45.6%	40.8%	100%

Source: Bakhît (1996), p. 20.
[a]Of the questioned journalists, 65 were from national, 60 from party papers, among them journalists of the ruling party paper *Mâyû*.

the government. And when the surveyed journalists had to rank the importance of news media, almost one third (the biggest singular group) said the most important purpose was to support government policy. Only one journalist considered it to be most important to serve as a critic of the government. In addition, the majority of the questioned journalists found it inappropriate for newspapers to inform about corruption at highest levels of government, about failed government development projects, or about negative consequences of economic reform in Egypt (Napoli, Amin, & Boylan, 1995a).

The aforementioned answers suggest that there are a number of journalists with constructive critical attitudes. This is also confirmed by impressionistic evidence from articles in the national and the party press: The national papers often contain several articles that are truly critical of government policies. And at least in some party papers, critical articles that are based on facts and not on rumors can be found. On the other hand, the data presented here also suggests that critical attitudes are not firmly established among a considerable segment of Egypt's journalists.

Work Performance

Work performance can be assessed in terms of the accuracy and balance of the journalists' products. Accurate and balanced reporting results in credibility, trustworthiness, and objectivity of the press. Inaccurate and biased reporting results in loss of trust and credibility.

Similar to any press in the world, the Egyptian press has had its scandals due to violations of basic journalistic standards. The question here is whether a weak work performance is an exception, whether it is normally confined to some papers (as in the West) or whether it exists throughout the Egyptian press. To gain a clearer picture of this issue, let us look next at some aspects of journalists' work standards.

PRESS ACCURACY

Surveys among journalists and media experts as well as impressionistic evidence of the press itself point to the recurrence of some flaws in the accuracy of reporting in the Egyptian press. These flaws are expressed in a tendency to exaggeration, sensationalism, and obscuring of sources, and in simple sloppiness. This is confirmed by the surveys of El Nawawy and Hammâda (Table 15.7). Top journalists asked by Bakhît would also confirm a tendency to sensationalism in the Egyptian press, and for the party press the tendency not to give sources (1996).

BALANCE AND BIAS

A problem of probably bigger scope than inaccuracy is bias in the Egyptian press. Because national papers are controlled by the government and opposition papers by political parties, this cannot come as a surprise. The majority of journalists questioned by Bakhît confirmed that working for a national or a party paper prevents journalists from being objective (1996). Journalists in general would also confirm the widespread tendency to self-censorship.

Editors-in-chief questioned by Bakhît pointed out that the national press mostly tries to justify the measures of the government while the opposition press, rather, tries to criticize them (1996). Content analyses by Ibrahîm (1994) and ᶜAli Ahmad (1996) confirm that party papers report considerably more about their party than about others, whereas the national papers report almost exclusively about the ruling National Democratic Party and neglect other parties. This, however, does not mean

TABLE 15.7.
Survey Results Regarding Press Accuracy

	Strongly disagree	Disagree	Agree	Strongly agree	Don't know
Distorting the content of news by being inaccurate or not thorough in reporting leads to the loss of credibility in the Egyptian press (n = 33)[a]	0	1	9	18	5
The tendency of the press to sensationalism and exaggeration prevents it from influencing decision making (n = 75)[b]	3	33	43	21	0
The national and the party papers lose their credibility by reporting unattributed incorrect news, which opens the market for independent foreign papers (n = 33)[a]	0	2	11	21	0

Sources: [a]El Nawawy (1995), pp. 111, 116. [b]Hammâda (1991), p. 595.
Note: Hammâda's fifth category was called "neutral" rather than "don't know."

that differing opinions are not given in the party or national press. Two thirds of the 125 journalists questioned by Bakhît said that the national papers did not neglect other opinions, and slightly more than half of those questioned would not describe the coverage of the opposition papers as "narrow-minded," while just under half indicated that coverage was indeed, narrow-minded (1996, p. 24). We thus gain the impression of a biased reporting style that nevertheless contains some variety in opinion.

Although some flaws in the work performance such as bias and self-censorship are probably due mainly to political constraints on journalists, inaccuracy and sensationalism in all likelihood are not, or are only partly so. The perception is therefore a lack of commitment and responsibility among an important segment of Egyptian journalists. This is an impression that is echoed by the editors-in-chief questioned by Bakhît (1996).

This lack of commitment, accuracy, and balance bodes ill for a credible and thus influential Egyptian press. The lack of critical attitudes on the part of journalists, and the palpable occurrence of corruption, further the weakness of the press. In this environment, the private press is springing up. The first impressions about its performance are mixed.

PERFORMANCE OF THE PRIVATE PRESS

No content analyses about the fledgling private press have been made available. But according to impressionistic evidence, it is possible to differentiate three categories of private papers: specialized magazines, Arabic-language papers of general interest, and English-language papers of general interest.

Specialized Magazines

These magazines can be in Arabic or in English and normally focus on lifestyles, the arts, women's issues, sports, business, or other specialized topics and touch politics rather infrequently. Some of them reach very high quality standards not only in terms of design and layout but also regarding accuracy and thoroughness of reporting. According to Napoli, Amin, and Napoli, this sector of the private press has been booming for more than a decade. It is also exposed to successful competition by some Saudi-financed magazines such as *Satellite Guide* or *Sayedati*, a woman's magazine (Napoli, Amin, & Napoli, 1995b, p. 52). A popular Egyptian Arab-language magazine is *Lamsa*. English-language magazines include *Egypt Today*, *Business Today,* and *Egypt Insight*. These magazines normally touch politics rather infrequently. Thus, the growth of politically critical attitudes should not be expected from this segment of the press.

Arabic-language Papers of General Interest

There are growing numbers of Arabic language papers, containing everything from political issues to sports and gossip; most of these are weeklies. However, the quality and the trustworthiness of these papers appear doubtful. While some papers such as *al-Maidân* and *al-Naba* try to entertain their readers mainly with pictures of scantily clad girls and juicy articles, others such as *al-Usbû^c* focus more on stories about alleged American and Zionist plots against Egypt and the Arabs, and are characterized by intemperate language and absurd speculations. In this category can be found all the flaws that could be observed in the national and the party press: structurally high advertiser influences, biased and inaccurate reporting, and uncritical commentaries. A reliable and comprehensive private Arabic newsmagazine is still lacking.

A possible exception in this category is the business daily *al-^{c}Âlam al-Yawm*. Its news section appears to be more reliable than those of the other papers. However, this paper focuses mainly on the economy and, with an estimated distribution of 5,000, reaches only a very small and elite segment of the population that is generally well informed, in any event.

English-language Papers of General Interest

In this category, we find only two major papers, the weekly *Middle East Times* and the fortnightly *Cairo Times*. The *Middle East Times* used to be a reliable source of information about political and economic events in Egypt and the Middle East. With many recent changes in the staff of the paper, it is doubtful if the paper can keep up this standard. The *Cairo Times*, however, which is published by an Egyptian, has developed into a very high-quality paper, certainly meeting high journalistic standards. It demonstrates that independent high-quality reporting and critical analysis can be realized in Egypt. Owing to its high cost-per-issue, when compared to the average Egyptian salary, and the fact that it is printed in English, the paper most likely reaches only a tiny, educationally elite segment of the Egyptian population.

CONCLUSION

This chapter has considered whether Egyptian journalists are ready to meet the challenge of a growing private press in terms of professional standards. The professional cultures of journalists in the party and in the national press were scrutinized on the basis of surveys among experts and journalists. As a result, weaknesses in the form of undue advertiser influence, bribes, uncritical attitudes, inaccurate and unbalanced reporting were found to be salient phenomena among noticeable segments of journalists. It could be shown that these flaws have a tradition that reaches back to the prerevolutionary era. Part of this culture could be attributed to the politically determined structure of the press, as, in particular, the governments of Nasser (national press) and Sadat (party press) devised it. And, restrictions on journalists in forms of tight press laws have not ceased to exist. Thus, a journalist is likely to self-censor his or her articles, to not develop critical attitudes, and to report in a biased way. However, unnecessary advertiser influence, inaccurate reporting, and corruption are by no means a necessary consequence of the political system. They can perhaps be best be explained by a lack of commitment to basic journalistic values by the individual journalist.

By looking at the development of the fledgling private press, it becomes clear that the prevalent weaknesses of journalists' standards in the national and party press have, to a certain extent, spilled over into the private press even though the latter should ideally be free of political allegiances. The not politically generated flaws of exaggerated advertiser influence, intemperate language, inaccurate reporting, speculations, and doubtful stories can be found particularly in the Arab-language general interest papers. These flaws could damage the reputation of the private press altogether.

The current situation means that journalists have a great opportunity for improvement. Instead of reorganizing journalistic education on a big scale—a project that would probably be doomed to fail from the outset—the establishment of a model paper could prove successful. A general interest Arab-language quality paper is still lacking. The *Cairo Times* has proven that it is possible to issue such a paper in English. If a privately owned, Arabic, quality newspaper should be started, it could serve as a practical school for Egyptian journalists and set an example for a new type of journalism in Egypt.

DISCUSSION QUESTIONS

1. How might the salient phenomenon of "inaccurate and unbalanced reporting" be explained in terms of Egyptian history and tradition that reaches back to the prerevolutionary era, or as it might be attributed to the politically determined structure of the press in the governments of Nasser (national press) and Sadat (party press)?
2. What types of advertiser influence may lead to inaccurate and unbalanced reporting in Egypt?
3. Is there a significant difference between "specialized magazines" and "general newspapers" as this issue pertains to the ethics of journalists in Egypt?
4. How does the idea of critical attitudes among Egyptian journalists contribute to journalists' stance toward the role of the media and journalism, according to the results of this survey? What impression do the available data provide concerning the importance of a critical attitude among Egyptian journalists?

5. Compare the compensation plans of Western and Egyptian journalists. How might a compensation package directly affect news reporting?

NOTES

[1] For an impression of the debate, look at, for example, *Middle East Times*, March 13–19 and March 27–April 2, 1998; *Al-Ahram Weekly*, April 2–8, 1998, and *Cairo Times* April 16–29, 1998.

[2] The term "national press" is used here interchangeably with semiofficial press.

[3] The law also provides the option of obtaining a license through a cooperative. However, as Ibrahim holds, it is very difficult to adjust the operating principles of a cooperative to the requirements of newspaper management (Ibrahîm, 1996, p. 172).

[4] Two of them were issued in 1996, still under the old law; information provided in September 1997 by the Director General of the Higher Press Council, Ossam Farag.

[5] Information provided in September 1998 by the Director General of the Higher Press Council, Ossam Farag. The names of the weeklies are *Al-Mida An-Naba, Usbua, Saut Al-Umma*. The monthly is called *Al-Malaib Al-Arabiya*.

[6] The officials in charge in the Ministry of Information refuse to release any data.

[7] This was, for example, reported in an article by the usually very reliable *Cairo Times* (April 16–29, 1998). Compare also Napoli, Amin, and Napoli (1995b, p. 52).

[8] Official figures about distribution of the private press are not given by authorities.

[9] When analyzing the figures in Table 15.2, one has to be aware that *Al-Ahram* attracts the bulk of advertisements, while some party papers receive almost none.

[10] Philip Meyer and other academics concerned with journalistic ethics strongly doubt the ability of a newspaper to prevent business interests—connected to advertisement—from unduly influencing the content of a paper if the business and the editorial sides are not strictly separated (Meyer, 1987; see also Hanlin, 1992).

[11] The Egypt journalists' draft code of ethics from 1996 states in its first articles that a journalist should be committed in his or her work to dignity, reliability, and truth as well as objectivity and accuracy, and that he or she should refrain from hurting the freedoms of other people.

[12] This was clearly confirmed by journalists in all the surveys.

REFERENCES

cAli Ahmad, A. (1996). *Al-Hamalât al-Suhufîya fî al-Sihâfa al-Misrîya wa Dawruhâ fî Mucâlaja Qadâyâ wa Mushkilât al-Mujtamc al-Misrî. Dirâsa Tahlîlîya Muqârina baina al-Sihâfa al-Qawmîya wa al-Sihâfa al-Hizbîya min Mâris 1984 hattâ Nihâya 1989*. [Campaigns in the Egyptian press and their role in treating issues and problems of Egyptian society. An analytical study comparing the national and the party press from March 1984 to the end of 1989]. Unpublished doctoral dissertation, al-Azhâr University, Faculty of Arabic Language, Cairo, Egypt.

Ayalon, A. (1995). Journalists and the press: The vicissitudes of licensed pluralism. In S. Shimon (Ed.), *Egypt from monarchy to republic: A reassessment of revolution and change*. Oxford: Oxford University Press.

Bakhît, al-S. (1996). *Qîyam al-Akhbâr fî al-Sihâfa al-Misrîya fî Itâr al-Siyâsât al-Tanmawîa. Dirâsya Tatbîqîya fî al-Sihâfa al-Qawmîya wa al-Sihâfa al-Hizbîya khilâl 1987–1990* [News values in the Egyptian press regarding development policies. A study of the national and party press from 1987 to 1990]. Unpublished doctoral dissertation, Cairo University, Faculty of Media, Egypt.

El Nawawy, M. A. (1995). *Journalism, professionalism, and information control.* Unpublished masters thesis, American University in Cairo, Egypt.

Hammâda, B. I. (1991). *Dawr Wasâ 'il al-Ittisâl al-Misrîya fî Sanâ^{c}a al-Qarârât. Dirâsa Tatbîqîya ^{c}alâ Sâni^c al-Qarâr fî Misr* [The role of Egyptian communication media in decision making. A study of the decision maker in Egypt]. Unpublished doctoral dissertation, Cairo University, Faculty of Media, Egypt.

Hanlin, B. (1992). Owners, editors and journalists. In A. Belsey & R. Chadwick (Eds.), *Ethical issues in journalism and the media* (pp. 33–48). New York: Routledge.

Ibrahîm, M. S. (1994). *Al-Dawr al-Tanmawî lî al-Sihâfa al-Misrîya fî Itâr al-Ta^c addudîya al-Hizbîya khilâl fitra 1977–88* [The role of the Egyptian press in development with regard to multipartyism during 1977 to 88]. Unpublished doctoral dissertation, Cairo University, Faculty of Media, Egypt.

Ibrahîm, M. S. (1996). *Hurrîya al-Sihâfa. Dirâsa fî Siyâsa al-Tashri^{c}îya wa ^{c}Alâqathâ bî al-Tatawwar al-Dîmuqrâtî* [The freedom of the press. A study of legislative policy and its relationship to democratization]. Cairo, Egypt: Dâr al-Kutub al-^{c}Ilmîya lî al-Nashr wa al-Tawzî^c.

Meyer, P. (1987). *Ethical journalism: A guide for students, practitioners, and consumers.* Lanham, MD: University Press of America.

Napoli, J. J., Amin, H., & Boylan, R. (1995a). *Final report assessment of the Egyptian print and electronic media.* Unpublished study, Department of Mass Communication, American University in Cairo, Egypt.

Napoli, J. J., Amin, H., & Napoli, L. (1995b, Summer). Privatization of the Egyptian media. *Journal of South Asian and Middle Eastern Studies, XVIII*(4), 39–57.

Nasser, M. K. (1990, December). Egyptian media under Nasser and Sadat: Two models of press management and control. *Journalism Monographs, 124,* 1–26.

Nasser, M. K. (1982). The Middle East press: Tool of politics. In J. L. Curry & J. R. Dassin (Ed.), *Press control around the world* (pp. 187–208). New York: Praeger.

Niqâba al-Suhufîyîn [Journalist's Syndicate]. (Ed.). (1996). *Mithâq al-Sharf al-Suhufî. Mashru^c Mithâq al-Sharf al-Suhufî Muqaddam ilâ al-Jam^{c}îya al-^{c}Amûmîya lî al-Niqâba* [The press code. The press code project presented to the Syndicate's General Assembly]. Cairo, Egypt: Egyptian Journalist's Syndicate.

Stagh, M. (1986). The press in Egypt: How free is the freedom of speech? In M. Laanatza (Ed.), *Egypt under pressure: A contribution to the understanding of economic social and cultural aspects of Egypt today* (pp. 70–93). Uppsala, Sweden: Scandinavian Institute of African Studies.

16

EGYPTIAN AND PALESTINIAN PRESS LAWS: PROSPECTS AND CONCERNS

James J. Napoli
Western Washington University

Carolyn Crimmins
Leonard Ray Teel
Georgia State University

INTRODUCTION

Governments in the established nation of Egypt and the emerging Palestinian Authority have both found it necessary to exercise control over their press. This chapter on Egyptian and Palestinian press laws focuses on the major developments of 1995. The chapter reflects numerous similarities and differences in the nature of the problems, and in the approach taken by the two governments. Certain differences are also evident. Egypt is an ancient nation with well-defined geography, independent since its revolution in 1952 from colonial domination. The Palestinian National Authority (PNA), not yet a nation and with control over noncontiguous urban areas and the Gaza Strip, is an ill-defined entity of only recent creation.

This emerging national impetus marks a fundamental difference between the two press systems. Egypt's press, now two generations removed from the revolution, no longer evidences the vigor and diversity associated with the "independence press" during the end of the era of imperialism and colonialism. Indeed, researchers concluded in 1995 that the Egyptian press is no longer characterized by spontaneous independent thought and action as much as by government control. The Egyptian press has become a "creature" of three successive socialist regimes that have alternately loosened and tightened press restrictions.

By contrast, the Palestinian newspapers, while few in number, still reflect some of the vigor of the struggle for independence, which is far from over. The Palestinian press allows for wider latitude of expression on issues such as national leadership, economic development, and religion and gender. There is still an opportunity in the independent press to discover information important to the electorate in making political, social and economic decisions.

In Egypt, however, communication specialists generally criticize the media for providing information that is biased either to the progovernment view or to the view of one of the opposition parties. The lack of a truly contributive independent media has been lamented. As a result, the Egyptian press has been characterized as lacking in "disinterested intelligence"—impartially presented information on which to base sound decisions. In line with the newness of its emerging nationalism, the Palestinian press has not yet tested its boundaries, despite the enactment of an administrative press law in 1995. By contrast with Egypt, the Palestinian press has not yet been defined by piles of legislative and judicial rulings. At the same time, however, both Egypt and the PNA share many of the same problems, challenges, and approaches. Both their press laws recognize the value of freedom of expression, grant such freedom, and then immediately circumscribe it.

In both cases, these legal limitations of press freedom are accompanied by actual enforcement of patterns of press control by the state. Both governments permit arrests of journalists whose stories or newspapers prove offensive for one reason or another; the journalist may be held while an investigation proceeds. In Egypt, such "preventive detention" was not permitted until 1995. In the PNA, "preventive security" has been used to train journalists to become more "responsible." Both governments justify such punitive actions as good for the general citizenry, and for the security or commonwealth of the state.

There is no better example than the governments' insistence on endorsing the Middle East peace process brokered by the United States. Significant dissent from the peace settlements is evident in both Egypt and the PNA. But the regimes of Hosni Mubarak and Yasir Arafat are committed to advancing the peace process. In tandem with the peace process is the thrust for economic development in both Egypt and the PNA. The new Egyptian press law specifically outlaws articles published "with the intention of causing harm to the national economy."

EGYPTIAN PRESS LAW IN TRANSITION

Egyptian journalists and press scholars during the 1990s have pointed with pride to the increasing democratization of social and political institutions, including the press. Certainly, the press since President Mubarak took over in 1981 has been freer from intervention than during the previous regime of Anwar Sadat (1970–1981) or his predecessor, Gamal Abdul Nasser (1952–1970).

Thus, in May 1995, it was a considerable shock when the Egyptian Parliament at the urging of the Mubarak government quickly passed through a new criminal law restricting freedom of the press by authorizing extraordinary fines and prison sentences for journalists. In addition, the government amended a previous law to permit jailing of journalists during investigations. As of February 1996, four journalists had been arrested under the provisions of this law, known as Law 93.

The new criminal law has become the focal point of a national debate over the status of freedom of the press. What freedom exists when the press can be muzzled by fear of fines and imprisonment? What is the relationship between the government clampdown and the Islamic movement? Was the government even more concerned about press accusations of corruption and favoritism? Opposition to Law 93 has taken several forms. Critics at once urged its abolition. Criticism soon changed to seeking ways to negotiate changes in the law. Was the government amenable to softening the harsh criminal penalties? Some saw an opportunity to leverage a new press law that could for all time establish the principle of a free, but responsible, press. Was the fundamental problem a misunderstanding of the relationship between press and government?

The new law reversed a general trend toward press freedom, which had given Egypt the reputation for having one of the freest presses in the Middle East. The swift legislative action shocked the world of Egyptian journalism. The Mubarak regime had a reputation for relaxing restrictions on the press, a welcome change from previous regimes. Although the 1980 Constitution declares that, "Freedom of the press, printing, publication and mass media shall be guaranteed" (Constitution of the Arab Republic of Egypt, 1980, p. 165), the nation's leaders have continually reinterpreted the Constitution through press laws and edicts. In September 1981, one of President Sadat's last decrees was to order the jailing of approximately 3,000 journalists. When he came to power in October 1981 after Sadat's assassination, Mubarak sought to reconcile differences between press and government. He released all jailed journalists and opposition leaders, and permitted suspended publications to resume their activities. This ushered in a new era of good will. In 1985, Mubarak declared that the press is free "without overt or covert censorship" (el-Nawawy, 1995, pp. 7–8). In May 1995, immediately after passage of Law 93, Mubarak clarified his position on press freedom. In an interview with the *Egyptian Gazette*, he stated that nobody will ever attempt to restrict freedom of the press as long as it is not abused. "No journalist will be subject to imprisonment so long as his stories are supported by conclusive and irrefutable evidence," Mubarak stated. Meeting with Press Syndicate Council members, the president reaffirmed his commitment to protect freedom of the press. He said he never opposes criticism that is based on documents or evidence. Law 93, he said, aims to eliminate false accusations, insults, or biased criticism (el-Nawawy, 1995, pp. 18–20).

What did Law 93 mean for Egyptian journalists' assumptions about the press-government relationship? What were the ramifications for freedom of the press? Was there some way to ameliorate the law? Nine months later none of these questions had been adequately, or safely, answered. Indeed, more questions had been raised as journalists joined together in reaction that took different forms. Some demanded immediate nullification of Law 93. Others, mainly through the Syndicate, tried to negotiate a new press law. Some believed that the debate since May 1995 had at least one positive effect, creating a prospect, long-range, for a more specific, healthier press-government relationship. Meanwhile, however, journalists were subject to arrest and detention more readily than before. Law 93 canceled earlier legal guarantees against "preventive detention" of journalists for publishing offenses (Khalil, 1995, p. 1).

Although the new criminal law was technically under judicial review in the court system, some journalists decried what they perceived as a general climate of prosecution and suppression of the press, while the government shielded itself from criticism. A leading opponent of the new press law has been Gamal Badawi, 62, editor-in-chief of the daily *Al-Wafd* opposition newspaper. The "true goal of Law 93," he insisted, is "as a protection and a shield for corrupt people" (Badawi, 1995, p. 3). Badawi made those comments in early September despite being beaten and warned a month earlier. On August 1, 1995, he was attacked at night by ten men in plain clothes who bruised him but broke no bones. Hours later, he said, he received an anonymous telephone call warning him that what had happened was just to "pinch his ear." The next time, the caller warned, Badawi would be sent to his grave (Alaily, 1995, p. 25). Since Law 93 was passed, three journalists have been arrested in separate cases. In December 1995, an Egyptian magazine editor was sentenced to 2 years' hard labor. Mahmoud Tohami, editor of the weekly *Rose Al-Youssef* magazine, had published an article that criticized Muslim militants for bringing cases against artists and intellectuals. Tohami pleaded not guilty. He argued that his article did not libel or insult anyone but was a warning to Egyptian society that the battle between fundamentalists and society generally had entered the legal arena. The sentence was interpreted as a victory for the plaintiff, Youssef al-Badri, a former member of Parliament turned Islamist, in his struggle against anti-fundamentalist intellectuals ("Egyptian Editor Gets Jail Term," 1995).

Later that year, two other editors-in-chief were arrested. Both were editors of newspapers published by opposition parties critical of the Mubarak regime. They were arrested in connection with a libel case brought by the former minister of endowments. The detained editors were Mostafa Bakry of *Al-Ahrar*, a socialist newspaper, and Magdi Hussein of *Al-Sha'ab*, the newspaper of the Socialist Labor Party. It was Hussein's second arrest. In September of that year, he was jailed on a charge of libel brought by the son of the former minister of Interior Affairs. In that case, Hussein was held in jail for a week while an investigation was carried out.

Hussein's arrest followed his outspoken criticism of Law 93. Immediately after passage of the criminal law, Hussein denounced it as the most regressive since the

British left. The law, he declared, "exceeded even those of Nasser's socialist state. Back then, no journalist was detained without trial. Under the new law, Mubarak's government can pick us up any time and keep us in jail as long as it wants" (Fandy, 1995, p. 18).

Criticism of "public figures" is hazardous to personal liberty and purse under Law 93, Article 303. If a public official alleges libel, a journalist may be detained during the investigation. This provision paved the way for any person to sue the journalist. El-Guindy, in the opposition *Al-Wafd*, wrote that "the increased severity of penalties in libel cases will have a negative effect on freedom of expression" (el-Guindy, 1995, p. 3).

If a formal charge of libel is demonstrated to the court's satisfaction, the journalist may be held for trial. If proven, the journalist may be imprisoned for at least one year and fined not more than LE 15,000 (Egyptian pounds), or about U.S.$5,000. The imprisonment doubles to a minimum of 2 years and the fine may be as much as LE 20,000 "if this libel has a negative impact on a public figure and it affects that figure in performing his public duties" (Ghalab & Moneim, 1995, p. 1). This provision has caused some journalists to criticize Law 93 as a shield law for corrupt politicians. "This law was adopted because there is a war between the press and corruption and the state is on the side of corruption," the *Middle East Times* quoted a journalist on the daily *Akhbar Al Yom* as stating (el-Nawawy, 1995, p. 19).

Indeed, public figures have been scandalized in the Egyptian media. In 1994, the Egyptian public was outraged, wrote political scientist Mamoun Fandy, when journalists revealed the connection between government housing corruption and the high death toll in the 1992 earthquake. "Journalists pointed to the unholy alliance between dishonest contractors and corrupt officials in the ministry of housing as the main reason so many new buildings collapsed," Fandy wrote. The story was broken by the troublesome *Al-Sha'ab*, whose editor was arrested. *Al-Sha'ab* charged that government officials were bribed to ignore safety standards. The newspaper cited close connections between high officials in Mubarak's government and some contractors, among them Egyptian billionaire Fawzi al-Sayed of Nasser City. Law 93, he concluded, "is a last-ditch effort to protect the government's already tarnished image" (Fandy, 1995, p. 18).

Information embarrassing to the government has also leaked to the more aggressive foreign press and has been, in turn, translated for Egyptian newspapers. A reporter for the *Washington Post*, Jim Hoagland, wrote a column in 1995 that suggested that the sons of Egyptian government officials were profiting from business deals with the government of Libya's Muammar Qaddafi. "Instead of ordering an investigation of such business ties," wrote one critic, "Mubarak sent a top aide to talk to Mr. Hoagland and other Americans who reported the story." Also in 1995, the *Wall Street Journal* published a story that Egyptian military officials were profiting on weapons sales from U.S. companies. Reprinting Western stories has not been without penalty. An Egyptian journalist, Abdul Satar abu-Hussein followed up the military profiteering story. As a result, he was arrested, convicted, and imprisoned for 3 months. The conviction was on April 4, 1995, just 6 weeks before Law 93 was enacted (Fandy, 1995).

Other provisions of Law 93 also appeared intended to increase the stability of the government. Article 188 addressed a wide range of concerns, including "national institutions" and "the public interest." The language stipulated that any journalist who published "rumors" or sensational news for the purpose of arousing horror among people, or causing damage and ridicule to the individuals or the national institutions, or harming the public interest would be penalized by imprisonment and a fine not less than LE 5,000 and not more than LE 10,000 (Ghalab & Moneim, 1995).

A sweeping provision of Law 93 also protected "the national economy." Such a target is ubiquitous and might involve anything, from a story that might have a negative impact on tourism, to one that correctly detailed the level of air pollution in Cairo. Certainly the press has reported the decline in tourism following the Islamic campaign to terrorize tourists. In lawsuits, the government presumably will need to prove intent to harm the economy. Article 188 declared that the journalist who published news with the intention of "causing harm to the national economy" would be penalized by imprisonment for not less than 5 years and a fine of not less than LE 10,000 and not more than LE 20,000 (Ghalab & Moneim, 1995).

The economic protection afforded by Law 93 gave to the government another tool with which to fight the Islamic threat, some critics observed. "This effectively puts a blackout on conflicts between Islamists and the government," noted political scientist Fandy, "since such reports portray the country as unstable and consequently harm the economy." He argued that the Mubarak regime is unreasonably haunted by the Islamists:

> The ghost of the 1991 Algerian elections, in which Islamists won the elections on an anti-corruption platform, seems to haunt the Egyptian government. But government fear of an Islamists election victory seems unjustified. Egyptian Islamists seem incapable of winning more than 30 percent of the vote. The Algerian scenario (collapse into civil war) is likely only if the government deprives large segments of Egyptian society of a political voice. (1995, p. 18)

Fandy links the quelling of criticism by Law 93 to potentially sinister political ramifications. Curiously, Mubarak edges closer to the feared Algerian-style abyss, Fandy argues, each time the president alienates moderate voices who articulate the middle ground between Islamists and other radicals against the system. "Mubarak has already antagonized other powerful groups who had been content to work for change within the system," Fandy notes, citing the government campaign against the "moderate, middle-class Islamic Brotherhood," accused "of being the political wing of the Radical Islamic Group, an organization of primarily disaffected southern peasants." If continued, the government strategy could limit its base of support to mainly "those who benefit from the patronage system of the ruling

National Democratic Party—old feudal families and military and ex-military officials" (Fandy, 1995, p. 18; see also Kirolos, 1995, p. 2).

In the months after the enactment of Law 93, no one was more critical of Law 93 than journalists with both government-owned and opposition newspapers. But even the journalists were divided in their proposed remedies. At first, many journalists vented outrage at the shackling of a "democratic" press; they demanded immediate revocation. When the government offered no negotiating points, the 1,500 members of the national organization of journalists, the Press Syndicate, threatened a 1-day newspaper strike. They canceled the strike after Mubarak responded and met with Syndicate representatives. The president dampened the fire by offering to refer the new law to the Supreme Constitutional Court for a ruling on its legality. Meanwhile, he agreed to consider changes; he would form a joint commission of journalists, legal experts, and government officials to draft a comprehensive substitute law within 3 months, from late June to late September ("Egyptian Journalists Cancel Strike," 1995).

While grievances were being negotiated during the summer of 1995, the tone became less strident and the range of issues widened. Discussion still focused on the dangerous Law 93, but journalists began talking about creating a new, comprehensive press law that dealt with other issues, including access to government records and information. In August, the Al-Ahram Regional Press Institute (ARPI) summoned scholars from around the Arab world for a symposium on other nations' press laws.

By early September 1995, leaders in Egyptian journalism were trying to channel protest into a larger frame. Al-Ahram Weekly took a leading role, offering space for editors to express opposing viewpoints. The managing editor of the daily Al-Ahram, Salaheddin Hafez, agreed that Law 93 was "dangerous" and he characterized protest as "strong and correct, albeit nervous at times." But he sought to refocus the target of criticism. Law 93 is not "the reason for the crisis," he said. The blame, Hafez said, "lies in a mutual misunderstanding which goes back many years, and denotes an inability to define the nature of the relationship between the press and the government" (1995, p. 3).

In retort, Gamal Badawi, the opposition editor who had recently been roughed up on the streets, accused the government of systematic interference with the gathering and dissemination of news, which culminated in Law 93. Law 93, he said, was a turning point for the worse because in the past "the president always refused to give in to pressures from some people in the government to place restrictions on the press" (Badawi, 1995, p. 3).

This refocusing of the national protest accelerated in early September 1995 when the national Press Syndicate hosted a national conference on the subject: "Beyond Law 93: Toward New Legislation for Press Freedom." The conference was suspected as being pro-Mubarak because it was held in the ruling party's headquarters, allegedly because of the need for a larger space. With this conference, the Press Syndicate chairman declared that Law 93 was no longer the main issue for Egyptian journalists. "What we are trying to achieve is something more comprehensive and more general," Chairman Ibrahim Nafie told *Al-Ahram Weekly* in an interview. "It's about the future of freedom, democracy and the press in Egypt, and the right of access to information" (Khalil, 1995, p. 1).

Nafie focused attention on President Mubarak's commission and the opportunity for the assembled journalists to present the commission with recommendations. The issue, he told *Al-Ahram*, "not only concerns journalists but also the whole society." He predicted that the conference would outline the future of journalism and "the march of freedom and democracy in Egypt." In his opening address to the conference, Nafie insisted that the Syndicate condemned Law 93, but he cautioned journalists against "a military-style operation where one party aims at destroying the other for the sake of establishing a new press law" (Khalil, 1995, p. 1).

The Syndicate identified three major areas of concern. Committees were created to discuss each. The first committee focused on "Rights and duties of journalists in the light of the constitution and the restrictions imposed on the press." During its meeting, legal expert Said el-Gamal argued that Law 93 violated the Egyptian constitution because it "made it the rule, not the exception, that a journalist be held in custody for his work" (Khalil, 1995, p. 1).

A second committee dealt with "The right to issue newspapers and the right to access to information." Soliman Saleh, a professor of mass communication at the University of Cairo, insisted that Egypt must encourage the expression of all shades of opinion by supporting "independent" newspapers as alternatives to its progovernment national press and its politically biased party press. The new press law, he insisted, must oblige officials to provide journalists with facts and documents (Khalil, 1995, p. 1).

The committee on "management and financing" focused on rules perceived as shackles on the press. Mustafa el-Bortoqali, legal adviser to *Al-Ahram*, criticized government taxation of newspapers and the rule that requires national press organizations to distribute too much of their income—50 percent—to their employees, leaving too little for reinvestment (Khalil, 1995).

The conference adjourned with none of these concerns satisfied, but with the result of channeling angry protest into peaceful discussion and new ideas. At the ARPI, which trains journalists across the Arab world, there was new talk of promoting professionalism through a new series of training sessions. For these, the ARPI proposed publishing a series of books on press skills, functions, and responsibilities (Al-Ahram Regional Press Institute, personal communication, October 25, 1995).

One week after the conference adjourned, these obstacles to free mass media were confirmed by a report that characterized "the Egyptian news media as a dysfunctional institution." Egypt's mass media do not serve the needs of the people or the needs of the government that shaped it. This was the conclusion of the year-long study conducted by the American University in Cairo with funding from the U.S. Agency for International Development (USAID). "The findings of this study suggest strong linkages between persistent and anachronistic government censorship and control, the generally poor quality of the news media, and the low regard the public has for the media" (Napoli, Amin, & Boylan, 1995, p. 2). The study's researchers summarized many of the frustrations facing Egyptian media:

- Historical, cultural, political, and other factors have shaped a system that is—although ultimately the creature of government—ineffective in promoting stated government goals.
- At the same time, it fails to meet the informational needs of the public.
- It is slow to respond to competitive pressures from within and without Egypt.
- Symptomatic of the dysfunction among media workers is a general lack of professionalism, pervasiveness of corruption and favoritism, a tendency to hoard information, an attitude of mistrust toward outsiders, and widespread passivity and acquiescence to government controls.
- Institutional practices such as bribery, unfair hiring and firing practices, and perks for obedient employees were identified by journalists as being at the heart of Egyptian media institutions and a major impediment to information flow.

The researchers noted that Law 93 was passed as they were concluding their year of surveying a "reasonable cross-section" of 48 newspaper (government and opposition) and broadcast personnel. The researchers agreed with journalists who saw Law 93 as a shield for government insiders. "To all appearances, the law was intended to protect high officials in the Mubarak regime from incessant and embarrassing charges of corruption by the opposition press; the allegations had been picked up and widely disseminated by foreign journalists." In conclusion, the report declared, Law 93 "reinforced" their findings. "Even under the relatively liberal regime of President Mubarak, the media remain firmly under government control. The high rhetoric of press freedom and democracy is belied by acts of repression and control, sending an ambiguous message to the public as well as to media professionals" (Napoli et al., 1995, p. 2).

The study measured the Egyptian press by standards developed in the West. By standards indigenous to the Middle East and North Africa, the Egyptian press is still ranked as among the freest in the region. Even after Law 93, Egypt is considered to be among the top three countries having the freest press in the Arab world. At a recent UNESCO meeting of journalists, Egypt, Jordan, and Yemen were cited as having "partially free" press systems. This freedom compares favorably with the controlled private press in many Arab nations, and contrasts with the state-run press in nations such as Libya and Iraq.

Whether this status meets the present and future needs of Egypt is another matter. Currently there are both internal and external economic and political pressures to reform various institutions, including the media. The American University in Cairo research team noted that "until Egypt has a mass media system that works properly, providing disinterested intelligence, the Egyptian government itself cannot function efficiently to promote economic development and democratization" (Napoli et al., 1995, p. 2). The team's recommendations for improvement were based in large measure on Egyptian journalists' own ideas. The journalists rated their own ideas for improvement on a scale from "very important" to "not very important." The very important and important recommendations included:

- Improved journalistic training,
- Improved education in such areas as economics and development issues,
- Improved technology,
- Improved access to government officials,
- Improved access to government data and information,
- More participation by journalists in decision-making,
- Greater freedom for journalists to research and report,
- Better wages for media personnel, and
- Privatization of the Egyptian media system.

These recommendations were judged by the researchers to be "implementable within the Egyptian media's institutional, social and political context." The investigators concluded that with strong and sustained political commitment, implementation of the recommendations would greatly improve the performance of the Egyptian media in providing information on public policy issues and government activities and decisions—information without which Egyptians cannot participate meaningfully and effectively in their own governance (Napoli et al., 1995, p. 2).

DISCUSSION QUESTIONS

1. What are the major similarities and differences between the Egyptian and the Palestinian press systems?
2. Why did the Egyptian journalists oppose the criminal law that was passed by the Egyptian Parliament in 1996?
3. What was the role of the Egyptian Press Syndicate in resolving the debate over Law 93?
4. What were the recommendations included in the American University in Cairo's study with regard to the improvement of the press system in Egypt?
5. Compare and contrast Egyptian journalists' professional standards with the U.S. RTNDA Code of Ethics.

REFERENCES

Alaily, J. (1995, September/October). Egypt's watchdogs may no longer be able to bark. *IPI Report*, 25.

Badawi, G. (1995, August 31-September 6). Guarantees needed. *Al-Ahram Weekly*, p. 3.

Constitution of the Arab Republic of Egypt, Article 48, p. 165 (1980).

Egyptian editor gets jail term for article criticizing militants. (1995, December 31). *New York Times*,

Egyptian journalists cancel strike. (1995, June 25). *Los Angeles Times*, p. A4.

El-Guindy, I. (1995, May). A slaughter: The new restrictions over press freedom—The worst legalities for closing mouths. *Al-Wafd*, p. 3.

Fandy, M. (1995, June 7). Mubarak's gag on Egypt's press could bring the disorder he fears: Educated class now finds the government as distasteful as Islamists. *Christian Science Monitor*, p. 18.

Ghalab, M., & Moneim, G. A. (1995, May). New restrictions over press freedom. *Al Wafd*, p. 1.

Hafez, S. (1995, August 31-September 6). No patchwork. *Al-Ahram Weekly,* p. 3.

Khalil, N. (1995, September 7-13). Beyond Law 93: After four months of protest action, journalists gathered this week to deliberate over the future of their profession and democracy. *Al-Ahram Weekly*, p. 1.

Kirolos, W. (1995, September 7-13). Brothers face military trial. *Al-Ahram Weekly*, p. 2.

Napoli, J. J., Amin, H. Y., & Boylan, R. F. (1995, September 17). *Executive summary report: Assessment of the Egyptian print and electronic media* (Grant No. 263-0225-G-00-4043-00, pp. 2, 7). Submitted to the U.S. Agency for International Development.

El-Nawawy, M. A. (1995, Fall). *Journalism professionalism and information control: The case of the Egyptian press.* Unpublished master's thesis, American University in Cairo, Egypt.

17

CULTURAL TREATMENT OF INTERNATIONAL EVENTS: A CONTENT ANALYSIS OF AMERICAN AND EGYPTIAN NEWSCASTING

Mohammed el-Nawawy
University of West Florida

INTRODUCTION

The world today is witnessing a dynamic increase in the flow of news across nations. This international exchange of news is accompanied by a rapid development in communication technologies. With the new millennium at hand, an interesting question surfaces once again. Is Marshall McLuhan's "Global Village" upon us? A communications world or society where all members share a similar knowledge, and are exposed to the same material (Fisher, 1979).

This chapter proposes to answer that question by investigating national coverage in the United States and Egypt for each's treatment of international news. The study will analyze the content of the *CBS Evening News*, the *NBC Nightly News* and the *ABC World News Tonight* in the United States, and the nine o'clock news bulletin, the main news report on channel one of Egyptian television. The study will compare U.S. and Egyptian news programs in terms of (1) the amount of reporting devoted to foreign news, (2) each's focus on negative versus positive news, (3) how both deal with protocol events, and (4) each's coverage of hard versus soft news. A period of 2 months was determined to be adequate for the study. During this time, 15 days were randomly selected for analysis; videotape recording was conducted in the United States and Egypt simultaneously.

The major network newscasts on U.S. television were selected for this research because of their powerful effects on the American people. Weaver (1975) described network news as the most powerful centralizing democratizing machine ever let loose in American society. Adams (1978) said "television network news reaches a massive heterogeneous audience each night, is heavily relied on as a national news source, and is trusted as credible and reliable" (p. 12). According to Adams, the network news has become a potent ingredient in the complexities of American society.

Iyengar and Kinder (1987) argued that American audiences consider network news to be the major source of providing objective, complete, and intelligent coverage of public affairs. The researchers also stated that television news shapes the American public's conception of events on the political scene, and thus is the news that really matters. In a hearing before the Congressional Committee on Foreign Affairs, Michael Beschloss, of the Annenberg Project on TV and U.S. Foreign Policy, argued that television news has strengthened the U.S. international engagement by "energizing Americans about issues that once might have been thought very distant" (*Impact on Television*, 1994, p. 28).

Besides the United States, Egypt was selected as the country to be studied because of its political, social, and cultural influence in the Middle East. Egyptian media are well developed, and attract large numbers of audiences. Moreover, the authority of Egyptian media is not limited to Egypt, but extends to include the whole Middle Eastern region (Boyd, 1978). News constitutes a major part of Egyptian television. Many Egyptians watch television news because they consider it to be the best way to learn what is going on in the world (Boyd, 1993).

TRENDS OF FOREIGN NEWS COVERAGE BY THE U.S. NETWORKS

American national networks have, for a long time, been accused of neglecting foreign news. Gans (1979) argued that American television devotes less airtime to foreign news than to domestic news. He said that foreign news on the U.S. networks is limited to stories that are relevant to Americans or to U.S. interests. American television news "judges other countries by the extent to which they live up to, or imitate American practices and values" (p. 42). This trend in the American news media is described by Gans as validated ethnocentrism.

Larson (1982) found that in foreign stories broadcast by the American networks from 1972 to 1979, 61 percent of the time the United States was mentioned. This is a strong confirmation that international news is usually defined in terms of American interests. Sahin (1982) reinforced the same notion when his findings concluded that international news is Americanized by broadcasting foreign events that are important only to Americans.

Prato (1994) argued that there is a crisis in international news reporting in the United States represented by stagnation and shrinkage in the number of international stories in U.S. media. Prato concluded, "what we're increasingly missing, as a culture, is connective tissue to bind us to the rest of the world" (p. 48).

Many reasons have been cited for the reduced coverage of foreign news on American television. Rubin (1979) argued that the shortage of airtime is an important factor in the lack of foreign news coverage. Network evening news runs between 22 and 25 minutes, plus time for commercials, which adds up to a full 30 minutes. Because of such a time constraint, the operating mode for television reporting of foreign news "is one of elimination rather than inclusion" (Batscha, 1975, p. 178). Not all significant foreign events can be covered in the limited time. Although the networks would like to extend their news time to 1 hour, the local affiliates have opposed this idea because it would cut into their local, commercial inventory of time sales (Rubin, 1979).

Another reason cited by Rubin for reduced coverage of foreign news is the commercial nature of American networks, which makes them highly dependent on ratings. Television executives feel that foreign news does not appeal to mass audiences, and therefore does not increase ratings. They believe that for news to succeed, it must be interesting and relate to people's lives—network VIPs do not believe that international news makes this contribution.

Hallin (1994) argued that television executives worry about pleasing and entertaining the maximum number of audiences to increase ratings, giving the people what they want, rather than what they need. The executives believe that people want entertainment; therefore, they increase the time allocated for entertainment at the expense of news. Bogart (1980) argued that "ratings rise when the broadcaster is successful in exposing the listener to what he wants to hear in the very personal way he wants to hear it. In terms of news, this means ratings are improved not when listeners are told what they should know, but what they want to hear" (p. 214).

Another factor impeding the television coverage in international news, as cited by Wallis and Baran (1990), is the high cost of maintaining permanent foreign correspondents and bureaus. In this context, Prato (1994) argued that although ABC, CBS, and NBC prefer to cover international stories using their own staff, it is neither feasible nor economically viable to base correspondents everywhere in the world. Networks have been forced to close numerous bureaus in foreign countries. Utley (1997) uncovered information revealing that the expenses of maintaining a foreign correspondent can reach $12,000 a day, including extras such as satellite fees and editing equipment. This makes television the most expensive medium for news, especially international news. Such high expenses have led network news producers to reach the conclusion that, "foreign news is expendable unless it is of compelling interest to a mass audience" (Utley, 1997, p. 6).

Still another factor, cited by Larson (1984), for the lack of foreign news coverage on the American networks is the political restrictions set by some Third World countries on foreign correspondents. Some countries refuse to issue visas to foreign correspondents, or demand at least a list of topic areas to be covered before issuing visas to a TV news team.

Many content analysis studies have been conducted to measure the amount of coverage devoted to international news by U.S. networks. One was conducted by Almaney (1970). During a period of 4 weeks, the evening newscasts of ABC, CBS, and NBC were observed. In the investigation, Almaney classified news into three types: (1) national affairs, meaning news events occurring within the United States in which no other country was involved; (2) international affairs, referring to any event in which the United States and another country were actively involved; and (3) foreign affairs, alluding to a happening in which the United States was not involved at all. Results of the study showed that the three networks gave priority to national affairs (63 percent of total stories), followed by international affairs (21 percent), and foreign affairs (16 percent). This chapter presents evidence that network television in the United States is basically "a domestic news medium in the sense that the dominant element in the news picture is national affairs" (Almaney, 1970, p. 509).

In 1973, another study conducted by Frank over a 7-week period showed that ABC devoted 69 percent of its coverage to domestic news and 31 percent to foreign news; CBS gave 70 percent of its coverage to domestic news and 30 percent to foreign news; and NBC allotted 64 percent to domestic news and 36 percent to foreign news. Larson and Hardy's (1984) content analysis of network newscasts between 1972 and 1975 utilized the Television News Index and Abstracts from the Vanderbilt Television News Archive. Results of this examination determined that international stories made up 35 percent of the stories at NBC, 37 percent at CBS, and 39 percent at ABC; the remaining stories were devoted to domestic issues. Results also demonstrated that industrialized countries were much more likely to be mentioned than developing countries. Researchers found that the United States was mentioned in most of the international stories, and Africa and Latin America were mentioned least often.

Larson's (1984) study of international news content of 1,000 television evening newscasts from 1972 to 1981 found that of the 17 stories on an average weeknight broadcast, approximately 7 stories (40 percent) dealt with international affairs, and accounted for 7 minutes, 19 seconds (33 percent) of broadcast time. The research also discovered the average length of an international news story to be 1 minute, 28 seconds. Moreover, Larson showed that countries in western Europe, the Middle East, and Asia were mentioned in 30 percent of the sample stories; eastern Europe in 20 percent; Latin America in 11 percent; and Africa in 7 percent.

Weaver (1984) conducted a content analysis of the foreign news presented on the evening news programs of the three commercial networks over the 10-year period comprising 1972 through 1981. The study presented evidence that foreign news (defined as news reported from outside the United States or originating from the United Nations) made up 28.3 percent of the total network newscast time. The study found that the percentage of the evening newscast time devoted to foreign news items decreased during the years in which there were exceptional domestic news events, such as presidential elections (1972, 1976, and 1980), and the Watergate years of 1973 and 1974.

Another content analysis, conducted by Barrett (1982), investigated network evening newscasts from September 1979 to September 1981. The study found that of the 313 special segments on NBC's *Nightly News*, 106 were devoted to international news; of the 116 extended enterprises on CBS's *Evening News*, 28 came from overseas; and that ABC's *World News Tonight* broadcast 154 special assignments during the study period, 44 of which were on foreign subjects.

Wallis and Baran (1990) pursued an inquiry that focused on the impact of technological and financial factors on network coverage of foreign news during the 1980s. The study established the fact that there has been a tremendous communication explosion in which satellite technology enabled news broadcasters to obtain pictures and sounds from remote places in a very short time. However, the researchers found that technology has not led to a marked increase in the number of foreign news stories covered by American networks. The researchers attributed this phenomenon to the high costs of communication technologies. In this context, Wallis and Baran referred to CBS, a $28-million source of profit in 1979, which became a $65-million dollar loser in 1987. Financial pressures led to cutbacks of foreign bureaus, and a greater reliance on news wholesalers, such as Visnews and WTN.

Utley (1997) cited statistics from the Tyndall Report, which showed that ABC's coverage of international news declined from 1,410 stories in 1988 to 918 in 1996; CBS's coverage decreased from 1,310 stories in 1988 to 824 in 1996; and NBC's coverage of foreign news dwindled from 827 in 1988 to 528 stories in 1996.

EGYPTIAN TELEVISION NEWS AND ITS COVERAGE OF FOREIGN EVENTS

Television is an important political and developmental tool in all Arab countries, including Egypt (Boyd, 1993). Egyptian television's Channel One broadcasts the main news bulletin nightly, and news and public affairs programs are the most common types of programs on the broadcast schedule (Amin, 1996). But one of the chief characteristics of Arab broadcast organizations is that they do not support media research studies; Egypt is no exception regarding this issue. Little information or systematic research has been published on news content concerning Egyptian television. The research office of the Egyptian Radio and Television Union (ERTU) conducts some content analysis studies, but these studies, as a rule, count only radio and television transmission hours and do not analyze the nature of broadcast news programming. Even researchers and students at the Egyptian national universities have not been encouraged to undertake such studies. A possible explanation for this attitude toward media research is the reluctance of a traditional people or culture to respond to official questioning, and the fear among broadcasting officials of negative criticism.

Nasser (1983) cited a survey conducted by Yehia Aboubakr in 1980 on the coverage of local and foreign news by the Egyptian television's main network. This survey showed that the daily average of news stories presented by Egypt's television network was 31. Of these, 17 items were local news, 4 were regional, and 10 came from outside the region. The daily average of television news included 26 items of a distinctly political nature, reflecting the involvement of the Middle East media with the Arab-Israeli conflict. This political involvement, according to Aboubakr, has been responsible for limiting television exchange within the Middle East region.

In selecting foreign news to be broadcast on the Egyptian television, the broadcasting authorities set criteria that are more sensitive than the standards of other media. Any foreign news item that discredits the national policies or disturbs public opinion is not broadcast. Some foreign stories are rejected, moreover, on the ground that they include too much violence, terrorism, unacceptable sex, or material offensive to religious, moral, and spiritual values. Furthermore, "the community of interests" criterion gives priority to the dissemination of good or positive news about countries with the same political, economic, cultural, or ideological interests. The broadcast authorities take into account the interests of other countries having the same political ideologies as their own government. In this regard, close relations with a foreign country are more decisive in the selection of foreign news items than the geographical proximity of the country (Nasser, 1983, p. 51).

Besides the political and social restrictions in the selection of foreign news on Egyptian television, there is the problem of language, and the need to translate and edit material coming from non-Arabic speaking countries. This problem limits the choice of foreign stories that can be shown on the Egyptian television (Nasser, 1983).

Despite all these taboos, restrictions, and problems, foreign news is still preferred by Egyptian broadcast authorities over local news because of the high professional quality of foreign footage. In Egypt, as in other developing countries, there is the belief that foreign news is less likely to arouse dissatisfaction than is domestic news. "In fact, foreign news may rally people to the government by appealing to their nationalism and team spirit; domestic news may accentuate the shortcomings of the government" (Martin & Choudhary, 1983, p. 7).

NEGATIVE NEWS COVERAGE BY U.S. NETWORKS

The U.S. national networks have always been accused of focusing on negative news in their coverage of foreign events, which include violence, conflict, and disaster

(Paletz & Pearson, 1978). Ali (1991) cites Arno's argument that the media "thrive on conflict because their very existence is defined by conflict participation. This is true notably in libertarian countries which, because of economic and political pluralism, are less inclined to engage in conflict with other states. The media, therefore, serve as outlets for cathartic feelings by playing up and playing out conflict scenarios" (p. 23).

Journalism professionals argue that it is easy to feature negative news, such as conflict, crime, or scandal, whereas it takes more effort to find news in peaceful nations. Likewise, they argue that people usually remember bad news, and forget good news since bad news leaves a stronger impression (Davison, 1974). Graber (1993) argued that natural or man-made disasters are "dramatic and rich in pictures that tug at human heart strings . . . they seem salient to the lives of media audiences because they threaten shared values, peace of mind, and often their lives and property" (p. 148). Nimmo and Combs (1985) posit that crises have a high degree of melodramatic style that emphasizes horror and fear, provokes anger and sadness, and appeals directly to human emotions. Roeh (1981) quotes an NBC producer who instructs his staff that "every news story should have structure and conflict, problem and denouement, rising action and falling action, a beginning, a middle and an end" (p. 78).

Of all negative news, coups d'etat and earthquakes are still perennial favorites of news editors. However, this kind of coverage often creates special problems. "Editors like their coups d'etat to be clear-cut, dramatic, and, if at all possible, with an immediate and distinct turn to the left or right. . . . Unfortunately, political upheaval is seldom tidy, and always difficult to follow" (Rosenblum, 1979, p. 122). Gans (1979) argued that some countries are reported on the U.S. network news only when they are the site of major disasters. He suggests that foreign disasters must be more serious and dramatic than equivalent American ones in order to be broadcast on the networks. According to Gans's research (1979), earthquakes and famines in Africa, Asia, or Latin America must kill hundreds of thousands of people to be reported by the American networks. "Generally speaking, the farther from America the country is geographically, politically, or racially, the larger the number of victims necessary for the story to receive attention" (Gans, 1979, p. 36).

An example of a foreign crisis given much coverage by the American networks was the assassination, in Cairo, of the Egyptian President, Anwar Sadat. The networks' evening news was committed fully to the event. CBS devoted 1 hour of prime time to considering the events of the day that led up to the assassination. Both ABC and NBC had late-night specials covering the event (Barrett, 1982).

Another more recent foreign crisis that was extensively covered by the U.S. networks was the Persian Gulf War in 1991, which absorbed virtually all network news time, and received more media and public attention than the domestic issues of economy, deficit, and drugs combined (Iyengar & Simon, 1994). One region having a voluminous amount of crises coverage by the U.S. networks is the Middle East. Most news devoted to the Middle East by the American networks has to do with disasters, coups d'etat, uprisings, conflicts, and terrorist activities. This negative news fosters misperceptions about Middle Eastern peoples and cultures. The Middle East is perhaps one of the most misunderstood, misperceived, and stereotyped regions of the world (Kamalipour, 1995). In a 1985 study, none of the television producers, writers, and directors interviewed could recall any positive image of the Arabs in any past or present news program on the U.S. networks. On an average weeknight in 1980, CBS devoted an average of 5 minutes, 10 seconds to the Middle East, and most of this coverage was about the American hostages in Teheran (Adams & Heyl, 1981).

PROTOCOL NEWS ON EGYPTIAN TELEVISION

Stevenson (1988) argued that protocol news originated in Third World countries, where it is also termed development news. According to Stevenson, development news is simply defined as news that promotes development. This type of reporting highlights the positive aspects of the society and focuses on the projects sponsored by the government in areas such as agriculture and education. Development news was initiated to demonstrate to the Western nations that "there was much more to the developing nations than coups d'etat and earthquakes" (Stevenson, 1988, p. 145).

Leaders of Third World countries use development and protocol news to strengthen national identity. Included in protocol news are the comings and goings of presidents and other national leaders, and their activities which assume symbolic importance. Protocol news includes "repetitious TV footage of dignitaries reviewing honor guards at airports, traveling to palaces in limousines, then sitting around big tables . . . where welcoming statements, banquet toasts and official communiques are exchanged" (Stevenson, 1988, p. 146). Protocol news is almost never exportable. Boyd (1993) defined such news as "a set of guidelines for each country's media that mandates that stories about the head of the state and his family come first, generally to be followed by stories about those countries with which the country has close relations" (p. 41).

In Egypt, as in other developing countries, the head of state has a high degree of visibility as a result of protocol news. He is almost always featured, if only in a still picture, receiving visitors; and presidential speeches are always given a great attention by all the media, especially television (Boyd, 1993).

HARD NEWS VERSUS SOFT NEWS

Bogart (1980) defined hard news as serious political and economic events that have a fixed schedule, such as election days and press conferences. Soft news, in turn, was defined as "human interest stories which are dramatic and involving, either because they deal with the universals of human experiences and passions or because of their bizarre and curious character" (Bogart, 1980, p. 216).

In the United States, television news has always focused on hard news, rather than on soft news (Batscha, 1975). Frank (1973) argued that soft news requires more airtime compared to hard news. He explains that soft news is always preceded by background information, or accompanied by detailed interviews with subjects of interest in the broadcast story. Given a limited amount of air time on the U.S. national networks, commercial broadcasters tend to focus on hard news more than on soft news.

Frank cites a study conducted in 1971 to measure the percentage of airtime devoted to the two types of reporting by the three American networks over a 3-week period. Results of the investigation pointed out that ABC devoted 82 percent of its time to hard news and 18 percent to soft news; CBS committed 77 percent of its time to hard news and 23 percent to soft news; and NBC provided 82 percent of its time for hard reporting and 18 percent to feature reporting.

In Weaver's (1984) content analysis of the three networks from 1972 through 1981, results revealed that soft news items, such as human interest, arts, and entertainment received very little coverage by the three major networks. In Gonzenbach's (1992) content analysis of the same networks from 1972 to 1989, findings demonstrated that soft news constituted about a quarter of the networks' coverage of foreign news. Furthermore, to increase ratings during recent years, network news has started to devote more time to entertainment values and other kinds of soft news, such as health, family life, or other subjects that are closer to the lives of the viewers and to which the viewers can relate (Hallin, 1994).

HYPOTHESES

Hypothesis 1. U.S. network newscasts present a contracted coverage of international events; while Egyptian newscasts provide expanded coverage of international events.

Hypothesis 2. U.S. network newscasts concentrate on negative aspects in their coverage of news about foreign countries.

Hypothesis 3. Egyptian network news gives priority to protocol news over international news.

Hypothesis 4. International news coverage of both U.S. and Egyptian network newscasts focuses on hard news rather than soft news.

Operational Definitions

International News: Any news item that is about a country other than the one broadcasting the news.

Contracted Coverage: Coverage of less than three international news events in one news broadcast.

Expanded Coverage: Coverage of three or more international news events in one news broadcast.

Negative Coverage: Concentrating on crises and disasters, whether they are natural (for example, earthquakes) or human disasters (such as coups d'etat).

Protocol News: News about the ceremonial activities of the top government officials concerning domestic issues only (for instance, the president's visits or inaugurations, or cabinet members' speeches).

Hard News: News on serious issues, including politics, protocol, military, economic matters, crime, natural disasters, coups d'etat, assassinations, terrorism, and the environment.

Soft News: News items such as culture, human interest, entertainment, art, religion, science, education, and sports.

METHODOLOGY

This study is a content analysis comparing U.S. and Egyptian network news in terms of each's coverage of foreign events. ABC's *World News Tonight*, CBS's *Evening News*, and NBC's *Nightly News* were chosen as representative of American news programming because of the extensive penetration the combined shows produce in a week's time. Certain other news programs (CNN and *Fox News*) were excluded from the sample because coverage extended beyond the U.S. borders, creating an inherent bias toward international events, or because the news service lacked parity with the major networks. The *9 P.M. Evening Bulletin* (Arabic) of Egyptian television (Channel One) was chosen as representative of Egyptian news programming. The other network (Channel Two) news program was excluded from the study because it is produced in English and is primarily dedicated to foreign affairs.

The time frame for the study was established for a period of 2 months, March and April 1997. During these 2 months, the researchers randomly selected a comparative sample of two composite weeks (actually 15 days) of network news in both countries. A random number generator (S Lottery) was used to select the days; all days of the week were represented in the sample. Videotape recordings were made in Carbondale, Illinois, and Cairo, Egypt.

After the random number generator selected the days, a stratified sample of ABC's *World News Tonight*, CBS's *Evening News*, and NBC's *Nightly News* programs was correlated with the established dates. Each network was represented equally (5 days) in the sample. The researchers avoided the American sweeps period, which started during the last 3 days of April 1997. Similar dates were used to record 15 days of the *9 P.M. Evening Bulletin* on Channel One of Egyptian television. In addition to the 15 days that were originally established for the sample, extra dates were selected using the random number generator; these dates were to be used as substitutes for the days that were missed during the process of taping the news.

Four students were utilized for coding the material (three coders for the English tapes and one for the Arabic tapes). The coders were graduate students in Radio-TV and Journalism at Southern Illinois University. Three training sessions were conducted, totaling 7 hours; one for clarifying definitions, others for actual recording practice. Some operational definitions were refined after the training session to increase the intercoder reliability.

Units of Analysis

The individual story within each newscast is the unit of analysis. Every story will be coded on the following variables: (1) theme—whether the news story is hard or soft; (2) issue—the subject of the story, and (3) negative stories.

Categories of Analysis

International News/Hard News: Politics, military, economic matters, crime, natural disasters, coups d'etat, assassinations, terrorism, environment, and others.
International News/Soft News: Culture, human interest, entertainment, art, religion, science, sports, science and education, and others.
Domestic News/Hard News: Politics, protocol, military, economic matters, crime, natural disasters, coups d'etat, assassinations, terrorism, environment, and others.
Domestic News/Soft News: Culture, human interest, entertainment, art, religion, science, sports, science and education, and others.

RELIABILITY

An intercoder reliability test (Holsti formula) was conducted among the three recorders used for coding the U.S. network news programs. Intercoder reliability was registered at .73 among the three coders. Intracoder reliability (test–retest) was registered at .93 by the single coder who analyzed the Egyptian network.

DATA ANALYSIS

The first hypothesis (U.S. network news presents contracted coverage of international events/Egyptian network news provide expanded coverage of international events) was supported in the study. Results showed that the U.S. network news paid little attention to international events, whereas Egyptian newscasts examined foreign affairs frequently. Every Egyptian newscast in this study covered three or more international news events. As for the U.S. newscasts, 6 of 15 newscasts covered less than three international news events. The statistics established the ratio of international to domestic news coverage by the U.S. networks at 1:5. As for Egyptian television's *9 P.M. Evening Bulletin*, the ratio of international to domestic news coverage was 3:1 (see Table 17.1).

The second hypothesis (U.S. newscasts focus on the negative aspects of international news) was rejected. Results showed that negative coverage is less frequent in international news coverage than in the domestic news. The ratio of negative international to negative domestic news coverage was 1:6 (see Table 17.2).

The third hypothesis (Egyptian network newscasts give priority to protocol news) was supported in the research. The Egyptian newscasts covered 11 protocol news items compared to only 1 protocol news story covered by the U.S. networks. This means that Egyptian protocol news is 40 times greater than U.S. protocol news coverage (see Table 17.3).

The fourth hypothesis (international news coverage of both U.S. and Egyptian network newscasts focuses on hard news rather than soft news) was confirmed as in many previous studies (see Table 17.4).

TABLE 17.1.

	U.S. Network News (192 total stories)		Egyptian Network News (186 total stories)	
	International	Domestic	International	Domestic
#	33	159	138	48
%	17.2	82.8	74.2	25.8

TABLE 17.2.

	U.S. Network News—All (192 total stories)		Egyptian Network News—Negative (116 total stories)	
	International	Domestic	International	Domestic
#	17	99	17	99
%	8.9	51.6	14.7	85.3

TABLE 17.3.

	Protocol News—Domestic	
	U.S. News (159 total domestic stories)	Egyptian News (48 total domestic stories)
# of protocol	11	1
% of protocol	22.9	0.6

TABLE 17.4.

	U.S. International News (33 total stories)		Egyptian International News (138 total stories)	
	Hard News	Soft News	Hard News	Soft News
#	26	7	104	34
%	78.8	21.2	75.4	24.6

DISCUSSION

Conducting empirical research that involves two continents and independent cultures presents numerous difficulties. Foremost is the coordination, planning, and execution of the investigation, while other problems include language differences, dissimilar technical recording and playback technology, and distinctly different reporting styles. Examining U.S. and Egyptian national newscasts brings this point to the surface quickly: English versus Arabic, NTSC versus PAL video standards, and a visual style of reporting versus an oral one.

Furthermore, cultural values play an important part in such investigations. But defining culture and the various terminology associated with culture is a delicate task. As Sitaram explains, "Until recently, no scientific effort had been made to determine the cultural values of either Eastern or Western peoples. It seems that values are hidden beneath the complex of beliefs, expectations, and customs of the world's cultures" (1995, p. 67). In the Western world, freedom of expression is a basic right and political and governmental criticism is openly practiced; in the Arab world such rights are limited, and censorship is easily tolerated, even expected as a form of civic responsibility.

However, the world is now a multicultural place, where global communication technologies break down borders and allow for countless intercultural exchanges. The 21st century is here. But is this new world order the global village posited by

Marshall McLuhan more than 30 years ago? It is the opinion of these researchers that we have not yet reached the McLuhan ideal. As Fisher (1979) has pointed out, McLuhan's concept of a global village is "an idealistic or utopian projection that goes too far beyond the reality of the here and now" (p. 6).

CONCLUSION

In today's world, where international events are becoming more complicated, many people turn to broadcast news to make sense of the confusion (Wallis & Baran, 1990). This makes a better system of international reporting essential for providing a realistic and comprehensive view of worldwide events (Rosenblum, 1979). The current study presents evidence that a planetary imbalance remains, at least in the coverage of international news between the U.S. and the Egyptian national networks. There are many, varied difficulties standing in the way of an equal and fair coverage of foreign news all over the world. This content analysis concludes that there is a lack of understanding, or at least there are differing points of view of what is going on in the world.

American network news emphasizes domestic issues. There may be several reasons why domestic coverage occurs five times more often than international coverage. Geographically, the United States is isolated on a single continent and is one of the largest, most populous nations in the world. It is the most powerful sovereign state militarily and economically. These characteristics may lead to a self-centered outlook and a somewhat provincial attitude by the American media. Egypt, on the other hand, is located at the confluence of three continents, and is surrounded by other independent states, one a former enemy on its northeastern border. It is an emerging Third World economy, which treats development as essential to its national identity. Egyptian media reflect this picture, and therefore, concentrate their reporting in the international arena three times more often than in the domestic arena. Also, Egyptian reporting deals with protocol news quite differently than the U.S. news effort. The 9 P.M. Evening Bulletin gives it priority, whereas the U.S. news reported only one protocol story during the 2-month research period.

Negative reporting, stories of crises and disasters, remains the predominate source of news in all American newscasts. However, the investigation revealed that negative reporting was less frequently found in international stories than in domestic stories. Only 8.9 percent of the total American network stories were negative international reports, whereas 51.6 percent of all American network stories were negative domestic reports. Such evidence is contrary to the beliefs held by most foreign observers, who feel stereotyping and unfavorable reporting are standard practices in U.S. network newscasts when it concerns international events.

Obviously, American networks are less concerned with international affairs than they are with local concerns. But if a global humanity is to enter the new millennium with a clearer understanding of world issues, then its most influential media will have to revise their thinking about foreign affairs. The average citizen's understanding of international events depends on television news. Therefore, there must be a careful and balanced presentation of foreign coverage in the broadcast media; without it, people around the world will be deprived of information they need.

This content analysis is basically a pilot study to examine research strategies for comparing source news across borders. One limitation of the study is the small size of the newscasts that were analyzed and the limited time frame. However, the researchers believe that the selected newscasts are sufficient for this preliminary research that may provide empirical data for future investigations in this area.

Another limitation is the usage of only one coder for the Egyptian newscasts as compared to three coders for the U.S. newscasts. The reason for this limitation is the lack of Arabic speakers during the time of the study.

A third limitation is the insufficient literature dealing with foreign news coverage in the Egyptian broadcast media. As was mentioned earlier in the chapter, the lack of research in this field is one problem facing many researchers in Egypt.

Recommendations for Future Research

Cross-border, cross-culture research is difficult, but it must be continued. Future research in this area may include all-news networks such as CNN to compare between these networks and the national networks in terms of their coverage of foreign news. One unrelated piece of research data found in the study was the 7:3 ratio of U.S. reporting of hard news to soft news. This is about a 15 percent change from studies done in the 1970s and 1980s. Further investigations may identify a trend in national news reporting in the United States.

DISCUSSION QUESTIONS

1. Why are the U.S. network newscasts powerful among the American public?
2. What are the factors responsible for the contracted coverage of foreign news on American television?
3. What are the basic criteria for selecting foreign news to be broadcast on Egyptian television?
4. Define "protocol" news within the framework of its application to the media in Egypt and other developing countries.
5. Do you think Marshall McLuhan's concept of the "global village" has been achieved? Why? Why not? Illustrate your answer with examples based on that study.

REFERENCES

Adams, W. (1978). Network news research in perspective. In W. Adams & F. Schreibman. (Eds.), *Television network news: Issues in content research* (pp. 11–46). Washington, DC: George Washington University Press.

Adams, W., & Heyl, P. (1981). From Cairo to Kabul with the networks, 1972–1980. In E. W. Adams (Ed.), *Television coverage of the Middle East* (pp. 1–39). Norwood, NJ: Ablex.

Ali, M. (1991). *Determinants of international news reporting in the U.S.* Unpublished doctoral dissertation, Southern Illinois University, Carbondale.

Almaney, A. (1970). International and foreign affairs on network television news. *Journal of Broadcasting, 14*(4), 499–509.

Amin, H. (1996). Egypt and the Arab World in the satellite age. In J. Sinclair, E. Jacka, & S. Cunningham (Eds.), *New patterns in global television: Peripheral vision* (pp. 101–125). New York: Oxford University Press.

Barrett, M. (1982). *Broadcast journalism, 1979–1981.* New York: Everest House.

Batscha, R. (1975). *Foreign affairs news and the broadcast journalist.* New York: Praeger.

Bogart, L. (1980). Television news as entertainment. In P. Tannenbaum (Ed.), *The entertainment functions of television* (pp. 209–250). Hillsdale, NJ: Lawrence Erlbaum.

Boyd, D. (1978). A q-analysis of mass media usage by Egyptian elite groups. *Journalism Quarterly, 55*, 501–507.

Boyd, D. (1993). *Broadcasting in the Arab World: A survey of the electronic media in the Middle East* (2nd ed.). Ames, IA: Iowa State University Press.

Davison, P. (1974). *Mass communication and conflict resolution: The role of the information media in the advancement of international understanding.* New York: Praeger.

Fisher, G. (1979). *American communication in a gobal society.* Norwood, NJ: Ablex.

Frank, R. (1973). *Message dimensions of television news.* Ashland, MA: Lexington Books.

Gans, H. (1979). *Deciding what's news: A study of* CBS Evening News, NBC Nightly News, Newsweek *and* Time. New York: Pantheon Books.

Gonzenbach, W. (1992). The world of U.S. network television news: Eighteen years of International and foreign news coverage. *Gazette, 50*, 53–72.

Graber, D. (1993). *Mass media and American politics* (4th ed.). Washington, DC: Congressional Quarterly.

Hallin, D. (1994). *We keep American on top of the world: Television journalism and the public sphere.* New York: Routledge.

Impact of television on U.S. foreign policy. (1994). Congressional hearing before the Committee on Foreign Affairs, Washington, DC.

Iyengar, S., & Simon, A. (1994). News coverage of the Gulf crisis and public opinion. In L. Bennett & D. Paletz (Eds.), *Taken by storm: The media, public opinion and U.S. foreign policy in the Gulf War* (pp. 167–185). Chicago: University of Chicago Press.

Iyengar, S., & Kinder, D. (1987). *News that matters: Television and American opinion.* Chicago: University of Chicago Press.

Kamalipour, Y. (1995). *The U.S. media and the Middle East: Image and perception.* London: Greenwood Press.

Larson, J. (1982). International affairs coverage on US evening network news, 1972–1979. In W. Adams (Ed.), *Television coverage of international affairs* (pp. 15–44). Norwood, NJ: Ablex.

Larson, J. (1984). *Television's window on the world: International affairs coverage on the U.S. networks.* Norwood, NJ: Ablex.

Larson, J., & Hardy, A. (1984). International affairs coverage on network television news: A study of news flow. *Gazette, 23*(4), 241–256.

Martin, J., & Chaudhary, A. (1983). *Comparative mass media systems.* New York: Longman.

Nasser, M. (1983). News values versus ideology: A third world perspective. In L. J. Martin & A. Chaudhary (Eds.), *Comparative mass media systems* (pp. 44–66). New York: Longman.

Nimmo, D., & Combs, J. (1985). *Nightly horrors: Crisis coverage by television network news.* Knoxville, TN: University of Tennessee Press.

Paletz, D., & Pearson, R. (1978). The way you look tonight: A critique of television news criticism. In W. Adams & F. Schreibman (Eds.), *Television network news: Issues in content research* (pp. 65–88). Washington, DC: George Washington University Press.

Prato, L. (1994). Expect more TV news from abroad. *American Journalism Review, 16*(10), 48.

Roeh, I. (1981). Israel in Lebanon: Language and images of storytelling. In W. Adams (Ed.), *Television coverage of the Middle East* (pp. 76–88). Norwood, NJ: Ablex.

Rosenblum, M. (1979). *Coups d'etat and earthquakes: Reporting the world for America.* New York: Harper & Row.

Rubin, B. (1979). International news and the American media. In D. Fascell (Ed.), *International news: Freedom under attack* (pp. 181–245). Beverly Hills, CA: Sage.

Sahin, S. (1982). Television as a source of international news: What gets across and what doesn't. In W. Adams (Ed.), *Television coverage of international affairs* (pp. 229–244). Norwood, NJ: Ablex.

Sitaram, K. S. (1995). *Culture and communication—A world view.* New York: McGraw-Hill.

Stevenson, R. (1988). *Communication, development, and the third world: The global politics of information.* New York: Longman..

Utley, G. (1997). The shrinking of foreign news: From broadcast to narrowcast. *Foreign Affairs, 76*(2), 2–9.

Wallis, R., & Baran, S. (1990). *The known world of broadcast news: International news and the electronic media.* New York: Routledge.

Weaver, J. (1984). Patterns in foreign news coverage on U.S. network TV: A 10-year analysis. *Journalism Quarterly, 61*(2), 356–363.

Weaver, P. (1975). Newspaper news and television news. In D. Cater & R. Adler (Eds.), *Television as a social force: New approaches to TV criticism* (pp. 81–94). New York: Praeger.

Global Forum:
Dialogues for the Next
Millennium

Article 1

CULTURE AND COMMUNICATION: A GLOBAL INFORMATION SOCIETY

Abdullah Hasanat
Jordan Times

During a conference devoted to the discussion of the 1997 temporary press law in October 1998, Jawad Anani, then Jordanian Information Minister, responded to criticism of the press law by citing Jordan's security concerns, which seem to be overriding democratic priorities.

There are many people who of course agree with Anani's argument. After all, this is the Middle East, a region that is still in the process of sorting itself out. Jordan, surrounded by hostile regimes, cannot liberalize but in an evolutionary, rather than a revolutionary way, the conservatives maintain. A patriarchal society at all levels has to move carefully towards modernity.

On the other hand, the liberals argue that with the onset of globalization and the proliferation of information technology, small countries such as Jordan should be a model for the Arab world, introducing more democracy, strengthening civil society, and ensuring a freer media.

Liberals recognize that reform is not an easy task because conservatives resist change. An open press and media endangers status quo interests. Stronger civil society threatens tribal affiliations from which they draw strength. No matter how enlightened the regime, the conservatives, both in the establishment and outside it, are opposed to the change that the new information age promises.

Consider if you will how all brands of conservatives view privatization and globalization. They all resist it. But even those who are for privatization would not approve of the media and the press going into private hands. While those in the establishment fear a privatized media might endanger the security of the country, conservatives fear a privatized media would endanger the country's value systems, whether it be Islamic or tribal. Unfortunately, the liberals are a minority, especially within the establishment. They are fragmented with no political party, association, or institution to represent them. There are a few of them in civil society organizations, research institutes, universities, or the media.

Even more, in a country of meager natural resources, where family or clan bonds are stronger than any other bond, parochialism dominates and self-interest overshadows all other interests. Furthermore, since all civil servants from the prime minister down are appointed, mostly for reasons other than merit, horizontal loyalty is to the clan, and vertical loyalty is to the immediate boss and the system as a whole. In such an environment there is a great deal of mistrust. Functionaries and nonfunctionaries alike are subjected to surveillance, not to determine how loyal they are to their mandate, but to ensure their loyalty to their bosses and to the system. Aware of this, all functionaries keep silent and refrain from criticizing even basic government policies lest they be branded disloyal, the easiest and most frequently applied tactic to end a person's career. In this context, it must be noted that the government and its various organizations provide about 50 percent of the nation's jobs.

Compounding the problem, instead of concentrating on doing their jobs, those civil servants start forming cliques based on clan or provincial affiliation. This hierarchical and patriarchal system characterizes not only civil servants, but all civil society organizations, including newspapers, nongovernmental organizations, and universities as well. Not only does this sort of arrangement stifle creativity in political, social, and economic fields, it weakens the regime itself by weakening its components.

We have to realize in this respect that the leadership, although more open and progressive at heart, is inclined to be more receptive to security worries and concerns. This fact seems at times to escape the minds of many civil society leaders who on occasion appear to be endangering national security by taking seemingly confrontational postures or resorting to inflammatory rhetoric.

Universities, meanwhile, fail to contribute to the national debate and manage to neutralize students and faculty. Apart from the Hashemite documents that Al-Bayt University publishes regularly, and the individual contributions of two or three historians, there seems to be no effort to document the modern history of Jordan in a scientific and academic manner. In his book, From *Abdullah to Hussein*, Robert Satloff of the Washington Institute notes that Jordanians depend for the reading of their contemporary history on foreign authors. Apart from the University of Jordan's Center for Strategic Studies, which tackles issues such as the complex Jordanian-Palestinian relationship, universities have very little to show in terms of contributions to explaining the country's multifaceted political, economic, and social problems.

It is no wonder, then, that a former dissident, Hani Hourani of the New Jordan Research Center, has contributed more to the kingdom's political and social debate than did the university community in toto. However, nowhere does our pathetic performance manifest itself as it does in the media.

Not only are our newspapers near–carbon copies of each other, their rhetoric is tiresome. Again, it took former dissidents like Uraib Rantawi and Saleh Qallab to offer a good defense of Jordan and its cause in the wake of the Al-Jazirah debacle. The media failed not only to explain to Jordanians the actions and ambitions of the leadership or the blessings of peace versus war, but also to create a breed of free-minded intelligentsia capable of defending the country at crucial junctures.

Various governments and successive information ministers have made media bashing their top priority. Over the years, newspapers witnessed closures, takeovers, and, as cynical journalists put it, chief editors landing on them by parachutes. Good and credible journalists either left the country or, as in the case of one fine editor, are about to leave or abandon journalism altogether. A few chose to become hired pens. This is not, of course, to belittle the efforts of many who aspire and push against all odds to produce good journalism, and to express their opinion.

Even when it comes to simple but plain news, almost all journalists and newspapers shy away from reporting or commenting on a multitude of issues including crimes of honor, despite the leadership's condemnations of these crimes on various occasions.

His Majesty, the king, calls on the government to combat poverty and unemployment. This call for action should have prompted newspapers to seek information and collect data to analyze the two problems. Instead, local newspapers are still filled with reports about the "achievements" of the government, its departments, and the inspection tours of government officials in the various governorates. Should not newspapers, radio, and television help the government by employing all their resources to gather and analyze information about unemployment and poverty? Should they not, individually or collectively, establish a reliable database about Jordan and its people, and their different activities, as the former Crown Prince Hassan had been constantly calling for?

At a brief time between 1991 and 1994, the tabloid press, in tandem with the 11th Parliament's daring probe into corruption, attempted to unveil misuse of power for personal gain. That, along with their reports and opinions over the peace process, elections, and civil society activity, were among the main reasons why the government cracked down on the press. That is why the government of Abdul Salam Majali and its functionaries insisted on passing the Press and Publications Law that now governs our national discourse and debate. Failing to defend or explain to the people and the Arab world the path of peace that the leadership charted for Jordan, the government chose to take the shortest and easiest course to silence the voices of criticism, cynicism, or dissent.

A careful reading of the press law reveals the extent to which the government wants to gag the press. Apart from the so-called 10 commandments (now they are

14) the law is loaded with restrictions and penalties that, if applied, will make the whole profession of journalism obsolete. Lacking the language construction of a piece of legislation, articles of the law contradict themselves, rendering freedom of expression guaranteed in the Constitution null and void. Worst of all, the press law places a muzzle on reporting cases being investigated by the authorities, or being reviewed by the courts, providing immunity to criminals and the corrupt.

It is unfortunate to notice that the 1953 Press and Publications Law is many times more liberal than the one we have today. The press law has become more restrictive over the years contrary to the country's progress in the different fields, the proliferation of education, and the skyrocketing number of university graduates in the country. No wonder, then, that newspaper readership is decreasing, not increasing. No wonder, then, that satellite television viewers are increasing, now at 12 percent of the population. No wonder, then, that a great number of our young people are taking to the Internet at home, and at any of the country's 70-plus Internet cafés. While Arab society meets the 21st century, the establishment entrenches itself, alienating more people along the way.

What most people, but especially the government, seem to be unaware of is that a gap has grown between parents and children, between old and young. What they seem not to notice is that children are increasingly looking to the West, hearing Western music and seeing Western video films. What they fail to understand is that the pathetic and distorted series made by Jordan Television depicting our Bedouin past are nothing but the laughing stock of our children who instead watch MTV, style their hair after the Marines, and yearn to own "Nike trainers."

The peace process and Jordan's peace treaty with Israel have also taken a heavy toll on freedom of expression in the Hashemite Kingdom of Jordan. In the main, this is because of the perception that peace with Israel is unpopular and will generate a great deal of opposition in the media, and that the media would become a mouthpiece for peace opponents. This perception has been proven wrong. During short respites of free expression during the past few years, the press demonstrated that it has a moderating influence, allowing opponents and proponents of peace to have their say.

I want to submit here that the apparent impoverishment of Jordanian intellectualism, arts, and literature are a direct result of the diverging press laws, especially in the sense of the establishment's insistence to be the guardian of what Jordanians think and utter. The establishment mistrusts its citizens, or think they are incapable of reacting rationally.

We should, therefore, be grateful to the new age of information that knows no boundary. To the airwaves that bring a different version of the news to our homes. To the Internet that will end, once and for all, government monopoly on information. We should be grateful to *Al-Jazirah*, despite the perceived agenda of its talk show hosts. It was *Al-Jazirah* that threw at us questions that we cannot avoid, questions that we should be discussing among ourselves and formulating answers to.

We have no choice. Either we open up lines of communication, or the airwaves will close on us. I am no prophet of doom or gloom, but Jordan, like many nations on earth, has only one natural resource, its citizens. Capital abounds and natural resources can be imported, but human beings are irreplaceable. The slogan, which His Majesty the late King Hussein launched decades ago, "man is our most precious asset," is even more valid today. We, therefore, must unleash the potential of our men and women—unleash their minds to undo all the chains that stifle people's potential and creativity.

Article 2

THE ROLE OF CYBER CAFÉS IN DEVELOPING INTERNET LITERACY IN EGYPT

Ahmed Mohammed el-Gody
American University in Cairo

INTRODUCTION

As with any other product and service, businessmen observed the computer-based, Internet mania. The spread of the technology, and the scarcity of Internet service in Egypt caused by the social and economic problems, made them believe it would be a good idea to open a place of business for computer services to make the Internet accessible for a new base of customers. These businesses operations are called cyber cafés. However, there are some challenges that face cyber café development in Egypt, including many legal, technical, and operational difficulties.

Owing to spotty Internet infrastructure, many cyber cafés still depend on a dial-up connection. This creates a problem of slow data transfer and frequent cut-offs from the net. Even those who use "Lase-line" or V-SAT (via satellite) connections have to face problems of poor connections, regular cut-offs and slow data transfer. Another challenge that faces the development of the cyber cafés is the problem of overhead expenditures. The investment used to open an Internet café is very expensive and the return on investment is low.

Licensing is another major challenge to the cyber cafés' existence. Government officials do not understand the nature of cyber cafés. They do not understand the meaning of having computer links to telephone networks, so they do not issue licenses for this type of business. One must take a risk and open without licensing by combining Internet services with food and beverages licenses. To serve a cup of tea, a cyber café needs licenses from several bureaucracies: tourism, health, food and beverage, district, and tax offices.

Another challenge facing cyber cafés is the lack of properly trained technicians and engineers. Cyber cafés are in severe need of well-equipped engineers and technicians who can handle the daily work of setting up computers and supporting the network. These obstacles are associated with another problem, the lack of trainers and consultants who are capable not only of understanding the Internet technology, but also of having the capability of training customers and assist them in online operations within the Internet.

Monitoring customers' misuse of the Internet is one of the main jobs in cyber cafés. Cyber cafés do not have written laws, but viewing pornographic sites or online gambling is prohibited. Customers must abide by the general 10 "Internet etiquette" commandments.

After seeing how cyber cafés operate in Egypt and the challenges facing them, the questions to be examined are these: What are the uses of cyber cafés in Egypt? And, what is the role of cyber cafés in developing computer-Internet literacy among Egyptians? Before answering these questions, we should understand that a cyber café is like any other business; its main goal is to make money. Cyber Cafés are private businesses and are not subsidized by the government, so these businesses are working for profit and are not educational institutions. However, to investigate these points, further study was required in order to ascertain the role of cyber cafés in developing Internet-computer literacy. For this reason, a case study on one of the cyber cafés was conducted.

RESULTS OF SURVEY

Results showed that 68 percent of the customers are between 15 and 21 years old. Children younger than 15 years of age made up 14 percent of customers, and 18 percent of the sample were found to be over 21 years old. Seventy-one percent of the sample were male, and 28 percent of cyber café customers were female. About 89 percent of the sample were students, 80 percent of whom are studying in preparatory and secondary schools. The final 11 percent were seeking a university degree, or were in the labor force. Those questioned, who have computers and Internet connection at their homes, go to cyber cafés to be with friends, or to entertain themselves by playing games. These activities cannot be found in their houses.

In terms of the users of the cyber cafés: 62 percent of cyber café customers use the computers for discussion groups; in other words, they go to cyber cafés to chat and socialize with others via the Internet. Twenty-five percent of the sample were found to be interested in the use of games; they consider cyber cafés to be a substitute for video games and arcade stores. Only 9 percent of the respondents use the Internet for e-mail purposes; 4 percent "surf the Net" for news, information, or to download data.

CONCLUSION

We can conclude that cyber cafés play a limited role in developing computer and Internet literacy among Egyptians. From the preceding discussion, we can see that many developing countries are using cafés to promote Internet and computer literacy. In many cases, cafés show themselves as a tool for development. In developed countries, users began associating cafés with small and micro-scale businesses. In Egypt, on the other hand, cyber café use is associated with video gaming and chatting over the Internet. Only 3 percent of the customers use the Internet for work or research applications. This strategy does not help in developing computer or Internet literacy and, therefore, does not contribute to the development projects and plans of Egypt.

However, Sheurie Fouad, manager of the Way Out Café in Egypt, said, in an interview, that the experience of cyber cafés is still considered to be only in the beginning stages. The picture is not quite so dark as it may seem. His experience with cyber cafés in Europe and the United States, in fact, is that the cafés started in these places as a natural evolution of arcade games. We must remember that the current generation will one day grow up, and they may then explore the true capabilities of the Internet.

Article 3
THE ROLE OF THE MEDIA IN THE INTERCULTURAL DIALOGUE IN THE MEDITERANEAN

Ahmed Bedjaoui

One cannot start talking about communication without mentioning that the advent of the media is, to a certain point, recent in the region. The first significant dailies appeared in the Mashrek in the 1930s, just after the *Nahdha*. In other countries, especially those of the Maghreb, the press remained, until the 1950s, in the exclusive hands of colonial publishers. The actual expansion of the media in these countries occurred when they regained their independence.

The generation of the new leaders has been obsessed by the necessity of using the press not only to reinforce the fragile independence of the state, but also to control the public audiences. The advent of television as a dominant medium has considerably increased the capacity of regimes to mobilize the *Masse*, a term which they use to refer to public opinion. It is easy to deduce that information could not escape, even for a small part, from the monopoly of those who claimed historical legitimacy to be the roots of their power. The rare efforts made by some journalists proved to be inefficient in most of our countries, until the beginning of the 1990s. The collapse of the communist system and the Gulf War led the way to major changes. It is still difficult to evaluate the effects of the Gulf War on cultural, religious, and mediated grounds. It turned out to be a fiasco for many, and for various reasons. For most of the Arab countries it marked the end of Pan Arabism,

275

the death of the Third World brand of socialism, and the agony of mediatory unanimity. All were gone with the winds of change.

The most curious consequence was the disillusionment of the southern audiences—disappointed by their national press, but also disgusted by the instrumentation of the Western sky-channels, which they had recently discovered as a source of exclusive pleasure. The result was a gigantic gap that widened between public opinions on both side of the Mediterranean. The journalists from the south who started enjoying the taste of freedom realized that they would never have the same financial and technical means as their colleagues from the rich northern countries to recapture readers or viewers.

The development of modern communication technology widened the gap between the industrialized and developing countries. The new tools were supposed to create a new era of openness and to democratized access to information. Even if they are much cheaper than 10 years ago, computers, the Internet, and cellular telephones are still too expensive for a citizen in the south, especially if we consider the price and the jungle of the software tools.

Attracted by the modernity of the new technologies, the richer citizens of the developing countries are tempted to feel that they are part of this new imperialism, just because they are up-to-date. That means that we are threatened by the global communication system from the outside and from within our societies as well. The amount of information coming from the wealthy nations is constantly growing at the expense of our share of the international communication flow.

In fact, the part played by the new technologies is only the visible aspect of this domination. We should not forget the role of the now traditional means of information with a special attention to the sky-television channels. Everybody agrees both in the north and in the south that television information is not neutral, and that the big channels have lost a large part of their credibility. However, this conviction has not diminished their great hold over the viewers in the developing countries simply because these viewers have become regular customers of a cultural, economic, and social model.

The viewers suffer, but swallow, when they know of the international community's decision to attack a given country and spare another one. The real question is, who belongs to this international community and why? It is clear that this international community is a very closed club to which we shall never belong. And yet, this terminology has been asserted and established by the dominant media whose legitimacy is rarely discussed in the Third World countries.

On the other hand, we should think about the role of the Western journalists in the conflicts involving Arab or Islamic countries. Let us take the example of Bosnia. It is admitted now that this conflict involves three warring factions—the Serbs, the Croats, and the Muslims. Why not call the Serbs and Croats "Christian crusaders"? The term Bosnians is never evoked. This terminology reveals the hidden outlook of Western journalists, who have been programmed in the role of the mourners while the genocide was being executed. It is the well-known diplomatic theory of *Fate ma fate faste.*

The result is that we are assaulted by Western propaganda and invaded through new technologies. There is no more need to send troops to invade a country. Technology and consent are sufficient. Does this mean that we should renounce the new technologies and globalization? Certainly not. Instead, we must adapt ourselves to the world system in order to protect our cultural identity. There is no need to ignore the fact that we are confronted with a major problem of' adaptation to modernity. I say modernity in terms of rationality, which we have forgotten since the times of Ibn Roshd and Ibn Khaldoun. It is amazing that the Arabs who offered modernity to Europe five centuries ago are reluctant to adopt the secular criteria. It is my conviction that it is the only way to reconcile tradition and modernity.

For me, secularity, communication, and democracy are inescapably linked to the development of' our countries. Every society shows its own capacity to build itself. We cannot ignore that the world is a global village, and that communication is the door through which we may enter the club. By the way, I am not sure that all the members of this club will welcome a large number of new members. If democracy and openness mean prosperity, then they will have to share. We must fight to get our share in the flood of communication. To reach that goal, we must rely primarily on training and cultural production. It is urgent that we prepare the new generation for modern communication in the schools and the universities. But we should also help our journalists to meet international standards. The problem is not strictly linked to financial difficulties. I am sure that the know-how is much more crucial for the time being. The West does not know much about us. We need to know a lot about the way the developed countries function and try to organize their knowledge of our culture and civilization. It is our job, not theirs.

To conclude, I would like to mention that new technologies are only tools in the hands of human beings, and that communication is only a means of transportation of cultural content. Their efficiency depends on the specific information or production being proposed. Increasing the know-how of our journalists is essential, but two conditions are still required: (1) the media must participate in the emergence of civil societies, and start working for the citizen, instead of constantly looking at the top of the political system; and (2) it is crucial that authorities organize a functional support for artistic and cultural creativity. In the battle for a more balanced share in the global communication, the countries that rely on a significant production of authentic national images, words, and concepts will certainly benefit the most.

Article 4

THE RISE OF PRIVATE MEDIA AROUND THE WORLD: PICKING UP WHERE TEXTBOOKS STOP

Craig Allen
Arizona State University

INTRODUCTION

The 1990s have witnessed a revolution in the global mass media. While recent events can bring interest and excitement to the study of international communication, the impetus for change—the emergence of private media systems in virtually every foreign country—poses a significant challenge to those who teach this subject in American classrooms. Not only must educators acquaint themselves with hundreds of startup media, including those that have rocked mass communication in key locales such as Great Britain, Germany, and Japan; teachers eventually must impart this knowledge to students with older textbooks and academic literature, in which a 1980s perspective, that from a different era, holds sway.

This article briefly outlines some teacher-friendly sources located during a root-to-branch revision of the international communication program at Arizona State University. Prior to 1997, courses in this program had relied on available textbooks and, through them, had placed first priority on differences between American media and those of the rest of the world. Students were taught language, cultural, regulatory, and technological barriers, while heavy emphasis on public and government-backed media systems was a building block to one of the sustaining elements in the older instruction: media traditions established under communist rule. That this concept was not meeting the needs of the nearly 250 students annually enrolled in the program was first expressed by the students themselves. Some had either lived or traveled abroad and had observed contrary conditions; many others were quick to point out that the cold war was over and that much of our instruction did not apply. Decisive, though, were extended contacts between faculty members and numerous media professionals directly involved in international communication. As these professionals proceeded to discuss nothing but the implications of privatization-deregulation, conglomeration, commercialization, and competition—it was clear our original approach had to be updated.

The result in the fall of 1997 was the launching of a new program of study aimed at exploring all aspects of the privatization trend. Elemental were further contacts with the industry, which happily led to several ongoing relationships, the teachers able to draw from the insights of several actually guiding parts of the global media. These practitioners, in turn, said they benefited by the interaction and welcomed what was to them a rare level of interest in their affairs shown by American educators. Following from this, not differences but similarities between American and overseas media have been underscored. The language, cultural, regulatory, and technological factors once taught as barriers now are seen as having the opposite effect.

Set forth in the following pages are some of the links in the evolving outreach program at Arizona State University. Included in the first section are three reference sources around which much of the eventual outreach took shape. The professional sources subsequently listed and sketched again were teacher friendly; information is provided as to how others may access them. Yet the purpose here is not to establish a template for international outreach but to demonstrate that such pursuit is possible. Because more and more educators are seeking timely parameters and perspectives, material here may help inspire outreach initiatives fitted to individual needs.

REFERENCE SOURCES

The old saying "You can't tell the players without a scorecard" has never been more relevant in international communication. Particularly in the broadcast arena, the proliferation of new channels, networks, and media combines has confused almost beyond recognition the traditional and long-accepted lineup of overseas media. No longer are educators safe in assuming that what counts, country by country, is a single public media institution such as the BBC. Although not part of the actual outreach, an essential preceding step was learning about the many new media institutions, with attention given to what they are, where they are based, and who owns them. At Arizona State University, three reference sources keyed this part of the planning.

Multichannel News International

This monthly periodical contributed in a special way as the only known source of diagnostic charts tracing the interconnections of virtually all of the world's broadcast and telecommunications media. At a glance, the impact of privatization can be seen. These charts are extremely detailed and were applied in understanding the complex of links between U.S. and non-U.S. corporations. They further spell out the emerging convergence between mass communication and telecommunication entities. The Multichannel group prepares annual charts for each continent as well as a unified version depicting the linkage of media throughout the world.

IP Key Facts

Each year the Paris-based IP Group circulates a 400-page guidebook on trends in international television. Laid out somewhat like *Broadcasting Yearbook,* although far more detailed and incisive, the IP reference volumes are fully up-to-date and a must toward mapping the progress of media privatization. In them each country's media are extensively treated both in narrative components and in compendiums of charts and graphs showing such factors as cable and satellite penetration, ratings trends, advertising and marketing characteristics, ownership histories, and competitive considerations. The IP factbooks are available in published form and on CD-ROM, and can be obtained directly from the IP Group at 136 Avenue Charles de Gaulle, 9253 Neuilly Sur Seine, France, 33-1-4-640-2020.

Variety—In Step with the Times

This weekly American trade publication has recently reoriented a considerable proportion of its reporting to coverage of global media activities. On a regular basis, *Variety* profiles, in multipart symposia, the media in specific countries, and the various articles are a valuable source of information on exported American programming, mergers and buyouts, and the continuing process of deregulation in the treated countries. Of particular interest are special international editions of *Variety,* which appear in the spring and fall in conjunction with meetings held by MIP-TV (Marche International de Programmes, a television program market in Cannes, France). In terms of regular narrative content on global media privatization, there may be no more authoritative source.

PROFESSIONAL SOURCES

The eventual outreach program, and the instruction which led from it, was committed to tapping professional sources. Again, this was with a view that only those directly involved in the global media can provide the insights and topical information necessary to advance understanding of this rapidly changing field. While the search for professional sources did evolve into continuing relationships, it was initially driven by two short-term needs: (1) immediate background information through interpersonal interactions and referrals, and (2) the acquisition of audio-visual materials and other displays that could be both libraried for study and used as classroom teaching tools. As the process proceeded, it was apparent that no end of professional sources could be cultivated. Although as noted in the introduction, educators do have many options, and sources indicated here do not comprise a master plan, those that proved most instrumental in the program revisions at Arizona State University have been as follows.

Audience Research & Development

Audience Research & Development (AR&D), a news-consulting firm based in Dallas, lent vital support to revising Arizona State University's instruction on global news. Since 1993, AR&D has developed a large overseas clientele and has played a key role in developing newscasts on new private networks mainly in Europe. AR&D provided background materials as well as an assortment of videotapes. In addition, its representatives were available for discussions relating to the recent history of privatization and the competitive climate of overseas news. Inquiries can be directed to Elizabeth Anderson at AR&D headquarters in Dallas, at 8828 Stemmons, Dallas, Texas 75247.

City TV

An arm of Canada's CHUM Ltd., City TV is a progressive Toronto-based international programming distributor whose directors were found to be friendly toward the academic community. Because City TV competes with American enterprises, its figures were a rich source of insight and reflection into not just programming concepts, but the dominance of U.S. television and other matters touching on the Canadian concept of American "cultural imperialism." Further, City TV's recent role in reducing the audience base of Canada's CBC brought a timely perspective into the global decline of public broadcasting. The relationship with City TV ultimately led to visits at its Toronto facilities. Inquiries can be addressed to Bev Nenson, City TV, 299 Queen Street West, Toronto, Canada M5V 2ZS.

Disney

Several representatives of the Disney Corporation contributed in a number of ways. Fundamental to moving the program forward was finding an authoritative source on international advertising and marketing. This help came from the sales department of ESPN International, which provided current data and compilation record-ings of overseas advertising. Importantly, the video contributions included material carried not just on ESPN but also on its competitors. Then, a second contact with Disney was made at the London offices of Disney International. Members of the director's staff were able to detail the recent expansion of American satellite and cable services. Inquires can address to Disney headquarters in New York or ESPN International at ESPN Plaza, Bristol, Connecticut 06010.

Frank N. Magid Associates

With divisions in London and Kuala Lumper, Magid is the world's largest news consulting firm, currently with 40 newsroom clients in 20 countries. Contacts with Magid representatives both in London and at the firm's headquarters in Marion, Iowa, largely anchored a subprogram on the impact of privatization on global news. Requests for some basic information on overseas news consulting led to exchanges of information and referrals to media professionals at some of the consulted outlets. Plans currently call for members of the Magid staff to come to campus for job recruitment as well as to appear as guests in classes. Inquiries can be directed to Joe George, Frank N. Magid Associates, One Research Center, Marion, Iowa 52302.

McHugh & Hoffman

This Detroit-based firm, another U.S. news consultant, was instrumental in bringing focus to news and programming affairs at new private networks in the former Eastern bloc communist countries of Europe, as well as Scandinavia, and Latin America. McHugh & Hoffman has around 15 major clients in these regions, and has served as a ready source of audio-visual material, background information, and referrals, most relating to overseas news broadcasts. Managed by individuals with past academic experience, McHugh & Hoffman has pledged considerable support to the Arizona State University program. Inquires can be directed to John Bowen, McHugh & Hoffman International, 2000 Tower Center, Suite 2600, Southfield, Michigan 48075.

NHK

Japan's public television corporation served as a link between Arizona State University and the Japanese broadcast media. Starting in Tokyo, contacts eventually were forged with NHK's U.S. division based in Los Angeles. Keying this relationship was direction offered on engineering technology, notably HDTV, which NHK has pioneered. A volume of materials on NHK's HDTV system called "Hi Vision," operational as of 1996, was obtained, as were commitments for future visits to campus by NHK representatives. Inquiries can be addressed to Mariko Hirai, NHK Enterprises, Inc., Los Angeles, California 90067.

RTL

The Luxembourg-based RTL is a significant global media institution and in many ways a key facet of the Arizona State University outreach program. As the owner of new private television networks in Germany, the Netherlands, Luxembourg, and France, and the television arm of the Bertelsmann Corporation, RTL is the world's largest broadcasting system. Interviews pertaining to new national news broadcasts in countries served by RTL, and the integration of American and European programming ventures, were conducted by long-distance telephone with a team of RTL representatives. Several recordings of RTL news and entertainment programs were obtained. Inquiries can be directed to Vie Reuter, RTL headquarters, 177 Route De Luxembourg, L-8077 Bertange, Luxembourg.

Storyfirst Communication

Based in New York, Storyfirst currently spearheads efforts to launch new private radio and television networks in the former Soviet Union. Beginning with mall and telephone communication with Storyfirst directors in the United States, contact eventually was established with the managers of the new CTC network in Moscow and the ICTV network in Kiev. These individuals have proven crucial in fleshing out a crossroads component in the Arizona State University instruction: the conversion of media from communist control to market systemization. Further ties with Storyfirst representatives in New York enabled acquisition of video recordings of Russian and Ukrainian programs. Inquiries can be directed to Thomas Kounelis, Storyfirst Communications, 12, 3rd Khoroshevskaya, 123298 Moscow, Russia.

Telemundo

This U.S.-based Hispanic network has recently formed a partnership with Mexico's new TV Azteca network, and in that position helped link those at Arizona State University to television affairs throughout Latin American relationships initially struck at Telemundo's base Phoenix expanded into contacts in other locales. Inquiries can be directed to Thomas Kounelis, Storyfirst Communications, 12, 3rd Khoroshevskaya, 123298 Moscow, Russia.

RCS/TCS

The Radio and Television Corporations of Singapore, a country which long has had close ties to Arizona State University, were important focal points as the two breakaway units in the recent privatization of the Singapore Broadcasting Company (SBC). Representatives made possible a visit to Singapore; there, a case study in overseas media privatization, one still unfolding, was implemented. Further contacts have solidified relations with these two bellweather Asian media, as well as the prospect for additional on-sight exchanges. Inquires can be addressed to May Wong, Caldecott Broadcast Center, Farrar Road, Singapore 912886.

OTHER SOURCES

In addition to these professional sources, several nonmedia agencies were consulted and gave vital assistance to the planning. An effort to draw in new media developments in the Islamic countries thus far has centered within the Islamic Cultural Center in Phoenix, whose representatives have proven well versed in the media and helpful in developing referrals. Meanwhile, the contacts with Japan's NHK precipitated from dialogue with the Los Angeles–based Japan Information and Culture Center. The Canadian Embassy, through its consulate in Los Angeles, has provided financial support for the examination of privatization in that country. Finally, a consortium of Hispanic community leaders in Phoenix, some with media backgrounds and connections, also has lent meaningful guidance.

CONCLUSION

The outreach program described here is far from complete. Indeed, in detailing mostly positive strides, the discussion here has not taken into consideration several complications and setbacks. A large number of media did not, and have not as yet, responded to requests for assistance, and this has left some countries underexamined. Even among the institutions that did cooperate, immediate priorities were not geared toward advancing an academic undertaking. Educators interested in similar types of outreach should be advised that persistence often has to be applied. Still, the long-term payoffs can be immense, particularly for educators who sense a "new" international communication and feel uncomfortable going before students with current textbooks and educational materials. Improved international telephone service, expanded express mailing capabilities, satellite availability, and the Internet—not to mention the increased prospect of overseas travel—can dissolve time and distance and make an outreach program especially exciting. At Arizona State University, the biggest benefit has been greater confidence that teachers are in tune with real and forward-looking conditions.

In the past, international communication has been interesting to American educators because most of the world's media have not been subjected to market factors, private ownership, and competition, and thus have not resembled those in the United States. Yet that day appears to be past. Until newer materials put privatization in perspective, educators will probably have to seek knowledge on their own. While it also is true that recent developments remain vexing, if not dizzying, educators today have a unique opportunity for sharpening their interests—with outreach programs that may carry many unforeseen rewards.

Article 5

CULTURE AND COMMUNICATION IN THE GLOBAL INFORMATION SOCIETY

Kamel Abu Jaber
Jordan Institute of Diplomacy

God distinguished humans from all of his other wondrous creatures by giving them the gift of speech and communication. It is through speech that ideas are, sometimes, transferred. It is through the Lebanese Phoenician invention of the alphabet that abstract thought is recorded, and passed from generation to generation to become a body of thought, a creed, literature, record, and history.

I say sometimes because often we talk at each other in a manner that escalates to reach the level of verbal violence rather than communicating and transferring ideas. On the evening of Tuesday, November 3, 1998, I, and my country, were viciously and unjustly attacked on the *Al-Jazirah* satellite station. The verbal violence and hatred was so intense and pervasive it shocked me as well as the rest of the country. Words wound, and leave terrible scars that, in time, become part of the collective memory of a people. Words are symbols and men have been known to kill for these brands, even to martyr themselves.

Ideas are contained in communication, and ideas can last for a very long time, governing the lives and actions of peoples and nations. No one knows or can tell how many were the number of martyrs who gave their lives for ideas. That is because words embody values, mores, and traditions. Always emotive, often they are tyrannical in their dictates, moving humans to behave in an uncivilized fashion in accordance with their content.

The Middle East has been the generator of some of the greatest ideas in the history of humanity. To this day these ideas govern and direct the lives and actions of humans not only in our region, but the world over. Judaism, Christianity, and Islam, as well as a colorful mosaic of ideas, have their origin here and, to this day and well into the future, will continue to light the lives and to civilize and humanize the actions of peoples round the world.

That is why we, perhaps more than any other peoples of the world, are oral communicators. We appreciate the texture, the sound, the form and content of both the spoken and written word. Especially in the Arab world, words expressed in poetic form sometimes have an intoxicating effect. Ideas here do not die, nor do they seem to fade away. Their power, centuries later, continue to drive people.

Communication should be handled carefully and with delicacy, always keeping in mind that others will react. Physical violence may eventually be forgotten in time, but that is not the case with communication or verbal violence. That is one of the most important features distinguishing a dialogue from a monologue. In the first place, there are rules that need to be followed—etiquette and a proper form of protocol that recognizes and accepts difference in a civilized manner. The former Crown Prince al-Hassan Bin Talal refers to these rules as "Adab al-Hiwar," good manners of dialogue. The idea is to cultivate some understanding, not to win an argument or register a point, for there is, or should be, a difference between mere hearing and listening.

In our time, the technology of communication has become one of the most distinguishing features of modern life. While it has made people everywhere virtual neighbors, it has not, sadly, brought about neighborliness. Often, it seems to have hardened the heart as people repeatedly view on their television screens the natural and man-made catastrophes, the wanton killings, ethnic cleansing, mutilation, and violence.

That is why it is good to ponder how to humanize the approach of the mass media. I am not simply referring to the merciless doggedness of the paparazzi. Entire cultures now tremble when contemplating with terror the so-called "cultural invasion." Muslims everywhere cringe with fear at the venom of "Islamophobia" that distorts their image and demonizes their culture.

How to ease the transition until certain features of globalization become accepted everywhere is the task and the challenge before mass media technology, which has no frontiers and respects no boundaries. The direction must be from within, in addition to a code of conduct that respects differences and sanctifies privacy. The media must become an instrument of bringing about harmony. I, for one, do not believe in the melancholy and gloomy predictions of the inevitability of a clash of civilizations. There must be better alternatives.

One final thought: Since the discovery of the alphabet, the art of communication has brought humankind neither peace nor security. The second revolution represented by the invention of the printing press further complicated matters, providing fuel for primordial hatreds to vent themselves in the name of creed or ideology. In historical terms, the media are still on the threshold of the greatest revolution in the development of mass communication thus far. We are still on the threshold and no one knows the impact or the multiplier effect of these developments on entire cultures. The globalization until now is more of a reality in the north; widening rather than narrowing the gap with the south is yet another serious, perhaps sinister development in need of study and examination. The signposts and indications are that the mass media can play a much greater role in civilizing and humanizing behavior than they have done thus far. Let us hope they do.

Article 6

SELLING OIL TO ARABS

Jihad Fakhreddine
Pan Arab Research Center

It is observed that Eskimos have up to 55 words to designate snow. Arabs, on the other hand, have less than a dozen words to designate oil. Given this variation in the number of words designated for each of the two respective "products," and assuming that the communication inputs needed to sell each product to the respective targets are on par, would it mean that the chances of selling snow to Eskimos are better than those for selling oil to Arabs?

It would be rash to attempt to arrive at any definite conclusion so quickly. A word's meaning depends upon the context of other words that surround it. It also depends on the communicator's knowledge of the words itself, and one's appreciation of its meaning and implications. And most importantly, it depends on whether an environment has been created in which the customer appreciates the benefits of consuming the product. Indeed, these are only a few of the determining factors for selling. But the bottom line is that communication is needed, with the selection of words being very critical.

But in the context of marketing and selling in the Arab world, be it oil or other products, what's in an Arabic word? I believe that a full answer to this question can only be obtained once Arab linguists and marketers come to realize that it is in the best interest of marketing in the Arab world that they consider courting each other. Until such an interaction becomes a reality, I would like to share with you a market researcher's perspective on a few Arabic language-related issues that can seriously undermine the efficiency of communicating with Arab consumers.

There have invariably been positive responses to the advertiser's demands that greater efficiency in communicating with the Arab consumers be achieved. In many ways the media have witnessed substantial progress. The same can be said about the technical capabilities and quality of producing such publicity; so, also, for the data and the software required for media planning.

Yet despite these positive changes, there is a feeling that advertisers in the Arab markets are not communicating enough. When the current size of the advertising budget spent is compared either to the relative size of the Arab economies, particularly the oil-rich ones, or to the per capita spending, the figures are not particularly high as yet. In Saudi Arabia, the largest Arab economy, for instance, advertising spending in 1995 was only 0.002 percent of its gross domestic product (GDP), and per capita advertising spending was $15, compared to $11 in 1990.

This comparatively low level of advertising money spent can be attributed to many factors, with local cultural restrictions being one of them. Some observers also argue that the rate cards themselves are comparatively low. Another factor is that the Arab advertising industry remains very much dependent on the international brands' advertising budgets. Local companies remain small-time players, but are increasingly taking note of the benefits of advertising and taking more of an interest in their marketing.

However, the main impediment to a faster growth in advertising spending may be the Arab language itself. I would even venture to state that the Arab language, with its present modes of usages and the insignificant growth in its vocabulary, are both bound to have adverse effects on all aspects of marketing communications, with advertising being only one part of it. Other communication elements include things such as positioning statements of a company, product, or brand; the language used in brochures; instructions on labels regarding how to use products; product contents; outlining of product features; descriptions of products; and so on.

At present, the Arab markets are being flooded with a massive number of products and services, imported and locally produced, many of which have no commonly accepted and proper designations in Arabic, let alone being given Arabic designations for their respective features. The products I am referring to are by no means limited to high-tech and sophisticated products and services. It is easy to make a long list of products that have become a staple in most homes, but are either referred to in English or are commonly referred to wrongly, when compared to their respective English designations. The persistence of such situations will naturally affect advertisers' capability to communicate with Arab target segments.

The issue of exploring and arriving at the appropriate Arabic vocabulary to designate a product or service should not be viewed as being of concern to a single marketer within a certain business activity, but to that business sector as a whole. The Arab banking sector, for instance, has yet to agree on the Arabic equivalent of "teller," "telephone banking," "charge card," "debit card," as well as a host of other newly introduced products and services. Similarly, marketers of breakfast cereals have yet to agree on finding and disseminating an Arabic equivalent to the English word "cereal." Because corn flakes was the first type of cereal to be introduced to the Arab markets, breakfast cereals of all types are now commonly referred to as "corn flakes." More importantly, a number of cereal producers are using the Arabic equivalent of the word *flakes*, whether it is in reference to corn puffs, cocoa puffs, golden grahams, or rice puffs. Hence, combined industry efforts are required to set forth the right definitions of certain products.

I would like to share with you a recent incident that may further illustrate this. On a recent visit to a fast food restaurant in Sharjah, I came across a small poster written in both English and Arabic. The English version stated: *"Get a Frisco Kid's puzzle every time you buy the Fun Meal. Collect all five."* The literal translation of the Arabic version stated the following: *"Get a Frisco characters collection game when you buy the cheerful kid's meal."* Noticing that I was copying the text, the restaurant manager, an Arab, approached me and politely enquired what I was doing. I pointed out that three Arabic words were used to designate one English word "puzzle," yet they failed to capture its meaning. Apparently he was aware of the fact that there is no Arabic equivalent to the word "puzzle." Learning that I am a market researcher, he invited me to come up with an alternative word.

Indeed, it would be very perplexing to non-Arabs that there is no Arabic word for a game as common as a "puzzle." But this is by no means an isolated case in which an advertiser finds himself helpless in finding Arabic words to designate his products or to differentiate them from competing ones. This case illustrates the necessity for communicating backups to the three Arabic words appearing in the poster. In this instance, the English and the Arabic versions of the communication were placed next to each other, with a visual of a "puzzle" in the background. The game itself, and its English designation are familiar to most, if not to all, Arab children targeted.

But while this particular communication in Arabic has a backup support to salvage it from being totally wasted, not all communications in Arabic, which may have a need for a proper and commonly used Arabic vocabulary, can have all the desired communication backups. In fact, in all marketing-related fields where communication needs to be carried out in Arabic, advertisers, advertising agencies, public relations executives, and market researchers are largely riding in the same boat. And, too often, all of them are bound to find their fishing nets empty of the Arabic words that can clearly define their thoughts and ideas.

Currently, the Arabic vocabulary sea is not replete with a sufficiently large enough body of words to fully support effective and efficient marketing communications. With this scenario in mind, one is tempted to conclude that since something has not been said or written in Arabic, then it has not been thought of by Arabs. Such an argument could have had certain validity had Arabs in the various marketing fields not been exposed to the Western body of knowledge on marketing. Most of the Arab marketing professionals, if not all of them, can think and communicate their thoughts and ideas about marketing communication in English, much better than they would in Arabic.

Marketing, as a body of knowledge, has been a latecomer to the curriculum of the Arab universities. This is unlike other closely related fields such as trade, commerce, or economics, for which many Arab universities have long had well-established schools. The early surge in interest in these fields had, in turn, resulted in extensive and serious attempts to translate, or Arabize, most of the trade and commerce-related terminologies and concepts that are enlightening the Arab professionals in marketing, advertising, and marketing research, but who themselves are unable to deflect this "light" in Arabic.

It should not come as a surprise to any Arab marketing professional that there are no commonly accepted Arabic words to designate the English words regularly used in marketing, such as brand, brand image, market positioning, equity, brand awareness, marketing mix, below-the-line advertising, above-the-line advertising, product concept, attitudes, perceptions, needs, and wants. Nor would it be an overstatement to say that no two Arabic textbooks on marketing would designate the same Arabic equivalents to the same English terms alluded to earlier. But the true impact of this predicament, whereby Arab marketers often find themselves unable to communicate their thoughts in fluent Arabic, still remains to be measured. At present, for an Arab to be qualified in any marketing field, fluency in English is a prerequisite. However, similar fluency in Arabic is not a necessary requirement and, most often is not required at all.

This paradoxical situation has its roots in the Arab culture and is being perpetuated by the existing Arab educational systems at all levels. At the university level, when studying for a marketing degree, Arabic is often a second language. In Lebanon, Arab students in marketing or advertising can make do without any proficiency in Arabic. In most other Arab universities, only introductory marketing courses are given in Arabic. All advanced courses are taught in English; required references are only available in English.

The persistence of this enigmatic situation is bound to have certain detrimental effects on many aspects of marketing communications with Arab consumers. The tendency is that Arab advertisers will score more successes in impressing foreign suppliers than in communicating in Arabic with their Arab consumers. I have alluded thus far to the cultural and educational gridlock. Arab marketing communicators are finding themselves in a gridlock that leaves them gasping for Arabic vocabulary with which to communicate. But if this is the scenario at the senders' side of the marketing communication process, it is more unsettling at the receivers' end; that is, among, the Arab consumers. In the final analysis, Arab marketing communicators and their Arab target segments find themselves in the same boat; both are faced with a situation wherein they do not have sufficient Arabic vocabulary at their command to guarantee them efficient and effective communication in Arabic. The elements contributing to creating gaps in marketing communication are multifaceted, and some of them were touched on earlier.

It is very handy for a non-Arab advertiser to think of the Arab markets as a single entity, the "Arab world," with one Arabic language. This would have been a correct perception had all Arabs been communicating in classical Arabic (al-Fousha) at all levels, written and verbal. For many centuries, however, communication among Arabs at the personal level—schools, offices, or homes—has been predominantly, if not solely, carried out using the speakers' respective local dialects. Not only do the local Arab dialects and slangs vary significantly from one region to another, they are at variance with the classical Arabic.

Hence, and in practical terms, the usefulness of classical Arabic as a medium of communication has become rather limited and is largely restricted to written communication. It is not surprising, for instance, that a news reporter or news presenter, while writing his or her news stories in classical Arabic, could turn around and communicate that same story in a local dialect to a colleague sitting across the table. Sadly enough, it would sound rather awkward were they to verbally communicate their thoughts in classical Arabic.

The predominance of local dialects as mode of communication is observed to have many serious implications for the marketer's capabilities to formulate an effective message. Critical decisions have to be made on which mode of Arabic language to use and, subsequently which medium to use, given that the medium used will more or less dictate what mode of language to use. At present, virtually all marketing communication carried out in the print media uses classical Arabic, with a few exceptions. The audio-visual media, on the other hand, rely mostly on local dialects, with the exception of messages in the form of announcements, for which classical Arabic is more likely to be used. Indeed, each mode of communication in Arabic has its advantages and drawbacks. Although the local dialects are at times more capable of capturing certain local thoughts and ideas, they may not be useful for a broader marketplace, limiting how effectively advertisers can put their messages across. I can only cite a few of the difficulties a marketing communicator would have to overcome.

Overall, marketing communicators, as well as Arab consumers, tend to have on hand a limited pool of Arabic words with which they can communicate. The size of this pool is not necessarily positively correlated with the level of education of the classical Arabic language in that it is living, but not alive. And in the face of the high-tech and fast-paced information age, which brought along it its own vocabulary, the Arabic vocabulary is expanding at a snail's pace. This situation is further compounded by the fact that the Arab book market does not have a thesaurus of any sort, and the English-Arabic dictionaries are stagnant. More disturbing is that Arabic-Arabic dictionaries are not only stagnant in their number of words, but scarcely owned at homes or institutions or ever referred to. Hence, the Arabic vocabulary falls short of meeting the demands of modern-day marketing communication in Arabic.

Even where new Arabic words are being adopted to designated newly introduced products, services, concepts, or ideas, their proliferation amongst the general public, or even the educated elite, is also very slow. For instance, an Arabic advertisement could list all the modern features in a new car having full options, such as an anti-lock breaking system, fuel injection, and so on, but one would be required to know one or two additional foreign languages to understand the full message. In fact, some television commercials in Lebanon typify just such a form of advertising.

A further frustrating aspect of using classical Arabic for marketing communication is its apparent inflexibility in accommodating more than one word into a single newly coined one. This is unlike the English language, where one can come across an avalanche of newly coined words and terms, either given as brand names for products and services or to differentiate their respective features. A quick browse in the Internet is enough to illustrate this point. The current trend in the Arab world is to follow suit in naming companies, products, or services using English names. English names are perceived to be either catchier or possibly more impressive than any other likely alternative in Arabic. I believe that we are increasingly reaching the stage where a new company with an Arabic name will even sound out of place to an Arab.

The inflexibility of the Arabic language is also apparent in its limitations on using abbreviations to designate names of products, services, their features, or names of supplying companies or organizations. It is rare that an Arabic company would use the initial letters in the words of its Arabic name to conjure a short-cut name. An Arab company would, however, use the initials of its English name to coin its name. A company should communicate an image about itself to Arab consumers. The question is, what impact would those adaptations have on the image? This is something only research can answer.

Another problematic aspect for marketing communications in Arabic is related to translation from other languages. Very often, along with a product or service imported from the West, a whole ready-made package of communication will be imported as well. It is also safe to state that because of their educational background and exposure to the mechanism of foreign advertising, Arabs working in creative advertising departments have a tendency to do their original thinking in English and not in Arabic. In such circumstances the translation aspect becomes vital because, while the Arabic translation of an English text could be very effective, it could also have either a neutral or even a negative impact. The communication I am referring to here is not limited to advertising only, but also includes issues such as the Arabic connotations of an imported brand name. In many instances, a brand name in a foreign language can be Arabized, but it might embody certain negative or even vulgar connotations in the Arabic context.

Not only is it possible for the brand name to backfire and thus kill the product, but mistranslating could relay wrong information about the exact features of a product or service, or how to use it. For instance, on the label of a very popular imported instant fruit drink, the Arab consumer will read the following English text: *"Percentages of U.S. recommended daily allowances per serving are . . . ."* Whereas the Arabic version states: *"Percentages of U.S. allowed daily allowances per serving is are . . . ."* For another advertiser, "firm cheese" (with reference to texture) in English becomes "solid cheese" in Arabic. Similarly, a particular brand of washing softener that has "a colorful range" of fragrance variants, as stated in

English, would have "items rich in colors" as far as the Arabic communication is concerned.

Furthermore, along with the imported package of communication for a brand often comes its positioning statement. Here, knowledge of the variations in the meanings of similar English and Arabic words is of critical importance. Often, within the same market, the message sent across in English could be somewhat, if not very, different from its Arabic version. The literal meaning of a word or a phrase does not always have to be adopted. A most dangerous ditch into which a number of translators are falling is the disregard of the cultural context of the words being translated.

It is not uncommon to come across several English words that have quite positive connotations within a Western culture, for instance, but do not have readily available equivalents in Arabic; or their meaning in Arabic does not embody that same intensity of positiveness; or they may even imply a negative meaning. The advice here is that an advertiser needs to beware of staying a prisoner to a positioning statement composed in English, rather than creating a new one more relevant to the Arabic language and Arab consumers.

At the Pan Arab Research Center, we are increasingly finding ourselves in situations where, to capture such variations in the meanings of certain words, phrases, or positioning statements, we produce our analytical reports in both Arabic and English languages. This is an attempt to ensure that we capture the full meaning or implications of Arabic words as used by the Arabs surveyed. As it stands now, Arab translators are at a disadvantage. Although their exposure to the Western culture is intensifying, they are often unaware that certain English words may take on different meanings or implications over time, and that hundreds of words are added to the English vocabulary every year. Against this backdrop, the best 1996 Arabic-English dictionaries are still reprints of editions that came out in the 1960s, 1950s, or even the 1940s.

Moreover, cultural variations could encompass many aspects other than the meanings of words and their implications. They include variations in taste for food, music, clothing, social behavior, and norms. In the English language, for instance, a cheese supplier could possibly designate up to 40 or 50 different words to position or differentiate the taste of different cheese products. A particular type of cheese could be creamy, milky, velvety; the list goes on. But it is evident that this same message has its limitations in communicating with Arab consumers. Arabs are accustomed to consuming only a very limited variety of cheeses compared to their Western counterparts. In addition, many words that are used in English to describe the taste or flavor of a type of cheese do not have an equivalent in Arabic. Hence, the communication capabilities of a cheese advertiser are limited, especially when restricted to translating exactly the same vocabulary used in English.

Another cultural variation to consider is the difference in environment. Consumers are observed to relate more to the natural environment in which they live. One could argue about the effectiveness of telling an Arab woman in the Arabian

Peninsula that a skin care cream gives her "excessive smoothness, like summer rain," as one advertisement states. It is possible that a woman living in Mount Lebanon may relate to summer rain, but in the Arabian Peninsula it hardly rains in winter, let alone in summer.

I would like to conclude with the following observations. Many centuries ago, culture and environment were the determining factors in how the Arab communicated. Modern-day factors are decidedly different, with economics and high-technology assuming forward positions in determining how we communicate amongst ourselves. In many ways, markets in the Arab world were caught off guard in the midst of these new developments. Through the mid-1980s, ideological expectations were set in high gear, with little attention given to the economic performance of their economy; but the end of the cold war dictated that the Arab world switch off the ideological engine and begin assembling components of a market economy.

We are still in the early period of this economic transformation, with the Gulf countries being more fortunate than others in the region. Where earlier, we only needed to know how to sell, now we need to learn how to market. Hence, there is the need to acquire new and more effective communication. Currently, there is little evidence that marketing communication in the Arab world is planning to change.

Fifteen hundred years ago, the Arabic language had up to 50 words to designate a sword; only a few are currently used. We are told that in the new promised land of economic development we will rely little on wars, and hence there will be little use for words designating swords. But we still live in the "oil era," and in order to market this product as well as others better, Arabic requires a more diverse vocabulary than is currently available. The time is ripe for Arab marketers to invite their fellow Arab linguists for at least a little chat.

AUTHOR INDEX

SUBJECT INDEX

ABOUT THE EDITORS

Leo A. Gher (MA, Southern Illinois University) is Associate Professor and Director of the Brown Media Management Lab, a state-of-the-art, electronic media research facility, housed at Southern Illinois University in Carbondale, Illinois. Radio-Television at SIUC is consistently ranked as one of the top five communication education programs in the United States, and maintains a preeminent international reputation for management and media training. Director Gher is credited with more than 75 educational and professional presentations and publications, including the documentary series, Centaur Symposium, which featured authors Marshall McLuhan, R. Buckminster Fuller, and Jonathan Kozol, among others. Gher is a member of the editorial board of *Transnational Broadcasting Studies*, and is the author of a forthcoming text, *The Art & Science of Media Economics: Marketing & Management Strategies for the 21st Century*. Gher comes to academia from a professional background, and is widely recognized as an expert in media economics, cross-cultural communications, and management. In addition to his academic responsibilities, Gher is the CEO of Avery Media International, Ltd., a management consulting firm, specializing in television distribution and global marketing in new media. Gher also sits on the executive committee of BetaTel PCS, LLC; a wireless, PCS company and is a board member of AirQuest Communications, LP, a cellular telephone firm.

Hussein Y. Amin (Ph.D., Ohio State University) is Associate Professor and Senior Fellow in the School of Business, Economics and Communication at the American University in Cairo, the premiere institution of higher education in the Arab world. Dr. Amin is a founding board member of the Arab–U.S. Association for Communication Educators, the senior editor of *Transnational Broadcasting Studies,* on the editorial board of the *Journal of African Studies*, and member of the advisory board of the *Journal of International Communication.* Amin also serves as a reviewer for the binational Fulbright Commission. He holds several key positions in Egyptian broadcasting, including chairman of Egyptian Radio and Television Union's Space Committee. He is a member of the Higher Committee for Specialized NileSat TV Networks, the Specialized Committee on Egyptian Radio and Television Privatization, and the General Assembly of the Egyptian Ministry of Information. In addition, Amin is a trustee of ERTU, the governing body of Egyptian radio-television broadcasting. Dr. Amin is credited with more than 30 book chapters or journal articles, and 50 conference presentations. He is the winner of the Stephen Coltron Award for Excellence in Communication Theory from the International Radio and Television Society. Dr. Amin is acknowledged as the foremost authority on Arab media regulation and privatization, and global broadcasting in developing and Third World countries.

ABOUT THE CONTRIBUTORS

Rasha A. Abdulla (M.A., American University in Cairo) is Lecturer of Journalism and Mass Communication at the American University in Cairo. This Fall, she starts her Ph.D. in communication at Georgia State University. Ms. Abdulla obtained her Master of Arts degree in journalism and mass communication from AUC in February 1996. Her thesis was entitled "The Uses and Gratifications of Music Television in Egypt: Why Kids Want Their MTV." She is a recipient of the Mostafa and Ali Amin Journalism Award, one of the most prestigious journalism awards in the Middle East. Her areas of interest include music and music videos as media, journalism and marketing on the Internet, writing and editing of English-language publications, as well as graphic design and computer layout. Ms. Abdulla is a professional singer and guitar player. She performs regularly in English and Arabic at the Cairo Opera House. E-mail: rasha@aucegypt.edu

Craig Allen (Ph.D., Ohio University) is an associate professor at the Walter Cronkite School of Journalism and Telecommunication at Arizona State University. His teaching specialties include international communication and broadcast news. He began his career in the media at the *Oregon Journal* in Portland. After 6 years as a sports reporter and news editor, he moved into broadcast news and held reportorial and managerial positions at television stations in Spokane, Portland, Colorado Springs, and Denver. He has contributed stories to the ABC television network and has been honored by the Society of Professional Journalists and the Colorado Association of Broadcasters for his work. Dr. Allen's research focuses on television news comprehension, television history, and the mass media in the electoral process. His works have appeared in *Presidential Studies Quarterly, Journalism Quarterly*, and the *Journal of Broadcasting*. His book, *Eisenhower and the Media*, was published by the University of North Carolina Press. E-mail: idcma@asu.edu

Ali Ahmed Attiga (Ph.D., University of Wisconsin) is the Secretary General, Arab Thought Forum in the Middle East. He has been the Social Envoy of the United Nations Secretary General, and has served the United Nations Development Project in several different capacities. He is based in Amman, Jordan. Dr. Attiga's research interests lie in economic development, diplomatic relations and the media, and Arab culture and the media.

Ahmed Bejaoui is a writer and well-known scholar in the Middle East. Mr. Bejaoui is head of the MedMedia Freidrich Naumann Foundation in Algeria. He specializes in articles concerning mass media, Western journalism and Arab affairs, and cultural invasion of developing countries, especially in the Middle East.

Douglas A. Boyd (Ph.D., University of Minnesota) is Professor and Dean of the College of Communications and Information Studies at the University of Kentucky. Dr. Boyd spent more than 20 years in the Middle East and is recognized as an expert on Arab world media and communication studies. His research specialties include comparative systems of broadcasting, international broadcasting, broadcasting and development, and new media.

Carolyn Crimmins (Ph.D., Georgia State University) is Associate Chair of the Department of Communication at Georgia State University. Dr. Crimmins's research interests involve the relationship between the mass media and society from both historical and contemporary perspectives, and the ethical considerations facing the media and their audiences. Dr. Crimmins teaches in the areas of media history, ethics, and communication theory. She is the President of the Arab–U.S. Association of Communication Educators, and an associate with the Center for International Media Education at Georgia State University. Dr. Crimmins has participated extensively in media education workshops, lectures, and panels throughout the Middle East and North Africa. E-mail: jouccc@panther.gsu.edu

James A. Danowski (Ph.D., Michigan State University) is Associate Professor of Communication, Graduate College Faculty member, and Honors College Fellow at the University of Illinois at Chicago. He serves on the editorial boards of the *Journal of Communication* and the Communication Division of Ablex Publishing Company. He has been a member of the International Communication Association Board of Directors, founding chair of ICA's Human Communication Technology Interest Group (now the Communication and Technology Division), and chair of the ICA Information Systems Division. E-mail: jimd@uic.edu

Jihad Fakhreddine (M.A., University of North Carolina) is Research Manager–Media of the Pan Arab Research Center located in Dubai, United Arab Emirates. PARC is the preeminent commercial marketing and audience research company in the Middle East. PARC has on-ground research facilities located through the Levant, the Maghreb, and the Gulf regions, and services governments and private advertising and broadcasting firms worldwide. E-mail: jihad@arabresearch.com

Shems Friedlander is senior lecturer at the American University in Cairo and Director of the Apple Center for Graphic Communications in Cairo, Egypt. Mr. Friedlander's professional career includes work with such notable companies as Columbia Records, *Look* magazine, *Holiday* magazine, *Architectural Forum*, and Columbia Broadcasting System. He was the former Silver Medal winner of the New York Art Directors' Club. Mr. Friedlander is a member of the Broadcast Education

Association and the Arab–U.S. Association for Communication Educators. Of special interest is his historical documentary of the founder of the Whirling Dervishes, *Rumi: The Hidden Treasure*, published by Safina Books, which is an introduction to Persian thought, mystic poetry, and Islam. E-mail: shems_f@acs.auc.eun.eg

Roger Gafke (M.A., University of Missouri) is Professor in the Missouri School of Journalism at the University of Missouri–Columbia. Professor Gafke is the chair of the broadcasting division, specializes in broadcasting news and writing, and is a member of university advisory boards on educational technology and distance education. His teaching specialties include new media, news reporting and writing. He was project director for a cooperative program in curriculum development between his school and Birzeit University, West Bank. He is a member of the Public Relations Society of America and the Association of Education for Journalism and Mass Communications. E-mail: gafker@missouri.edu

Ahmed Mohammed el-Gody (B.A., American University in Cairo) is a research assistant in the Department of Journalism and Mass Communication at American University in Cairo. Mr. el-Gody is the former editor of *Ru'ya* magazine, a development magazine published by the Institute of Cultural Affairs of Egypt. He was a reporter for *Akhbar Al-Youm*, an Arabic daily newspaper in Egypt. Mr. el-Gody has written extensively on international communication with a specific interest in Middle Eastern affairs.

Abdullah Hasanat is well known as a journalist in the Middle East and especially in Jordan. He is also the Executive Director of the *Jordan Times*, one of the most recognized and important English-language newspapers in the Middle East. Mr. Hasanat has written extensively on issues related to the Jordanian media.

Walid A. Hashem (Ph.D., Georgetown University) is Executive Director of Arab Radio and Television, a seven-channel satellite television network broadcasting to the Arab world, Europe, North and South America, and Asia. ART transmitting facilities are located in Fucino, Italy, at the renowned satellite uplink center, Telespazio. ART is wholly owned by Arab Media Corporation (AMC), incorporated in the Cayman Islands–British West Indies, a company established through investments of the Dallah Al Baraka Group, chaired by the eminent Saudi investor, Sheik Saleh Kamel. Corporate support for ART networks includes six companies created under the umbrella of AMC.

Kamel Abu Jaber (Ph.D., Syracuse University) is President of the Jordan Institute of Diplomacy. Dr. Abu Jaber serves as a senator in the Jordanian Upper House of Parliament, and is the author of numerous papers and publications in both English and Arabic.

Yahya R. Kamalipour (Ph.D., University of Missouri) is Professor of Mass Communications and the Director of Graduate Studies in the Department of Communication and Creative Arts at Purdue University–Calumet. Dr. Kamalipour is the recipient of the Distinguished Scholarship Award in International and Intercultural Communication from the National [Speech] Communication Association,

the recipient of the 1996 Edgar Mills Award for Outstanding Service in Communi-
cations, and recognized for outstanding research at Purdue University in 1995. He
is acknowledged as one of the leading scholars in America on Middle Eastern
affairs, and has written numerous books, including: *Images of the U.S. Around the
World: A Multicultural Perspective, Cultural Diversity and the U.S. Media, The
U.S. Media and the Middle East: Image and Perception*, and *Mass Media in the
Middle East: A Comprehensive Handbook*. A forthcoming text, coedited by Dr.
Kamalipour and J. P. Thierstein, is called *Religion, Law, and Freedom: A Global
Perspective* (Greenwood Press). E-mail: Kamaliyr@calumet.purdue.edu

Marwan M. Kraidy (Ph.D., Ohio University) is Assistant Professor and Acting
Director of Graduate Studies in the School of Communication at the University of
North Dakota. Dr. Kraidy is the former secretary of the International Communication Division of the Association for Education in Journalism and Mass Communication. He is the 1998 winner of the Ralph Cooley Award for top research paper in
the International and Intercultural Communication Division of the National Com-
munication Association. Dr. Kraidy has been a judge for the prestigious Athens
International Film and Video Festival on three occasions, has appeared as talent for
Image Inc. in Lebanon, and was a columnist for NDU News and Views, in Lebanon,
from 1991 to 1992. His creative works include the documentaries *The Post-War
Dream, The Future in the Mirror*, and *L'Enfance et la Guerre*, and a short novel,
Childhood and War, which won the 1987 top prize (Best Young Francophone Writer
Award) at Antoura in Lebanon. E-mail: kraidy@hadlands.nodak.edu

Yorck von Korff is (M.A., University of Heidelberg) a doctoral student from
Germany. He is doing field research in journalism in Cairo. Mr. Korff specializes
in media ethics, political science, economics, and Islamic studies with a special
emphasis on the Middle East. Mr. Korff has taught media ethics and responsibility
at the American University in Cairo since 1998. He has made several conference
paper presentations on Egyptian journalism, press standards, and democratization.
E-mail:yorkk@uns2.auc.eun.eg

Safran S. al-Makaty (Ph.D., University of Kentucky) is Assistant Professor and
Chairman of the Department of Communication at Umm al-Quara University in
Mecca, Saudi Arabia. He is also Editor-in-Chief of *Almanar*, a periodical newspaper
published by Umm al-Quara University. Dr. Safran is a board member of the
Arab–U.S. Association for Communication Educators. E-mail: safran@uqu.edu.sa

Issam Suleiman Mousa is professor in the Department of Journalism at Yarmouk
University in Irbid, Jordan. Dr. Mousa specializes in journalism, mass communication, and cross-cultural media development and is the author of numerous books
and professional articles related to media in the Arab world. Dr. Mousa is currently
the President of the Arab–U.S. Association of Communication Educators. E-mail:
issam@yu.edu.jo

James Napoli (M.A., Boston College) is associate professor of Journalism at
Western Washington University. He was also on the faculty at the American
University in Cairo for 12 years. Mr. Napoli is a former report for American

newspapers and magazines. Mr. Napoli research interests are in political communication and issues of press freedom.

Mohammed el-Nawawy (Ph.D., Southern Illinois University) is Assistant Professor in the Communications Arts Department at the University of West Florida. Dr. el-Nawawy's professional background includes working for several international news organizations, such as the Associated Press and the Middle East News Agency of Egypt and several publishing houses, including Longman Publishers. He is the 1998 winner of the First International Travel Grant Award offered by the Broadcast Education Association, and the Dissertation Research Award offered by Southern Illinois University's Graduate School. Dr. el-Nawawy is a member of Kappa Tau Alpha; his research interests include international and intercultural communication with a focus on culture and media in the Middle East, communication theories, and the social construction of reality. E-mail: mohammedn99@hotmail.com

Leonard Ray Teel (Ph.D., Georgia State University) is Associate Professor and Director of the Center for International Media Education at Georgia State University in Atlanta. Dr. Teel is a founding board member and past president of the Arab–U.S. Association for Communication Educators, a founding member of the Economic Information Network, and past president of the American Journalism Historians Association. His publications include *Debating Qadhafi: Satellite TV Challenges Convention*, *Middle East Insight*, and the book, *Into the Newsroom: An Introduction to Journalism*. E-mail: Joulrt@panther.gsu.edu

G. Norman Van Tubergen (Ph.D., University of Iowa) is Associate Professor in the College of Communications and Information Studies at the University of Kentucky. Dr. Tubergen specializes in Q methodology, multivariate research methods, mass communication, mass culture, and market research.